IAGO

Major Literary Characters

**THE ANCIENT WORLD THROUGH
THE SEVENTEENTH CENTURY**

ACHILLES
Homer, *Iliad*

CALIBAN
William Shakespeare, *The Tempest*
Robert Browning, *Caliban upon Setebos*

CLEOPATRA
William Shakespeare, *Antony and
     Cleopatra*
John Dryden, *All for Love*
George Bernard Shaw, *Caesar and
     Cleopatra*

DON QUIXOTE
Miguel de Cervantes, *Don Quixote*
Franz Kafka, *Parables*

FALSTAFF
William Shakespeare, *Henry IV, Part I,
     Henry IV, Part II, The Merry Wives
     of Windsor*

FAUST
Christopher Marlowe, *Doctor Faustus*
Johann Wolfgang von Goethe, *Faust*
Thomas Mann, *Doctor Faustus*

HAMLET
William Shakespeare, *Hamlet*

IAGO
William Shakespeare, *Othello*

JULIUS CAESAR
William Shakespeare, *Julius Caesar*
George Bernard Shaw, *Caesar and
     Cleopatra*

KING LEAR
William Shakespeare, *King Lear*

MACBETH
William Shakespeare, *Macbeth*

ODYSSEUS/ULYSSES
Homer, *Odyssey*
James Joyce, *Ulysses*

OEDIPUS
Sophocles, *Oedipus Rex, Oedipus
     at Colonus*

OTHELLO
William Shakespeare, *Othello*

ROSALIND
William Shakespeare, *As You Like It*

SANCHO PANZA
Miguel de Cervantes, *Don Quixote*
Franz Kafka, *Parables*

SATAN
The Book of Job
John Milton, *Paradise Lost*

SHYLOCK
William Shakespeare, *The Merchant
     of Venice*

THE WIFE OF BATH
Geoffrey Chaucer, *The Canterbury
     Tales*

**THE EIGHTEENTH AND
NINETEENTH CENTURIES**

AHAB
Herman Melville, *Moby-Dick*

ISABEL ARCHER
Henry James, *Portrait of a Lady*

EMMA BOVARY
Gustave Flaubert, *Madame Bovary*

DOROTHEA BROOKE
George Eliot, *Middlemarch*

CHELSEA HOUSE PUBLISHERS

Major Literary Characters

DAVID COPPERFIELD
Charles Dickens, *David Copperfield*

ROBINSON CRUSOE
Daniel Defoe, *Robinson Crusoe*

DON JUAN
Molière, *Don Juan*
Lord Byron, *Don Juan*

HUCK FINN
Mark Twain, *The Adventures of Tom Sawyer, Adventures of Huckleberry Finn*

CLARISSA HARLOWE
Samuel Richardson, *Clarissa*

HEATHCLIFF
Emily Brontë, *Wuthering Heights*

ANNA KARENINA
Leo Tolstoy, *Anna Karenina*

MR. PICKWICK
Charles Dickens, *The Pickwick Papers*

HESTER PRYNNE
Nathaniel Hawthorne, *The Scarlet Letter*

BECKY SHARP
William Makepeace Thackeray, *Vanity Fair*

LAMBERT STRETHER
Henry James, *The Ambassadors*

EUSTACIA VYE
Thomas Hardy, *The Return of the Native*

TWENTIETH CENTURY

ÁNTONIA
Willa Cather, *My Ántonia*

BRETT ASHLEY
Ernest Hemingway, *The Sun Also Rises*

HANS CASTORP
Thomas Mann, *The Magic Mountain*

HOLDEN CAULFIELD
J. D. Salinger, *The Catcher in the Rye*

CADDY COMPSON
William Faulkner, *The Sound and the Fury*

JANIE CRAWFORD
Zora Neale Hurston, *Their Eyes Were Watching God*

CLARISSA DALLOWAY
Virginia Woolf, *Mrs. Dalloway*

DILSEY
William Faulkner, *The Sound and the Fury*

GATSBY
F. Scott Fitzgerald, *The Great Gatsby*

HERZOG
Saul Bellow, *Herzog*

JOAN OF ARC
William Shakespeare, *Henry VI*
George Bernard Shaw, *Saint Joan*

LOLITA
Vladimir Nabokov, *Lolita*

WILLY LOMAN
Arthur Miller, *Death of a Salesman*

MARLOW
Joseph Conrad, *Lord Jim, Heart of Darkness, Youth, Chance*

PORTNOY
Philip Roth, *Portnoy's Complaint*

BIGGER THOMAS
Richard Wright, *Native Son*

CHELSEA HOUSE PUBLISHERS

Major Literary Characters

IAGO

8300

Edited and with an introduction by
HAROLD BLOOM

CHELSEA HOUSE PUBLISHERS
New York ◇ Philadelphia

Cover illustration: José Ferrer as Iago (Billy Rose Theater Collection, The New York Public Library for the Performing Arts, Astor, Lenox and Tilden Foundation). *Inset:* Title page of the first quarto edition of *Othello* (London: Printed by N. O. for Thomas Walkley, 1622) (By permission of the Folger Shakespeare Library).

Chelsea House Publishers

Editor-in-Chief   Remmel T. Nunn
Managing Editor   Karyn Gullen Browne
Picture Editor   Adrian G. Allen
Art Director   Maria Epes
Manufacturing Manager   Gerald Levine

Major Literary Characters

Senior Editor   S. T. Joshi
Associate Editor   Richard Fumosa
Designer   Maria Epes

Staff for IAGO

Picture Researcher   Ellen Barrett
Assistant Art Director   Howard Brotman
Production Manager   Joseph Romano
Production Coordinator   Marie Claire Cebrián

Printed and bound in the United States of America

First Printing

1   3   5   7   9   8   6   4   2

Library of Congress Cataloging-in-Publication Data

Iago / edited and with an introduction by Harold Bloom.
p.   cm.—(Major literary characters)
Includes bibliographical references and index.
ISBN 0-7910-0920-3.—ISBN 0-7910-0975-0 (pbk.)
1. Shakespeare, William, 1564–1616. Othello.   2. Shakespeare, William, 1564–1616—Characters—Iago.   3. Iago (Fictitious character).
4. Villains in literature.   I. Bloom, Harold.   II. Series.
PR2829.I2   1992
822.3′3—dc20
91-35915
CIP

CONTENTS

THE ANALYSIS OF CHARACTER

Harold Bloom

"Character," according to our dictionaries, still has as a primary meaning a graphic symbol, such as a letter of the alphabet. This meaning reflects the word's apparent origin in the ancient Greek *charactēr,* a sharp stylus. *Charactēr* also meant the mark of the stylus' incisions. Recent fashions in literary criticism have reduced "character" in literature to a matter of marks upon a page. But our word "character" also has a very different meaning, matching that of the ancient Greek *ēthos,* "habitual way of life." Shall we say then that literary character is an imitation of human character, or is it just a grouping of marks? The issue is between a critic like Dr. Samuel Johnson, for whom words were as much like people as like things, and a critic like the late Roland Barthes, who told us that "the fact can only exist linguistically, as a term of discourse." Who is closer to our experience of reading literature, Johnson or Barthes? What difference does it make, if we side with one critic rather than the other?

Barthes is famous, like Foucault and other recent French theorists, for having added to Nietzsche's proclamation of the death of God a subsidiary demise, that of the literary author. If there are no authors, then there are no fictional personages, presumably because literature does not refer to a world outside language. Words indeed necessarily refer to other words in the first place, but the impact of words ultimately is drawn from a universe of fact. Stories, poems, and plays are recognizable as such because they are human utterances within traditions of utterances, and traditions, by achieving authority, become a kind of fact, or at least the sense of a fact. Our sense that literary characters, within the context of a fictive cosmos, indeed are fictional personages is also a kind of fact. The meaning and value of every character in a successful work of literary representation depend upon our ideas of persons in the factual reality of our lives.

Literary character is always an invention, and inventions generally are indebted to prior inventions. Shakespeare is the inventor of literary character as we know it; he reformed the universal human expectations for the verbal imitation of personality, and the reformation appears now to be permanent and uncannily inevitable. Remarkable as the Bible and Homer are at representing personages, their characters are relatively unchanging. They age within their stories, but their habitual modes of being do not develop. Jacob and Achilles unfold before us, but without metamorphoses. Lear and Macbeth, Hamlet and Othello severely modify themselves not only by their actions, but by their utterances, and most of all through *overhearing themselves,* whether they speak to themselves or to others. Pondering what they themselves have said, they will to change, and actually do change, sometimes extravagantly yet always persuasively. Or else they suffer change, without willing it, but in reaction not so much to their language as to their relation to that language.

I do not think it useful to say that Shakespeare successfully imitated elements in our characters. Rather, it could be argued that he compelled aspects of character to appear that previously were concealed, or not available to representation. This is not to say that Shakespeare is God, but to remind us that language is not God either. The mimesis of character in Shakespeare's dramas now seems to us normative, and indeed became the accepted mode almost immediately, as Ben Jonson shrewdly and somewhat grudgingly implied. And yet, Shakespearean representation has surprisingly little in common with the imitation of reality in Jonson or in Christopher Marlowe. The origins of Shakespeare's originality in the portrayal of men and women are to be found in the *Canterbury Tales* of Geoffrey Chaucer, insofar as they can be located anywhere before Shakespeare himself. Chaucer's savage and superb Pardoner overhears his own tale-telling, as well as his mocking rehearsal of his own spiel, and through this overhearing he is emboldened to forget himself, and enthusiastically urges all his fellow-pilgrims to come forward to be fleeced by him. His self-awareness, and apocalyptically rancid sense of spiritual fall, are preludes to the even grander abysses of the perverted will in Iago and in Edmund. What might be called the character trait of a negative charisma may be Chaucer's invention, but came to its perfection in Shakespearean mimesis.

The analysis of character is as much Shakespeare's invention as the representation of character is, since Iago and Edmund are adepts at analyzing both themselves and their victims. Hamlet, whose overwhelming charisma has many negative components, is certainly the most comprehensive of all literary characters, and so necessarily prophesies the labyrinthine complexities of the will in Iago and Edmund. Charisma, according to Max Weber, its first codifier, is primarily a natural endowment, and implies a primordial and idiosyncratic power over nature, and so finally over death. Hamlet's uncanniness is at its most suggestive in the scene of his long dying, where the audience, through the mediation of Horatio, itself is compelled to meditate upon suicide, if only because outliving the prince of Denmark scarcely seems an option.

Shakespearean representation has usurped not only our sense of literary character, but our sense of ourselves as characters, with Hamlet playing the part of the largest of these usurpations. Insofar as we have an idea of human disinterestedness, we tend to derive it from the Hamlet of Act V, whose quietism has about it a ghostly authority. Oscar Wilde, in his profound and profoundly witty dialogue, "The Decay of Lying," expressed a permanent insight when he insisted that art shaped every era, far more than any age formed art. Life imitates art, we imitate Shakespeare, because without Shakespeare we would perish for lack of images. Wilde's grandest audacity demystifies Shakespearean mimesis with a Shakespearean vivaciousness: "This unfortunate aphorism about art holding the mirror up to Nature is deliberately said by Hamlet in order to convince the bystanders of his absolute insanity in all art-matters." Of *Hamlet*'s influence upon the ages Wilde remarked that: "The world has grown sad because a puppet was once melancholy." "Puppet" is Wilde's own deconstruction, a brilliant reminder that Shakespeare's artistry of illusion has so mastered reality as to have changed reality, evidently forever.

The analysis of character, as a critical pursuit, seems to me as much a Shakespearean invention as literary character was, since much of what we know about how to analyze character necessarily follows Shakespearean procedures. His hero-villains, from Richard III through Iago, Edmund, and Macbeth, are shrewd and endless questers into their own self-motivations. If we could bear to see Hamlet, in his unwearied negations, as another hero-villain, then we would judge him the supreme analyst of the darker recalcitrances in the selfhood. Freud followed the pre-Socratic Empedocles, in arguing that character is fate, a frightening doctrine that maintains the fear that there are no accidents, that over-determination rules us all of our lives. Hamlet assumes the same, yet adds to this argument the terrible passivity he manifests in Act V. Throughout Shakespeare's tragedies, the most interesting personages seem doom-eager, reminding us again that a Shakespearean reading of Freud would be more illuminating than a Freudian exegesis of Shakespeare. We learn more when we discover Hamlet in the Freudian Death Drive, than when we read *Beyond the Pleasure Principle* into *Hamlet*.

In Shakespearean comedy, character achieves its true literary apotheosis, which is the representation of the inner freedom that can be created by great wit alone. Rosalind and Falstaff, perhaps alone among Shakespeare's personages, match Hamlet in wit, though hardly in the metaphysics of consciousness. Whether in the comic or the modern mode, Shakespeare has set the standard of measurement in the balance between character and passion.

In Shakespeare the self is more dramatized than theatricalized, which is why a Shakespearean reading of Freud works out so well. Character-formation after the passing of the Oedipal stage takes the place of fetishistic fragmentings of the self. Critics who now call literary character into question, and who proclaim also the death of the author, invariably also regard all notions, literary and human, of a stable character as being mere reductions of deeper pre-Oedipal desires. It becomes clear that the fortunes of literary character rise and fall with the prestige of normative conceptions of the ego. Shakespeare's Iago, who wars against being, may be the first deconstructionist of the self, with his proclamation of "I am not what I am." This constitutes the necessary prologue to any view that would regard a fixed ego as a virtual abnormality. But deconstructions of the self are no more modern than Modernism is. Like literary modernism, the decentered ego came out of the Hellenistic culture of ancient Alexandria. The Gnostic heretics believed that the psyche, like the body, was a fallen entity, mechanically fashioned by the Demiurge or false creator. They held however that each of us possessed also a spark or pneuma, which was a fragment of the original Abyss or true, alien God. The soul or psyche within every one of us was thus at war with the self or pneuma, and only that sparklike self could be saved.

Shakespeare, following after Chaucer in this respect, was the first and remains still the greatest master of representing character both as a stable soul and a wavering self. There is a substance that endures in Shakespeare's figures, and there is also a quicksilver rendition of the unsettling sparks. Racine and Tolstoy, Balzac and Dickens, follow in Shakespeare's wake by giving us some sense of pre-Oedipal sparks or drives, and considerably more sense of post-Oedipal character and personality, stabilizations or sublimations of the fetish-seeking drives. Critics like Leo Bersani and René Girard argue eloquently against our taking this mimesis as the only proper work of literature. I would suggest that strong fictions of the self, from the Bible through Samuel Beckett, necessarily participate in both modes, the sublimation of desire, and the persistence of a primordial desire. The mystery of Hamlet or of Lear is intimately invested in the tangled mixture of the two modes of representation.

Psychic mobility is proposed by Bersani as the ideal to which deconstructions of the literary self may yet guide us. The ideal has its pathos, but the realities of literary representation seem to me very different, perhaps destructively so. When a novelist like D. H. Lawrence sought to reduce his characters to Eros and the Death Drive, he still had to persuade us of his authority at mimesis by lavishing upon the figures of *The Rainbow* and *Women in Love* all of the vivid stigmata of normative personality. Birkin and Ursula may represent antithetical and uncanny drives, but they develop and change as characters pondering their own pronouncements and reactions to self and others. The cost of a non-Shakespearean representation is enormous. Pynchon, in *The Crying of Lot 49* and *Gravity's Rainbow*, evades the burden of the normative by resorting to something like Christopher Marlowe's art of caricature in *The Jew of Malta*. Marlowe's Barabas is a marvelous rhetorician, yet he is a cartoon alongside the troublingly equivocal Shylock. Pynchon's personages are deliberate cartoons also, as flat as comic strips. Marlowe's achievement, and Pynchon's, are beyond dispute, yet they are like the prelude and the postlude to Shakespearean reality. They do not wish to engage with our hunger for the empirical world and so they enter the problematic cosmos of literary fantasy.

No writer, not even Shakespeare or Proust, alters the available stock that we agree to call reality, but Shakespeare, more than any other, does show us how much of reality we could encounter if only we retained adequate desire. The strong literary representation of character is already an analysis of character, and is part of the healing work of a literary culture, which implicitly seeks to cure violence through a normative mimesis of ego, *as if it were stable,* whether in actuality it is or is not. I do not believe that this is a social quest taken on by literary culture, but rather that we confront here the aesthetic essence of what makes a culture *literary,* rather than metaphysical or ethical or religious. A culture becomes literary when its conceptual modes have failed it, which means when religion, philosophy, and science have begun to lose their authority. If they cannot heal violence, then literature attempts to do so, which may be only a turning inside out of the critical arguments of Girard and Bersani.

I conclude by offering a particular instance or special case as a paradigm for the healing enterprise that is at once the representation and the analysis of literary character. Let us call it the aesthetics of being outraged, or rather of successfully representing the state of being outraged. W. C. Fields was one modern master of such representation, and Nathanael West was another, as was Faulkner before him. Here also the greatest master remains Shakespeare, whose Macbeth, himself a bloody outrage, yet retains our imaginative sympathy precisely because he grows increasingly outraged as he experiences the equivocation of the fiend that lies like truth. The double-natured promises and the prophecies of the weird sisters finally induce in Macbeth an apocalyptic version of the stage actor's anxiety at missing cues, the horror of a phantasmagoric stage fright of missing one's time, of always reacting too late. Macbeth, a veritable monster of solipsistic inwardness but no intellectual, counters his dilemma by fresh murders, that prolong him in time yet provoke him only to a perpetually freshened sense of being outraged, as all his expectations become still worse confounded. We are moved by Macbeth, however estrangedly, because his terrible inwardness is a paradigm for our own solipsism, but also because none of us can resist a strong and successful representation of the human in a state of being outraged.

The ultimate outrage is the necessity of dying, an outrage concealed in a multitude of masks, including the tyrannical ambitions of Macbeth. I suspect that our outrage at being outraged is the most difficult of all our affects for us to represent to ourselves, which is why we are so inclined to imaginative sympathy for a character who strongly conveys that affect to us. The Shrike of West's *Miss Lonely-hearts* or Faulkner's Joe Christmas of *Light in August* are crucial modern instances, but such figures can be located in many other works, since the ability to represent this extreme emotion is one of the tests that strong writers are driven to set for themselves.

However a reader seeks to reduce literary character to a question of marks on a page, she will come at last to the impasse constituted by the thought of death, her death, and before that to all the stations of being outraged that memorialize her own drive towards death. In reading, she quests for evidences that are strong representations, whether of her desire or her despair. Such questings constitute the necessary basis for the analysis of literary character, an enterprise that always will survive every vagary of critical fashion.

EDITOR'S NOTE

This book brings together a representative selection of the best criticism that has been devoted to Iago, the magnificent villain of Shakespeare's tragedy, *Othello*. The critical extracts and essays are reprinted here in the chronological order of their original publication. I am grateful to S. T. Joshi for his learning and energy in helping me to edit this volume.

My introduction centers upon Iago's ontological ambivalences toward Othello, the war-god who is both worshipped and hated by his passed-over follower. The critical extracts begin with Thomas Rymer's strictures and Dr. Johnson's moral perceptions, and proceed through Hazlitt and Coleridge, Swinburne and Shaw, on to such major modern Shakespeareans as Empson, Goddard, and Heilman.

Full-scale critical essays begin with A. C. Bradley's classic meditation upon Iago's resourcefulness, and with Carroll Camden's informed portrait of Iago as Renaissance antifeminist. Marvin Rosenberg's Iago incarnates High Freudian aggressivity, while W. H. Auden's celebrated vision of Iago presents him as the apotheosis of that dangerous creature, the practical joker.

In Madeleine Doran's interpretation, Iago's triumph over Othello is founded upon the Moor's inability to live with doubt, while Iago's very atmosphere is the realm of "if." Jane Adelman's view is complementary, since she emphasizes Iago's flaw as being the failure of mere "will" to carry everything before it.

Randolph Splitter's Iago is Othello's symbiotic fantasy-double, while Michael Neill sees Iago as native Venetian, taking advantage of the displacement of Othello and Cassio, both outsiders from the peculiar Venetian perspective. For Garry Gray, Iago is an image of the escape from social control into a dangerous, unlimited psychic "freedom."

The "questionable shapes" of Iago become, for Kenneth Palmer, the means for splitting the play's other characters off from what they know, and their very modes of knowledge.

This book concludes with Michael E. Mooney's ironic demonstration that Iago is still adept at persuading some of our advanced Shakespearean critics that his distorted perception of Othello ought to become their own.

INTRODUCTION

To see Iago as affiliated with his fellow-Machiavel, Edmund, is traditional; to see his troubling affinities with some aspects of Hamlet, the counter-Machiavel, is not altogether untraditional. Hamlet and Iago alike are theatrical geniuses, though the Prince of Denmark's genius is universal, whereas Iago, who prides himself upon his military talents, displays throughout a dramatic grasp of the power of fantasy that rivals Shakespeare's own. I cannot therefore agree with the late C. L. Barber and Richard P. Wheeler when, in their very useful book, *The Whole Journey,* they say of Iago: "What he seeks is to become the Moor by making the Moor enact his fantasies, fantasies that will destroy them both. When that is accomplished, he can stop." Iago is too aware of the incommensurateness between his godlike general and himself to seek to become Othello, and dreadfully enough the fantasies that Iago makes the Moor enact are authentically Othello's own uneasy imaginings. Shakespeare's grand negations, at their strongest, are figures in a kind of negative poetics, even a kind of dramatic negative theology. Iago, like Hamlet, is a great improviser. He does not set out to become the Moor, or to destroy the Moor; it may be that he does not even begin with the desire to destroy Desdemona. I think we need to start farther back with Iago, in order to see more fully how original a character he was, and is. Iago is not a skeptic, but a believer. His religion is war, and his god is Othello, and so his fury when Cassio is preferred to him is the fury of the priest or worshipper who has been found unworthy, or at least less worthy than another who lacks the intensity of his own devotion. Iago becomes instead a priest of Resentment, fit ancestor for many current pale clerks whose faith has been thwarted.

Iago, as Harold Goddard wisely said, is the incarnation of the spirit of modern war, indeed a prophecy of total war, the religion of war. His truest forerunner in Shakespeare is not Richard III but Ulysses, the theoretician of war, indeed its positive theologian, as opposed to its negative theologians in Iago and Edmund, and its fantastic imagination in Macbeth. Just as the relationship between Lear's Fool and Lear, or between Falstaff and Hal, cannot be understood without our recognizing the extraordinary ambivalence of the Fool towards Lear, and of Hal towards

1

Falstaff, so we need to comprehend Iago primarily in terms of his apocalyptic ambivalence in regard to Othello. Even as the play opens, we confront in Iago's ambivalence something very close to its descendant in Melville's Ahab. Ahab's Othello is Moby Dick, conceived as a great Gnostic Demiurge, a cosmic principle that inspires hatred and revenge. Iago's Moby Dick is the superb Othello, greatest of captains, worshipped by Iago as the God of War, but the worship has become hatred and a spur to revenge. Moby Dick has crippled Ahab, perhaps castrated him, but the permanent mystery of Shakespeare's tragedy is that Othello has done nothing to Iago, except failed to give him preference over Cassio. Yet in a perspective granted by the negative theology of war-as-religion, Iago's malignancy is anything but motiveless. For Iago, God or Othello is everything, because war is everything, and if Othello prefers Cassio, then Iago is nothing, as Cain felt he was nothing when Abel was preferred by Yahweh, or as Satan in *Paradise Lost* believes himself to be nothing when he belatedly hears Christ preferred by Milton's God. Iago is neither Cain nor the Devil, but something far worse: a priest of Moloch or Mars who is also a master psychologist, a great playwright, and a theologian of the primal Abyss. Iago's cognitive power is his most astonishing attribute; his intellect is as quick and fecund as Hamlet's, though vastly less comprehensive.

Iago's incessant war is against being itself, which he has identified with Othello. That identification, granted Iago's perspective, is no hyperbole; cultural change and loss accounts for our tendency to undervalue Othello. Iago's Othello is far closer to the *Iliad*'s Achilles than he is to Shakespeare's Achilles in *Troilus and Cressida*, though I mean a closeness in ontological force, rather than in personality. The given in Shakespeare's *The Tragedy of Othello, the Moor of Venice*, is Othello's splendor of being, his unquestioned magnitude, his absolute authority and perfection in the camp and field of war. We do not much exalt the purity of arms, but Shakespeare sometimes does, or at least allows some of his plays to entertain the possibility of such exaltation. Iago believes in nothing but his captain Othello, loves nothing but the captain in Othello, and destroys Othello, but not as captain, not as the pure warrior. Even his destruction of Othello the man remains a negative celebration of Othello the captain, a negative affirmation of the reality of the God of War.

A worship that is hatred is best expressed by Iago's marvelous boast: "I am not what I am," which echoes and undoes St. Paul's "By the grace of God I am what I am." By Othello's refusal of grace or preference, Iago is driven to the negation: "I am not what I am." That statement is not a mere insistence that he is not Othello's "honest Iago," the ensign or standard-bearer pledged to die rather than to yield Othello's colors to the enemy. I hear a kind of religious despair in it as well: "I am not what I am," I am nothing, if the only ontological being that I acknowledge has failed to acknowledge me. Reality has abandoned Iago, and his revenge is a rebellion that in the first place is against himself. He will not, cannot walk away from Othello to another captain; he now hates God, but continues to believe in him. That ambivalent regard for Othello demands expression through a passion for destruction that is also a creative passion. Primal ambivalence fires the whole substance of

Iago's being, and fathers his genius: the would-be second-in-command emerges as a Machiavel, as a poet who writes with people rather than with words, and most fascinatingly as the first High Aesthete, a dramatic critic adoring his own achievement as a dramatist. Richard III's gusto, his savage delight in his own villainy, is replaced by Iago's subtly perverse sadistic pleasure in his power of manipulation. Richard manipulates both his equals and his underlings. Iago manipulates as he chooses, but he knows that his negative greatness achieves apotheosis only by manipulating the fall of his mortal god, Othello. Iago's motive is Sublime: he debases, humiliates, and finally destroys the only authority he recognizes; his enterprise finally intends nothing less than the death of God. The God of War, having failed to recognize his true son in Iago, must be horribly punished. Falstaff, the God of Wit, is punished for having recognized his true son in Hal, who may once have accepted the recognition, but now recoils from it in a profound ambivalence. Hal cannot allow himself to know that he both loves and hates Falstaff, but consciously regards the fat knight as a kind of superior fool or jester. The ambivalence, transferred from Henry IV to Falstaff, destroys Falstaff and strengthens Hal. Iago, when we first encounter him, has been rejected for Cassio, and is conscious only of his great hatred for Othello. As he works upon Othello, Iago is delighted and surprised by his ease and aesthetic wonder of accomplishment. The delight could not have its intensity and largeness of dimension if Iago did not retain a reverence and passion for the magnitude of what he was ruining. A great captain, for Iago and for Shakespeare, is a masterpiece of nature, an Adamic splendor falling from godlike to something less than human status.

I think we must dismiss any speculation that Iago has a repressed sexual desire for Othello, which is about as useless as the notion that there was a sexual relationship between Falstaff and Hal. An extreme negative theologian or Gnostic does not lust after God, and what Freud learned from Shakespeare was the terrible ambivalence of our longing for reconcilement with the father while wishing also to murder the father. Freudian readings of Shakespeare, as I have remarked elsewhere, give us neither Shakespeare nor Freud, but a Shakespearean reading of Freud is capable of giving us both. Iago is subtler than Freud, as negative theology is frequently subtler than moral psychology. Reconcilement with Othello is not possible, Iago realizes, because it is Othello who must atone for the rejection of Iago. The degradation of God, a Gnostic concept, is Iago's project: the involuntary atonement of Othello through his debasement. The murder of Othello is not, cannot be Iago's project. A negative theologian does not seek to slay the father, nor to replace the father. It is enough that the father descend into the Abyss, there to suffer uncreation, to return to the void formlessness of night.

For me, the Shakespearean question to ask concerning Iago is: how does he change in the course of the drama? Unlike Macbeth, Iago does not progressively lose control of his own imagination. What makes *The Tragedy of Othello, the Moor of Venice* so harrowing a work is the total triumph of Iago, until he is brought down so unexpectedly by his wife's outrage at the victimage of Desdemona. Iago's changes, until Emilia's courage ends him, are marches of triumphalism, in which he perpetually astonishes himself by his own manipulative genius. Yet that is only part of the story, the emergence of Iago as appreciative dramatic critic of his own power in composition. There is another side to this triumphalism, and that is the extent to which Iago, as great improviser, traps himself also in his own web. More successful at manipulating Othello than he could have imagined, he is forced into a situation where he must prove Othello's love a whore, or himself be slain by Othello. His extraordinary status as pure negation gives at once unlimited intellect, an over-whelming sense of nothingness, and a primal ambivalence towards Othello's mas-sive, ontological presence that drives him beyond even his worked-out plottings. In this he differs from Edmund, who keeps to plan until the bodies of Goneril and Regan are brought in. Iago changes with each fresh confrontation, whether with Othello or with Desdemona, until he enters the final changelessness of his silence, prompted by outrage at Emilia's courageous devotion to the murdered and slan-dered Desdemona.

Iago tells us that he is nothing if not critical, and that he has never found a man that knew how to love himself. We can apply both these self-judgments to one of the most extraordinary moments in the play, when Emilia has given Iago the handkerchief and then been sent away by him (Act III, scene iii, lines 318–29). Alone on stage, Iago exults at his own mastery, and then is moved to a marvelous and horrible aesthetic apprehension of the ruined Othello, the fallen god of hon-orable war, and now Iago's masterpiece:

> I will in Cassio's lodging lose this napkin
> And let him find it. Trifles light as air
> Are to the jealous confirmations strong
> As proofs of Holy Writ. This may do something.
> The Moor already changes with my poison:
> Dangerous conceits are in their natures poisons,
> Which at the first are scarce found to distaste,
> But, with a little, act upon the blood,
> Burn like the mines of sulfur. I did say so.
>   *Enter Othello.*
> Look where he comes! Not poppy nor mandragora,
> Nor all the drowsy syrups of the world,
> Shall ever medicine thee to that sweet sleep
> Which thou owedst yesterday.

We shudder and yet, for this great moment, we *are* Iago, or perhaps Iago is already John Keats and Walter Pater, particularly as he rolls out those sensuous negatives: "Not poppy nor mandragora, / Nor all the drowsy syrups of the world . . ." For he is nothing if not critical, and he chants an appreciation of his own poisonous art, relishing each syllable of "poppy" and "mandragora" and "drowsy syrups" and "sweet sleep." Aesthetic awareness in our modern sense, the poetic self-consciousness of Keats and Pater and the sublime Oscar Wilde, is invented by

Iago in this grand negative moment. The excited apprehension of: "This may do something" leads to the conscious pride of "I did say so," as Iago hymns the power of his own "dangerous conceits." It is only a step from this to that still more dangerous prevalence of the murderous imagination that will triumph even more sublimely in the strongest of all Shakespearean negations, Macbeth.

—H. B.

CRITICAL EXTRACTS

THOMAS RYMER

But what is most intolerable is *Jago*. He is no Black-amoor Souldier, so we may be sure he should be like other Souldiers of our acquaintance; yet never in Tragedy, nor in Comedy, nor in Nature was a Souldier with his Character; take it in the Authors own words;

> EM.:   some Eternal Villain
> Some busie, and insinuating Rogue,
> Some cogging, couzening Slave, to get some Office.

Horace Describes a Souldier otherwise:

> Impiger, iracundus, inexorabilis, acer.

Shakespear knew his Character of *Jago* was inconsistent. In this very Play he pronounces,

> If thou dost deliver more or less than Truth,
> Thou are no Souldier.——

This he knew, but to entertain the Audience with something new and surprising, against common sense, and Nature, he would pass upon us a close, dissembling, false, insinuating rascal, instead of an open-hearted, frank, plain-dealing Souldier, a character constantly worn by them for some thousands of years in the World.

—THOMAS RYMER, *A Short View of Tragedy* [1692], *The Critical Works of Thomas Rymer*, ed. Curt A. Zimansky (New Haven: Yale University Press, 1956), pp. 134–35

SAMUEL JOHNSON

The beauties of this play impress themselves so strongly upon the attention of the reader, that they can draw no aid from critical illustration. The fiery openness of Othello, magnanimous, artless, and credulous, boundless in his confidence, ardent in his affection, inflexible in his resolution, and obdurate in his revenge; the cool malignity of Iago, silent in his resentment, subtle in his designs, and studious at once of his interest and his vengeance; the soft simplicity of Desdemona, confident of merit, and conscious of innocence, her artless perseverance in her suit, and her slowness to suspect that she can be suspected, are such proofs of Shakespeare's skill in human nature, as, I suppose, it is vain to seek in any modern writer. The gradual progress which Iago makes in the Moor's conviction, and the circumstances which he employs to inflame him, are so artfully natural, that, though it will perhaps not be said of him as he says of himself, that he is "a man not easily jealous," yet we cannot but pity him when at last we find him "perplexed in the extreme."

There is always danger lest wickedness conjoined with abilities should steal upon esteem, though it misses of approbation; but the character of Iago is so conducted, that he is from the first scene to the last hated and despised.

—SAMUEL JOHNSON, *The Plays of William Shakespeare*
(London: J. & R. Tonson, 1765), Vol. 8, p. 472

WILLIAM HAZLITT

We certainly think Mr. Kean's performance of the part of Iago one of the most extraordinary exhibitions on the stage. There is no one within our remembrance who has so completely foiled the critics as this celebrated actor: one sagacious person imagines that he must perform a part in a certain manner,—another virtuoso chalks out a different path for him; and when the time comes, he does the whole off in a way that neither of them had the least conception of, and which both of them are therefore very ready to condemn as entirely wrong. It was ever the trick of genius to be thus. We confess that Mr. Kean has thrown us out more than once. For instance, we are very much inclined to adopt the opinion of a contemporary critic, that his *Richard* is not gay enough, and that his *Iago* is not grave enough. This he may perhaps conceive to be the mere caprice of idle criticism; but we will try to give our reasons, and shall leave them to Mr. Kean's better judgment. It is to be remembered, then, that *Richard* was a princely villain, borne along in a sort of triumphal car of royal state, buoyed up with the hopes and privileges of his birth, reposing even on the sanctity of religion, trampling on his devoted victims without remorse, and who looked out and laughed from the high watch-tower of his confidence and his expectations on the desolation and misery he had caused around him. He held on his way, unquestioned, 'hedged in with the divinity of kings,' amenable to no tribunal, and abusing his power *in contempt of mankind*. But as for *Iago*, we conceive differently of him. He had not the same natural advantages.

He was a mere adventurer in mischief, a pains-taking plodding knave, without patent or pedigree, who was obliged to work his up-hill way by wit, not by will, and to be the founder of his own fortune. He was, if we may be allowed a vulgar allusion, a sort of prototype of modern Jacobinism, who thought that talents ought to decide the place,—a man of 'morbid sensibility,' (in the fashionable phrase), full of distrust, of hatred, of anxious and corroding thoughts, and who, though he might assume a temporary superiority over others by superior adroitness, and pride himself in his skill, could not be supposed to assume it as a matter of course, as if he had been entitled to it from his birth. We do not here mean to enter into the characters of the two men, but something must be allowed to the difference of their situations. There might be the same insensibility in both as to the end in view, but there could not well be the same security as to the success of the means. *Iago* had to pass through a different ordeal: he had no appliances and means to boot; no royal road to the completion of his tragedy. His pretensions were not backed by authority; they were not baptized at the font; they were not holy-waterproof. He had the whole to answer for in his own person, and could not shift the responsibility to the heads of others. Mr. Kean's *Richard* was, therefore, we think, deficient in something of that regal jollity and reeling triumph of success which the part would bear; but this we can easily account for, because it is the traditional commonplace idea of the character, that he is to 'play the dog—to bite and snarl.'—The extreme unconcern and laboured levity of his *Iago*, on the contrary, is a refinement and original device of the actor's own mind, and therefore deserves consideration. The character of *Iago*, in fact, belongs to a class of characters common to Shakspeare, and at the same time peculiar to him—namely, that of great intellectual activity, accompanied with a total want of moral principle, and therefore displaying itself at the constant expence of others, making use of reason as a pander to will—employing its ingenuity and its resources to palliate its own crimes and aggravate the faults of others, and seeking to confound the practical distinctions of right and wrong, by referring them to some overstrained standard of speculative refinement.—Some persons, more nice than wise, have thought the whole of the character of *Iago* unnatural. Shakspeare, who was quite as good a philosopher as he was a poet, thought otherwise. He knew that the love of power, which is another name for the love of mischief, was natural to man. He would know this as well or better than if it had been demonstrated to him by a logical diagram, merely from seeing children paddle in the dirt, or kill flies for sport. We might ask those who think the character of *Iago* not natural, why they go to see it performed, but from the interest it excites, the sharper edge which it sets on their curiosity and imagination? Why do we go to see tragedies in general? Why do we always read the accounts in the newspapers of dreadful fires and shocking murders, but for the same reason? Why do so many persons frequent executions and trials, or why do the lower classes almost universally take delight in barbarous sports and cruelty to animals, but because there is a natural tendency in the mind to strong excitement, a desire to have its faculties roused and stimulated to the utmost?

Whenever this principle is not under the restraint of humanity, or the sense of moral obligation, there are no excesses to which it will not of itself give rise, without the assistance of any other motive, either of passion or self-interest. *Iago* is only an extreme instance of the kind; that is, of diseased intellectual activity, with an almost perfect indifference to moral good or evil, or rather with a preference of the latter, because it falls more in with his favourite propensity, gives greater zest to his thoughts, and scope to his actions.—Be it observed, too, (for the sake of those who are for squaring all human actions by the maxims of Rochefoucault), that he is quite or nearly as indifferent to his own fate as to that of others; that he runs all risks for a trifling and doubtful advantage; and is himself the dupe and victim of his ruling passion—an incorrigible love of mischief—an insatiable craving after action of the most difficult and dangerous kind. Our 'Ancient' is a philosopher, who fancies that a lie that kills has more point in it than an alliteration or an antithesis; who thinks a fatal experiment on the peace of a family a better thing than watching the palpitations in the heart of a flea in an air-pump; who plots the ruin of his friends as an exercise for his understanding, and stabs men in the dark to prevent *ennui*. Now this, though it be sport, yet it is dreadful sport. There is no room for trifling and indifference, nor scarcely for the appearance of it; the very object of his whole plot is to keep his faculties stretched on the rack, in a state of watch and ward, in a sort of breathless suspense, without a moment's interval of repose. He has a desperate stake to play for, like a man who fences with poisoned weapons, and has business enough on his hands to call for the whole stock of his sober circumspection, his dark duplicity, and insidious gravity. He resembles a man who sits down to play at chess, for the sake of the difficulty and complication of the game, and who immediately becomes absorbed in it. His amusements, if they are amusements, are severe and saturnine—even his wit blisters. His gaiety arises from the success of his treachery; his ease from the sense of the torture he has inflicted on others. Even, if other circumstances permitted it, the part he has to play with *Othello* requires that he should assume the most serious concern, and something of the plausibility of a confessor. 'His cue is villainous melancholy, with a sigh like Tom o' Bedlam.' He is repeatedly called 'honest *Iago*,' which looks as if there were something suspicious in his appearance, which admitted a different construction. The tone which he adopts in the scenes with *Roderigo, Desdemona,* and *Cassio,* is only a relaxation from the more arduous business of the play. Yet there is in all his conversation an inveterate misanthropy, a licentious keenness of perception, which is always sagacious of evil, and snuffs up the tainted scent of its quarry with rancorous delight. An exuberance of spleen is the essence of the character. The view which we have here taken of the subject (if at all correct) will not therefore justify the extreme alteration which Mr. Kean has introduced into the part. Actors in general have been struck only with the wickedness of the character, and have exhibited an assassin going to the place of execution. Mr. Kean has abstracted the wit of the character, and makes *Iago* appear throughout an excellent good fellow, and lively bottle-companion. But though we do not wish him to be represented as a monster, or fiend, we see no reason why he should instantly be converted into a pattern of comic gaiety and good-humour. The light which illumines the character should rather resemble the flashes of lightning in the mirky sky, which make the darkness more terrible. Mr. Kean's *Iago* is, we suspect, too much in the sun. His manner of acting the part would have suited better with the character of *Edmund* in *King Lear*, who, though in other respects much the same, has a spice of gallantry in his constitution, and has the favour and countenance of the ladies, which always gives a man the smug appearance of a bridegroom!

—WILLIAM HAZLITT, "On Mr. Kean's Iago" [1814], *The Round Table*
(Edinburgh: Archibald Constable & Co.; London: Longman, Hurst, Rees,
Orme, & Brown, 1817)

SAMUEL TAYLOR COLERIDGE

Iago's speech:—

Virtue? a fig! 'tis in ourselves, that we are thus, or thus, &c.

This speech comprises the passionless character of Iago. It is all will in intellect; and therefore he is here a bold partizan of a truth, but yet of a truth converted into a falsehood by the absence of all the necessary modifications caused by the frail nature of man. And then comes the last sentiment,—

Our raging motions, our carnal stings, our unbitted lusts, whereof I take this, that you call—love, to be a sect or scion!

Here is the true Iagoism of, alas! how many! Note Iago's pride of mastery in the repetition of 'Go, make money!' to his anticipated dupe, even stronger than his love of lucre: and when Roderigo is completely won—

I am chang'd. I'll go sell all my land—

when the effect has been fully produced, the repetition of triumph—

Go to; farewell; put money enough in your purse!

The remainder—Iago's soliloquy—the motive-hunting of a motiveless malignity— how awful it is! Yea, whilst he is still allowed to bear the divine image, it is too fiendish for his own steady view,—for the lonely gaze of a being next to devil, and only not quite devil,—and yet a character which Shakespeare has attempted and executed, without disgust and without scandal!

—SAMUEL TAYLOR COLERIDGE, "Notes on *Othello*" [1819], *Literary Remains*,
ed. Henry Nelson Coleridge (London: William Pickering, 1836),
Vol. 2, pp. 259–60

VICTOR HUGO

Now what is Othello? He is the night. An immense fatal figure. Night is amorous of day. Darkness loves the dawn. The African adores the white woman. Othello has for his light and for his frenzy, Desdemona. And then, how easy to him is jealousy! He is great, he is dignified, he is majestic, he soars above all heads; he has as an escort bravery, battle, the braying of trumpets, the banners of war, renown, glory; he is radiant with twenty victories, he is studded with stars, this Othello: but he is black. And thus how soon, when jealous, the hero becomes the monster, the black becomes the negro! How speedily has night beckoned to death!

By the side of Othello, who is night, there is Iago, who is evil—evil, the other form of darkness. Night is but the night of the world; evil is the night of the soul. How deeply black are perfidy and falsehood! It is all one whether what courses through the veins be ink or treason. Whoever has jostled against imposture and perjury, knows it: one must blindly grope one's way with knavery. Pour hypocrisy upon the break of day, and you put out the sun; and this, thanks to false religions, is what happens to God.

Iago near Othello is the precipice near the landslip. "This way!" he says in a low voice. The snare advises blindness. The lover of darkness guides the black. Deceit takes upon itself to give what light may be required by night. Falsehood serves as a blind man's dog to jealousy. Othello the negro and Iago the traitor pitted against whiteness and candor: what more formidable? These ferocities of darkness act in unison. These two incarnations of the eclipse conspire, the one roaring, the other sneering, for the tragic suffocation of light.

Sound this profound thing. Othello is the night, and being night, and wishing to kill, what does he take to slay with? Poison? the club? the axe? the knife? No; the pillow. To kill is to lull to sleep. Shakespeare himself perhaps did not take this into account. The creator sometimes, almost unknown to himself, yields to his type, so truly is that type a power. And it is thus that Desdemona, spouse of the man Night, dies, stifled by the pillow upon which the first kiss was given, and which receives the last sigh.

—VICTOR HUGO, *William Shakespeare* [1864], tr. Melville B. Anderson
(Chicago: A. C. McClurg, 1887), pp. 242–43

EDWARD DOWDEN

Of the tragic story what is the final issue? The central point of its spiritual import lies in the contrast between the two men, Iago and his victim. Iago, with keen intellectual faculties and manifold culture in Italian vice, lives and thrives after his fashion in a world from which all virtue and all beauty are absent. Othello with his barbaric innocence and regal magnificence of soul must cease to live the moment he ceases to retain faith in the purity and goodness which were to him the highest and most real things upon earth. Or if he live life must become to him a cruel agony.

Shakspere compels us to acknowledge that self-slaughter is a rapturous energy—that such prolonged agony is joy in comparison with the earthly life-in-death of such a soul as that of Iago. The noble nature is taken in the toils because it is noble. Iago suspects his wife of every baseness, but the suspicion has no other effect than to intensify his malignity. Iago could not be captured and constrained to heroic suffering and rage. The shame of every being who bears the name of woman is credible to Iago, and yet he can grate from his throat the jarring music:

> And let me the canakin clink, clink:
> And let me the canakin clink.

There is therefore, Shakspere would have us understand, something more inimical to humanity than suffering—namely, an incapacity for noble pain. To die as Othello dies is indeed grievous. But to live as Iago lives, devouring the dust and stinging—this is more appalling.

Such is the spiritual motive that controls the tragedy. And the validity of this truth is demonstrable to every sound conscience. No supernatural authority needs to be summoned to bear witness to this reality of human life. No pallid flame of hell, no splendour of dawning heaven, needs show itself beyond the verge of earth to illumine this truth. It is a portion of the ascertained fact of human nature, and of this our mortal existence. We look upon "the tragic loading of the bed," and we see Iago in presence of the ruin he has wrought. We are not compelled to seek for any resolution of these apparent discords in any alleged life to come. That may also be; we shall accept it, if it be. But looking sternly and strictly at what is now actual and present to our sight, we yet rise above despair. Desdemona's adhesion to her husband and to love survived the ultimate trial. Othello dies "upon a kiss." He perceives his own calamitous error, and he recognizes Desdemona pure and loyal as she was. Goodness is justified of her child. It is evil which suffers defeat. It is Iago whose whole existence has been most blind, purposeless, and miserable—a struggle against the virtuous powers of the world, by which at last he stands convicted and condemned.

—EDWARD DOWDEN, *Shakspere: A Critical Study of His Mind and Art*
(London: H. S. King, 1875), pp. 242–44

ALGERNON CHARLES SWINBURNE

As surely as Othello is the noblest man of man's making, Iago is the most perfect evildoer, the most potent demi-devil. It is of course the merest commonplace to say as much, and would be no less a waste of speech to add the half comfortable reflection that it is in any case no shame to fall by such a hand. But this subtlest and strangest work of Shakespeare's admits and requires some closer than common scrutiny. Coleridge has admirably described the first great soliloquy which opens to us the pit of hell within as "the motive-hunting of a motiveless malignity." But subtle and profound and just as is this definitive appreciation, there is more in the matter yet than even this. It is not only that Iago, so to speak, half tries to make himself half believe that Othello has wronged him, and that the thought of it gnaws him inly like a poisonous mineral: though this also be true, it is not half the truth—nor half that half again. Malignant as he is, the very subtlest and strongest component of his complex nature is not even malignity. It is the instinct of what Mr. Carlyle would call an inarticulate poet. In his immortal study on the affair of the diamond necklace, the most profound and potent humourist of his country in his century has unwittingly touched on the mainspring of Iago's character—"the very pulse of the machine." He describes his Circe de la Mothe-Valois as a practical dramatic poet or playwright at least in lieu of play-writer: while indicating how and wherefore, with all her constructive skill and rhythmic art in action, such genius as hers so differs from the genius of Shakespeare that she undeniably could not have written a *Hamlet*. Neither could Iago have written an *Othello*. (From this theorem, by the way, a reasoner or casuist benighted enough to prefer articulate poets to inarticulate, Shakespeare to Cromwell, a fair Vittoria Colonna to a "foul Circe-Megæra," and even such a strategist as Homer to such a strategist as Frederic-William, would not illogically draw such conclusions or infer such corollaries as might result in opinions hardly consonant with the Teutonic-Titanic evangel of the preacher who supplied him with his thesis.) "But what he can do, that he will": and if it be better to make a tragedy than to write one, to act a poem than to sing it, we must allow to Iago a station in the hierarchy of poets very far in advance of his creator's. None of the great inarticulate may more justly claim place and precedence. With all his poetic gift, he has no poetic weakness. Almost any creator but his would have given him some grain of spite or some spark of lust after Desdemona. To Shakespeare's Iago she is no more than is a rhyme to another and articulate poet. His stanza must at any rate and at all costs be polished: to borrow the metaphor used by Mr. Carlyle in apologetic illustration of a royal hero's peculiar system of levying recruits for his colossal brigade. He has within him a sense or conscience of power incomparable: and this power shall not be left, in Hamlet's phrase, "to fust in him unused." A genuine and thorough capacity for human lust or hate would diminish and degrade the supremacy of his evil. He is almost as far above or beyond vice as he is beneath or beyond virtue. And this it is that makes him impregnable and invulnerable. When once he has said it, we know as well as he that thenceforth he never will speak word. We could smile almost as we can see him to have smiled at Gratiano's most ignorant and empty threat, being well assured that torments will in no wise ope his lips: that as surely and as truthfully as ever did the tortured philosopher before him, he might have told his tormentors that they did but bruise the coating, batter the crust, or break the shell of Iago. Could we imagine a far other lost spirit than Farinata degli Uberti's endowed with Farinata's might of will, and transferred from the sepulchres of fire to the dykes of Malebolge, we might conceive something of Iago's attitude in hell—of his unalterable and indomitable posture for all eternity. As though it were possible and necessary that in some one point the extremities of all conceivable good and of all imaginable evil should meet and mix together in a new "marriage of heaven and hell," the action in passion of the most devilish among all the human damned could hardly be other than that of the most godlike among all divine saviours—the figure of Iago than a reflection by hell-fire of the figure of Prometheus.

—ALGERNON CHARLES SWINBURNE, *A Study of Shakespeare* (London: Macmillan, 1880), pp. 177–80

GEORGE BERNARD SHAW

⟨. . .⟩ the character defies all consistency. Shakespeare, as usual, starts with a rough general notion of a certain type of individual, and then throws it over at the first temptation. Iago begins as a coarse blackguard, whose jovial bluntness passes as "honesty," and who is professionally a routine subaltern incapable of understanding why a mathematician gets promoted over his head. But the moment a stage effect can be made, or a fine speech brought off by making him refined, subtle and dignified, he is set talking like Hamlet, and becomes a godsend to students of the "problems" presented by our divine William's sham characters. Mr. ⟨Franklin⟩ McLeay does all that an actor can do with him. He follows Shakespeare faithfully on the rails and off them. He plays the jovial blackguard to Cassio and Roderigo and the philosopher and mentor to Othello just as the lines lead him, with perfect intelligibility and with so much point, distinction and fascination that the audience loads him with compliments, and the critics all make up their minds to declare that he shows the finest insight into the many-sided and complex character of the prince of villains.

—GEORGE BERNARD SHAW, "Mainly about Shakespeare," *Saturday Review* (London), May 29, 1897, p. 605

W. HUGHES HALLETT

So far from Iago being removed from humanity, there is not in the whole range of Shakespeare, no, not in the whole range of literature, a man more familiar to humanity. He is the type of a class which has existed in all societies, a class which never flourished more than to-day; he is the man who makes of self a cult; who in every serious circumstance of life works for his own personal gratification, irrespective of all other considerations. Such a man is usually good-natured enough so long as his own interests are not affected, and this not only because it pays better but because it pleases him and ministers to his insatiate vanity. When Sir Henry Irving played Iago, he had a very happy inspiration. The news that Othello had landed sent half the Cypriots running to meet him, while the rest remained on the stage, standing tip-toe, craning their necks, to watch the great man approach; a toddlekin of three or four, forgotten of its mother, trotted up and down behind the crowd in misery because it, too, could not see what was going on. Iago took it up with a word of cheery sympathy and perched it on his shoulder, making the little creature crow with delight. That is just what the man would do. I can imagine Iago taking his nephews and nieces to a modern pantomime, and sitting out the ordeal with a smile on his face as though it were amusing. But when his own interests are involved—ah, that is another matter. Then everything else must give way. From the life of a fellow-creature downwards, all obstacles are equally unimportant, all must go. Iago does not wish Desdemona dead, not in the least, he rather likes her; but since it will add to Othello's torments to kill her—why, killed let her be. He does not wish Roderigo dead, the money-bags cannot yet be really exhausted, but since the failure to run Cassio through is sure to lead to awkward inquiries the quat must be silenced. (Least of all does he want Othello dead—that is directly against his interests, is the loss of his patron, and it is a striking satire on the marvellous cleverness with which commentators have thought fit to endow him, that he should not have foreseen so probable an outcome of his schemes.) This unscrupulous selfishness superhuman! On the contrary, it is common all round us. There are thousands of men in London this day not one whit behind Iago in unhesitating rascality. They do not kill because there is now a sentiment about the sacredness of human life unknown three centuries ago, but they do things which indirectly cause death, and even worse than death. Their object is to make money, and for that object they work with a single eye. That people who never did them injury, people whom they have never seen, are inevitably ruined in the process does not affect them in the slightest degree. They draw up a lying prospectus, sell rotten food, supply bad materials on contract, let houses with poisonous drains, commit any knavery that the cracks and crannies of a tinkered system of laws renders possible, without caring a button how much their victims suffer in pocket and health. The sole difference between such men and Iago is the difference due to the times; in the matter of unscrupulousness, of entire indifference to the means so long as the end is attained, there is not a pin to choose between them.

Here are a few extracts from an analysis of the character of a very great man:—

> He was singularly destitute of generous sentiments. . . . he has not the merit of common truth and honesty. He is unjust. . . . egotistic and monopolising. . . . He is a boundless liar. . . . His theory of influence is not flattering: "There are two levers for moving men—interest and fear. Love is a silly infatuation, depend upon it. Friendship is but a name. I love nobody." . . . He was thoroughly unscrupulous. He would steal, slander, assassinate, drown, and poison, as his interest dictated. He had no generosity; but mere vulgar hatred; he was intensely selfish; he was perfidious. . . . His manners were coarse. . . . In short, . . . you were not dealing with a gentleman, but with an impostor and a rogue.

Thus wrote Emerson of Napoleon. He might have been writing of Iago.

—W. HUGHES HALLETT, "Honest, Honest Iago," *Fortnightly Review* 79, No. 2 (February 1903): 284–86

W. E. HENLEY

⟨. . .⟩ Iago is entirely credible. Despite the majestic assurance and completeness of his presentment as a chief actor in the play, we should not know him as we do if we were denied the privilege of sitting with him in the privy chamber of his thought, and taking our fill, and more, of those terrible mental practices by which he seeks, in the dry light of an excellent and daring intelligence, to reconcile his action with his conscience, his processes with his results, and, half in earnest, half in jest, as it were to excuse himself before his soul. He is a piece of pure intellect: he has gaiety, wit, invention, a kind of lethal humour; he is versed in 'politic authors,' and, besides, he is deeply read in the books of Character and Life, so that he 'knows all qualities of human dealing with a most learned spirit'; he discovers in himself a fine observer, a shrewd and gluttonous critic; first and last he is high in resolve, stern of heart, swift and resolute of hand; in speech he is liberal to the point of intemperance, with an odd trick of obscenity, whether suggested or phrased, which he has practised till it has mastered him, and in which the World, if it were but wise, would find proof indubitable of the inherent baseness of his mind. Said a fine critic to me long years ago, in the great Salvini times: 'You may meet Iago on any Yorkshire racecourse'; and, the inevitable mutations duly made, I take the remark to be intrinsically just. Palmer of Rugely, the poisoning creature, was of Iago's type and strain; and the Ring breeds many such potential beasts of prey. These are the men who kill, and are half surprised and half angered to find, as they generally do, that Killing is called *Murder*, is an offence before the Law, and has to be expiated on the Gallows. These wretches play with Evil much as a young man plays with Life; and are just as sorry for themselves when they come to the unchanging end.

For the rest, Iago, like his kind at large, is wholly the creature of the Event he quickens and stage-manages. He gulls Roderigo, he gulls Cassio, he gulls Othello into killing Desdemona, and essaying to compass his Lieutenant's murder. But, though he never so much as suspect it, the mortal issue he has made imminent, masters him ever, and, being determined, leaves him the most wretched slave this side Eternity. He starts by 'guying' an aged and respectable Senator on a most delicate and peculiar point of honour, in terms so rank that Shakespeare himself, good as he was at filth (and none better ever lived), has not improved on them; he ends as the murderer whole or parcel-gilt of Othello, Desdemona, Roderigo, and Emilia, with a bad wound in his body, the assurance of being done to death, and the knowledge that, thanks to him, the Cassio he so miserably loathed and scorned is Governor of Cyprus. For all his vocabulary and for all his brains, his contempt for elementary human law is ever too strong for him. He makes the best of circumstances he can; he wins his points; he is always alert, maleficent, superior to his opportunity; and in the long-run he is found to be merely the peer of the Hogarthian Thomas Idle.

—W. E. HENLEY, *"Othello"* [1903], *Essays* (London: Macmillan, 1921), pp. 369–71

STOPFORD A. BROOKE

Then there is Iago. It is odd that a young man of twenty-eight years should be capable of such cool hypocrisy, unreasonable hatred, such luxuriousness of cruelty; should have such advanced experience of evil, such lip-smacking pleasure in plotting it and fulfilling it; should so soon have arrived at the pitilessness of grey-haired inhumanity. It is possible, of course, but it is very improbable; as if a monstrous mind had arrived by chance in the body of a non-commissioned officer. It is all the more improbable that the reasons of his wickedness cannot clearly be discovered by us, nor indeed by himself. Endless discussion has gathered round the question—'Why did Iago torture Othello?' Even when he is proved in the play to have done so, no one can quite understand why. His wife is lost in surprise. Othello cries—

demand that demi-devil
Why he hath thus ensnar'd my soul and body.

Iago himself cannot tell. Hate is his native air; the desire to torture stings him within. He seeks to explain it; he searches for his motives; 'motive-hunting,' Coleridge calls it. He finds this and that motive, but not one of them explains what is in his heart, not one of them is an adequate reason for the devilish pleasure he has in putting Othello on the rack, in egging him on to kill Desdemona. His suspicion that the Moor was intimate with his wife is an invented suspicion. To give it some colour he accuses Cassio of the same sin. His action is outside of probable humanity, even of wicked humanity. It is like that of a soulless devil in a man, that is, of the last improbability. Envy is the most real of his motives, but is in him excited to a height almost incredibly beyond its ordinary nature. Cassius was envious, so was Casca, but they only desired to slay Cæsar, not to torture him. All this is the more improbable when we find that every one believes Iago is especially frank, honest, and open; that every one, and especially his chief victim, trusts him to the bone.

—STOPFORD A. BROOKE, *"Othello," Ten More Plays of Shakespeare*
(London: Constable, 1913), pp. 172–73

MAUD BODKIN

We may note first that even when a critic sets out, as A. C. Bradley does, to study Iago's character as if he were an actual living man, what seems to emerge most clearly is the dominance of the man by a certain force, or spirit. We can feel, says Bradley, the part of himself that Shakespeare put into Iago—the artist's delight in the development of a plot, a design, which, as it works itself out, masters and possesses him. In regard to this plot it concerns us, as psychological critics, to note that it is built not merely, as Bradley remarks, on falsehoods, but also on partial truths of human nature that the romantic vision ignores. It is such a truth that a woman, 'a super-subtle Venetian,' suddenly wedding one in whom she sees the image of her ideal warrior, is liable to experience moments of revulsion from the strange passionate creature she as yet knows so little, movements of nature toward those more nearly akin to her in 'years, manners, and beauties'. There is an element of apt truth in Iago's thought that a woman's love may be won, but not held, by 'bragging and telling her fantastical lies'. There is terrible truth in the reflection that if a man is wedded to his fantasy of woman as the steadfast hiding-place of his heart, the fountain whence his current flows, so that he grows frantic and blind with passion at the thought of the actual woman he has married as a creature of natural varying impulse—then he lies at the mercy of life's chances, and of his own secret fears and suspicions.

What is the meaning of that reiteration by Othello of his trust in Iago's honesty? Before Iago has fashioned accident into a trap for Othello, and woven a web of falsehood to ensnare him, at his very first insinuations, Othello shows signs of terror. He fears the monster 'too hideous to be shown' that he discerns lurking in Iago's thought. He begins to harp upon his honesty:

> . . . for I know thou are full of love and honesty,
> And weigh'st thy words before thou giv'st them breath,
> Therefore these stops of thine fright me the more;

As soon as Iago has left him:

> Why did I marry? This honest creature doubtless,
> Sees and knows more, much more, than he unfolds.

And again:

> This fellow's of exceeding honesty,
> And knows all qualities, with a learned spirit
> Of human dealings . . .

The whole of this dialogue between Othello and Iago, at the very beginning of Iago's plot, shows the uncanny insight of genius, illustrating in anticipation the discoveries of science. Our halting psychological theory has begun to describe for us the manner in which those aspects of social experience that a man's thought ignores leave their secret impress on his mind; how from this impress spring feelings and impulses that work their way toward consciousness, and if refused entrance there project themselves into the words, looks, and gestures of those around, arming these with a terrible power against the willed personality and its ideals. Iago seems to Othello so honest, so wise beyond himself in human dealings, possessed of a terrible power of seeing and speaking truth, because into what he speaks are projected the half truths that Othello's romantic vision ignored, but of which his. mind held secret knowledge.

If we attempt to define the devil in psychological terms, regarding him as an archetype, a persistent or recurrent mode of apprehension, we may say that the devil is our tendency to represent in personal form the forces within and without us that threaten our supreme values. When Othello finds those values, of confident love, of honour, and pride in soldiership, that made up his purposeful life, falling into ruin, his sense of the devil in all around him becomes acute. Desdemona has become 'a fair devil'; he feels 'a young and sweating devil' in her hand. The cry 'O devil' breaks out among his incoherent words of raving. When Iago's falsehoods are disclosed, and Othello at last, too late, wrenches himself free from the spell of Iago's power over him, his sense of the devil incarnate in Iago's shape before him becomes overwhelming. If those who tell of the devil have failed to describe Iago, they have lied:

> I look down towards his feet; but that's a fable.
> If that thou be'st a devil, I cannot kill thee.

We also, watching or reading the play, experience the archetype. Intellectually aware, as we reflect, of natural forces, within a man himself as well as in society around, that betray or shatter his ideals, we yet feel these forces aptly symbolized for the imagination by such a figure as Iago—a being though personal yet hardly human, concentrated wholly on the hunting to destruction of its destined prey, the proud figure of the hero.

—MAUD BODKIN, "The Images of the Devil, of the Hero, and of God,"
Archetypal Patterns in Poetry: Psychological Studies of Imagination
(Oxford: Oxford University Press, 1934), pp. 221–24

WILLIAM EMPSON

Most people would agree with what Bradley, for example, implied, that the way everybody calls Iago honest amounts to a criticism of the word—Shakespeare means "a bluff forthright manner, and amusing talk, which get a man called honest, may go with extreme dishonesty." Or indeed that this is treated as normal, and the satire is on our nature not on language. But they would probably maintain that Iago is not honest and does not think himself so, and only calls himself so as a lie or an irony. It seems to me, if you leave the matter there, that there is much to be said for what Rymer decided, when the implications of the hearty use had become simpler and more clear-cut—that the play is ridiculous, because that sort of villain (silly-clever, full of secret schemes, ignorant of people) is not mistaken for that sort of honest man. This, if true, is of course a plain fault, whatever you think about "character-analysis." It is no use taking short cuts in these things, and I should fancy that what Rymer said had a large truth when he said it, and also that Iago was a plausible enough figure in his time. The only main road into this baffling subject is to find how the characters use the term themselves.

Both Iago and Othello oppose honesty to mere truth-telling:

OTH.: I know, Iago,
Thy honesty and love doth mince this matter,
Making it light to Cassio.

IAGO: It were not for our quiet, nor your good,
Nor for my manhood, honesty, or wisdom
To let you know my thoughts.

No doubt the noun tends to be more old fashioned than the adjective, but the old "honourable" sense is as broad and vague as the new slang one; it was easy enough to be puzzled by the word. Iago means partly "faithful to friends," which would go with the Restoration use, but partly I think "chaste," the version normally used of women; what he has to say is improper. Certainly one cannot simply treat his version of *honest* as the Restoration one—indeed, the part of the snarling critic involves a rather puritanical view, at any rate towards other people. It is the two notions of being ready to blow the gaff on other people and frank to yourself about your own desires that seem to me crucial about Iago; they grow on their own, independently of the hearty feeling that would normally humanise them; though he can be a good companion as well.

One need not look for a clear sense when he toys with the word about Cassio; the question is how it came to be so mystifying. But I think a queer kind of honesty is maintained in Iago through all the puzzles he contrives; his emotions are always expressed directly and it is only because they are clearly genuine that he can mislead Othello as to their cause.

OTH.: Is he not honest? [Faithful etc.]
IAGO: Honest, my lord? [Not stealing etc. Shocked.]
OTH.: Honest? Ay, honest. ["Why repeat? The word is clear enough."]
IAGO: My lord, for aught I know. ["In *some* sense. . . ."]
IAGO: For Michael Cassio
I dare be sworn I think that he is honest.
OTH.: I think so too.
IAGO: Men should be what they seem,
Or those that be not, would they might seem none.
OTH.: Certain, men should be what they seem.
IAGO: Why then, I think Cassio's an honest man.

The point of these riddles is to get "not hypocritical"—"frank about his own nature" accepted as the relevant sense; Iago will readily call him honest on that basis, and Othello cannot be reassured. "Chaste" (the sense normally used of women) Cassio is not, but he is "not a hypocrite" about Bianca. Iago indeed despises him for letting her make a fool of him in public; for that and for other reasons (Cassio is young and without experience) Iago can put a contemptuous tone into the word; the feeling is genuine but not the sense it may imply. This gives room for a hint that Cassio has been "frank" to Iago in private about more things than may honestly be told. I fancy too that the idea of "not being men" gives an extra twist. Iago does not think Cassio manly nor that it is specially manly to be chaste; this allows him to agree that Cassio may be honest in the female sense about Desdemona and still keep a tone which seems to deny it—if he is, after so much encouragement, he must be "effeminate" (there is a strong idea of "manly" in *honest*, and an irony on that gives its opposite). Anyway, Iago can hide what reservations he makes but show that he makes reservations; this suggests an embarrassed defence—"Taking a broad view, with the world as it is, and Cassio my friend, I can decently call him honest." This forces home the Restoration idea—"an honest dog of a fellow, straightforward about women," and completes the suspicion. It is a bad piece of writing unless you are keyed up for the shifts of the word.

The play with the feminine version is doubtful here, but he certainly does it the other way round about Desdemona, where it had more point; in the best case it is for his own amusement when alone.

> And what's he then that says I play the villain,
> When this advice is free I give and honest,
> Probal to thinking, and indeed the course
> To win the Moor again? For 'tis most easy
> The inclining Desdemona to subdue
> In any honest suit. She framed as fruitful
> As the free elements . . .

Easy, inclining, fruitful, free all push the word the same way, from "chaste" to "flat, frank and natural"; all turn the ironical admission of her virtue into a positive insult against her. The delight in juggling with the word here is close to the Machiavellian interest in plots for their own sake, which Iago could not resist and allowed to destroy him. But a good deal of the "motive-hunting" of the soliloquies must, I think, be seen as part of Iago's "honesty"; he is quite open to his own motives or preferences and interested to find out what they are.

The clear cases where Iago thinks himself honest are at a good distance from the Restoration use; they bring him into line with the series of sharp unromantic critics like Jacques and Hamlet:

> For I am nothing if not critical

he tells Desdemona to amuse her; his faults, he tells Othello, are due to an excess of this truthful virtue—

> I confess, it is my nature's plague
> To spy into abuses, and oft my virtue
> Shapes faults that are not.

There seems no doubt that he believes this and thinks it creditable, whatever policy made him say it here; indeed we know from the soliloquies it is true. Now this kind of man is really very unlike the Restoration honest fellow, and for myself I find it hard to combine them in one feeling about the word. But in a great deal of Iago's talk to Roderigo—"drown thyself! drown cats and blind puppies . . . why, thou silly gentleman, I will never love thee after"—he is a wise uncle, obviously honest in the cheerful sense, and for some time this is our main impression of him. Perhaps the main connection between the two sorts of honest men is in not being indulgent towards romantic love:

> OTH.: I cannot speake enough of this content,
> It stops me heere; it is too much of joye.
> And this, and this, the greatest discords be,
> That e'er our hearts shall make. (Kissing her.)
> IAGO: Oh you are well tun'd now;
> But Ile set down the peggs that make this Musicke,
> As honeste as I am.

The grammar may read "because I am so honest" as well as "though I am so honest" and the irony may deny any resultant sense. He is ironical about the suggestions in the patronising use, which he thinks are applied to him—"low-class, and stupid, but good-natured." But he feels himself really "honest" as the kind of man who can see through nonsense; Othello's affair is a passing lust which has become a nuisance, and Iago can get it out of the way.

The suggestion of "stupid" in a patronising version of *honest* (still clear in "honest Thompson, my gardener," a Victorian, if not a present-day, use) brings it near to *fool*; there is a chance for these two rich words to overlap. Though there is an aspect of Iago in which he is the Restoration "honest fellow," who is good company because he blows the gaff, we see Iago like this mainly when he makes sport for his betters; especially when he clowns in the second act to amuse Desdemona, and she takes his real opinion of love and woman for a piece of hearty and good-natured fun. Iago's kind of honesty, he feels, is not valued as it should be; there is much in Iago of the Clown in Revolt, and the inevitable clown is almost washed out in this play to give him a free field. It is not, I think, dangerously far-fetched to take almost all Shakespeare's uses of *fool* as metaphors from the clown, whose symbolism certainly rode his imagination and was explained to the audience in most of his early plays. Now Iago's defence when Othello at last turns on him, among the rich ironies of its claim to honesty, brings in both Fool and the Vice used in *Hamlet* as an old name for the clown.

> IAGO: O wretched foole,
> That lou'st to make thine Honesty, a Vice!
> Oh monstrous world! Take note, take note (O World)
> To be direct and honest, is not safe.
> I thank you for this profit, and from hence
> Ile loue no Friend, sith Loue breeds such offence.
> OTH.: Nay stay: thou should'st be honest.
> IAGO: I should be wise; for Honestie's a Foole,
> And loses that it works for.
> OTH.:   By the world,
> I think my wife be honeste, and thinke she is not.

What comes out here is Iago's unwillingness to be the Fool he thinks he is taken for; but it is dramatic irony as well, and that comes back to his notion of *honest;* he is fooled by the way his plans run away with him; he fails in knowledge of others and perhaps even of his own desires.

Othello swears *by the world* because what Iago has said about being honest in the world, suggesting what worldly people think, is what has made him doubtful; yet the senses of *honest* are quite different—chastity and truth-telling. Desdemona is called a supersubtle Venetian, and he may suspect she would agree with what Iago treats as worldly wisdom; whereas it was her simplicity that made her helpless; though again, the fatal step was her lie about the handkerchief. *Lou'st* in the second line (Folios) seems to me better than *liu'st* (Quarto), as making the frightened Iago bring in his main claim at once; the comma after *Honesty* perhaps makes the sense "loves with the effect of making" rather than "delights in making"; in any case *loue* appears a few lines down. *Breeds* could suggest sexual love, as if Iago's contempt for that has spread to his notions of friendship; Othello's marriage is what has spoilt their relations (Cassio "came a-wooing with" Othello, as a social figure, and then got the lieutenantship). In the same way Othello's two uses of *honest* here jump from "loving towards friends, which breeds honour" to (of women) "chaste." It is important I think that the feminine sense, which a later time felt to be quite distinct, is so deeply confused here with the other ones.

It is not safe to be direct either way, to be *honest* in Othello's sense or Iago's. The sanctimonious metaphor *profit* might carry satire from Iago on Puritans or show Iago to be like them. Iago is still telling a good deal of truth; the reasons he gives have always made him despise those who are faithful to their masters, if not to their friends. It is not clear that he would think himself a bad friend to his real friends. He believes there is a gaff to blow about the ideal love affair, though his evidence has had to be forced. Of course he is using *honest* less in his own way than to impose on Othello, yet there is a real element of self-pity in his complaint. It is no whitewashing of Iago—you may hate him the more for it—but he feels he is now in danger because he has gone the "direct" way to work, exposed false pretensions, and tried to be "frank" to himself about the whole situation. I do not think this is an oversubtle treatment of his words; behind his fear he is gloating over his cleverness, and seems to delight in the audience provided by the stage.

In the nightmare scene where Othello clings to the word to justify himself he comes near accepting Iago's use of it.

EMIL.: My Husband!
OTH.:   Ay, 'twas he that told me first:
An honest man he is, and hates the slime
That sticks on filthy deeds. . . .
EMIL.: My husband says that she was false?
OTH.:   He, woman;
I say thy husband: dost understand the word?
My friend, thy husband, honest, honest Iago.

From the sound of the last line it seems as bitter and concentrated as the previous question; to the audience it is. Yet Othello means no irony against Iago, and it is hard to invent a reason for his repetition. He may feel it painful that the coarse Iago, not Desdemona or Cassio, should be the only honest creature, or Iago's honesty may suggest the truth he told; or indeed you may call this a trick on the audience, to wind up the irony to its highest before Iago is exposed. Yet Iago would agree that one reason he was honest was that he hated the slime. The same slime would be produced, by Desdemona as well as by Othello, one would hope, if the act of love were of the most rigidly faithful character; the disgust in the metaphor is disgust at all sexuality. Iago, playing "honest" as prude, is the rat who stands up for the ideal; once Othello agrees he is finely cheated; Iago is left with his pleasures and Othello's happiness is destroyed. Iago has always despised his pleasures, always treated sex without fuss, like the lavatory; it is by this that he manages to combine the "honest dog" tone with honesty as Puritanism. The twist of the irony here is that Othello now feels humbled before such clarity. It is a purity he has failed to attain, and he accepts it as a form of honour. The hearty use and the horror of it are united in this appalling line.

The only later use comes when Othello's sword is taken from him by the State officer; a mark of disgrace, a symbol of cuckoldry; two possible negations of honour and honesty.

> OTH.:   I am not valiant neither,
> For every puny whipster gets my sword.
> But why should honour outlive honesty?
> Let it go all.

This question so sums up the play that it involves nearly all of both words; it seems finally to shatter the concept whose connecting links the play has patiently removed. There are ten other uses of *honour*. Four by Othello about himself, three by others about Othello, one by Othello about Desdemona, echoed once ironically by Iago, one ironically from Iago about heroes in general. The play has made Othello the personification of honour; if honour does not survive some test of the idea nor could Othello. And to him *honest* is "honourable," from which it was derived; a test of one is a test of the other. Outlive Desdemona's chastity, which he now admits, outlive Desdemona herself, the personification of chastity (lying again, as he insisted, with her last breath), outlive decent behaviour in, public respect for, self-respect in, Othello—all these are honour, not honesty; there is no question whether Othello outlives them. But they are not tests of an idea; what has been tested is a special sense of *honest*. Iago has been the personification of honesty, not merely to Othello but to his world; why should honour, the father of the word, live on and talk out itself; honesty, that obscure bundle of assumptions, the play has destroyed. I can see no other way to explain the force of the question here.

There is very little for anybody to add to A. C. Bradley's magnificent analysis, but one can maintain that Shakespeare, and the audience he had, and the audience he wanted, saw the thing in rather different proportions. Many of the audience were old soldiers disbanded without pension; they would dislike Cassio as the new type of officer, the boy who can displace men of experience merely because he knows enough mathematics to work the new guns. The play plays into their hands by making Cassio a young fool who can't keep his mistress in order and can't drink. Iago gets a long start at the beginning of the play, where he is enchantingly amusing and may be in the right. I am not trying to deny that by the end of the first act he is obviously the villain, and that by the end of the play we are meant to feel the mystery of his life as Othello did—

> Will you, I pray, demand that demi-devil
> Why he hath thus ensnared my soul and body?

Shakespeare can now speak his mind about Iago through the conventional final speech by the highest in rank:

> O Spartan dog,
> More fell than anguish, hunger, or the sea.

Verbal analysis is not going to weaken the main shape of the thing. But even in this resounding condemnation the *dog* is not simple. The typical Shakespearean dog-men are Apemantus and Thersites (called "dog" by Homer), malign underdogs, snarling critics, who yet are satisfactory as clowns and carry something of the claim of the disappointed idealist; on the other hand, if there is an obscure prophecy in the treatment of *honest*, surely the "honest dog" of the Restoration may cast something of his shadow before. Wyndham Lewis' interesting treatment of Iago as "fox" leaves out both these dogs, though the dog is more relevant than the fox on his analogy of tragedy to bull-baiting; indeed the clash of the two dogs goes to the root of Iago. But the *dog* symbolism is a mere incident, like that of *fool;* the thought is carried on *honest*, and I throw in the others only not to over-simplify the thing. Nor are they used to keep Iago from being a simple villain; the point is that more force was needed to make Shakespeare's audience hate Iago than to make the obviously intolerable Macbeth into a tragic hero.

There seems a linguistic difference between what Shakespeare meant by Iago and what the nineteenth century critics saw in him. They took him as an abstract term "Evil"; he is a critique on an unconscious pun. This is seen more clearly in their own personification of their abstract word; e.g. *The Turn of The Screw* and *Dr. Jekyll and Mr. Hyde*. Henry James got a great triumph over some critics who said his villains were sexual perverts (if the story meant anything they could hardly be anything else). He said "Ah, you have been letting yourself have fancies about Evil; I kept it right out of my mind." That indeed is what the story is about. Stevenson rightly made clear that *Dr. Jekyll* is about hypocrisy. You can only consider Evil as all things that destroy the good life; this has no unity; for instance, Hyde could not be both the miser and the spendthrift and whichever he was would destroy Jekyll without further accident. Evil here is merely the daydream of a respectable man, and only left vague so that respectable readers may equate it unshocked to their own daydreams. Iago may not be a "personality," but he is better than these; he is a product of a more actual interest in a word.

—WILLIAM EMPSON, "The Best Policy," *Life and Letters To-day* 14, No. 4
(Summer 1936): 39–45

G. R. ELLIOTT

The modern idealization of Iago, as of Milton's Satan, springs from the modern, and often sentimental, cult of unorthodoxy with its admiration of rebels. Iago, according to that cult, is a superb, brainy rebel against our smug rules and gods: he dares to be himself alone! However, this attitude is entirely foreign to Shakespeare. Certainly he is always interested, sometimes comically, sometimes seriously, in flashes of independence. But this quality is not, for him, what it is for many modern writers, a criterion of value. It is a neutral, natural power; like the wind, for example; which we may admire for itself, in a passing fashion, while we are proceeding to the more important recognition of what it does, for good and for ill, to ships and houses and steeples. In this fashion Falstaff, notably, is admired and judged by Shakespeare. For him independence is not really independent; daring to be one's self is not a value isolable, in anything more than a passing manner, from the moral value of that self. And Iago's self-reliant intelligence is certainly less significant in the eyes of his creator than the fateful limitations of that intelligence owing to immoral self-reliance.

Iago's "almost superhuman art" may properly be termed subhuman. This fact the spectator, presumably a person of normal humanity, is intended to see more and more, and to enjoy dramatically, in the last three acts of the play. He is supposed not only to condemn the villain morally but to feel superior to him in insight into the human heart. For the audience has been enabled by Shakespeare in the first two acts to perceive that inward force and danger of Othello's love to which Iago has been entirely oblivious. (Note how different from ours is his reaction to the reunion episode: "O, you are well tuned now!" The tune has for him no *inward* tone of premonition.) So that the violence of Othello's vengeful outburst in the last phase of the great temptation scene in Act III does not surprise the audience as it does Iago. The actor who at this point labors to eliminate Iago's perturbation, by representing it as entirely feigned, runs counter to the plain sense of the lines. Of course the thing can be done if the actor makes the right faces, but Shakespeare would exclaim like Hamlet, "Pox, leave thy damnable faces. . . ." The fact is that Iago, in spite of his ability in adapting himself to the situation, is astounded and dismayed by the force he has helped to unloose. The murder of Desdemona, which Othello determines upon, had never for an instant been contemplated in the villain's plans. He had intended to

> Make the Moor thank me, love me, and reward me
> For making him egregiously an ass
> And practising upon his peace and quiet
> Even to madness. . . .

that is, to such a madness as such "an ass" could have; not the fearful human passion that actually ensues. Iago finds that in order to be thanked, loved, and rewarded, to hear from Othello the coveted words "Now art thou my lieutenant" (in the last line but one of the temptation scene), he must take part in Othello's "black vengeance" with an air of passionate conviction imitated from his master. But he strives to concentre that vengeance on Cassio; whose death—if only it would satisfy the

Moor's absurd and bothersome rage—would clinch the success of his plot. Whereas the killing of Desdemona is quite unnecessary—Iago has adduced no evidence which she could disprove—and may well be embarrassing. His plea, "But let her live", means exactly that. And the actor who accompanies these climactic words with a leer of insincerity and intellectual triumph is trying to defeat the legitimate triumph of the audience. We are intended to see, with immense satisfaction, that the villain has overshot his mark. Subdued by his master's violent refusal of his request, he closes the scene with a submissive and dramatic-ironic line, "I am yours forever." For the remainder of the action he is the tool of Othello's passion more than Othello is the tool of his cunning. His self-defeating blindness to the strength of his wife Emilia's love for Desdemona, so brilliantly foreshadowed by the author in the middle of the temptation scene, where the villain appears to be on the crest of fortune's wave, is recognized in the last act as the natural nemesis of one who has failed to fathom the hearts of all the other persons in the play, from Othello down to Roderigo.

Such, I think, is Shakespeare's best intention in the story of Iago. But the fact is that this character is imperfectly drawn. Not all the efforts of his admiring interpreters have succeeded in divesting him of a certain air of staginess. Their subtle lucubrations upon his so-called "motive-hunting" have helped to demonstrate that he is not coherently motivated. For example, if he can suspect the faithfulness of his wife in the past when only his "honor" was at stake, why has he not the faintest presentiment of her defection in the future when his very life is involved? But the truth is that in the former case he is merely providing comic relief for the audience. His two rôles, smart buffoon and "heavy villain", are not well harmonized. No doubt Shakespeare himself was aware of this defect; in his next play, *King Lear,* he remedied it remarkably. Here the rôle of witty buffoon, divorced entirely from plot-function, is assigned to the wise Fool; while Edmund, Iago's direct successor as intriguing villain, is delimited and thoroughly motivated as such.

—G. R. ELLIOTT, "*Othello* as a Love-Tragedy," *American Review* 8, No. 3
(January 1937): 265–68

F. R. LEAVIS

According to the version of *Othello* elaborated by Bradley the tragedy is the undoing of the noble Moor by the devilish cunning of Iago. Othello we are to see as a nearly faultless hero whose strength and virtue are turned against him. Othello and Desdemona, so far as their fate depended on their characters and untampered-with mutual relations, had every ground for expecting the happiness that romantic courtship had promised. It was external evil, the malice of the demi-devil, that turned a happy story of romantic love—of romantic lovers who were qualified to live happily ever after, so to speak—into a tragedy. This—it is the traditional version of *Othello* and has, moreover, the support of Coleridge—is to sentimentalize Shakespeare's tragedy and to displace its centre.

Here is Bradley:

> Turning from the hero and the heroine to the third principal character we observe (what has often been pointed out) that the action and catastrophe of *Othello* depend largely on intrigue. We must not say more than this. We must not call the play a tragedy of intrigue as distinguished from a tragedy of character.

—And we must not suppose that Bradley sees what is in front of him. The character he is thinking of isn't Othello's. 'Iago's plot,' he goes on,

> Iago's plot is Iago's character in action.

In fact the play (we need hardly stop short of saying) is Iago's character in action. Bradley adds, it is true, that Iago's plot 'is built on his knowledge of Othello's character, and could not otherwise have succeeded.' But Iago's knowledge of Othello's character amounts pretty much to Bradley's knowledge of it (except, of course, that Iago cannot realize Othello's nobility quite to the full): Othello is purely noble, strong, generous, and trusting, and as tragic hero is, however formidable and destructive in his agonies, merely a victim—the victim of Iago's devilish 'intellectual superiority' (which is 'so great that we watch its advance fascinated and appalled'). It is all in order, then, that Iago should get one of the two lectures that Bradley gives to the play, Othello sharing the other with Desdemona. And it is all in the tradition: from Coleridge down, Iago—his motivation or his motivelessness—has commonly been, in commentaries on the play, the main focus of attention.

The plain fact that has to be asserted in the face of this sustained and sanctioned perversity is that in Shakespeare's tragedy of *Othello* Othello is the chief personage—the chief personage in such a sense that the tragedy may fairly be said to be Othello's character in action. Iago is subordinate and merely ancillary. He is not much more than a necessary piece of dramatic mechanism—that at any rate is a fit reply to the view of Othello as necessary material and provocation for a display of Iago's fiendish intellectual superiority. Iago, of course, is sufficiently convincing as a person; he could not perform his dramatic function otherwise. But something has gone wrong when we make him interesting in this kind of way:

> His fate—which is himself—has completely mastered him: so that, in the later scenes, where the improbability of the entire success of a design built on so many different falsehoods forces itself on the reader, Iago appears for moments not as a consummate schemer, but as a man absolutely infatuated and delivered over to certain destruction.

We ought not, in reading those scenes, to be paying so much attention to the intrinsic personal qualities of Iago as to attribute to him tragic interest of that kind.

This last proposition, though its justice is perhaps not self-evident, must remain for the time being a matter of assertion. Other things come first. Othello has in any case the prior claim on our attention, and it seems tactically best to start with something as easy to deal with as the view—Bradley's and Coleridge's—and of course, Othello's before them—that Othello was 'not easily jealous.' Easy to deal with because there, to point to, is the text, plain and unequivocal. And yet the text was there for Coleridge, and Bradley accompanies his argument with constant particular reference to it. It is as extraordinary a history of triumphant sentimental perversity as literary history can show. Bradley himself saves us the need of insisting on this diagnosis by carrying indulgence of his preconception, his determined sentimental preconception, to such heroic lengths:

> Now I repeat that *any* man situated as Othello was would have been disturbed by Iago's communications, and I add that many men would have been made wildly jealous. But up to this point, where Iago is dismissed [III, iii, 238] Othello, I must maintain, does not show jealousy. His confidence is shaken, he is confused and deeply troubled, he feels even horror, but he is not yet jealous in the proper sense of that word.

The 'proper sense of that word' is perhaps illustrated by these lines (not quoted by Bradley) in which, Bradley grants, 'the beginning of that passion may be traced':

> Haply, for I am black
> And have not those soft parts of conversation
> That chamberers have, or for I am declined
> Into the vale of years—yet that's not much—
> She's gone; I am abused, and my relief
> Must be to loathe her. O curse of marriage,
> That we can call these delicate creatures ours,
> And not their appetites. I had rather be a toad,
> And live upon the vapour of a dungeon,
> Than keep a corner in the thing I love
> For others' uses.

Any reader not protected by a very obstinate preconception would take this, not for a new development of feeling, but for the fully explicit expression of something he had already, pages back, registered as an essential element in Othello's behaviour—something the evoking of which was essential to Iago's success. In any case, jealous or not jealous 'in the proper sense of that word,' Othello has from the beginning responded to Iago's 'communications' in the way Iago desired and with a promptness that couldn't be improved upon, and has dismissed Iago with these words:

> Farewell, farewell:

> If more thou dost perceive, let me know more;
> Set on thy wife to observe

—to observe Desdemona, concerning whom Iago has just said:

> Ay, there's the point: as—to be bold with you—
> Not to affect many proposed matches

Of her own clime, complexion and degree,
Whereto we see in all things nature tends—
Foh! one may smell in such a will most rank,
Foul disproportions, thoughts unnatural.
But pardon me: I do not in position
Distinctly speak of her, though I may fear
Her will, recoiling to her better judgment,
May fall to match you with her country forms,
And happily repent.

To say that it's not jealousy here is hardly (one would have thought) to bring Othello off clean; but Bradley's conclusion is not (as might have seemed inevitable) that there may be other faults than jealousy that are at least as damaging to a man in the character of husband and married lover. He is quite explicit:

Up to this point, it seems to me, there is not a syllable to be said against Othello.

With such resolute fidelity does Bradley wear these blinkers that he can say,

His trust, where he trusts, is absolute,

without realizing the force of the corollary: Othello's trust, then, can never have been in Desdemona. It is the vindication of Othello's perfect nobility that Bradley is preoccupied with, and we are to see the immediate surrender to Iago as part of that nobility. But to make absolute trust in Iago—trust at Desdemona's expense—a manifestation of perfect nobility is (even if we ignore what it makes of Desdemona) to make Iago a very remarkable person indeed. And that Bradley, tradition aiding and abetting, proceeds to do.

However, to anyone not wearing these blinkers it is plain that no subtilization and exaltation of the Iago-devil (with consequent subordination of Othello) can save the noble hero of Bradley's devotion. And it is plain that what we should see in Iago's prompt success is not so much Iago's diabolic intellect as Othello's readiness to respond. Iago's power, in fact, in the temptation-scene is that he represents something that is in Othello—in Othello the husband of Desdemona: the essential traitor is within the gates. For if Shakespeare's Othello too is simple-minded, he is nevertheless more complex than Bradley's. Bradley's Othello is, rather, Othello's; it being an essential datum regarding the Shakespearean Othello that he has an ideal conception of himself.

The tragedy is inherent in the Othello-Desdemona relation, and Iago is a mechanism necessary for precipitating tragedy in a dramatic action. Explaining how it should be that Othello, who is so noble and trustful ('Othello, we have seen, was trustful, and thorough in his trust'), can so immediately doubt his wife, Bradley says:

But he was newly married; in the circumstances he cannot have known much of Desdemona before his marriage.

Again we read:

> But it is not surprising that his utter powerlessness to repel it (Iago's in-
> sinuation) on the ground of knowledge of his wife . . . should complete his
> misery . . .

Bradley, that is, in his comically innocent way, takes it as part of the datum that
Othello really knows nothing about his wife. Ah, but he was in love with her. And
so poetically. 'For,' says Bradley, 'there is no love, not that of Romeo in his youth,
more steeped in imagination than Othello's.' Othello, however, we are obliged to
remark (Bradley doesn't make the point in this connection) is not in his youth; he
is represented as middle-aged—as having attained at any rate to maturity in that
sense. There might seem to be dangers in such a situation, quite apart from any
intervention by an Iago. But then, we are told, Othello is 'of a great openness and
trustfulness of nature.'—It would be putting it more to the point to say that he has
great consciousness of worth and confidence of respect.

> —F. R. LEAVIS, "Diabolic Intellect and the Noble Hero: A Note on *Othello*,"
> *Scrutiny* 6, No. 3 (December 1937): 260–64

EDITH SITWELL

Ludovici, apostrophizing Iago, the 'Spartan dog,' cried:
  'More fell than Anguish, Hunger, or the Sea': and almost all commentators
have written of Iago's 'greatness'—Swinburne saying that 'Desdemona was between the devil and the deep sea.' There he is right, but Mr. Wilson Knight speaks
with equal truth when he calls Iago 'The spirit of negation.'
  Iago appears in a shrunken shape, with a dulled and hooded eye, as the first
tempter appeared in Eden. With the exception of two earth-shaking sentences, and
one speech of great beauty in which his voice has taken on the sound of Othello's,
Iago never speaks 'above a mortal mouth.' For the rest, there is in his verbal
intercourse with others, the terrible 'deadness' that Dr. Bradley noted in the *feeling*
of Iago.
  He is a subterranean devil. . . . His voice comes to us muffled by the earth of
the world, and of his nature. It comes to us from underground, like that of the 'old
mole' that Hamlet knew. That is why it sounds so small. But it is none the less
deadly. Iago is a million miles beneath the surface of our nature. Though ineffably
tainted by the world's evil, he is yet so shut off from the world of ordinary
men—he who is yet shaping their lives—that he cannot reach them by any words
save those with a jet of poison in them. Though he can overthrow them with a
touch, it hardly seems to be *his* touch.
  He cannot express himself. 'Do not weep, do not weep! Alas the day!' (Act
IV. Scene II) he says to Desdemona, after the scene when she first realizes that night
is falling.

Indeed, he does not need her tears. They give him no particular pleasure: if anything, they disturb him in his intellectual pride at what he has done. ⟨. . .⟩

Iago is, perhaps, too far under the earth for hatred. . . . But pride, he tells himself, must surely give him *some* feeling: he owes it to his pride to hate.

And he is filled with an immeasurable contempt: but this is scarcely a *feeling*. To Roderigo, he says (Act I. Scene III)

What sayst thou, noble heart?

And by the very fact of applying the words to that despised being, he tells us what is his opinion of a noble heart.

He has a curiosity to see what will be the movements under pain, of these extraordinary beings of an alien world—beings who have passions, nobilities, and are ruled by a power that is not that of the will.

Sometimes he even tries to emulate their feelings, the speech born from these,—as when he pretends to himself, and to Emilia, that he knows jealousy (but even then the pretence breaks down, and we see the face behind the mask: it is that of Pride),—or as when, in the first scene, he says

Though I doe hate him, as I hate hell-pains.

But here, we feel that he is disguising from us that those pains are his climate—he is used to them, is a native of them; they do not touch him as they would those who have hearts to be consumed. He would, indeed, hardly know the difference between those pains and the pleasures of Heaven. For he is not a damned soul. He is a devil.

—EDITH SITWELL, "Iago," *New Writing and Daylight* 7 (1941): 141–42, 145

HARLEY GRANVILLE-BARKER

He is a passionless creature. Cinthio gives his wicked Ensign some motive for evil doing in jealousy, and a love for Desdemona ignored and so "changed into the bitterest hate". But Shakespeare admits neither love nor lust into Iago's composition, nothing so human; shows him to us, on the contrary, frigidly speculating upon the use such indulgence might be to him, and as frigidly deciding: none. Even his hate is cold, and will be the more tenacious for that, its strength not being spent in emotional ebb and flow. His endeavours then, to respond suitably to Othello's outbursts—the flamboyant "Take note, take note, O world . . ." and the kneeling to echo and mock the oath by "yond marble heaven"—are simply histrionic, and overdone at that. And this, made plain to us, might be plain to Othello, were he not "eaten up with passion". For of intellectual excitement Iago *is* capable; and, elated by swift success, he begins to run risks. That stirs his cold blood; it is all that does. And the pleasures of the game, as it develops, are multiplying. He has this "noble" Moor stripped now, but for a rag or so, of his nobility; no stimulus to savagery seems to be too strong for him. Iago can, consequently, admit more of himself into the part he is playing, can, in the actor's phrase, "let himself go", while the actor faculty enables him still to keep a cool enough eye upon whither he is going. He can thus vent the full foulness of his mind, in itself a relief and pleasure: and there is the sheer pleasure of seeing Othello suffer and madden beneath the spate of it. And his daring pays. The success of the enterprise betters all expectation. Not merely is Cassio's death to be granted him—when he had schemed for no more than his disgrace—but at that zestful crisis, with the artist in evil in him strung to perfect pitch, one timely phrase assures him of Desdemona's thrown in too.

Yet in the very ease and abundance of his success—in his complacent enjoyment and exploitation of it, looking neither ahead nor around—lie the means to his ultimate ruin. To harry the distraught Othello until he actually collapses at his feet in a fit, then to rally the unlucky cuckold and condescendingly urge him to "be a man"; to be able to jerk him, like a black puppet, back and forth from his eavesdropping—what could be more amusing? And, having once had to defer for his ends to each changing shade of Othello's mood, now to find the victim swaying to his every sinister touch, even to be able—artist in evil as he is—to devise that felicitous strangling of Desdemona "in her bed, even the bed she hath contaminated"—this is gratifying too. There are secret satisfactions besides. To see Desdemona struck and be the hidden force behind the blow, to deplore Othello's conduct and be the unsuspected prompter of it; that is meat and drink to thwarted, perverted vanity. And that the blind fools who have ever galled him by their patronising praise should be deaf to the irony in his

> Alas, alas!
> It is not *honesty* in me to speak
> What I have seen and known.

—he finds egregious pleasure here.

> —HARLEY GRANVILLE-BARKER, "Iago," *Prefaces to Shakespeare: Fourth Series*
> (London: Sidgwick & Jackson, 1945), pp. 167–69

HOOVER H. JORDAN

But what of Iago? Can Othello be absolved for not uncovering his true nature only because he is the pasteboard figure of a drama, lacking any conceivable prior existence and credible in the play simply by the grace of a powerful illusion? A dramatic character can of course exist only inside the work of fiction and has no life, prior or subsequent, but that premise does not preclude the fact that characters seem to have prior existence. The Iago of the play must be a logical growth from the Iago known by his friends in former times. As the curtain rises they apparently believe him to be a rough, stout-hearted fellow, who is full of jest, loves a full tankard on the table, and spices his conversation with an amusing cynicism. No intimate has the slightest reason to doubt the sturdiness of his honor. The crux of the argument in reference to him, therefore, is whether such a man in actuality can sink rapidly to a frightful degeneration. If possible, then excuse for Othello and the others may be sought. If not possible, that is, putting the matter another way, if he has been habitually knavish behind an honest front, Othello, Emilia, and most of the others must be extraordinarily dull indeed for not having detected the duplicity. Shakespeare was forced to dismiss this latter conjecture summarily, for he could not make the plot of Iago succeed while simultaneously picturing a dull Othello. In III, iii, Iago relies for success on Othello's alertness and delicacy of perception. He knows that Othello will feel the first heat in his blood by seizing the full force of "Ha! I like not that" or "But for a satisfaction of my thought" or "Indeed"; so, even without putting the full enormity of Desdemona's acts into words, he stimulates Othello's vigorous imagination into envisioning every possibility in regard to his conjugal relationship. Shakespeare has then caused Othello to become entrapped by quickness of mind and overwhelming power of imagination.

Offered no alternative, Shakespeare had to presume a relatively honest Iago prior to the drama's inception. Nor does it appear that he considered this a singular pretense, for like all writers of fiction he must follow the laws of probability rather than those of possibility. If he so disconcerted his audience that it entered upon a train of conjecture apart from the play, he was guilty of an inartistic performance; if his audience easily accepted the situation, he could feel satisfaction. For instance, during the last war a Navy pilot fell two thousand feet into the Pacific without parachute and lived to tell the tale; no writer of fiction would dare to allow his protagonist in a climactic moment to duplicate that feat. Shakespeare most assuredly cannot promote the climax of his play by a supposition about Iago that belongs in the lands of legend. Given the boundless limits of the novel (such as Hawthorne enjoyed in tracing the somewhat parallel degeneration of Chillingworth, who was a far more refined and honorable man before his fall than was Iago), he could trace in detail the conscious and even subconscious forces within Iago that wrought his change, and even a critic, reading meticulously, would not be likely to cavil at the transformation in character. Compressing that same change within the boundaries of a five-act drama may place an added burden upon the critic of supplying some of the psychological impulses of Iago, but it does not necessarily therefore destroy the credibility of the change for the audience.

To make the doctrine more palatable to both critic and audience, he has endowed Iago with a cynical disposition, well recognized by Desdemona, Cassio, and Emilia, who rather enjoy it because of the fun which Iago occasions by it, as in II, ii. Nor has he granted Iago the same measure of honesty which characterizes Othello, Hamlet, Horatio, or Kent. The opening lines of the play testify to a flaw in his character, not a major one perhaps, but yet a crack that may widen. In addition, as the play opens, Iago has just completed a long period of inactivity from war-like maneuvers, an ideal time of stagnation for brooding about himself and his future. Finally, and by no means least, he is an egoist. Presumably in the past Iago advanced as rapidly as he anticipated by the orderly turning of the wheels of military promotion. As long as that was true, he would feel no need for underhanded practices, and honesty would remain his best policy. In the period of stagnation, however, his affairs have reached a critical juncture. In his estimation, and perhaps quite properly, his years of service have brought him to such rank that the step to the lieutenancy is but easy, natural, and expected. As an egoist, he believes himself fully deserving of the honor; moreover, if his story be correct that three great ones of Venice did plead his suit with Othello, then others shared a sense of his worth and so were the coals of his egoism fanned the more. But Cassio is plucked from the ranks and passed over his head. Disappointment, thwarted self pride, and jealousy, added to his native cynicism and his penetrable honesty, become a raging torrent within him. Observing that honesty has not paid him full dividends, and being a clever rather than a wise man, he begins at once to think of devious means to accomplish his goal in lieu of the direct and honorable ones that have failed him. He also senses at once that his reputation for honesty is the very means whereby he can practice deceit.

But he does not become villainous all in a moment. Unaccustomed to knavery, he thinks first of a trivial vengeance, almost a piece of mischief, in arousing Brabantio against Othello. He knows that nothing serious will come of the scheme because of the absolute necessity of Othello to the Venetian military plans, but it eases him a bit to play it out, and, more important to the drama, it evolves so nicely according to his anticipation that he experiences a wave of enthusiasm and self-confidence, and an obsession to manipulate his superiors in rank and birth. He then advances, like a swimmer accustoming himself to cold water, toward a more villainous plan, seeing it but dimly at first and only conceiving it full-blown after he has habituated himself to the ways of knavery. In the end, thoroughly steeped in evil, he loses all sense of values as guides for his personal conduct. His original intention, the demotion of Cassio, is lost as the degradation progresses, in favor of larger ends—the demotion and death of Cassio, the death of Desdemona, and as a consequence the destruction of Othello himself. In presenting this panorama, Shakespeare seems to have taken liberties not so much with human psychology as with the compression of events to fit the necessary limits of the five-act drama.

Another consideration bearing on the matter of Othello's obtuseness is his decision to place his reliance on Iago rather than his wife. Two points bear directly upon our understanding of this choice. The first is that Othello chooses to believe the one he has known the longer. Iago explains their intimate association in his opening lines,

> I, of whom his eyes had seen the proof
> At Rhodes, at Cyprus and on other grounds
> Christian and heathen. . . .

Desdemona he has not known long, and in that brief time she has been able to deceive her father. To that extent is his error of judgment extenuated. The second point is that he is esteeming friendship above love. Suppose for a moment an illustration which is of course not highly analogous but may clarify an idea. After Hamlet had taken Horatio to his heart, suppose Horatio had muttered, "I like not that," had undertaken to conceal a foul thought about a guilty young lady beloved by Hamlet, and then refused to impart that thought after involuntarily hinting it. Would not the audience resent Horatio's secrecy? Would it not believe he was violating the code of friendship? Would it not remain in anxiety until he did reveal his thoughts, and would it not rejoice when Hamlet exploded in violent anger? Yet Othello is condemned as a fool when he forces information about his newly won wife from a trusted soldier and friend and becomes inflamed through that disclosure. Here is a curious anomaly. Hamlet, a man of thought, has been condemned for not rushing out immediately after the Ghost's disclosure and killing Claudius; instead, he waits for proof. Othello, however, a man of action, aroused by a far more substantial being than a Ghost, is in his turn condemned because he makes up his mind too quickly and does not procrastinate while awaiting genuine proof. The spirit of such criticism is that of the historian who derides a medieval man for believing the world to be flat.

Out of this web of circumstance and character comes a situation so complex that Othello is never afforded an opportunity to sit down with his wife in unimpassioned talk about their affairs. After the first disclosures in III, iii, Othello, alarmed and upset, begs off from Desdemona as they leave for dinner with the islanders and apparently retires to do what any intelligent man might be inclined to do under similar circumstances—muse on his lot and endeavor to separate fact from illusion. Has he known Desdemona long enough to be sure that she will not tire of him because of his age and color? He is not a Venetian and in his own estimation knows not the soft phrase of peace, but his friend, whom he trusts, seems to know Venice, its arts and subtleties; he says Venetian women are loose. Presumably then they are loose, and Desdemona is a Venetian. Does he know her well enough to say for certain that she is the exception rather than the rule, particularly when she has deceived her father and "may thee"? Othello has talked very calmly with Iago, who has made no reckless charges. Logically there must be something to what he hints, and even a slight blot on his wife's honor is torture to Othello. But before Othello can complete his reasoning or get emotional control of himself, Iago approaches him once more and completes the ruin.

—HOOVER H. JORDAN, "Dramatic Illusion in *Othello,*" *Shakespeare Quarterly*
1, No. 3 (July 1950): 148–51

HAROLD C. GODDARD

Iago's jealousy of Cassio is real enough, but it is the occasion rather than the cause of his plot against Othello; and the other reasons he assigns for his hatred in the course of the play are not so much motives as symptoms of a deeply underlying condition. The psychology of Iago is that of the slave-with-brains who aspires to power yet remains at heart a slave.

We cannot all be masters, nor all masters
Cannot be truly follow'd

"Some cogging cozening slave," says Emilia, describing the as yet hypothetical and unidentified villain who is actually her husband. "O cursed, cursed slave!" cries Othello, at the end, to that part of himself that Iago had corrupted. We are led to conjecture that some situation or event early in Iago's life that produced a profound sense of injustice or inferiority, and instigated a revolt against it, could alone have produced so twisted a nature, as in the case of Emily Brontë's Heathcliff or Dostoevsky's Smerdyakov, figures spiritually akin to Shakespeare's villain. It would be consumingly interesting to have a peep into Iago's childhood, as we have into theirs. It must have been full of power-fantasies like those that Dostoevsky describes in *A Raw Youth*. "The secret consciousness of power is more insupportably delightful than open domination." "I don't know," the Raw Youth declares, "whether the spider perhaps does not hate the fly he has marked and is snaring. Dear little fly! It seems to me that the victim is loved, or at least may be loved. Here I love my enemy; I am delighted, for instance, that she is so beautiful." Compare this with Iago's words on Desdemona:

> Now, I do love her too;
> Not out of absolute lust, though peradventure
> I stand accountant for as great a sin,
> But partly led to diet my revenge,

or his,

> So will I turn her virtue into pitch,
> And out of her own goodness make the net
> That shall enmesh them all.

Iago is a spider whose web is spun out of his brain. (Though that is by no means all he is.) Whatever he began by being, however human the motives that at first led him on, he ends by being an image of Death revenging itself on Life through destruction. Why does a small boy knock down, in pure wantonness, the tower of blocks his younger brother has so slowly and laboriously built up? Iago is like that:

> If Cassio do remain,
> He hath a daily beauty in his life
> That makes me ugly.

These are the most consciously self-revealing words he speaks. Ugliness cannot tolerate beauty. Death cannot tolerate life.

> That that likes not me
> Pleases me best.

If you are defeated, change the rules of the game, call defeat success (as if to get the fewest runs in baseball were the object), and then you win! Drag down the good—it is so much easier than rising. Define darkness as light.

Shakespeare's archvillain had many Shakespearean forerunners: the melodramatic Richard III, the casuistical Pandulph, the sly and crafty Ulysses. But they all fade before him. He is perhaps the most terrific indictment of pure intellect in the literature of the world—"pure intellect," which, as Emerson said, "is the pure devil." "Think, and die," as Enobarbus puts it, though he may not have realized all he was packing into three words. The intellect, as all the prophets have divined, should be the servant of the soul. Performing that function it is indispensable. There can scarcely be too much of it. Indeed, the primacy in the world of art of men like Beethoven, Michelangelo, and Shakespeare himself is that their imaginations are held in check by their critical power. But the moment the intellect sets up a claim of sovereignty for itself, it is the slave in revolt, the torchbearer turned incendiary, Lucifer fallen. Iago is a moral pyromaniac.

I wonder, if he had been of more limited intelligence, whether he might not have been, literally, a pyromaniac. He exhibits a dozen traits of that type of criminal, including a secret joy in being on the scene of the conflagration he has kindled. Shakespeare himself hints as much in the speech in which, of all in the play barring the soliloquies, Iago most fully reveals himself for what he is. It is in the opening scene, while his plot, if conceived, is still unconscious. And he is boasting to his dupe, Roderigo. He is off guard. But first we must recall the conscious revelation that leads up to the unconscious one:

> For when my outward action doth demonstrate
> The native act and figure of my heart
> In compliment extern, 'tis not long after
> But I will wear my heart upon my sleeve
> For daws to peck at: I am not what I am.

How characteristic of Shakespeare that in his very next speech Iago should place his heart squarely on his sleeve, and put into words, and still more into tone, precisely what he is.

> ROD.: What a full fortune does the thick-lips owe,
> If he can carry't thus!
> IAGO: Call up her father:
> Rouse him, make after him, poison his delight,
> Proclaim him in the streets, incense her kinsmen,
> And, though he in a fertile climate dwell,
> Plague him with flies; though that his joy be joy,
> Yet throw such changes of vexation on 't,
> As it may lose some colour.
> ROD.: Here is her father's house; I'll call aloud.
> IAGO: Do, with like timorous accent and dire yell
> As when, by night and negligence, the fire
> Is spied in populous cities.

Poison! Plague! Fire! Never again, unless to himself, do we hear Iago speak with such gusto. The bewildering shift in antecedents of the pronouns ("Rouse him, make after him"), the first referring to Brabantio, the second to Othello, is intentional on Shakespeare's part, revealing in a flash that Iago's hatred of Othello is already an obsession. For these few seconds, before he puts on his perpetual mask and cloak, Iago stands before us naked.

But if he is a moral pyromaniac, it is *only* morally that he is mad, and, whatever may be said of the fires he kindles in others, the fire in his own veins is an icy fire. "Now could I drink hot blood," cried Hamlet. Iago goes fathoms lower than that. "For I am nothing if not critical," he observes calmly, as he scrutinizes Desdemona's beauty on the threshold of her destruction; and as he begins to weave the web that is to enmesh her, he cries:

> By the mass, 'tis morning;
> Pleasure and action make the hours seem short.

Hot revenge is a fearful thing. But its devastation has bounds, because its passion reveals its secret, makes it act prematurely, mars its aim, and soon burns it out. Cold revenge is incredibly more awful. For it can conceal, it can calculate, it can lie in wait; it can control itself, it can coil and strike without warning at the crucial moment. Cold revenge is the union of intellect and hate—the most annihilating of all alliances. Dante was right in making his nethermost hell of ice.

The deliberate placing of the highest intellectual gifts and achievements at the service of the lowest human instincts is a phenomenon with which the twentieth century is acquainted on a scale never previously attained. And whether the instinct be fear (the main defensive one) or revenge, greed, cruelty, thirst to possess more power or to assert power already possessed (the main offensive ones) makes little difference in the end, so readily do they pass into one another.

It is no recent discovery that brain as well as brawn is essential to the efficient fighter. The Trojan Horse is the perennial symbol of that truth, and it is appropriate that Shakespeare put on the lips of Ulysses an encomium on the "still and mental parts" of war. But it remained for war in our time to effect the total mobilization of those still and mental parts. The ideological warfare that precedes and precipitates the physical conflict (*cold* war as it has significantly come to be called); the propaganda that prepares and unifies public opinion; the conscription, in a dozen spheres, of the nation's brains; the organization of what is revealingly known as the *intelligence* service; but most of all the practical absorption of science into the military effort: these things, apart from the knowledge and skill required for the actual fighting, permit us to define modern war, once it is begun, as an unreserved dedication of the human intellect to death and destruction.

But that is exactly what Iago is—an unreserved dedication of intellect to death and destruction. To the extent that this is true, Iago is an incarnation of the spirit of modern war.

This does not mean that those who participate in modern war are Iagos. The scientist calmly conducting his experiment in a clean laboratory without an iota of hate in his heart bears no resemblance to Shakespeare's Italian fiend. But there may be hate, and there will almost certainly be fear, in the heart of the man who months later and thousands of miles away utilizes the results of that experiment on the fighting front (not to imply for a moment that there may not be heroism in it also). Nobody wants war. No individual does, that is, or very few. But that great Composite Personality which is the nation is driven into it nevertheless against the wishes of the thousands of individuals who make it up. It is within that Personality, not generally within the individual, that the union of intellect with animal instincts takes place, the prostitution especially of man's supreme intellectual achievement, modern science, to the most destructive of his ancestral practices. It is something within this Composite Personality that is like Iago, and, like him, it did not foresee when it set out to make war efficient that it was playing with the possibility of its own extinction. The uniqueness of Iago, like the uniqueness of modern war, does not lie in the spirit of destruction. That has always been common enough. It lies in the genius he dedicates to destructive ends. Modern war would not recognize itself in the portraits of Shakespeare's classical and feudal fighters, in Hector and Hotspur, in Faulconbridge and Coriolanus, or in Othello himself. But let it look in the glass and it will behold Iago. In him Shakespeare reveals, with the clarity of nightmare, that unrestrained intellect, instead of being the opposite of force, and an antidote for it, as much of the modern world thinks, *is* force functioning on another plane. It is the immoral equivalent of war, and as certain to lead to it in due season as Iago's machinations were to lead to death. "All other knowledge is hurtful," says Montaigne, "to him who has not the science of honesty and goodness."

—HAROLD C. GODDARD, *"Othello," The Meaning of Shakespeare* (Chicago: University of Chicago Press, 1951), pp. 461–65

ARTHUR SEWELL

Othello and Iago ⟨. . .⟩ characterize by their imagery the worlds they engage and in which they live. It may, indeed, be suggested at the outset that there is a certain important difference in the manner in which these worlds are affirmed. Othello's world is dynamic and he is, in a sense, the creative centre of it. He creates his world from moment to moment, and it may be said in him that Mind and Nature are one. Iago, on the other hand, lives in a static world, in which men's characters are catalogued and their behaviours predicted. Othello's is a perceptual, Iago's a conceptual universe. This difference marks, as we shall see, a profound difference in the function they fulfil in the vision of their author; for imagery characterizes not only that world to which the persons address themselves but also the kind of world to which that address is made and the mode of vision in which that address is comprehended.

In Iago's world everything is catalogued from observation. No image seems to have passed through his being, there to have been forged and fused. He has, as Mr. Morozov notes, a very large number of images of beasts; but these images are no more than emblems of men's weaknesses and vices. When he refers to Othello as an 'old black ram' this is smoking-room or barrack-room talk; it has nothing in common with Othello's 'Goats and monkeys!' His images very often, too, come, as do his judgements, from social behaviour and, with what emotional force there is behind them, reinforce these judgements.

You shall mark
Many a duteous and knee-crooking knave
That, doting on his own obsequious bondage,
Wears out his time, much like his master's ass,
For naught but provender; and when he's old, cashiered.

Such images illustrate both the idea and the emotion—and that is their function; they have none of the enrichment of fruitful ambiguity.

Iago rarely reveals a present emotion. His images always *refer to* an emotion of old standing, never generate the emotion in the moment, from the centre. Except at the end he has no present discomfitures, no present excitements. He is never in doubt. Consequently he can, as it were, move out of the time of the play, especially in his soliloquies, in a way impossible to Othello. He can, and to all intents and purposes does, speak about himself in the third person, as though he should take the audience into his confidence and say: 'You and I know this Iago well enough, but they can't catch him, not this poor trash of Venice, this nigger and this silly girl. Iago is much too fly for them.' Inevitably language which is not caught and contained within the concrete *time* of the play employs a different kind of imagery, less particular, more external. A less external, more particular kind of image would, in fact, misrepresent him. He addresses himself—and so must his language—to each situation as steadily as a compass to its pole.

It must be clear from what precedes that it is not only the *provenance* of the images that individualizes character but also their form and their activity.

Othello's world, which he creates in his imagery, is not at all the social world in which Iago has his being. There are, except as objects abstractly recognized, no heavens, no oceans, in the world of Iago. Othello's world is the universe itself, which he all but creates, where the sun and the moon at his imagining suffer their huge eclipses, where heaven and hell are in their places, where vast seas wash the shores, and oceans meet each other. When Iago calls on his world:

Take note, take note, O world!
To be direct and honest is not safe,

he means the world of men. But when a few lines later Othello uses the same word, the 'world' becomes as large as its history, and contains both seas and continents:

By the world,
I think my wife be honest and think she is not—

so different are the worlds which they address. Iago's is a pragmatic world, and his imagery finds its authority in social usage. Othello's world is the poetical aggrandizement of himself, and as he addresses he creates it.

While Iago, being a character statically conceived, must necessarily be, as it were, external to the imagery he uses, Othello's nature is in every word. We might say that imagery illustrates and elaborates Iago's character: but it creates Othello's. In his speech words come active from those deeps of language in which they return to their early origin and are reinforced in their primitive energies. The living image comes out of the chrysalis of the concept and takes on unique being. And whereas in Iago's soliloquies time is external to language and no more than time taken to utter the words, in Othello's speeches time is very often transformed and becomes the dimension of the living language itself, as it creates its own space in its own time. Do we not feel, for example, that in the famous temptation scene Iago lives not so much in the dimension of his own time as in Othello's? Or, perhaps, is there not here a subtle interplay between two kinds of time, as I believe there to be in *King Lear* when Lear and the fool are out in the storm? This interplay of two kinds of time, indeed, seems to me symbolical of a deeper interplay, which is part of the business of tragedy; and this interplay has its concrete representation, is made external, through the processes of language.

—ARTHUR SEWELL, "Character and Vision," *Character and Society in Shakespeare* (Oxford: Clarendon Press, 1951), pp. 30–33

ROBERT B. HEILMAN

To call Iago the Economic Man would over-emphasize one aspect of him and under-emphasize others. But the term suggests the kind of self-revelation which Iago makes in that inner drama of exchange and values in which the good-name-is-jewel speech is a key point. That self-revelation begins in the opening scene of the play, the first eighty lines of which are spoken by Iago and Roderigo. For a minor character whom we tend to forget, Roderigo has a rather substantial role; the fact is that he is more important than he may seem. Shakespeare gives him the utmost dramatic usefulness by making him a lesser, semi-tragic analogue of Othello; by providing us, through Iago's deception of him, with another view of Iago as deceiver and hence strengthening our sense of his technical competence as manipulator; and by endowing Roderigo with a moral and intellectual negligibility that lets Iago be entirely off-guard before him, so that from their dialogue we learn much about Iago. The quality of their relationship, as Coleridge noted, is expressed in the first speech of the play, when Roderigo rebukes Iago, "who hast had my purse / As if the strings were thine" (I.i.2–3). This monetary definition of friendship, besides telling us something about Roderigo, is a tip-off to a real interest of Iago's. But even at that we are a little surprised to see with what grossness Iago later insists on a supply of cash when he encourages Roderigo not to despair of having Desdemona just because she is married: "Put money in thy purse . . . I say, put money in thy purse. It cannot be that Desdemona should long continue her love to the Moor—put money in thy purse—nor he his to her . . . Put but money in thy purse. These Moors are changeable in their wills. Fill thy purse with money . . . She must have change, she must. Therefore put money in thy purse ... Make all the money thou canst ... Therefore make money. A pox of drowning thyself! ... Thou art sure of me. Go, make money ... Traverse! go! provide thy money!" (I.iii.345–379). Crude as this is, Roderigo falls into line immediately, as if charmed: "I am chang'd. I'll go sell all my land" (388). But what actually is Iago's project? Up to this moment we have seen Iago as a man with an apparent grievance and with a heart for revenge—a situation which, despite Iago's lowbrow manner and his banal ideas about love, is not without associations of nobility. What, then, is he up to now? To sponging or petty bilking? Is the revenger, with his tradition of desperation and abandon, sinking into the calculating parasite and confidence man? As if quite aware of the problem, Shakespeare rushes to answer the question in an immediate soliloquy by Iago:

> Thus do I ever make my fool my purse;
> For I mine own gain'd knowledge should profane
> If I would time expend with such a snipe
> But for my sport and profit.　　　　　　　　　　　　(389–392)

So we have it: Iago is literally pursuing "purse" and "profit." He feels a momentary need to defend himself to himself: "sport" has a gentlemanly ring. But, in arguing that it is all right to "time expend with such a snipe" if there is some gain to show for it, Iago exhibits, besides his shrewdness in calculation, a streak of vulgarity. We see his economics in much sharper focus: the weighty judge of rich and poor is a small-scale profiteer.

Iago knows how to influence people, indeed, but how good is his judgment of their quality? Is Roderigo merely a "snipe," or, as Iago calls him later, "this poor trash of Venice" (II.i.312)? The answer is Roderigo's coming up with the acute perception that Desdemona is "full of most blessed condition" (II.i.254–255). Since this feeling for human quality is precisely what is absent in "poor trash"—"poor white trash," as we have come to say—we have an excellent glimpse into Iago's economics of character. Roderigo progresses from a recognition of Desdemona to a recognition of himself: not only can he face facts—"My money is almost spent"—but he can almost gain something immaterial from his loss: "I shall have so much experience for my pains; and so, with no money at all, and a little more wit, return again to Venice" (II.iii.371–375). Albeit for a very small way, and from a great distance, Roderigo approaches the Shakespeare tragic character who at the very moment of loss ironically comes into a better kind of possession. Then Iago interposes with another sample of his moral economics: "How poor are they that have not patience!" (376), cleverly converting Roderigo's material poverty into a poverty of morale; and this challenge, plus a few words of encouragement for the quest which Roderigo even yet cannot relinquish, again reduces the latter to a tool. But once more, failure opens Roderigo's eyes, and he begins to sense Iago's game: "I have wasted myself out of means. The jewels you have had from me to deliver to Desdemona would half have corrupted a votarist. You have told me she hath receiv'd them ... I tell you 'tis not very well. I will make myself known to Desdemona. If she will return me my jewels, I will give over my suit and repent my unlawful solicitation" (IV.ii.187–202).

Roderigo's rates of exchange show how he fails of the tragic stature which in some ways he approaches: though he has come to understand Desdemona, himself, and to an extent Iago, he cannot by free repentance seal his recognitions but expects Desdemona to buy his repentance. His alliance with Iago is not entirely a mismating, and though quite unwilling to leave him a stereotyped gull, Shakespeare keeps him, as moral economist, within the range of vacillation that makes plausible Iago's finally persuading him to attempt murder and thus expose himself to murder.

Now Iago. Not until the final act do we learn the truth of what Roderigo has irresolutely suspected. Iago thus resolves on Roderigo's death:

> Live Roderigo,
> He calls me to a restitution large
> Of gold and jewels that I bobb'd from him
> As gifts to Desdemona.   (V.i.14–17)

This is said so much in the flat style of a man coolly canvassing alternatives that we almost slide over it; yet we should linger here, at what is a key-point in this system of value-terms, for here is made a specific definition of the evil which Iago practices. His eye upon the money in Roderigo's purse has not been that of the needy friend, the costly agent, the inveterate touch-artist; it is that of the thief. He is not the ne'er-do-well or the "bum"—the picaro—but the vicious man whom Dante punished in the eighth circle.

Iago's economic history shows him to be both vulgar and vicious—a notable definition of evil. He has not the shadow of a motive to rob Roderigo; contrariwise, he has at least monetary reasons for feeling gratitude to Roderigo. What we can see at work is a kind of "pure malice" or "floating hatred." If this is true, the whole Roderigo line of action takes on a new dramatic utility, for it is directly related to the problem of what Coleridge called, thereby becoming the target of many a rebuttal, "motiveless malignity." If Iago acts with "motiveless malignity" toward Roderigo, it is probable that he acts so toward Othello. His cheapness and unscrupulousness together cast doubt upon the probability of his having originally, as has been argued, a strong sense of injustice, for such a sense implies an integrity or "justness" of feeling foreign to everything else in Iago. We have only Iago's word for his "case" against Othello, and there is no reason whatever to trust his word. It is inevitable for Iago to say, as he does to Roderigo, "I know my price, I am worth no worse a place" (I.i.11), for this is the standard economics of self in the disappointed man. Emilia, who is no fool, never shares the grievance which he says he feels. In fact, it is impossible not to suspect that in arguing his merits against Cassio's he is primarily bent upon convincing himself; all his complaint resembles the archetypal disparagement of better men by one who has failed of an end, public or private. After noisily outlining his complaint (I.i.8–39), Iago does not rest there, as a man might who really wished his point to sink in, but rushes on, as if the grievance were after all only a point of departure, into a shocking enunciation of his intent to continue, to Othello, "forms and visages of duty," "shows of service," but to be of those who, "when they have lin'd their coats,/ Do themselves homage" (50–54). In

Iago's "what's in it for me?" economics, moral and material accounts are identical. He now inaugurates a revenge so incommensurate, in its savagery, with the alleged slight to himself that it becomes the more difficult to think of even Iago as taking his proffered "motive" seriously.

But "motiveless" is not the same as "meaningless." Indeed, to deny that Iago is an instance of commonplace cause-and-effect is not to disparage the portrayal but rather to move it into a much ampler realm of meaning. In the largest sense, Iago suggests autonomous evil, which is one of the facts of experience that are not reducible to the common formulae of conduct; his difficulty is for those readers for whom the concept of a spontaneous malice is not positive enough and who must therefore endeavor to locate specific situational causes for all actions. The fact, however, that we have never thought Iago's terrible hatred of Othello improbable in itself, suggests that, even while rather literally bent upon motive-hunting, we have subconsciously tended to solve the problem by viewing Iago as human depravity in action. Iago is clearly a condensation of evil that is much more than an isolatable, localized impulse to crime. Yet this view does not compel us to conceive of him only metaphysically; at the human level we see in him the entity whose only excursion from moral indifference is destructive hatred of the achievements of the spirit—namely, the mass-mind. For the spiritual gracelessness of Iago, who is at once demonic and vulgar, Shakespeare has found an excellent dramatic formulation in the maneuverings of the thief.

—ROBERT B. HEILMAN, "The Economics of Iago and Others," *PMLA* 68, No. 2
(June 1953): 557–61

HELEN GARDNER

My subject being the Noble Moor, I cannot spend as long as I should wish upon his Ancient. There is an assumption current today that Iago expresses in some way a complementary view of life to Othello's. His power over Othello is said to derive from the fact that 'into what he speaks are projected the half-truths that Othello's romantic vision ignored, but of which his mind held secret knowledge'. I am quoting Miss Maud Bodkin, since she has been much quoted by later writers. She also speaks of the reader 'experiencing the romantic values represented in the hero, and recognizing, in a manner secretly, the complementary truths projected into the figure of Iago'. Professor Empson has put this view more breezily:

> The thinking behind the 'melodrama' is not at all crude, at any rate if you give Iago his due. It is only because a rather unreal standard has been set up that the blow-the-gaff man can take on this extraordinary power. It is not merely out of their latent 'cynicism' that the listeners are meant to feel a certain sting of truth in Iago's claim to honesty, even in the broadest sense of being somehow truer than Othello to the facts of life.

I cannot resist adapting some Johnsonian expressions and saying this is 'sad stuff': 'the man is a liar and there's an end on't.' What Iago injects into Othello's mind, the poison with which he charges him, is either false deductions from isolated facts—she deceived her father—and from dubious generalizations—Venetian women deceive their husbands—or flat lies. Whatever from our more melancholy experiences we choose to call the facts of life, in this play there is one fact which matters, upon which the plot is built and by which all generalizations are tested:

Moor, she was chaste; she lov'd thee, cruel Moor.

The notion that by striking a mean between the 'high-mindedness' of Othello and the 'low view' of Iago we shall arrive at a balanced view, one that is not 'crude', could only have arisen in an age which prefers to the heroic that strange idol of the abstracting intelligence, the normal, and for the 'beautiful idealisms of moral excellence' places before us the equally unattainable but far more dispiriting goal of 'adaptation to life'. But, in any case, the sum will not work out, for Iago has not a point of view at all. He is no realist. In any sense which matters he is incapable of speaking truth, because he is incapable of disinterestedness. He can express a high view or a low view to taste. The world and other people exist for him only to be used. His definition of growing up is an interesting one. Maturity to him is knowing how to 'distinguish betwixt a benefit and an injury'. His famous 'gain'd knowledge' is all generalizations, information docketed and filed. He is monstrous because, faced with the manifold richness of experience, his only reaction is calculation and the desire to manipulate. If we try to find in him a view of life, we find in the end only an intolerable levity, a power of being 'all things to all men' in a very unapostolic sense, and an incessant activity. Iago is the man of action in this play, incapable of contemplation and wholly insusceptible to the holiness of fact. He has, in one sense, plenty of motives. His immediate motives for embarking on the whole scheme are financial, the need to keep Roderigo sweet, and his desire for the lieutenancy. His general motive is detestation of superiority in itself and as recognized by others; he is past master of the sneer. Coleridge has been much criticized for speaking of his 'motiveless malignity' and yet the note of glee in Iago confirms Coleridge's moral insight. Ultimately, whatever its proximate motives, malice is motiveless; that is the secret of its power and its horror, why it can go unsuspected and why its revelation always shocks. It is, I fear, its own reward.

Iago's power is at the beginning of the action, where he appears as a free agent of mischief, creating his plot out of whatever comes to hand; after the middle of the third act he becomes the slave of the passion which he has aroused, which is the source of whatever grandeur he has in our imagination. Othello's agony turns the 'eternal villain', the 'busy and insinuating rogue', the 'cogging cozening slave' of the first acts into the 'Spartan dog, more fell than anguish, hunger, or the sea' of the close. The crisis of the action comes when Othello returns 'on the rack', determined that he will not 'make a life of jealousy', and demands that Iago furnish him with proof. Iago's life is from now on at stake. Like Desdemona's it hangs upon the handkerchief. He must go forward, to everyone's ruin and his own.

Iago ruins Othello by insinuating into his mind the question, 'How do you know?' The tragic experience with which this play is concerned is loss of faith, and Iago is the instrument to bring Othello to this crisis of his being. His task is made possible by his being an old and trusted companion, while husband and wife are virtually strangers, bound only by passion and faith; and by the fact that great joy bewilders, leaving the heart apt to doubt the reality of its joy. The strange and extraordinary, the heroic, what is beyond nature, can be made to seem the unnatural, what is against nature. This is one of Iago's tricks. But the collapse of Othello's faith before Iago's hints, refusals, retreats, reluctant avowals, though plausible and circumstantiated, is not, I believe, ultimately explicable; nor do I believe we make it so by searching for some psychological weakness in the hero which caused his faith to fail, and whose discovery will protect us from tragic experience by substituting for its pleasures the easier gratifications of moral and intellectual superiority to the sufferer. There is only one answer to Iago's insinuations, the answer Othello made to Brabantio's warning: 'My life upon her faith.' It is one thing to retort so to open enmity; more difficult to reply so to the seemingly well-meant warnings of a friend. That Othello does not or cannot reply so to Iago, and instead of making the venture of faith, challenges him to prove his wife false, is his tragic error.

—HELEN GARDNER, "The Noble Moor," *Proceedings of the British Academy*
41 (1955): 195–98

J. K. WALTON

Iago, whether seen as dramatic mechanism or consummate villain, has often been taken to be an essentially isolated figure. This is surely a mistake. He is rather an extreme embodiment of a number of attitudes which other of the Venetians are shown, directly or by implication, as possessing. When he first appears he is presented as a Venetian who is complaining that he has been passed by in favour of an outsider, a Florentine, despite the fact that

> Three great ones of the city,
> In personal suit to make me his lieutenant,
> Off-capp'd to him   (I. i. 8–10)

—to 'his Moorship'. Like Roderigo, a representative of 'the wealthy curled darlings of our nation', he 'loves' Desdemona and resents Othello's possession of her. Roderigo's exclamation as he resolves to kill Cassio—' 'Tis but a man gone' (V. i. 10)—is of a piece with Iago's customary cynicism. Like Brabantio, Iago considers the marriage of Othello and Desdemona unnatural, and, like him, he tends to see people as property. He awakens Brabantio with the cry of 'Thieves' to tell him that he is 'robb'd', a cry which Brabantio takes up—'Down with him, thief' (I. ii. 57), 'O thou foul thief' (I. 62), 'She is . . . stol'n from me' (I. iii. 60). The Duke, despite his restraint due to the State's need of Othello, speaks of the marriage in the same terms:

The robb'd that smiles steals something from the thief;
He robs himself that spends a bootless grief.   (I. iii. 208–9)

Here again it is Iago who gives the most extreme expression to this attitude. He knows his 'price', and makes Roderigo his purse.

Of Iago's various motives, there are only two which none of the other characters possesses: his jealousy—unless we take Roderigo to be jealous—and his desire for revenge. But, so far as Shakespeare's audience was concerned, there would have been no need to introduce characters with these motives in order to show Iago as an extreme expression of his environment, since these were motives which such an audience was accustomed to have associated with Italians in general. Iago's use of sea imagery may also have suggested to Shakespeare's audience a connexion with Venice not apparent to an audience of today; for in the early seventeenth century Venice, though in decline, was still a sea-power, and still noted for its association with the sea.

It is in relation to Iago's representative role that we should consider his motivation. The sinister ambiguity of his motives arises precisely because he is so representative a figure. If Shakespeare had given Iago only one motive, or had emphasized one more than another, he would have been less representative and less sinister. The concentration of them all in one person produces an effect greater than that of a simple addition; the whole is greater than the parts, and gives Iago the single effect of malignancy which makes him appear 'More fell than anguish, hunger, or the sea' (V. ii. 365). It is when we see Iago in this way that we can best appreciate the adversary with whom, unknown to themselves, Othello and Desdemona are faced when they reach Cyprus. Their marriage has been made possible only by a crisis in the Venetian State brought about by the threatened Turkish invasion. This threat vanishes, and the situation which would have made their marriage impossible reappears, together with Iago in whom is found in deadly concentration all the various hostile forces presented in the first Act.

But Iago, for all his force, is not the prime mover of the tragedy. This is to be found in the strength, rather than the weakness, of Othello and Desdemona. Iago's role is limited to that of manipulating the situation so that their strength destroys them. Without that strength his plot would be powerless to bring about their destruction. Iago himself is essentially negative; even in his manipulation of the situation he is merely reacting to the initial action, which is their marriage.

That the tragedy is due to the strength of Othello and Desdemona is brought out in a rich variety of ways throughout the play. The nature of the earlier part of his plot is quite clearly stated by Iago himself. In the soliloquy in which he discusses the scheme whereby he will encourage Cassio to plead with Desdemona to have him reinstated, he observes that

by how much she strives to do him good
She shall undo her credit with the Moor.
So will I turn her virtue into pitch;
And out of her own goodness make the net
That shall enmesh them all.   (II. iii. 347–51)

But Desdemona's earlier virtue is also turned by Iago to work her undoing. In III. iii, after he has by means of his insinuations prepared for the direct assault, he proceeds to make definite imputations against her which are based on a cynical interpretation of just those aspects of her conduct in which her greatest courage has consisted. First of all, echoing Brabantio, he suggests that her love for Othello and her resolution to marry him—her 'downright violence and storm of fortunes' (I. iii. 249)—were simply a matter of deceit:

> She did deceive her father, marrying you;
> And when she seem'd to shake and fear your looks,
> She lov'd them most.   (III. iii. 210–12)

Iago's second imputation consists of a cynical distortion of the fact that Desdemona had the strength of character to marry someone of different country, colour, and rank:

> Not to affect many proposed matches
> Of her own clime, complexion, and degree,
> Whereto we see in all things nature tends—
> Foh! one may smell in such a will most rank,
> Foul disproportion, thoughts unnatural.   (III. iii. 233–7)

Later we can see how, quite apart from her generous appeals on Cassio's behalf, her generosity and modesty contribute to her downfall. She dismisses Othello's ill-humour with the thought that

> Men's natures wrangle with inferior things,
> Though great ones are their object.   (III. iv. 145–6)

Even after she has been struck and reviled, she does not think of asking for the protection of her fellow-countrymen, the Venetian messengers. To Emilia's 'I would you had never seen him' she replies,

> So would not I: my love doth so approve him
> That even his stubbornness, his checks, his frowns—
> Prithee unpin me—have grace and favour in them. (IV. iii. 18–20)

When shortly before her death, Othello tells her, 'Think on thy sins', and she replies 'They are loves I bear to you', she indicates an aspect of the truth that her destruction comes from her strength. Later, when Emilia asks 'O, who hath done this deed?', and she declares, 'Nobody. I myself', she is valiantly trying to shield Othello; but she is also illuminating the inner recesses of her tragic destiny.

So too with Othello there are abundant indications that he owes his downfall to his virtues rather than to weakness. Iago tells us that

> The Moor is of a free and open nature
> That thinks men honest that but seem to be so;
> And will as tenderly be led by th' nose
> As asses are.   (I. iii. 393–6)

That is, he can be duped because he is 'of a free and open nature'. Iago is a grudging witness to Othello's virtues; and according to ordinary reason and also the stage conventions of the time, when he describes Othello as having nature of this kind—a nature the opposite of that of the self-regarding, self-dramatizing Othello of some recent critics—we should accept that description as correct. The same point concerning Othello's strength is twice made in the 'temptation' scene itself, at dramatically important points. Just before Iago begins to make specific insinuations against Desdemona, based on the supposed behaviour of Venetian women and her treatment of her father, he tells Othello to 'observe her well with Cassio', for 'I would not have your free and noble nature / Out of self-bounty be abus'd' (III. iii. 203–4). If we take it that Othello is not, at this very point, being abused out of the 'self-bounty' of a 'free and noble nature', we here impoverish for ourselves the dramatic texture of the play by failing to see the irony. Later, when the success of Iago's plot is hanging by a thread and he faces Othello's 'wak'd wrath', he exclaims as if to himself,

> O wretched fool,
> That liv'st to make thine honesty a vice!
> O monstrous world! Take note, take note, O world,
> To be direct and honest is not safe.
>
> (III. iii. 379–82)

Here, too, that interpretation is 'reductive' which holds that the danger to Othello arises otherwise than because he is 'direct and honest' and has lived to make his 'honesty a vice'.

When we examine the decisive moments of Othello's deception by Iago, we can see the large part played by his modesty in his fall, so that it would be truer to say that he falls through modesty than through pride. Those critics who speak of Othello's loss of faith in Desdemona tend to make a mechanical division between his faith in her and his faith in himself, whereas they are interrelated. In the conditions presented in the play—where at the time of their marriage they are virtual strangers to each other, and he a stranger to Venice—the one is necessarily based on the other. The only proof of her love that he can have consists in the fact of her devotion to him, and that must ultimately depend on his view of his own merits. When Iago succeeds in destroying Othello's faith in himself, he inevitably succeeds in destroying his faith in her as well. The first part of the 'temptation' scene (III. iii. 35–168) consists essentially of an assault on his self-confidence. Iago, by means of his insinuations, conveys to Othello that he knows more about Cassio, and by implication Desdemona, than he says—and also that he knows more than Othello knows. It is not until l. 169—'O, beware, my lord, of jealousy'—that he begins to develop a direct attack on Desdemona. From Othello's long speech beginning 'Why, why is this? / Think'st thou I'd make a life of jealousy' it is clear that, despite Iago's many insinuations, he still has faith in her:

> 'Tis not to make me jealous
> To say my wife is fair, feeds well, loves company,
> Is free of speech, sings, plays, and dances well;
> Where virtue is, these are more virtuous.
>
> (III. iii. 187–90)

But in the very next lines in the same speech, he reveals the point which Iago will be able to work on with devastating effect. All that has gone before leads up to this moment when Othello has been manœuvred into a position where he finds it necessary to state the grounds of his confidence in Desdemona:

> Nor from mine own weak merits will I draw
> The smallest fear or doubt of her revolt;
> For she had eyes, and chose me.

This is modesty, and modesty is strength; but this very strength gives Iago the opportunity of seizing on that aspect of the situation which, in the circumstances of the play, can make that strength become weakness. Othello, besides being modest, is a stranger, and the combination is fatal, for his being a stranger means that he has now no source of assurance of Desdemona's love but the fact that she chose him; and his modesty prevents him from assuming that this must have been for his merits. The way for Iago's advance is now open. He first of all emphasizes Othello's ignorance of Venice, telling him in the following speech, 'Look to your wife; observe her well with Cassio', for

> I would not have your free and noble nature
> Out of self-bounty be abus'd; look to't.
> I know our country disposition well:
> In Venice they do let God see the pranks
> They dare not show their husbands; their best conscience
> Is not to leave't undone, but keep't unknown.   (III. iii. 203–8)

When Othello admits his ignorance of Venice with 'Dost thou say so?', Iago rein-forces the point with special reference to Desdemona, by echoing Brabantio's words in the first Act, 'She has deceiv'd her father, and may thee' (I. iii. 293). Iago pursues his advantage by making further insinuations; and as soon as Othello expresses a doubt (I. 231)—'And yet, how nature erring from itself' (meaning human nature)—Iago seizes upon this general reflection on human weakness to make, in a manner which recalls words of Brabantio's, his most vicious suggestion— that Desdemona married him out of perversity, and not for any merits he may have possessed. When Iago is able to suggest without opposition from Othello that repentance by Desdemona for having married him would really be in the nature of a 'recoiling to her better judgment', the point has been reached where Othello has lost faith in himself. It is now only a short step to his loss of faith in Desdemona. In the following speech he instructs Iago,

> If more thou dost perceive, let me know more;
> Set on thy wife to observe. Leave me, Iago.   (III. iii. 243–4)

and from now on Iago can proceed to the practical details of his plot, which are based on Othello's desire for evidence that follows from his loss of faith in his wife.

How decisive is Iago's victory? Once he has gained the ascendancy over Othello's soul, it is certainly true that Othello begins to see the world through Iago's eyes, and that he begins in a sense to turn into Iago. This change, as W. H. Clemen and M. M. Morozov have pointed out, is indicated by Othello's use of Iago's kind of imagery, which predominantly consists of images of 'beasts, represented as embodiments of foolishness, lechery and all kinds of loathsome vices'. This metamorphosis, however, is also shown in other, more direct ways. The fact that Othello is now jealous, and that he thinks of revenge, of itself makes him akin to his tormentor. The change is also seen in his adoption of the view of love as a matter of private property. Employing the same terms as Iago and Brabantio, he declares that

> He that is robb'd, not wanting what is stol'n,
> Let him not know't, and he's not robb'd at all.
>
> (III. iii. 346–7)

His newly acquired view of love as a commodity is most fully developed in the 'brothel' scene (IV. ii). The full extent of the change here may be appreciated when we compare Othello's 'there's money for your pains' (IV. ii. 94) with his declaration on his first appearance:

> But that I love the gentle Desdemona,
> I would not my unhoused free condition
> Put into circumscription and confine
> For the seas' worth.
>
> (I. ii. 25–28)

But Iago's triumph is never complete. His failure becomes apparent at the very moment when on one level he seems entirely successful. In the scene where Desdemona is killed, the old Othello is already reappearing, brought to life by a sense of the solemnity of the deed he is to perform, which he sees as a sacrifice. Iago has not ultimately been successful, for Othello ultimately remains uninfected by the cynicism which is Iago's all-pervading trait; and he kills Desdemona, not out of a base Iago-like jealousy, but because his love for her is so great. He has seen her as representing the source of order—'Perdition catch my soul / But I do love thee; and when I love thee not / Chaos is come again'—and of all that is good—'If she be false, O, then heaven mocks itself!' He kills her so that what is good may no longer 'mock itself'. More specifically, 'I will kill thee, / And love thee after' (V. ii. 18–19). That is, he kills her so that he can love her after. The fact that in the death scene he uses once more 'the noble Othello music' with its 'lofty and poetic imagery' emphasizes the nature of his motivation. It is heard in the opening speech, 'It is the cause, it is the cause, my soul—'; and in his declaration to Emilia which recalls both his valuation of his love above 'the seas' worth', and Desdemona's own refusal to consider the 'world' as 'a great price for a small vice' (IV. iii):

> Nay, had she been true,
> If heaven would make me such another world
> Of one entire and perfect chrysolite,
> I'ld not have sold her for it.
>
> (V. ii. 146–9)

It is also heard in the speech which culminates in his self-destruction, when this 'extravagant and wheeling stranger' is completing his tragic circle. The steps leading to that completion are clear. He realizes that Iago has been false and Desdemona true, and undergoes a terrible repentance:

> When we shall meet at compt,
> This look of thine will hurl my soul from heaven,
> And fiends will snatch at it.   (V. ii. 276–8)

He now sees that the self-division of what is good is to be found, not in Desdemona, but in himself; and he acts in the same way as he had with her.

> So they lov'd as love in twain
> Had the essence but in one;
> Two distincts, division none:
> Number there in love was slain.   (*The Phoenix and the Turtle*)

When we come to consider Othello's last great speech, we should remember that it is a part of the entire dramatic movement of the play. This speech, in which he asks his listeners to speak 'of me as I am; nothing extenuate, / Nor set down aught in malice', takes us back to that in which he delivers to the Senate 'a round unvarnish'd tale' of his wooing. The 'Arabian trees' and 'Aleppo' recall the story of his travels, which have now reached their end. If we accuse Othello in the later speech of self-dramatization and untruth, we must also say the same about him in the earlier. In this we shall have been anticipated by Iago, who instructs Roderigo to note 'with what violence she first lov'd the Moor, but for bragging and telling her fantastical lies' (II. i. 219–21). From the viewpoint of Iago, which is that of a cynic, Othello is of course a sentimentalist and self-dramatizer. But Iago is not Shakespeare, however much some critics may choose to associate themselves with his utterances: he represents, seen in his most general aspect, the conditions in which strength destroys itself. Far from Othello's self-inflicted death and his speech leading up to it indicating a self-dramatizing attitude of mind, they are the result of a process of internal development central to his being. Like all tragic heroes, he is consumed by that which nourishes him. With splendid accuracy he describes himself as 'one that lov'd not wisely, but too well'. When he kills himself, saying with his last words,

> I kiss'd thee ere I kill'd thee. No way but this—
> Killing my self, to die upon a kiss.

we have the appropriate consummation of the tragedy of Othello and Desdemona, for each dies for the love of the other.

—J. K. WALTON, " 'Strength's Abundance': A View of *Othello*," *Review of English Studies* 11, No. 1 (February 1960): 9–17

G. M. MATTHEWS

Why does Iago hate Othello? This has always been the crux of the play. The characters themselves are baffled by hatred of such intensity; the dying Roderigo calls Iago an 'inhuman dog', and to Lodovico he seems 'More fell than anguish, hunger, or the sea'—more implacable than the blind forces of nature. Yet when Othello asks him point-blank why he acted as he did, he shuts up completely. Not that Iago has ever been unwilling to talk, indeed he has just 'part confessed his villainy': all he refuses to explain is the motive of his hatred. 'What you know you know'. What could he possibly say? 'I was passed over for the lieutenancy'? 'Some people thought Othello had seduced my wife'? The possible rational motives are so ludicrously incommensurate with the effects. But although the quick-witted Iago cannot explain his conduct rationally, Coleridge's verdict of 'motiveless malignity' overlooks the first scene of the play, which shows that his conduct was powerfully motivated. He is no devil from hell, except metaphorically. We learn within twenty lines that he is sensitive to aliens, because one of his first objections to Cassio is that he is a foreigner, 'a Florentine'. And although Iago's avowed policy is to thrive by Othello until he has lined his coat, his first dramatic action is to stir up an unprofitable racial riot against Othello merely in order to 'poison his delight' in his marriage, which is described to Brabantio in bestially obscene language:

IAGO: Even now, now, very now, an old black ram
Is tupping your white ewe. . . .
　　. . . you'll have your daughter cover'd with a Barbary horse; you'll have
　　your nephews [= grandchildren] neigh to you; . . . your daughter and the
　　Moor are now making the beast with two backs.
BRABANTIO:　Thou art a villain.
IAGO:　　　　　　　　　　　　　　You are—a Senator.　　(I. I. 89–119.)

The moment is crucial. The profane wretch and the magnifico suddenly recognize, behind their hostile confrontation, a kind of mutual identity: Brabantio is face to face with his own unconfessed reaction to the news of his daughter's elopement with a black man. Before the Duke that reaction becomes explicit, and Iago afterwards uses it as an invaluable source of quotation in baiting Othello. When Brabantio's 'loved' visitor is also loved by Desdemona he is immediately regarded as a heathen dealer in witchcraft and aphrodisiacs, and the senator's class-prejudice and religious intolerance are revealed in his horrified fear that if such unions are permitted, 'Bond-slaves and pagans shall our statesmen be'. These early scenes demonstrate, therefore, that Iago's view of Othello is not—except in pathological intensity—a unique aberration, but an attitude held by the Venetian ruling class when forced into human relationship with a Moor. The Duke and the rest of his council who are conciliatory and tolerant cannot afford to be otherwise, 'cannot with safety cast him': they need Othello's professional services.

　　Iago hates Othello because he is a Moor. This irrational but powerful motive, underlying the obsessive intensity of his feeling and the improvised reasons with which he justifies it, continually presses up towards the surface of his language. It breaks through into action at the opening of the play in order to give the audience the key to his character; after this its energies go into the intrigue that will bring the hated object and all its associates to destruction; but it often nearly betrays itself.

Iago's 'motive-hunting' has been much discussed, but the fact is that he never gives a direct reason of any kind for his hatred. He tells Roderigo the story of Cassio's appointment and then asks whether this gives him any reason to *love* the Moor? Later he reflects: 'I hate the Moor; And it is thought abroad that twixt my sheets He's done my office'—the hatred and its possible cause are unconnected. Again he tells himself: 'The Moor, howbeit that I endure him not, Is of a constant, loving, noble nature', where this phrase *I endure him not* ('I just can't stand him') is even more revealing than *I hate*, especially when accompanied by an acknowledgment of his true qualities. 'I have told thee often, and I re-tell thee again and again, I hate the Moor'. Iago's mind broods constantly over Othello's colour. After the disembarkation at Cyprus, when Cassio drinks 'To the health of our general' Iago drinks 'to the health of black Othello'. But it is in conversation with Othello himself that the hidden disgust most nearly betrays itself. One exchange is of particular importance. Othello's trust in Desdemona is just beginning to waver:

> OTHELLO: And yet, how nature erring from itself—
> IAGO: Ay, there's the point: as—to be bold with you—
> Not to affect many proposed matches
> Of her own clime, complexion, and degree,
> Whereto we see in all things nature tends—
> Foh! one may smell in such a will most rank,
> Foul disproportion, thoughts unnatural.
> But pardon me—   (III. 3. 231–8.)

Othello has been judged stupid for failing to see that this is an open insult, but it is *not* an open insult; Iago is repeating what Brabantio had said in council:

> she—in spite of nature,
> Of years, of country, credit, every thing—
> To fall in love with what she fear'd to look on!
> It is a judgment maim'd and most imperfect
> That will confess perfection so could err
> Against all rules of nature ...   (I. 3. 96–101.)

The point lies in two antithetical interpretations of 'nature'. For Othello, as for Desdemona, what was 'natural' was a marriage between two lovers, involving the same duties as their parents had owed each other, and by *nature erring from itself* Othello meant 'a wife forgetting her proper loyalty'. To Brabantio it was against all rules of nature for a Venetian girl to love a Moor, and Iago therefore inverted Othello's phrase *nature erring from itself* to mean 'a woman flouting the laws of colour and class' ('clime, complexion, and degree'). The tragedy is epitomized in this exchange. Human love is what Othello stands by. But for Iago Othello is not a human being at all, he is an animal: a ram, a horse, an ass; his sexual union with Desdemona will produce not children but colts. Since Iago himself admits Othello's qualities ('a constant, loving, noble nature'), he is involved in complete irrationality, forced to argue that it is the very virtues of men that make them beast-like:

The Moor is of a free and open nature
... And will as tenderly be led by th' nose
As asses are.

(I. 3. 393–6.)

This particular beast is loved by his wife and honoured as a brilliant military com-
mander. The real relationship between him and Iago was established at the beginning of the play when Othello quelled the uproar Iago had raised by saying: 'For
Christian shame put by this barbarous brawl'; Othello is the civilized man, Iago the
barbarian. Iago's task is to reduce him in actuality to a shape that at first exists only
in Iago's fantasy, that of an irrational beast, by

> making him egregiously an *ass*
> And practising upon his peace and quiet
> Even to *madness*.

(II. 1. 303–5; my italics.)

So when Othello exclaims, at the beginning of his ordeal, that Iago would have to
'exchange [him] for a goat' before he would make jealousy the business of his soul,
he is describing with unconscious irony exactly what Iago proposes to do. This is not
a study of a civilized barbarian reverting to type (for Othello has never been a
barbarian, though he has been a slave), but the more subtle one of a white
barbarian who tries to make a civilized man into his own image.

The psychology of the Nazi underlings who ran the concentration camps has
been similarly explained. By reducing intelligent human beings to the condition of
animals they could enjoy a superiority that inverted the real relation between them:
it was a fantasy enactment, resembling magic as magic has been defined by Professor Gordon Childe, 'a way of making people believe they are going to get what
they want'. The element of fantasy and the reliance on magic is one of the 'realist'
Iago's most striking characteristics. Some of his logic, even when it is not designed
to mock the half-witted Roderigo, shows an opportunism that is simply bizarre. He
will postulate almost anything for immediate effect, not just on others but even on
himself, and then back it up with moralizings that sound shrewd only because they
are cynical, like a sort of lunatic Polonius. It is a superb study of an irrational mind,
lucid and cunning on the surface but mad just underneath; and in this it contrasts
directly with Othello's, which is deeply rational but guileless on the surface.

Other characters find Iago's surface convincing, but when they describe him as
honest they are in effect confessing that all they see in him is surface. The main
function of the famous epithet is of course ironic: the pitiless deceiver is the man
everybody turns to for help and everybody trusts. But the word *honest*, constantly
repeated, is eventually felt to express a definite limitation; Iago is imprisoned within
the boundaries of the epithet as a modern commodity is imprisoned within the
slogan advertising it. When Othello says 'Iago is most honest', the honesty is that of
an N.C.O. who is thoroughly reliable at his own job but never in the running for a
commission. Iago seems to recognize the limiting force of the description so automatically attached to him by the savage way he quotes it himself when under-
taking to make discord of the lovers' harmony:

> O, you are well tun'd now!
> But I'll set down the pegs that make this music,
> As honest as I am.   (II. 1. 197–9.)

Thus there is an ironical parallel between Iago who, though lavishly praised for honesty, is not in fact able enough even for minor promotion, and Othello, the truly 'noble Moor', who is not considered good enough to marry into the Venetian ruling class. And the parallel almost converges in the end, for Othello's nobility deceives everyone and becomes, in its effects, practically indistinguishable from Iago's honesty.

The weapon Iago uses is systematic unreason, magic. Brabantio's first assumption on learning that his daughter had fallen in love with a Moor was that she must have been corrupted by sorcery:

> thou hast practis'd on her with foul charms,
> Abus'd her delicate youth with drugs or minerals . . .

> For nature so preposterously to err, . . .
> Sans witchcraft could not.   (I. 2. 73–4, 62–4.)

The Duke's council soon realizes that mutual love was the only 'witchcraft' in the case. Shakespeare is careful to show that the advances came equally from both sides, though at first he plays down the sensual element in Othello's love because men from hot climates were traditionally hot-blooded and this must not be supposed of Othello. The perfect equality of the lovers is symbolized in their playful exchange of roles on arrival in Cyprus, where Othello is Desdemona's 'dear' and Desdemona is Othello's 'fair warrior', while the imagery of Cassio's benediction on them is rich with fertility-feeling:

> Great Jove, Othello guard,
> And swell his sail with thine own powerful breath,
> That he may bless this bay with his tall ship,
> Make love's quick pants in Desdemona's arms,
> Give renew'd fire to our extincted spirits,
> And bring all Cyprus comfort!   (II. 1. 77–82.)

It is hard to see how Shakespeare could have made the case clearer. It is not their union but their disunion that is effected by 'drugs or minerals', as the imagery now begins to demonstrate. Iago curbs Roderigo's impatience by reminding him that 'we work by wit and not by witchcraft', meaning 'the job can't be done without planning'; but in this most ironical of Shakespeare's tragedies the statement carries an opposite implication: 'I work by witchcraft, not by reason'. The degrading of Cassio in Act II is a kind of symbolic rehearsal of the method Iago will use with his principal victim. Betrayed into drunkenness and senseless violence Cassio cries in self-disgust: 'To be now a sensible man, by and by a fool, and presently a beast!' The 'medicine' that so 'unwitted' Cassio was alcohol; the drug used on Othello will be more subtle and instead of wine into his mouth Iago will pour pestilence into his ear, but the sequence of results is to be identical. 'The Moor already changes with my poison', Iago says after his first insinuation, and for this the victim has no counter-drug:

> Not poppy, nor mandragora,
> Nor all the drowsy syrups of the world,
> Shall ever medicine thee to that sweet sleep
> Which thou owed'st yesterday.   (III. 3. 344–7.)

This poetry, it has been noticed, is in Othello's own style: Iago is putting on the verbal habits of his victim, as Othello's later 'Goats and monkeys!' will adopt Iago's; but its *content* is quite alien to Othello's thinking, who is not a drug-addict. Othello's characteristic images are of achieved perfection: Desdemona is a pearl, she is as smooth as monumental alabaster, he would not exchange her for a world made of chrysolite; and it is this integrity of love that Iago attacks with the solvents and corrosives of unreason.

> —G. M. MATTHEWS, "*Othello* and the Dignity of Man," *Shakespeare in a Changing World*, ed. Arnold Kettle (New York: International Publishers, 1964), pp. 130–36

T. McALINDON

The foundation of all Iago's achievements as a liar—his greatest lie—is to convince the world that he is a personification of the quality invoked at the start of the play by the deluded Brabantio: 'honest plainness' (I i 98). Throughout the play, no one is readier than he to affirm the need 'to speak the truth', 'to be direct and honest' (II iii 215; III iii 384), and to deal 'most directly' in the affairs of a friend (IV ii 208). Privately, however, he conceives of himself as a dark apothecary who pours poison into the ears of trusting fools; and when he observes his poisonous medicine begin to burn like mines of sulphur he watches the torments of his victim with artistic satisfaction: 'Work on / My medicine, work. Thus credulous fools are caught . . .' (IV i 44–5). There is probably no greater testimony to the virulence of his poison than the way in which it continues to affect Desdemona even after she has been murdered. Her last words consist of a lie (or ambiguity) intended to conceal Othello's guilt from Emilia; and Othello interprets them as a sign that she is 'double damn'd'—'a liar gone to burning hell' (IV ii 39, V ii 32).

However, Iago's are not the only lies in the complicated web of deceit which finally destroys himself, Emilia and Roderigo as well as Othello and Desdemona. Out of loyalty to her husband, and with little sign of being troubled by a sense of divided duties, Emilia lies to her mistress about the lost handkerchief (III iv 20–1). Later in the same scene she is present when Othello delivers his cloudy warning to Desdemona about the importance of the handkerchief to their happiness. Yet when the distressed Desdemona says: 'Sure there is some wonder in this handkerchief; / I am most unhappy in the loss of it', Emilia takes refuge in indignant generalisations on the baseness of men (III iv 103–7; cf. III iv 156–63)—thus behaving exactly as her husband would in the same situation.

Emilia's awareness that the loss of the handkerchief and the estrangement of her lord and lady are connected is later emphasised in an oblique but powerful manner when she discovers that Iago did tell Othello 'an odious damned lie' (V ii 183). Rapidly fitting together the pieces of the plot, she exclaims: 'I think upon't. I think—I smell't. O villainy! / I thought so then. I'll kill myself for grief' (V ii 194–5). Feelings of guilt and remorse must surely contribute to her audacious determination to trumpet the truth in spite of the threatening swords of Othello (V ii 168) and Iago (V ii 227). Very consciously, she puts truth and loyalty to her mistress above obedience to her husband and indicates that despite appearances to the contrary such behaviour is proper:

> IAGO: What, are you mad? I charge you get you home.
> EMIL.: Good gentlemen, let me have leave to speak.
> 'Tis proper I obey him, but not now.   (V ii 197–9; cf. V ii 222–5)

Of course it is not the truth alone which redeems Emilia, but a willingness to die for it; and she knows that: 'So come my soul to bliss, as I speak true; / So speaking as I think, alas, I die' (V ii 253–4).

The manner of Iago's end is antithetical to Emilia's. Although he can spread no more false reports, he seals his damnation by refusing to lighten the darkness in which his motives lie hidden: he bequeaths to his contemporaries, not a lie, but an unanswered question, an everlasting riddle. Othello, on the other hand, is intensely conscious at death of the need for truthful, balanced and appropriate speech. Like Hamlet's, his last wish (V ii 341–58) is that his cause should be reported aright to the unsatisfied and that his wounded name should not be associated with 'a purpos'd evil' (*Hamlet*, V ii 233). But he does not ask for panegyric simplification. If Lodovico and Montano are to report his unlucky deeds in a manner which accords with truth and justice, they must (he indicates) avoid extremes: they must extenuate nothing nor set aught down in malice. They will thus report that he loved, but lacked wisdom in his loving; that he was not jealous by nature, but when wrought to jealousy, jealous in the extreme. They will set it down, too, that he was noble and base, a champion and an enemy of the state, unjust and just: at once a malignant Turk and an upright Venetian who punished him.

But this great speech-act, in which Othello strives heroically to acknowledge and even to resolve the contradictions in his nature, may not be without its imperfections. His claim that he loved 'not wisely but too well' has a touch of paradoxical confusion and is somewhat akin to his description of himself as 'an honourable murderer' (V ii 297); one accepts Timon's apologia much more readily: 'unwisely, not ignobly, have I given' (*Timon of Athens*, II ii 173). And it hardly seems fit that a Christian who righteously slew a circumcised dog of a Turk should slay himself, that a murderer should play the part of judge and executioner; the inturned sword gives a 'bloody period' to the noble speech and must make some feel (with

Lodovico and Gratiano) that 'all that's spoke is marr'd' (V ii 360). But despite its possible imperfections (on which, I think we are expected to ponder and debate), Othello's last marriage of word and deed fits a valiant general and proves that 'he was great of heart' (V ii 364). Seen in relation to the artistic requirements of the play, it is at once inevitable, flawless and superbly imaginative.

The tragic end of Othello and Desdemona is caused not just by untruth but by rashness or impatience as well. Emilia's reaction to Othello's charge that Desdemona 'was false as water' points very tersely to the combined operation of these two familiar Shakespearean evils: 'Thou art rash as fire to say/That she was false' (V ii 137–8). Iago's slanderous insinuations are really no more than sparks which derive all their destructive potential from the inflammatory human material on which they descend. Had the principal characters been able to 'sprinkle cool patience' on 'the heat and flame' of their distempers and impulses (*Hamlet*, III iv 123–4), and so allowed their judgements to function properly, their history would have had a happy ending. To say this much might well make one seem to fit the role of what Iago calls 'too severe a moraller' (II iii 288); yet it is an idea which Shakespeare plants in the audience's imagination as early as the third scene of Act I. Just before Brabantio storms into the senate with his band of armed supporters and his accusations of witchcraft, the duke and his colleagues are shown dealing with the news of the Turkish threat in a cool and rational fashion—sifting the evidence, pointing to inconsistencies, and distinguishing facts from exaggerations and fictions before deciding on a plan (I iii 1–19).

Rashness is firmly identified throughout the play with disregard for the circumstance of time and the law of timeliness. Indeed, apart from *Romeo and Juliet* and (perhaps) *The Winter's Tale*, no other play of Shakespeare's devotes so much attention to the fatal consequences of failure to keep time in word and deed. And no other play of Shakespeare's moves to such a hectic tempo. As A. C. Bradley has observed, there is no trace in Act IV of that pause which follows the crisis in the other great tragedies. After Act III, Scene iii, where lies ignite passion beyond all control, the action advances towards its catastrophe with a compulsive movement which is simply the translation into deeds of Othello's desire for instant revenge. Aptly, Othello's movement toward the act of revenge is compared to that strange sea whose current is unaffected by sun and moon—the arbiters of time—and shows 'no retiring ebb' until it is swallowed up in the Propontic and the Hellespont (III iii 457–64).

One is made aware of the problem of timeliness chiefly through the moralisings of Iago, who habitually advises his victims to practise patience and 'keep time in all'. This habit is an aspect of Iago's daring hypocrisy. It also exemplifies a kind of indecorum with which we are now well acquainted: gracious words in an ungracious mouth, wisdom from the coxcomb, morality from the Vice. And it is in keeping with the notion (not peculiar to Shakespeare among the Elizabethans) that the villainous and the vindictive frequently display far more interest in the appropriate and inappropriate moment—in Occasion, Opportunity and Importunity—than do ordinary folk:

How poor are they that have not patience!
What wound did ever heal but by degrees?
Thou know'st we work by wit and not by witchcraft;
And wit depends on dilatory time. . . .
Though other things grow fair against the sun,
Yet fruits that blossom first will first be ripe.
Content thyself awhile!   (II iii 358–66)

Iago here shows a regard for timeliness which is impressive but thoroughly perverted and misleading, for his reminder that ripeness is all is really designed to
safeguard a plan which will ensure that the fruits of lawful love will very quickly
become bitter as coloquintida (I iii 348). Hence the contradiction latent in the
sentence 'Though other things . . .', and the accusing evidence of fundamental dis-
harmony with 'proportion'd course of time' (*Lucrece*, I 774) unintentionally introduced by the spontaneous observation which follows immediately in the same
speech: 'By the mass, 'tis morning! / Pleasure and action make the hours seem short'
(II iii 366–7). Liar and murderer, demon and supersubtle magician, Iago instinctively
plies his business by night and so greets the sunrise exactly as a dedicated workman
greets the dusk. All his plots to reduce 'justice, truth, / Domestic awe, night-rest' to
their confounding contraries (Timon's curse is most apt here) are hatched and
executed in the dark. Brabantio is incensed, Cassio is cashiered, Roderigo is killed,
Cassio is wounded, and Desdemona murdered at night.
    Iago continually utilises his understanding of the appropriate and inappropriate
moment in order to provoke others to ignore time. Knowing that Cassio has
no head for drink and that he is 'rash and very sudden in choler' (II ii 265) when
intoxicated, he arranges events so that Roderigo easily finds 'occasion' and 'opportunity' to get him into trouble (II i 262, 277). Then by lavishly praising Desdemona's generous nature, he gets Cassio to neglect the elementary rule that a suit
to gain or regain favour must on no account be pressed inopportunely. Cassio has
scarcely been cashiered when he exhorts him: 'Importune her help to put you
in your place again' (II iii 307). Then, having put Othello on the look-out for 'any
strong or vehement importunity' (III iii 255) in his wife, he returns to Cassio with
the original advice more forcefully urged: 'There is no other way; this she must
do't . . . Go and importune her' (III iv 108–9). And Cassio's is certainly a most
'importunate suit' (IV i 26). Reminding Desdemona of 'service past', 'present sor-
rows', and 'purpos'd merit in futurity', he seems to compress all of time into one
unbearable moment: 'I would not be delay'd' (III iv 115–18). Desdemona's sad
reply—for Othello has now spoken 'so startlingly and rash' (III iv 79) about the
handkerchief—carries an unintended criticism of Cassio's failure to keep time and
relates it to the impending destruction of love's harmonies: 'Alas, thrice-gentle
Cassio! / My advocation is not now in tune' (III iv 123–4). Indirect but even more
apt criticism of his behaviour is contained in his own brief conversation with Bianca
after Desdemona has left him. He promises the importunate courtezan that he will
visit her 'in a more continuate [Q1, 'convenient'] time' and so the scene concludes

with Bianca's resigned comment: ' 'Tis very good; I must be circumstanc'd' (III iv 179, 202).

Iago's success in accelerating the natural pace of things is obviously dependent on the sensation, common to those who suffer in mind or body, that time has begun to move with unnatural slowness. Estranged from Othello's love (III iv 119), Cassio is oppressed with 'leaden thoughts' (III iv 178) and experiences what Bianca complains of: 'lovers' absent hours, / More tedious than the dial eight score times. / O weary reckoning' (III iv 175–7). But it is Othello who suffers most keenly from this sensation. And lest by any chance he should acquire the patience necessary to endure it, Iago reminds him of just how intolerable it is: 'But, O, what damned minutes tells he o'er, / Who dotes, yet doubts, suspects, yet strongly loves?' (III iii 173–4). Iago is instantly rewarded by Othello's exclamation, 'O, misery!', and by his assurance that he will never 'follow still the changes of the moon / With fresh suspicions' (III iii 175, 181–3). Later, too, Othello abjures patience with the implicit claim that the sufferings of Job are trivial in comparison to the protracted agonies and humiliations of the cuckold—and he likens the cuckold to the figure at which the clock-hand points his slow but seemingly motionless finger (IV ii 48–56). Othello's crucifixion is to a clock-face.

—T. McALINDON, *"Othello, the Moor of Venice," Shakespeare and Decorum*
(London: Macmillan, 1973), pp. 84–89

HOWARD FELPERIN

For those with an archeological interest in Shakespeare, the recognition that Iago resembles the Vice of the moralities is an invaluable aid in discovering coherence in language and conduct that would have to be considered insane by naturalistic or psychological norms. Iago's gleeful self-revelations to the audience, his self-contradictions in setting forth a bewildering array of motives, and his casualness, even lightheartedness, in enacting what is supposed to be a rooted hatred can all be traced back to the behavior of his prototype, the Vice of homiletic and allegorical drama. But to invoke the older convention that governs Iago's behavior, though it may explain *what* he does, cannot satisfactorily explain *why* he does it—unless we are willing to postulate, with Spivack, an involuntary author at the mercy of dramatic evolution or, with Eliot, an incompetent author unable to naturalize his archaic sources. In fact, why Iago acts as he does is not only a problem *of* the play but a problem *in* the play: "Will you, I pray, demand that demi-devil / Why he hath thus ensnared my soul and body?" (V.ii.300–301). As Othello's vocabulary suggests, he has little difficulty recognizing in retrospect the role that Iago has enacted all along; why he has put it on in the first place, however, is the anterior question, which Iago expressly refuses to answer. Moreover, the very fact that Othello finally does recognize the convention which has governed Iago's conduct all along can only mean that for Othello and the rest of the cast Iago's role-playing must have been more than transparently conventional for it to have taken in everyone so completely. This only confirms what virtually any spectator must feel in watching the play, that Iago's behavior, conventional as it may retrospectively seem, manages to transcend mere conventionality and achieve a thoroughly convincing naturalism.

The problem of why Iago casts himself in the role of the Vice in the first place thus leads to the related problem, also unaddressed and insoluble by a purely archaeological criticism, of why he succeeds so easily and totally in enacting that role. Why, that is, should Othello fall such easy prey to his snare? The hero of another Elizabethan domestic tragedy contemporaneous with *Othello*, Thomas Heywood's *A Woman Killed with Kindness* (1603), in an almost identical situation demands and gets an "ocular proof" far more compelling—he is shown his wife in bed with his friend—before taking action. It does not help in explaining Othello's extraordinary credulity to look for some naturalistic or psychological basis for it in his characterization, such as his supposed jealousy, since no such flaw is visible in him before Iago's overtures. In fact, Iago himself is somewhat surprised at their success: "Can he be angry? . . . And is he angry?" (III.iv.134–137). What is visible in Othello is a marked propensity to allegorize his experience in other-worldly terms, to define his being in terms of the same morality structure that sustains Iago. For Othello is an allegorist, not a literalist, throughout the play and as such is ready at any point to assimilate the natural and human world to a world of abstract and unchanging values. The storm at sea is an apocalyptic storm of winds that "blow till they have wakened death," of seas that rise and "duck again as low / As hell's from heaven," and the reunion with Desdemona, his "soul's joy" and a "content so absolute" (II.i.182–189). Othello lives and moves and has his being within an allegorical mode in which sign and significance are inseparable, words and deeds magically and instantaneously joined. All Iago need do is supply in detachment a few appropriate visual and verbal signs—some muttered misgivings, a few vivid images, a misplaced handkerchief—for Othello to conjure up their referential "reality" for himself, an eternal plot of sin and the wages of sin. The action he undertakes against the "fair devil" Desdemona thus become for him not a "murder" but a "sacrifice," not personal revenge but divine justice: "It is the cause, it is the cause . . . / O balmy breath, that dost almost persuade / Justice to break her sword" (V.ii.1–17). The morality design that informs Othello is the collaborative product of its two principal characters.

The temptation at this point is to accept this allegorization of character and action at face value, to see the play simply as a re-presentation of a timeless or mythic or archetypal—and therefore "true"—pattern in human affairs. Iago becomes of course the incarnation of evil, Othello the tragic human scapegoat, and Desdemona the embodied principle of goodness and patience doomed to suffer long and be kind. The fact that it would not be implausible to place Othello rather than Desdemona in the Christ-like role of persecution and sacrifice should at least alert us to the difficulties involved in such a critical procedure. For to allegorize the play or, more accurately, to return it to its allegorical prototype is to mystify it, to make it illustrate what St. Paul termed the "mystery of iniquity" and leave it at that.

Whereas medieval poets may predetermine the meaning of their work by including the exegetical apparatus of allegory within it, this is not what we expect from modern writers, who may well suggest interpretive viewpoints on their work from within it but without curtailing the interpretive freedom of their audience. Nor is it what we expect from Shakespeare, whose work forms a kind of interface between medieval and modern literature. To mystify *Othello* by reducing it to the allegorical drama enacted and expressed by its two main characters, with perhaps some lip-service to its "fleshing out" or naturalization of this basically allegorical structure, is to beg the critical questions with which we began. Why does Iago, or for that matter Othello, adopt an allegorical outlook on his world to begin with, and why, for all their self-conventionalization and self-allegorization, does their play strike us as more than or other than conventional and allegorical?

If the question of Iago's motivation cannot be satisfactorily answered in the older terms of allegory, neither can it be answered in the more modern terms of characterization. For it is circular to try to explain the role-playing of the principals by appeal to that which is itself revealed only through their role-playing and therefore inseparable from it. The question would have to be approached in terms of something that exists prior to and outside of their characters and roles and that is thereby capable of conditioning both. That something might be termed the pre-poetic situation out of which Iago and Othello act, since they create their fictive constructs not in a vacuum but from within a social structure which is already in place before Iago hatches a single plot, and about which we learn a great deal before we even lay eyes on Othello. We quickly learn that both characters exist in a marginal relation to the play's dominant Venetian society, and it is this marginality that helps to explain their role-playing. Almost the first information we receive about Othello is that he is an outsider, set apart by background, idiom, and—pre-eminently—color from the Venetian society he serves. Yet he is also clearly at pains to integrate himself within it by outdoing the Venetians themselves, as we see in his scene before the assembled senate, in civility and self-control. As the living symbol of high Venetian culture, Desdemona is not simply a wife to Othello but the legitimating agent of his acculturation. Her loss would thrust Othello outside the structure within which he is now defined and legitimated, however precariously, in his social roles of general, Christian, and husband and back into the dangerous anarchy and isolation of his pre-Venetian and pre-Christian life. Othello recognizes the precariousness of his position and the grace Desdemona reflects on him, and expresses this recognition in the form of a drama of salvation and damnation: "Perdition catch my soul / But I do love thee! and when I love thee not / Chaos is come again" (III.iii.90–92). His wholehearted adoption of the dramatic vocabulary of Christian allegory projects his essential relations to the Venetian society that she represents and that he would have adopt him. At the same time, the rhetorical and histrionic overcompensation with which he employs that formal convention and throws himself into its roles reveals the very marginality he would overcome through them.

Though Iago is of course a Venetian, he too exists in a marginal relation to the dominant Venetian society. He serves under "an erring barbarian" and has been passed over in favor of a mere Florentine "arithmetician," another outsider to whom he deems himself superior in all relevant professional categories as well as in intelligence and self-discipline. This is not to suggest, reductively, that Iago does what he does because Othello has made Cassio lieutenant instead of him. That rebuff is merely a symptom of the prior and more fundamental decadence of a social structure that keeps down "merit" and prefers outsiders graced with "letter and affection." Deprived of a social role commensurate with his conviction of superiority, Iago creates a rival structure in which he is central and potent rather than marginal and impotent, one through which he can demonstrate the very subordination of passion to reason he prides himself on and finds wanting in everyone around and above him:

> the power and corrigible authority . . . lies in our wills. If the balance of our lives had not one scale of reason to poise another of sensuality, the blood and baseness of our natures would conduct us to most prepost'rous conclusions. But we have reason to cool our raging motions, our carnal stings or unbitted lusts, whereof I take this that you call love to be a sect or scion.
>
> (I.iii.320–328)

Iago's "psychology" takes the form of an anatomy of the soul whose terms are taken over from countless morality plays, and which no medieval or renaissance theologian would dispute. Except, that is, for its glaring omission of grace and reduction of love, all exogenous and redemptive functions having been displaced entirely onto the self and replaced by the "authority" of the individual will. The morality play he creates is thus a slick perversion of the values of his own Venetian and Christian culture and of the traditional form that embodies those values. From his own point of view, however, the bewildering multiplicity of Iago's motives becomes intelligible in their very multiplicity. To assert "authority" is to "plume up my will" (I.iii.384), a process that requires an object, or better still, as many objects as possible, since one cannot simply will but must will *something*. Given the primacy of the will, its particular objects must always be arbitrary, *ad hoc*, and of secondary concern. But what better objects than the passionate creatures around him, whom he proceeds to caricature into veritable monsters of appetite leaping almost at random into each other's beds, and who are living symbols of the social structure that keeps him subservient?

The point is that the play presents not only its own allegorization but the basis for demystifying that allegory, the situational logic out of which Iago's and Othello's impulse to allegorize themselves in the first place can be seen to arise. The question remains, however, of why Iago and Othello are discussed as if they were the autonomous and impenetrable figures of the world of allegory they make themselves out to be, when the play provides the basis for rendering them accessible and interpretable in this-worldly terms. This acceptance of the principals' self-allegorization is not really surprising when we consider how unanalytical and acquiescent the rest of the cast is. The web that Iago and Othello spin around themselves is only reinforced by the others, who are at once too closely enmeshed in it and too prone to allegorizing themselves to see it as allegory. So absorbed are Desdemona and Cassio in projecting and enacting roles for themselves—the role of patient virtue who refuses to commit adultery "for the whole world," who takes the guilt of her world on herself ("A guiltless death I die"), and who forgives even her own murderer; and the role of innocent idealist with his own Othello-like "daily beauty in his life" and his own Petrarchan adoration of "the divine Desdemona"— that neither is in a position of sufficient detachment to question or probe either his own motives or those of others:

> OTHELLO: How comes it, Michael, you are thus forgot?
> CASSIO: I pray you pardon me. I cannot speak.   (II.iii.178–179)

> EMILIA: He called her whore. . . .
> IAGO: Why did he so?
> DESDEMONA: I do not know; I am sure I am none such.   (IV.ii.119–123)

The characters of the play provide the cue for their own mystification in their inability to step back from or outside of the roles they equate with themselves. In this respect, Roderigo is comically paradigmatic of the rest in his relation to "honest Iago." He is so caught up in his own role of languishing lover that he cannot see the blatant contradiction between Iago's stated disdain of "passion" and his professed commitment to furthering Roderigo's passion.

> —HOWARD FELPERIN, "Plays within Plays: *Othello, King Lear, Antony and Cleopatra,*" *Shakespearean Representation: Mimesis and Modernity in Elizabethan Tragedy* (Princeton: Princeton University Press, 1977), pp. 74–81

STEPHEN J. GREENBLATT

⟨. . .⟩ it is the dark essence of Iago's whole enterprise that is, as I shall argue, to play upon Othello's buried perception of his own sexual relations with Desdemona as adulterous.

What I have called the marks of the impromptu extend to Iago's other speeches and actions through the course of the whole play. In act 2, he declares of his conspiracy, " 'tis here, but yet confus'd; / Knavery's plain face is never seen, till us'd," and this half-willed confusion continues through the agile, hectic maneuvers of the last act until the moment of exposure and silence. To all but Roderigo, of course, Iago presents himself as incapable of improvisation, except in the limited and seemingly benign form of banter and jig. And even here he is careful, when Desdemona asks him to improvise her praise, to declare himself unfit for the task:

> I am about it, but indeed my invention
> Comes from my pate as birdlime does from frieze,
> It plucks out brain and all: but my Muse labours,
> And thus she is deliver'd . . .   (II, i, 125–28)

Lurking in the homely denial of ability is the image of his invention as birdlime, and hence a covert celebration of his power to ensnare others. Like Jonson's Mosca, Iago is fully aware of himself as an improvisor and revels in his ability to manipulate his victims, to lead them by the nose like asses, to possess their labor without their ever being capable of grasping the relation in which they are enmeshed. Such is the relation Iago establishes with virtually every character in the play, from Othello and Desdemona to such lowly figures as Montano and Bianca. For the Spanish colonialists, improvisation could only bring the Lucayans into open enslavement; for Iago, it is the key to a mastery whose emblem is the "duteous and knee-crooking knave" who dotes "on his own obsequious bondage" (I, i, 45–46), a mastery invisible to the servant, a mastery, that is, whose character is essentially ideological. Iago's attitude toward Othello is nonetheless colonial: though he finds himself in a subordinate position, the ensign regards his black general as "an erring barbarian" whose "free and open nature" is a fertile field for exploitation. However galling it may be to him, Iago's subordination is a kind of protection, for it conceals his power and enables him to play upon the ambivalence of Othello's relation to Christian society: the Moor is at once the institution and the alien, the conqueror and the infidel, the agent of "civility" and the Lucayan. Iago can conceal his malicious intentions toward "the thick-lips" behind the mask of dutiful service and hence prolong his improvisation as the Spaniards could not. To be sure, the play suggests, Iago too must ultimately destroy the beings he exploits and hence undermine the profitable economy of his own relations, but that destruction may be long deferred, deferred in fact for precisely the length of the play.

If Iago then holds over others a possession that must constantly efface the signs of its own power, how can it be established, let alone maintained? We will find a clue, I think, in what we have been calling the *process of fictionalization* that transforms a fixed symbolic structure into a flexible construct ripe for improvisational entry. This process is at work in Shakespeare's play where we may more accurately identify it as *submission to narrative self-fashioning*. When in Cyprus Othello and Desdemona have been ecstatically reunited, Iago astonishes Roderigo by informing him that Desdemona is in love with Cassio. He has no evidence, of course—indeed we have earlier seen him "engender" the whole plot entirely out of his fantasy—but he proceeds to lay before his gull all of the circumstances that make this adultery plausible: "mark me, with what violence she first lov'd the Moor, but for bragging, and telling her fantastical lies; and will she love him still for prating?" (II, i, 221–23). Desdemona cannot long take pleasure in her outlandish match: "When the blood is made dull with the act of sport, there should be again to inflame it, and give satiety a fresh appetite, loveliness in favour, sympathy in years, manners and beauties" (II, i, 225–29). The elegant Cassio is the obvious choice: "Didst thou not see her paddle with the palm of his hand?" Iago asks. To Roderigo's objection that this was "but courtesy," Iago replies, "Lechery, by this hand: an index and prologue to the history of lust and foul thoughts" (II, i, 251–55). The metaphor makes explicit what Iago has been doing all along: constructing a narrative into which he inscribes ("by this hand") those around him. He does not need a profound or even reasonably accurate understanding of his victims; he would rather deal in probable impossibilities than improbable possibilities. And it is eminently probable that a young, beautiful Venetian gentlewoman would tire of her old, outlandish husband and turn instead to the handsome, young lieutenant: it is, after all, one of the master plots of comedy.

What Iago as inventor of comic narrative needs is a sharp eye for the surfaces of social existence, a sense, as Bergson says, of the mechanical encrusted upon the living, a reductive grasp of human possibilities. These he has in extraordinarily full measure. Above all, he is sensitive to habitual and self-limiting forms of discourse, to Cassio's reaction when he has had a drink or when someone mentions Bianca, to Othello's rhetorical extremism, to Desdemona's persistence and tone when she pleads for a friend; and, of course, he is demonically sensitive to the way individuals interpret discourse, to the signals they ignore and those to which they respond.

We should add that Iago includes himself in this ceaseless narrative invention; indeed, as we have seen from the start, a successful improvisational career depends upon role-playing that is in turn allied to the capacity, as Professor Lerner defines *empathy*, "to see oneself in the other fellow's situation." This capacity requires above all a grasp that one is not forever fixed in a single, divinely sanctioned identity, an ability to imagine one's nonexistence so that one can exist for a moment in another and as another. In the opening scene Iago gives voice to this hypothetical self-cancellation in a line of eerie simplicity: "Were I the Moor, I would not be Iago" (I, i, 57). What is disturbing in this comically banal expression—as, for that matter, in Professor Lerner's definition of empathy—is that the imagined self-loss conceals its opposite: a ruthless displacement and absorption of the other. *Empathy*, as its derivation from *einfühlung* suggests, may be a feeling of oneself into an object, but that object may have to be drained of its own substance before it will serve as an appropriate vessel. Certainly in *Othello*, where all relations are embedded in power and sexuality, there is no realm where the subject and object can merge in the unproblematic accord affirmed by the theorists of empathy. As Iago himself proclaims, his momentary identification with the Moor is a strategic aspect of his malevolent hypocrisy:

> In following him, I follow but myself.
> Heaven is my judge, not I for love and duty,
> But seeming so, for my peculiar end.   (I, i, 58–60)

Exactly what that "peculiar end" is remains opaque. Even the general term *self-interest* is suspect: Iago begins his speech in a declaration of self-interest—"I follow him to serve my turn upon him"—and ends in a declaration of self-division: "I am not what I am." We tend, to be sure, to hear the latter as "I am not what I seem," hence as a simple confirmation of his public deception. But "I am not what I am" goes beyond social feigning: not only does Iago mask himself in society as the honest ancient, but in private he tries out a bewildering succession of brief narratives that critics have attempted, with notorious results, to translate into motives. These inner narratives—shared, that is, only with the audience—continually promise to disclose what lies behind the public deception, to illuminate what Iago calls "the native act and figure" of his heart, and continually fail to do so; or rather, they reveal that his heart is precisely a series of acts and figures, each referring to something else, something just out of our grasp. "I am not what I am" suggests that this elusiveness is permanent, that even self-interest, whose transcendental guarantee is the divine "I am what I am," is a mask. Iago's constant recourse to narrative, then, is both the affirmation of absolute self-interest and the affirmation of absolute vacancy; the oscillation between the two incompatible positions suggests in Iago the principle of narrativity itself, cut off from original motive and final disclosure. The only termination possible in his case is not revelation but silence.

—STEPHEN J. GREENBLATT, "Improvisation and Power," *Literature and Society: Selected Papers from the English Institute 1978,* ed. Edward W. Said (Baltimore: Johns Hopkins University Press, 1980), pp. 67–72

TERRY EAGLETON

If Othello in the end is unable to distinguish between delusion and reality, Iago has severed them too rigorously all along. 'I am not what I am' signals not a crisis of identity but a smug self-affirmation: Iago is the exact opposite of whatever he appears to be, which is a consistent enough way of possessing oneself. Appearances for Iago are just empty rituals to be pragmatically manipulated: 'I must show out a flag and sign of love, / Which is indeed but sign' (I.i.157–8). But nothing for Shakespeare is *but* sign: the signifier is always active in respect of its meaning, not some hollow container to be discarded at will. Iago is one of a long line of possessive individualists in Shakespeare who locate reality only in bodily appetite, believing that they can exploit signs and forms from the outside while remaining themselves unscathed by the consequent mystification. Whereas Othello lives straight out of an imaginary self-image, his very being indissociable from rhetoric and theatricality, Iago scorns such burnished discourse as 'mere prattle, without practice'. But both Othello's histrionic 'bombast' and Iago's brisk materialism miss the measure. Othello starts off with a wholly 'imaginary' relation to reality: his rotund, mouth-filling rhetoric signifies a delusory completeness of being, in which the whole world becomes a signified obediently reflecting back the imperious signifier of the self. Even Desdemona becomes his 'fair warrior', as though he can grasp nothing which he has not first translated into his own military idiom. From this deceptively secure standpoint, Othello is then pitched violently into the 'symbolic order' of desire, where signifier and signified never quite coincide. The problem, then, is how to recognize, unlike the cynically naturalistic Iago, that signs and illusions are structural to reality—that all experience, because driven by desire, has an inescapable dimension of fantasy and mystification—without falling prey to the tragic lunacy of an Othello, for whom appearance and reality come to merge into a seamless whole. Iago fails to see that all bodily appetite is caught up in discourse and symbolism, which are not 'superstructural' pieties but part of its inward form. Othello knows this too well, and comes to mistake the sign for the reality. How does one distinguish between taking appearances for reality, and acknowledging the reality of appearances? Failing to make such a distinction, *Othello* suggests, is a psychopathological condition; but it also suggests, more alarmingly, that this psychopathology may be intrinsic to everyday life.

—TERRY EAGLETON, " 'Nothing': *Othello, Hamlet, Coriolanus,"*
William Shakespeare (Oxford: Basil Blackwell, 1986), pp. 69–70

TOM McBRIDE

The apparent sum total of Iago's motives for despising the Moor is two, and both deal with his being denied his appropriate place: the exclusive occupation of the lieutenancy and of his bedroom. The lieutenancy is certainly an office, and whatever we may think of Iago's right to have sole sexual access to Emilia, he calls this an "office," too (I.iii.382). These matters raise for commentators an occupational question, since it is frequently observed that neither of these motives can explain Iago's plot to unman the Moor. How, then, does one occupy oneself in explaining it? Does one turn archetypal, with Coleridge, and name a philosophical force "motiveless malignity"; or become Aristotelian stage-historian, like Stoll, and state that Iago is but a theatrical chimera who derives his only reality from a hermetically sealed poetic unity; or join with Auden to see Iago's real intention as value-free experimentation; or just assent to Othello's momentary guess that Iago is a cloven-footed devil? All commentators have something in common with these critical occupations: they have located Iago's motive far from where he himself situates it. They have placed his motive in a theological force or a recessed psyche, or explained away the "problem" of his motive in poetic praxis. But Iago *says* that he hates the Moor because, in effect, Othello has denied him his place, his office, his proper occupation. It is a fact that Cassio, not Iago, has gotten the lieutenancy; and whether or not Othello has had a sexual liaison with Emilia, that is the humiliating gossip "thought abroad" (I.iii.381), a fact later confirmed by Emilia herself. The general critical occupation treats these as Iagoan rationalizations, but why should not Iago be full of resentment about losing what he considers his deserved place, in the military and the bedchamber? That Iago has filled himself with social resentments is seen by the lyric he sings just before his trick on Cassio: King Stephen can demand whatever he wants concerning his breeches, but anyone of low degree must be content to "take thine auld cloak about thee" (II.iii.91). The song is a motivational overture before Iago's main acts of vengeance. Indeed, the ontology of such social resentments as Iago's should be clear, for the Renaissance is now rightly viewed as a time when "ascriptive status emerged as a commodity." Once work is no longer felt as a transpersonal role on behalf of a sacred monarch, but only a job compelled by those in power, then social resentments and alienations become more likely and serious.

It is useful shorthand to call military places and sexual places "social space."

Although the definitive territoriality implied by "space" is often metaphorical, it is not always so because the military does have its definite barracks and marriage its definite bedroom. But such spaces, whether explicitly marked by territory or not, always have in common a sense of alliance, interdependence, welfare, and status. There are confederacies based on mutual needs and versions of the good; there are hierarchies, often based on reciprocal needs (for a simple example, the master needs the slave to define him as master, while the slave needs the master for material necessities); and there are diverse but definite regulations of discourse, as dictated by different societal or subcultural contexts. Above all, there are manipulations of desire, so that fitting one social space or another comes to be deemed as desirable or even necessary for coherent self-definition and self-worth.

Iago has a personal crisis in social space so defined because he has been passed over in the military hierarchy, and especially at a time during the Renaissance, when ideas of supraindividual duty are not enough—even in the military—to confer adequate self-esteem. Thus Iago reacts as a person may plausibly do in such circumstances: he extracts revenge to make others suffer for his sufferings. The vengeance itself involves the manipulation of others in social space. Iago's sufferings have also given him his insights about how to move others. The play begins early by Iago's early morning announcement to Senator Brabantio that Desdemona is not in her assigned social space, her home bedchambers. Later Brabantio learns that his own social space, as influential father and senator, has been lost because of Othello: Desdemona loves him, and Venice cannot get along without him. Thus Brabantio and Iago both find their places lost through the actions of Othello; they both become excluded thirds in the pervasive social space logic of this play, where a change in relations—the personal or professional, marriage or promotion—seems to ally two parties (Othello and Desdemona, Othello and Cassio) and to displace a third (Brabantio, Iago). Brabantio's occupation is gone long before Othello's: Othello causes Brabantio to lose his; Iago leads Othello to lose his. But first Iago moves Cassio from the social space of the latter's lieutenancy; that it is social space indeed is affirmed by Cassio's bemoaning the loss of no less than his "Reputation." Later Iago not only replaces Cassio as Othello's lieutenant (though in secretive unofficial conspiracy) but also makes Othello think that Cassio has moved into *his* social space in his own honeymoon bedchamber. In the last act that social space, in turn, is changed from honeymoon celebration to homicidal censure. In sum, out of his double motives, Iago has confirmed for another (Brabantio) his loss of social space, moved still others (Cassio and Othello) out of theirs, and caused one social space (the bridal bedroom) to be transformed into yet another (site for ritual execution). These movements, ejections, and mutabilities within social spaces suggest that the play, with a military man as its major protagonist, is about war by other means. For Iago, a declaration of war against him means that he will strike back. He does: he defeats the man who places another ahead of him on the job and may have replaced him in the bed.

—TOM MCBRIDE, "Othello's Orotund Occupation," *Texas Studies in Literature and Language* 30, No. 3 (Fall 1988): 415–17

BARBARA EVERETT

His brilliance as a character is his blankness, his commonplaceness, in the end his uninterestingness: his complete adjustment to the Venice he remakes in his own image. Despite all their jokey intimacy, his soliloquies are fake—though we may sharply recognize him, we never see into Iago, who is a construct of social attitudes and social appetites. From this follows the fact of the invisibility of his villainy to the other characters. It is not that they are particularly stupid as individuals (though they are not particularly intelligent, either); but that Iago wears the 'invisibility' of the sheerly social unit—as we call a social lie, 'politeness'. Emilia's strange, striking, and reiterated 'My husband?' in the fifth Act makes it seem almost that she has genuinely never seen Iago before; she has only accepted the 'anybody' in the role, the driving male non-person who inhabits her bed. And Iago has a public persona which matches this private one, one which shows Shakespeare's power of social imagination at its most extreme. Iago plainly sees Othello's relation to himself as that of Master and Man, a relation he perverts and inverts. As a result he exists as a vortex of continual power-energies. Dramaturgically perhaps descended from Shakespeare's Rumour, and related to his Lucio too, Iago is the contemporary crowd packed into a single consciousness: he is the voice of the Mob, and trouble flows mindlessly from him,

> As when (by Night and Negligence) the Fire
> Is spied in populus Citties.

Iago is, in short, any member of the Venetian back-street crowd, but he is that in a crowd which pushes to the front. It says something about Iago's extraordinary originality as a character that the critical study which throws most light on him is possibly Canetti's psycho-philosophical (and very twentieth-century) *Crowds and Power*.

The "honest" man is one who admits that in society only certain things can be said and done, and they can be said and done only in certain ways. But Iago exists before such concepts were usable because systematically formulated. And he exists as the servant of a man who declares his own alienness to any such society: 'Rude am I in my speech'—Othello's token is not Honesty but Sincerity or Authenticity, the belief that anything can be felt and that anything that can be felt should be said. If Iago lies, Othello is perhaps held by fallacy. It is very terrible that when Othello feels himself to be suffering most, what his mouth says is 'It is not words that shakes me thus, (pish) Noses, Eares, and Lippes: is't possible. Confesse? Handkerchiefe? O divell.' Face to face with simple Othello, nothing is more dishonest than the pseudo-civilized honesty of honest Iago. But then perhaps nothing is more foolishly arrogant than Othello's falling in love in Venice—even falling in love *with* Venice—without once stopping and looking fully at Venetian Iago, who is his own dark shadow, the Master's Man.

—BARBARA EVERETT, "*Othello:* Mixing," *Young Hamlet: Essays on Shakespeare's Tragedies* (Oxford: Clarendon Press, 1989), pp. 46–47

KENNETH GROSS

Now even on a stylistic level, Iago's mobile, ironic, accommodative manner can seem disturbingly close to that of Montaigne (the Renaissance author most capable of saying something like "I am not what I am")—but it is Iago's overall "stance" in the play that is crucial here, insofar as it mirrors much of what compels us in Montaigne. Iago is, as William Empson notes, a deeply "honest" character, not just because he never tells obvious lies but because the word "honest" in the sixteenth century could also refer to manner that is bluff and forthright, healthily scornful of principle, high-mindedness, and romance, a way of being both frank about yourself and ready to deflate the pretensions of others, always ready to shift the ground of what is "important" on the basis of experience. Iago is also the play's subtlest scholar of jealousy, warning Othello against its self-destructive lures, its hunger, its reductive mania, urging him to bear its human burden, to be a "civil monster," to be at home in what is an inevitable betrayal. Of course, as we all know (but how well do we know it?) Iago's "honesty" is a subtle mask of hypocrisy; his appeal to others is coercive rather than sublimely solipsistic; his "critical good humor" passes over both into coarse cynicism and into a darker strain of puritanism, a prudish mockery of pleasure and a subtle, self-hating interest in his own and others' sins. And not only does he impose his cynicism on others, but even in reiterating the commonplace wisdom about the errors of jealousy he manages slyly to reinforce them. His skeptical solicitude becomes a theft, a suffocation, a provocation to madness rather than freedom. All of which suggests that Iago is at best a nightmare image of so vigilant and humanizing a pyrrhonism as Montaigne's. Still, the likeness cannot be rejected out of hand. As an imagination of skepticism, Iago is at least a dark, limiting case of the stance of self-less doubt that we find in the *Essais*, a figure who points to the ambivalent motivations—malice, duplicity, abjection, the smug, unparticular-ized slyness of what William Blake called the "idiot Questioner"—which may move or hide behind such a voice of doubt, even when it is doubting the hyperbolic doubt of jealousy or skepticism.

—KENNETH GROSS, "Slander and Skepticism in *Othello*," *ELH* 56, No. 4
(Winter 1989): 836

DAVID POLLARD

Charles Baudelaire felt certain that the world was destined to be swallowed up by the "delicate monster" boredom. Boredom ("ennui"), for the French poet, meant a complex state of soul: its victim is deprived of interest in life as he finds it and turning inward surveys a vast emptiness. This "encounter with nothingness" (Rein-hard Kuhn) is oppressive. Agitated and restless, the bored person recoils with horror from the blank and void and thereafter is fretted by the mental anguish which Baudelaire calls "spleen"—the peevish sense that he is "le roi d'un pays pluvieux . . . impuissant, jeune et pourtant très-vieux." Such a state can arise out of

little or no commensurate pressure from external forces, for it is essentially en-
dogenous. The splenetic person suddenly discovers in himself feelings of estrangement and world hatred. His response is one of lassitude or edgy hostility attended
by a conviction of metaphysical absurdity—in short, the helpless apprehension that
there may be final truth in such a statement as August von Platen's chillingly succinct
line: "Denn jeder sucht ein All zu sein, und jeder ist im Grunde nichts."

In *Les Fleurs du mal* many poems address the description of this spiritual
affliction; many more record strategies of aesthetic escape. Baudelaire fashions
flights to imaginary paradises ("Invitation au voyage"); he explores the delights of
voyeuristic sex ("Les Bijoux"); and in several impressive poems, he engages in
meditative people watching on the streets of Paris. One liberation from boredom,
however, takes a more disturbing turn. "L'Héautontimorouménos," as the title
reveals, derives its inspiration from a play by Terence, and treats of self-activation
by recourse to deliberate self-torment. Its subtext is that pain can supply meaning
when it is otherwise lacking. The poem's speaker feels that he must first abuse
someone else. Thus he threatens to thrash his lover and make her weep in order
that, like Moses striking the rock, he can turn his spiritual desert ("mon Sahara") into
an ocean on which he can set sail to new experiences. The woman's sobs promise
to be like a drum that will sound the speaker's rush into the excitement of battle.
Partly, the speaker wants to force the woman to recognize herself as tormentor by
beholding in him a reflection of her own identity ("Je suis le miroir / Où la mégère
se regarde!") More importantly, however, he longs to see himself in her agony as
a way of filling the inner blank with a self-image of some kind, albeit loathsome and
painful. The torture works. The speaker has his releasing epiphany:

Je suis la plaie et le couteau!
Je suis le soufflet et la joue!
Je suis les membres et la roue,
Et la victime et le bourreau!

Willfully accepting himself as source and most fitting recipient of clarifying hatred,
Baudelaire's speaker asserts with a sense of triumph his morally marginal status as
nature's pariah ("Un de ces grands abandonnés").

Leo Bersani has discussed "L'Héautontimorouménos" suggestively in terms of
Freud's ideas about sadomasochism. Baudelaire's poem, as Bersani insists, presents
one extended sadomasochistic moment during which the erotogenic process of
self-location through the abuse of another, self-declaiming theatricalization, and
preemptive self-punishment, is enacted. I would add that the poem's startling
mimesis connects thoughts that its author had mulled over darkly in his intimate
journal: "When I have inspired universal horror and disgust, I shall have conquered
solitude. . . . As for torture, it has been devised by the evil half of man's nature,
which is thirsty for voluptuous pleasures. Cruelty and sensual pleasure are identical
like extreme heat and extreme cold." "L'Héautontimorouménos," poised on these
values, riots in an exultant exhibitionism of determined moral ugliness.

Freud, rather more dispassionately, takes up sadomasochism as an anomalous challenge to the overriding supremacy of the "pleasure principle." Freud at first thought that sadism was a primary instinct; later he changed his mind and, in *Beyond the Pleasure Principle,* speculated that masochism was primary, deriving directly from the death instinct. In any case, the sadistic and masochistic impulses are convertible, and when the one is transformed into the other, the process is always accompanied by a sense of guilt. This leads Freud to conclude about masochism that it is in essence a "punishment for [a] forbidden genital relation" with the father and in fact its "pleasurable substitute." Instructively, Freud brackets sadomasochism with scoptophilia-exhibitionism as parallel examples of how instincts may revert into their opposites. In such a reversal, Freud claims, the "passive aim (to be tortured, or looked at) has been substituted for the active aim (to torture and to look at)." Masochism is, then, sadism, only "turned round upon the subject's own ego," fired by an attendant libidinal delight. On the reconvertibility of these instincts, Freud adds an intriguing observation: "Where once the suffering of pain has been experienced as a masochistic aim, it can be carried back into the sadistic situation and result in a sadistic aim of *inflicting pain,* which will then be masochistically enjoyed by the subject while inflicting pain upon others, through his identification of himself with the suffering object." This brilliant formulation, it seems to me, helps to assign the place in the sadomasochistic "loop" where the gargoyled psychodynamics of Baudelaire's poem are located.

Shakespeare's absorption in the psychology of self-torment is virtually coterminous with his art. From Richard III to Leontes, the Shakespearean *Gemäldegalerie* is filled with a variety of tormenting and tormented characters. Certainly, however, Hamlet and Iago stand as excelling hyperboles of the type—siblings, as it were— the former, the glamorous; the latter, the decidedly unglamorous, version. Shakespeare's *Othello,* like *Hamlet,* has yielded fruitful results from characterological considerations along psychoanalytic lines. And the figure of Iago, in particular, strikes me as an apt subject for analysis under the light of Baudelairean example and Freudian precept. Iago challenges us the way Baudelaire's "héautontimorouménos" does, in that he is a human gargoyle too, and with him also we are compelled to experience horrific designs from the emotional perspective of an excitingly intelligent and self-conscious deviance. This character, besides, provokes disturbing speculations with respect to the sexual component in the aesthetics of audience response.

At the outset of *Othello* Iago is indeed splenetic—disillusioned, restive, hostile, young, and yet very old—Baudelaire's *l'homme ennuyé.* Cassio and Desdemona, rivals for Othello's favor, have already received their promotions; she, in fact is the "general's general." Iago, on the other hand, has been consigned (symbolically) at the age of twenty-eight to the role of "ancient," and in this capacity we see him as squire to the ladies and as sage counselor. The practiced soldier has become in effect the real "moth of peace." As with Richard III, however, this deflection offers Iago an opportunity for deep, malevolent disguise.

At the beginning of the temptation scene, watching Cassio withdraw from Desdemona's presence, Iago reacts with concern:

IAGO: Hah? I like not that.
OTH.:   What dost thou say?
IAGO: Nothing, my lord; or if—I know not what.   (3.3.35–36)

The concern is of course staged for its auditor; nevertheless, the subtext makes this a critical exchange in the play. "Nothing" is precisely what Iago is looking at. On the other hand, "nothing"—inner emptiness, deprivation, absence, and denied access to a woman's genitals—is what drives Iago to invention. His compulsion becomes the desire to stuff the word "nothing" with materialist fact.

Considered as metaphysics, Iago's riddling announcement, "I am not what I am" (1.1.65), is a worrying of the old paradox of how to be present by means of duplicitous self-cancellation. In Iago's case, the moral program of disguising whatever is real entails the assumption that the "nothing" of others is actually only a competitive version of fraudulence that the discerning eye of imagination can penetrate with the help of projection. To put the matter slightly differently, for Iago, as for Baudelaire (not to mention Schopenhauer), human existence boils down to the view of the world as will and idea. As Iago explains to his dupe Roderigo: " 'Tis in ourselves that we are thus, or thus. Our bodies are our gardens, to the which our wills are gardeners" (1.3.319–21). A gardener can choose what will be present or absent—nettles or lettuce. Likewise, the will is free to guess or even influence the contents of other "gardens." Whatever—in the beginning, there is "nothing."

Iago's concept of the self-fashioning will is radically sexualized. His response to *le néant*, therefore, is to infuse it with libido. Thus, quite in the way of Freud's description, his behavior is sadomasochistic. This is apparent in his paralleled relationships with Cassio, Desdemona, and Othello. In each case, the tormented Iago—a "poisonous mineral" gnawing his innards—identifies with a victim and achieves pleasure from the recognizability of the pain he has caused. In each instance, he could conceivably gloat, "Work on, / My medicine, work!" (4.1.43–44), for the goal of such a self-reflexive and narcissistic identification is to attain that totality of being that von Platen claims is humanity's deep desire.

Iago's interaction with Cassio is paradigmatic of his method. Cassio is one of those "duteous and knee-crooking knaves" whom Iago despises, and yet he has succeeded in filling his space. While he vilifies his rival to Roderigo, inwardly Iago is forced to acknowledge an envious respect. Cassio is a "proper" man, sexually attractive, who "hath a daily beauty in his life" (admits Iago) "That makes me ugly" (5.1.19–20). The villain, therefore, proceeds to deface that beauty and put ugliness in its stead. On the parapet, alcohol is the "medicine" that makes Cassio cease to be himself.

Cassio sustains thereby the disfiguration he most dreads: in reputation he is hurt "past all surgery." Later this is extended to bodily wounding when Cassio is "maim'd for ever" (5.1.28). After his dismissal (act 2), in any event, Cassio has foisted on him a new identity as Desdemona's secret lover. This is entirely a projection of Iago, based on his own fantasies. Iago warms to the excitement of inventing Cassio's dream-life and thus creates a blind for an intense scoptophilic lechery:

> In sleep I heard him say, "Sweet Desdemona,
> Let us be wary, let us hide our loves";
> And then, sir, would he gripe and wring my hand;
> Cry, "O sweet creature!" then kiss me hard,
> As if he pluck'd up kisses by the roots
> That grew upon my lips; then laid his leg
> Over my thigh, and sigh'd, and kiss'd, and then
> Cried, "Cursed fate that gave thee to the Moor!"   (3.3.419–26)

In a curious mixture of projection and identification with Cassio together with a sadistic torment of Othello, Iago enjoys Desdemona while simultaneously managing the provocation which will bring about his delayed installation as lieutenant.

Like Cassio, Desdemona holds a place close to Othello that Iago experiences as personal displacement. Desdemona, however, represents a vastly more complex incitement to sadomasochistic emotions. For one thing, she possesses a reputation for "honesty"—with all of that word's ambiguity—which contends with Iago's own. The task becomes, therefore, for masculine "honesty" to find means to discredit its feminine counterpart. Desdemona's honesty is correlated with her whiteness. As Iago understands, whiteness is a kind of nothing which black Othello invests with moral signification: "that whiter skin of hers than snow" must point to Desdemona's chaste disposition. For this reason, in his jealousy, Othello becomes desperately perplexed: "Was this fair paper, this most goodly book, / Made to write 'whore' upon?" (4.2.71–72). It is Iago, of course, who has made the false inscription.

In a direct manner, as Terry Eagleton has suggested, the genitals of Othello's heroine stand for a kind of inscrutable "nothing" too. On the one hand, they confirm male power by their need to be filled ("She loved me for the dangers I had passed"). On the other, their vacancy may adumbrate a yawning gulf of appetite that can arouse fears of inner lack and threaten male adequacy. Playing on such fears, Iago torments Othello with his keenest sadism by sharing his imaginings of prodigious female erotomania. For Iago, women "rise to play, and go to bed to work" (2.1.115); Desdemona, therefore, both a "supersubtle Venetian" and "sport for Jove," must really be guided by a changeable appetite and a need to enjoy "stolen hours of lust." One such hour Iago recreated through the fiction of Cassio's dream. What is most interesting about the fiction is its demonstration of Iago's identification with Desdemona. After all, in the supposed encounter, Cassio had mistakenly confused Iago with Othello's wife. The sadomasochistic implications are clear. Thereafter, the inventor of a feminine criminal self who has enjoyed forbidden pleasures—a self with which he has identified—Iago proceeds to devise the appropriate punishment. Throughout the play, Iago has ached to enter Desdemona's bedroom. In the end he succeeds and there receives from Othello the phallic wound ("I bleed, sir, but not killed"), which completes the identification.

Iago's soliloquy of 2.1.286–312 ("That Cassio loves her, I do well believe't; /

That she loves him, 'tis apt and of great credit. . . . Now I do love her too . . . [and] I do suspect the lusty Moor / Hath leap'd into my seat . . ." puts forth a festival of private Baudelairean misery: envy, suspicion, self-justifying vindictiveness, and an oversexed paranoia. It is pivotally placed. The Othello of the first act is, I think, "valiant" Othello of heroic poise and dignified eloquence—the authentic man to whom Desdemona gave away her heart. What invades him gradually on the isle of Cyprus is a second self. This self is the projection of Iago. Here the transaction differs essentially from those involving Cassio and Desdemona, for their effects are extrinsic. As the vengeance oath dramatizes ("I am your own forever"), Iago and Othello achieve an *égoisme à deux;* this enables Iago's identification with his general and in turn opens the way for the absorption of an interfering self on the part of the latter.

Accurately Iago calls Othello's epileptic trance an "ecstasy" (4.1.79), for it signifies the departure of the original ego, leaving the victim "nothing of a man." By the beginning of the fourth act, consequently, Iago has reached the plateau of his success; his scheme—the establishment of fictive versions of Cassio and Desdemona and the hypnotic ingress into Othello's mind and language—all expressive of Iago's sadistic narcissism—is fully realized:

IAGO: Will you think so?
OTH.:   Think so, Iago?
IAGO: What,
To kiss in private?
OTH.:   An unauthoriz'd kiss?
IAGO: Or to be naked with her friend in bed
An hour, or more, not meaning any harm?
OTH.: Naked in bed, Iago, and not mean harm?   (4.1.1–5)

Again, Iago is occluding "nothing" with a monstrous something, only now Othello shares fully in the scoptophilic imaginings, as he does later in the eavesdropping scene (4.1.102–70).

As the play draws toward an end, Othello, still the embodiment of the Iago self, nevertheless recovers something of his first identity and we hear in the restoration of his authentic language (5.2.1–22) a melodramatic grandeur. This is too weak, however, and Othello becomes the instrument of violence for Iago that Roderigo had been. In the event Othello achieves some understanding of his divided self. When asked: "Where is this rash and most unfortunate man?" Othello responds: "That's he that was Othello; here I am" (5.2.283–84). Yet Desdemona is not altogether wrong in saying that "nobody" killed her (5.2.124). It is, after all, the essential act of the sadomasochistic personality to seek to destroy all that is without and within. Finally, then, Iago, like Baudelaire's speaker, is both the wound and the knife that inflicts it: and the sadomasochist who is attempting to escape "boredom" and vacuity will find (with Iago) that "Pleasure and action make the hours seem short" (2.3.379).

Plays too—the writing and the viewing of them—make the hours seem short.

One cannot evade, consequently, the reality that, as with "L'Héautontimo-rouménos," it is the artist who has slapped his heroine in *Othello* (4.1); Shakespeare's also are the unseen hands that strangle her throat. The dramatist is in fact the "nobody" that Desdemona's lie is ultimately meant to conceal. To his great credit, Baudelaire had the honesty to admit that the artist is always the primal self-tormentor who creates in his work a means of exhibitionist escape from isolation at the risk of raising a universal horror. A play like *Othello* shows Shakespeare in prophetic agreement with the French poet. It too is a flower of evil. We the audience, on the other hand, share in its exciting pathology. Our instincts healthily repressed or sublimated under compulsion from the reality principle, we do not shrink, like the self-tormented and emotionally violent Dr. Johnson, from the play's finale. Rather we release the libidinal energies of our own scoptophilia as we join vicariously Othello and Iago in Desdemona's bedroom. Thus do we indulge our own sadomasochistic fantasies in the aesthetically pleasing mayhem on the heroine's wedding sheets as it unfolds before our view. *Othello* thereby becomes the focusing instrument for complex and collusive "communal" aggression. The only possible justification for experiencing such a work is whatever clarifying catharsis it might momentarily effectuate. The likelihood is, however, that the clarification we attain will induce something like self-loathing—as with Baudelaire and (one fancies) Shakespeare himself.

—DAVID POLLARD, "Iago's Wound," Othello: *New Perspectives,*
ed. Virginia Mason Vaughan and Kent Cartwright (Rutherford, NJ:
Fairleigh Dickinson University Press, 1991), pp. 89–96

CRITICAL ESSAYS

A. C. Bradley

OTHELLO

I

Evil has nowhere else been portrayed with such mastery as in the character of Iago. Richard III., for example, beside being less subtly conceived, is a far greater figure and a less repellent. His physical deformity, separating him from other men, seems to offer some excuse for his egoism. In spite of his egoism, too, he appears to us more than a mere individual: he is the representative of his family, the Fury of the House of York. Nor is he so negative as Iago: he has strong passions, he has admirations, and his conscience disturbs him. There is the glory of power about him. Though an excellent actor, he prefers force to fraud, and in his world there is no general illusion as to his true nature. Again, to compare Iago with the Satan of *Paradise Lost* seems almost absurd, so immensely does Shakespeare's man exceed Milton's Fiend in evil. That mighty Spirit, whose

> form had yet not lost
All her original brightness, nor appeared
Less than archangel ruined and the excess
Of glory obscured;

who knew loyalty to comrades and pity for victims; who

> felt how awful goodness is, and saw
Virtue in her shape how lovely; saw, and pined
His loss;

who could still weep—how much further distant is he than Iago from spiritual death, even when, in procuring the fall of Man, he completes his own fall! It is only in Goethe's Mephistopheles that a fit companion for Iago can be found. Here there is something of the same deadly coldness, the same gaiety in destruction. But then

---

From *Shakespearean Tragedy* (London: Macmillan, 1904), pp. 207–37.

Mephistopheles, like so many scores of literary villains, has Iago for his father. And Mephistopheles, besides, is not, in the strict sense, a character. He is half person, half symbol. A metaphysical idea speaks through him. He is earthy, but could never live upon the earth.

Of Shakespeare's characters Falstaff, Hamlet, Iago, and Cleopatra (I name them in the order of their births) are probably the most wonderful. Of these, again, Hamlet and Iago, whose births come nearest together, are perhaps the most subtle. And if Iago had been a person as attractive as Hamlet, as many thousands of pages might have been written about him, containing as much criticism good and bad. As it is, the majority of interpretations of his character are inadequate not only to Shakespeare's conception, but, I believe, to the impressions of most readers of taste who are bewildered by analysis. These false interpretations, if we set aside the usual lunacies,[1] fall into two groups. The first contains views which reduce Shakespeare to common-place. In different ways and degrees they convert his Iago into an ordinary villain. Their Iago is simply a man who has been slighted and revenges himself; or a husband who believes he has been wronged, and will make his enemy suffer a jealousy worse than his own; or an ambitious man determined to ruin his successful rival—one of these, or a combination of these, endowed with unusual ability and cruelty. These are the more popular views. The second group of false interpretations is much smaller, but it contains much weightier matter than the first. Here Iago is a being who hates good simply because it is good, and loves evil purely for itself. His action is not prompted by any plain motive like revenge, jealousy or ambition. It springs from a 'motiveless malignity,' or a disinterested delight in the pain of others; and Othello, Cassio and Desdemona, are scarcely more than the material requisite for the full attainment of this delight. This second Iago, evidently, is no conventional villain, and he is much nearer to Shakespeare's Iago than the first. Only he is, if not a psychological impossibility, at any rate, not a *human* being. He might be in place, therefore, in a symbolical poem like *Faust*, but in a purely human drama like *Othello* he would be a ruinous blunder. Moreover, he is not in *Othello:* he is a product of imperfect observation and analysis.

Coleridge, the author of that misleading phrase 'motiveless malignity,' has some fine remarks on Iago; and the essence of the character has been described, first in some of the best lines Hazlitt ever wrote, and then rather more fully by Mr. Swinburne,—so admirably described that I am tempted merely to read and illustrate these two criticisms. This plan, however, would make it difficult to introduce all that I wish to say. I propose, therefore, to approach the subject directly, and, first, to consider how Iago appeared to those who knew him, and what inferences may be drawn from their illusions; and then to ask what, if we judge from the play, his character really was. And I will indicate the points where I am directly indebted to the criticisms just mentioned.

But two warnings are first required. One of these concerns Iago's nationality. It has been held that he is a study of that peculiarly Italian form of villainy which is considered both too clever and too diabolical for an Englishman. I doubt if there is much more to be said for this idea than for the notion that Othello is a study of

Moorish character. No doubt the belief in that Italian villainy was prevalent in Shakespeare's time, and it may perhaps have influenced him in some slight degree both here and in drawing the character of Iachimo in *Cymbeline*. But even this slight influence seems to me doubtful. If Don John in *Much Ado* had been an Englishman, critics would have admired Shakespeare's discernment in making his English villain sulky and stupid. If Edmund's father had been Duke of Ferrara instead of Earl of Gloster, they would have said that Edmund could have been nothing but an Italian. Change the name and country of Richard III., and he would be called a typical despot of the Italian Renaissance. Change those of Juliet, and we should find her wholesome English nature contrasted with the southern dreaminess of Romeo. But this way of interpreting Shakespeare is not Shakespearean. With him the differences of period, race, nationality, and locality have little bearing on the inward character, though they sometimes have a good deal on the total imaginative effect, of his figures. When he does lay stress on such differences his intention is at once obvious, as in characters like Fluellen or Sir Hugh Evans, or in the talk of the French princes before the battle of Agincourt. I may add that Iago certainly cannot be taken to exemplify the popular Elizabethan idea of a disciple of Macchiavelli. There is no sign that he is in theory an atheist or even an unbeliever in the received religion. On the contrary, he uses its language, and says nothing resembling the words of the prologue to the *Jew of Malta:*

I count religion but a childish toy,
And hold there is no sin but ignorance.

Aaron in *Titus Andronicus* might have said this (and is not more likely to be Shakespeare's creation on that account), but not Iago.

I come to a second warning. One must constantly remember not to believe a syllable that Iago utters on any subject, including himself, until one has tested his statement by comparing it with known facts and with other statements of his own or of other people, and by considering whether he had in the particular circumstances any reason for telling a lie or for telling the truth. The implicit confidence which his acquaintances placed in his integrity has descended to most of his critics; and this, reinforcing the comical habit of quoting as Shakespeare's own statement everything said by his characters, has been a fruitful source of misinterpretation. I will take as an instance the very first assertions made by Iago. In the opening scene he tells his dupe Roderigo that three great men of Venice went to Othello and begged him to make Iago his lieutenant; that Othello, out of pride and obstinacy, refused; that in refusing he talked a deal of military rigmarole, and ended by declaring (falsely, we are to understand) than he had already filled up the vacancy; that Cassio, whom he chose, had absolutely no practical knowledge of war, nothing but bookish theoric, mere prattle, arithmetic, whereas Iago himself had often fought by Othello's side, and by 'old gradation' too ought to have been preferred. Most or all of this is repeated by some critics as though it were information given by Shakespeare, and the conclusion is quite naturally drawn that Iago had some reason to feel aggrieved. But if we ask ourselves how much of all this is true we shall answer, I believe, as follows. It is absolutely certain that Othello appointed Cassio his lieutenant, and *nothing* else is absolutely certain. But there is no reason to doubt the statement that Iago had seen service with him, nor is there anything inherently improbable in the statement that he was solicited by three great personages on Iago's behalf. On the other hand, the suggestions that he refused out of pride and obstinacy, and that he lied in saying he had already chosen his officer, have no verisimilitude; and if there is any fact at all (as there probably is) behind Iago's account of the conversation, it doubtless is the fact that Iago himself was ignorant of military science, while Cassio was an expert, and that Othello explained this to the great personages. That Cassio, again, was an interloper and a mere closet-student without experience of war is incredible, considering first that Othello chose him for lieutenant, and secondly that the senate appointed him to succeed Othello in command at Cyprus; and we have direct evidence that part of Iago's statement is a lie, for Desdemona happens to mention that Cassio was a man who 'all his time' had founded his good fortunes on Othello's love and had 'shared dangers' with him (III. iv. 93). There remains only the implied assertion that, if promotion had gone by old gradation, Iago, as the senior, would have been preferred. It may be true: Othello was not the man to hesitate to promote a junior for good reasons. But it is just as likely to be a pure invention; and, though Cassio was young, there is nothing to show that he was younger, in years or in service, than Iago. Iago, for instance, never calls him 'young,' as he does Roderigo; and a mere youth would not have been made Governor of Cyprus. What is certain, finally, in the whole business is that Othello's mind was perfectly at ease about the appointment, and that he never dreamed of Iago's being discontented at it, not even when the intrigue was disclosed and he asked himself how he had offended Iago.

II

It is necessary to examine in this manner every statement made by Iago. But it is not necessary to do so in public, and I proceed to the question what impression he made on his friends and acquaintances. In the main there is here no room for doubt. Nothing could be less like Iago than the melodramatic villain so often substituted for him on the stage, a person whom everyone in the theatre knows for a scoundrel at the first glance. Iago, we gather, was a Venetian[2] soldier, eight-and-twenty years of age, who had seen a good deal of service and had a high reputation for courage. Of his origin we are ignorant, but, unless I am mistaken, he was not of gentle birth or breeding.[3] He does not strike one as a degraded man of culture: for all his great powers, he is vulgar, and his probable want of military science may well be significant. He was married to a wife who evidently lacked refinement, and who appears in the drama almost in the relation of a servant to Desdemona. His manner was that of a blunt, bluff soldier, who spoke his mind freely and plainly. He was often hearty, and could be thoroughly jovial; but he was not seldom rather rough and caustic of speech, and he was given to making remarks somewhat disparaging to human nature. He was aware of this trait in himself, and frankly admitted that he was nothing if not critical, and that it was his nature to spy into abuses. In these admissions he characteristically exaggerated his fault, as plain-dealers are apt to do; and he was liked none the less for it, seeing that his satire was humorous, that on serious matters he did not speak lightly (III. iii. 119), and that the one thing perfectly obvious about him was his honesty. 'Honest' is the word that springs to the lips of everyone who speaks of him. It is applied to him some fifteen times in the play, not to mention some half-dozen where he employs it, in derision, of himself. In fact he was one of those sterling men who, in disgust at gush, say cynical things which they do not believe, and then, the moment you are in trouble, put in practice the very sentiment they had laughed at. On such occasions he showed the kindliest sympathy and the most eager desire to help. When Cassio misbehaved so dreadfully and was found fighting with Montano, did not Othello see that 'honest Iago looked dead with grieving'? With what difficulty was he induced, nay, compelled, to speak the truth against the lieutenant! Another man might have felt a touch of satisfaction at the thought that the post he had coveted was now vacant; but Iago not only comforted Cassio, talking to him cynically about reputation, just to help him over his shame, but he set his wits to work and at once perceived that the right plan for Cassio to get his post again was to ask Desdemona to intercede. So troubled was he at his friend's disgrace that his own wife was sure 'it grieved her husband as if the case was his.' What wonder that anyone in sore trouble, like Desdemona, should send at once for Iago (IV. ii. 106)? If this rough diamond had any flaw, it was that Iago's warm loyal heart incited him to too impulsive action. If he merely heard a friend like Othello calumniated, his hand flew to his sword; and though he restrained himself he almost regretted his own virtue (I. ii. 1–10).

Such seemed Iago to the people about him, even to those who, like Othello, had known him for some time. And it is a fact too little noticed but most remarkable, that he presented an appearance not very different to his wife. There is no sign either that Emilia's marriage was downright unhappy, or that she suspected the true nature of her husband. No doubt she knew rather more of him than others. Thus we gather that he was given to chiding and sometimes spoke shortly and sharply to her (III. iii. 300f.); and it is quite likely that she gave him a good deal of her tongue in exchange (II. i. 101f.). He was also unreasonably jealous; for his own statement that he was jealous of Othello is confirmed by Emilia herself, and must therefore be believed (IV. ii. 145).[4] But it seems clear that these defects of his had not seriously impaired Emilia's confidence in her husband or her affection for him. She knew in addition that he was not quite so honest as he seemed, for he had often begged her to steal Desdemona's handkerchief. But Emilia's nature was not very delicate or scrupulous about trifles. She thought her husband odd and 'wayward,' and looked on his fancy for the handkerchief as an instance of this (III. iii. 292); but she never dreamed he was a villain, and there is no reason to doubt the sincerity of her belief that he was heartily sorry for Cassio's disgrace. Her failure, on seeing Othello's agitation about the handkerchief, to form any suspicion of an intrigue, shows how little she doubted her husband. Even when, later, the idea strikes her that some scoundrel has poisoned Othello's mind, the tone of all her speeches, and her mention of the rogue who (she believes) had stirred up Iago's jealousy of her, prove beyond doubt that the thought of Iago's being the scoundrel has not crossed her mind (IV. ii. 115–147). And if any hesitation on the subject could remain, surely it must be dispelled by the thrice-repeated cry of astonishment and horror, 'My husband!', which follows Othello's words, 'Thy husband knew it all'; and by the choking indignation and desperate hope which we hear in her appeal when Iago comes in:

> Disprove this villain, if thou be'st a man:
> He says thou told'st him that his wife was false:
> I know thou did'st not, thou'rt not such a villain:
> Speak, for my heart is full.

Even if Iago *had* betrayed much more of his true self to his wife than to others, it would make no difference to the contrast between his true self and the self he presented to the world in general. But he never did so. Only the feeble eyes of the poor gull Roderigo were allowed a glimpse into that pit.

The bearing of this contrast upon the apparently excessive credulity of Othello has been already pointed out. What further conclusions can be drawn from it? Obviously, to begin with, the inference, which is accompanied by a thrill of admiration, that Iago's powers of dissimulation and of self-control must have been prodigious: for he was not a youth, like Edmund, but had worn this mask for years, and he had apparently never enjoyed, like Richard, occasional explosions of the reality within him. In fact so prodigious does his self-control appear that a reader might be excused for feeling a doubt of its possibility. But there are certain observations and further inferences which, apart from confidence in Shakespeare, would remove this doubt. It is to be observed, first, that Iago was able to find a certain relief from the discomfort of hypocrisy in those caustic or cynical speeches which, being misinterpreted, only heightened confidence in his honesty. They acted as a safety-valve, very much as Hamlet's pretended insanity did. Next, I would infer from the entire success of his hypocrisy—what may also be inferred on other grounds, and is of great importance—that he was by no means a man of strong feelings and passions, like Richard, but decidedly cold by temperament. Even so, his self-control was wonderful, but there never was in him any violent storm to be controlled. Thirdly, I would suggest that Iago, though thoroughly selfish and unfeeling, was not by nature malignant, nor even morose, but that, on the contrary, he had a superficial good-nature, the kind of good-nature that wins popularity and is often taken as the sign, not of a good digestion, but of a good heart. And lastly, it may be inferred that, before the giant crime which we witness, Iago had never been detected in any serious offence and may even never have been guilty of one, but had pursued a selfish but outwardly decent life, enjoying the excitement of war and of casual pleasures, but never yet meeting with any sufficient temptation to risk his position and advancement by a dangerous crime. So that, in fact, the tragedy of *Othello* is in a sense his tragedy too. It shows us not a violent man, like Richard, who spends his life in murder, but a thoroughly bad, *cold* man, who is at last tempted to let loose the forces within him, and is at once destroyed.

III

In order to see how this tragedy arises let us now look more closely into Iago's inner man. We find here, in the first place, as has been implied in part, very remarkable powers both of intellect and of will. Iago's insight, within certain limits, into human nature; his ingenuity and address in working upon it; his quickness and versatility in dealing with sudden difficulties and unforeseen opportunities, have probably no parallel among dramatic characters. Equally remarkable is his strength of will. Not Socrates himself, not the ideal sage of the Stoics, was more lord of himself than Iago appears to be. It is not merely that he never betrays his true nature; he seems to be master of *all* the motions that might affect his will. In the most dangerous moments of his plot, when the least slip or accident would be fatal, he never shows a trace of nervousness. When Othello takes him by the throat he merely shifts his part with his usual instantaneous adroitness. When he is attacked and wounded at the end he is perfectly unmoved. As Mr. Swinburne says, you cannot believe for a moment that the pain of torture will ever open Iago's lips. He is equally unassailable by the temptations of indolence or of sensuality. It is difficult to imagine him inactive; and though he has an obscene mind, and doubtless took his pleasures when and how he chose, he certainly took them by choice and not from weakness, and if pleasure interfered with his purposes the holiest of ascetics would not put it more resolutely by. 'What should I do?' Roderigo whimpers to him; 'I confess it is my shame to be so fond; but it is not in my virtue to amend it.' He answers: 'Virtue! a fig! 'tis in ourselves that we are thus and thus.' It all depends on our will. Love is 'merely a lust of the blood and a permission of the will. Come, be a man. . . . Ere I would say I would drown myself for the love of a guinea-hen, I would change my humanity with a baboon.' Forget for a moment that love is for Iago the appetite of a baboon; forget that he is as little assailable by pity as by fear or pleasure; and you will acknowledge that this lordship of the will, which is his practice as well as his doctrine, is great, almost sublime. Indeed, in intellect (always within certain limits) and in will (considered as a mere power, and without regard to its objects) Iago *is* great.

To what end does he use these great powers? His creed—for he is no sceptic, he has a definite creed—is that absolute egoism is the only rational and proper attitude, and that conscience or honour or any kind of regard for others is an absurdity. He does not deny that this absurdity exists. He does not suppose that most people secretly share his creed, while pretending to hold up and practise another. On the contrary, he regards most people as honest fools. He declares that he has never yet met a man who knew how to love himself; and his one expression of admiration in the play is for servants

Who, trimmed in forms and visages of duty,
Keep yet their hearts attending on themselves.

'These fellows,' he says, 'have some soul.' He professes to stand, and he attempts to stand, wholly outside the world of morality.

The existence of Iago's creed and of his corresponding practice is evidently connected with a characteristic in which he surpasses nearly all the other inhabitants of Shakespeare's world. Whatever he may once have been, he appears, when we meet him, to be almost destitute of humanity, of sympathetic or social feeling. He shows no trace of affection, and in presence of the most terrible suffering he shows either pleasure or an indifference which, if not complete, is nearly so. Here, however, we must be careful. It is important to realise, and few readers are in danger of ignoring, this extraordinary deadness of feeling, but it is also important not to confuse it with a general positive ill-will. When Iago has no dislike or hostility to a person he does *not* show pleasure in the suffering of that person: he shows at most the absence of pain. There is, for instance, not the least sign of his enjoying the distress of Desdemona. But his sympathetic feelings are so abnormally feeble and cold that, when his dislike is roused, or when an indifferent person comes in the way of his purpose, there is scarcely anything within him to prevent his applying the torture.

What is it that provokes his dislike or hostility? Here again we must look closely. Iago has been represented as an incarnation of envy, as a man who, being determined to get on in the world, regards everyone else with enmity as his rival. But this idea, though containing truth, seems much exaggerated. Certainly he is devoted to himself; but if he were an eagerly ambitious man, surely we should see much more positive signs of this ambition; and surely too, with his great powers, he would already have risen high, instead of being a mere ensign, short of money, and playing Captain Rook to Roderigo's Mr. Pigeon. Taking all the facts, one must conclude that his desires were comparatively moderate and his ambition weak; that he probably enjoyed war keenly, but, if he had money enough, did not exert himself greatly to acquire reputation or position; and, therefore, that he was not habitually burning with envy and actively hostile to other men as possible competitors.

But what is clear is that Iago is keenly sensitive to anything that touches his pride or self-esteem. It would be most unjust to call him vain, but he has a high opinion of himself and a great contempt for others. He is quite aware of his superiority to them in certain respects; and he either disbelieves in or despises the qualities in which they are superior to him. Whatever disturbs or wounds his sense of superiority irritates him at once; and in *that* sense he is highly competitive. This is why the appointment of Cassio provokes him. This is why Cassio's scientific attainments provoke him. This is the reason of his jealousy of Emilia. He does not care for his wife; but the fear of another man's getting the better of him, and exposing him to pity or derision as an unfortunate husband, is wormwood to him; and as he is sure that no woman is virtuous at heart, this fear is ever with him. For much the same reason he has a spite against goodness in men (for it is characteristic that he is less blind to its existence in men, the stronger, than in women, the weaker). He has a spite against it, not from any love of evil for evil's sake, but partly because it annoys his intellect as a stupidity; partly (though he hardly knows this) because it weakens his satisfaction with himself, and disturbs his faith that egoism is the right and proper thing; partly because, the world being such a fool, goodness is popular and prospers. But he, a man ten times as able as Cassio or even Othello, does not greatly prosper. Somehow, for all the stupidity of these open and generous people, they get on better than the 'fellow of some soul.' And this, though he is not particularly eager to get on, wounds his pride. Goodness therefore annoys him. He is always ready to scoff at it, and would like to strike at it. In ordinary circumstances these feelings of irritation are not vivid in Iago—*no* feeling is so—but they are constantly present.

IV

Our task of analysis is not finished; but we are now in a position to consider the rise of Iago's tragedy. Why did he act as we see him acting in the play? What is the answer to that appeal of Othello's:

Will you, I pray, demand that demi-devil
Why he hath thus ensnared my soul and body?

This question Why? is *the* question about Iago, just as the question Why did Hamlet delay? is *the* question about Hamlet. Iago refused to answer it; but I will venture to say that he *could* not have answered it, any more than Hamlet could tell why he delayed. But Shakespeare knew the answer, and if these characters are great creations and not blunders we ought to be able to find it too.

Is it possible to elicit it from Iago himself against his will? He makes various statements to Roderigo, and he has several soliloquies. From these sources, and especially from the latter, we should learn something. For with Shakespeare soliloquy generally gives information regarding the secret springs as well as the outward course of the plot; and, moreover, it is a curious point of technique with him that the soliloquies of his villains sometimes read almost like explanations offered to the audience.[5] Now, Iago repeatedly offers explanations either to Roderigo or to himself. In the first place, he says more than once that he 'hates' Othello. He gives two reasons for his hatred. Othello has made Cassio lieutenant: and he suspects, and has heard it reported, that Othello has an intrigue with Emilia. Next there is Cassio. He never says he hates Cassio, but he finds in him three causes of offence: Cassio has been preferred to him; he suspects *him* too of an intrigue with Emilia; and, lastly, Cassio has a daily beauty in his life which makes Iago ugly. In addition to these annoyances he wants Cassio's place. As for Roderigo, he calls him a snipe, and who can hate a snipe? But Roderigo knows too much; and he is becoming a nuisance, getting angry, and asking for the gold and jewels he handed to Iago to give to Desdemona. So Iago kills Roderigo. Then for Desdemona: a fig's-end for her virtue! but he has no ill-will to her. In fact he 'loves' her, though he is good enough to explain, varying the word, that his 'lust' is mixed with a desire to pay Othello in his own coin. To be sure she must die, and so must Emilia, and so would Bianca if only the authorities saw things in their true light; but he did not set out with any hostile design against these persons.

Is the account which Iago gives of the causes of his action the true account? The answer of the most popular view will be, 'Yes. Iago was, as he says, chiefly incited by two things, the desire of advancement, and a hatred of Othello due principally to the affair of the lieutenancy. These are perfectly intelligible causes; we have only to add to them unusual ability and cruelty, and all is explained. Why should Coleridge and Hazlitt and Swinburne go further afield?' To which last question I will at once oppose these: If your view is correct, why should Iago be considered an extraordinary creation; and is it not odd that the people who reject it are the people who elsewhere show an exceptional understanding of Shakespeare?

The difficulty about this popular view is, in the first place, that it attributes to Iago what cannot be found in the Iago of the play. Its Iago is impelled by *passions*, a passion of ambition and a passion of hatred; for no ambition or hatred short of passion could drive a man who is evidently so clear-sighted, and who must hitherto have been so prudent, into a plot so extremely hazardous. Why, then, in the Iago of the play do we find no sign of these passions or of anything approaching to them? Why, if Shakespeare meant that Iago was impelled by them, does he suppress the signs of them? Surely not from want of ability to display them. The poet who painted Macbeth and Shylock understood his business. Who ever doubted Macbeth's ambition or Shylock's hate? And what resemblance is there between these passions and any feeling that we can trace in Iago? The resemblance between a volcano in eruption and a flameless fire of coke; the resemblance between a consuming desire to hack and hew your enemy's flesh, and the resentful wish, only too familiar in common life, to inflict pain in return for a slight. Passion, in Shakespeare's plays, is perfectly easy to recognize. What vestige of it, of passion unsatisfied or of passion gratified, is visible in Iago? None: that is the very horror of him. He has *less* passion than an ordinary man, and yet he does these frightful things. The only ground for attributing to him, I do not say a passionate hatred, but anything deserving the name of hatred at all, is his own statement, 'I hate Othello'; and we know what his statements are worth.

But the popular view, besides attributing to Iago what he does not show, ignores what he does show. It selects from his own account of his motives one or two, and drops the rest; and so it makes everything natural. But it fails to perceive how unnatural, how strange and suspicious, his own account is. Certainly he assigns motives enough; the difficulty is that he assigns so many. A man moved by simple passions due to simple causes does not stand fingering his feelings, industriously enumerating their sources, and groping about for new ones. But this is what Iago does. And this is not all. These motives appear and disappear in the most extraordinary manner. Resentment at Cassio's appointment is expressed in the first conversation with Roderigo, and from that moment is never once mentioned again in the whole play. Hatred of Othello is expressed in the First Act alone. Desire to get Cassio's place scarcely appears after the first soliloquy, and when it is gratified Iago does not refer to it by a single word. The suspicion of Cassio's intrigue with Emilia emerges suddenly, as an after-thought, not in the first soliloquy but the second, and then disappears for ever. Iago's 'love' of Desdemona is alluded to in the second soliloquy; there is not the faintest trace of it in word or deed either before or after. The mention of jealousy of Othello is followed by declarations that Othello is infatuated about Desdemona and is of a constant nature, and during Othello's sufferings Iago never shows a sign of the idea that he is now paying his rival in his own coin. In the second soliloquy he declares that he quite believes Cassio to be in love with Desdemona: it is obvious that he believes no such thing, for he never alludes to the idea again, and within a few hours describes Cassio in soliloquy as an honest fool. His final reason for ill-will to Cassio never appears till the Fifth Act.

What is the meaning of all this? Unless Shakespeare was out of his mind, it must have a meaning. And certainly this meaning is not contained in any of the popular accounts of Iago.

Is it contained then in Coleridge's word 'motive-hunting'? Yes, 'motive-hunting' exactly answers to the impression that Iago's soliloquies produce. He is pondering his design, and unconsciously trying to justify it to himself. He speaks of one or two real feelings, such as resentment against Othello, and he mentions one or two real causes of these feelings. But these are not enough for him. Along with them, or alone, there come into his head, only to leave it again, ideas and suspicions, the creations of his own baseness or uneasiness, some old, some new, caressed for a moment to feed his purpose and give it a reasonable look, but never really believed in, and never the main forces which are determining his action. In fact, I would venture to describe Iago in these soliloquies as a man setting out on a project which strongly attracts his desire, but at the same time conscious of a resistance to the desire, and unconsciously trying to argue the resistance away by assigning reasons for the project. He is the counterpart of Hamlet, who tries to find reasons for his delay in pursuing a design which excites his aversion. And most of Iago's reasons for action are no more the real ones than Hamlet's reasons for delay were the real ones. Each is moved by forces which he does not understand; and it is probably no accident that these two studies of states psychologically so similar were produced at about the same period.

What then were the real moving forces of Iago's action? Are we to fall back on the idea of a 'motiveless malignity;' that is to say, a disinterested love of evil, or a delight in the pain of others as simple and direct as the delight in one's own pleasure? Surely not. I will not insist that this thing or these things are inconceivable, mere phrases, not ideas; for, even so, it would remain possible that Shakespeare had tried to represent an inconceivability. But there is not the slightest reason to suppose that he did so. Iago's action is intelligible; and indeed the popular view contains enough truth to refute this desperate theory. It greatly exaggerates his desire for advancement, and the ill-will caused by his disappointment, and it ignores other forces more important than these; but it is right in insisting on the presence of this desire and this ill-will, and their presence is enough to destroy Iago's claims to be more than a demi-devil. For love of the evil that advances my interest and hurts a person I dislike, is a very different thing from love of evil simply as evil; and pleasure in the pain of a person disliked or regarded as a competitor is quite distinct from pleasure in the pain of others simply as others. The first is intelligible, and we find it in Iago. The second, even if it were intelligible, we do not find in Iago.

Still, desire of advancement and resentment about the lieutenancy, though factors and indispensable factors in the cause of Iago's action, are neither the principal nor the most characteristic factors. To find these, let us return to our half-completed analysis of the character. Let us remember especially the keen sense of superiority, the contempt of others, the sensitiveness to everything which wounds these feelings, the spite against goodness in men as a thing not only stupid but, both in its nature and by its success, contrary to Iago's nature and irritating to his pride. Let us remember in addition the annoyance of having always to play a part, the consciousness of exceptional but unused ingenuity and address, the enjoyment of action, and the absence of fear. And let us ask what would be the greatest pleasure of such a man, and what the situation which might tempt him to abandon his habitual prudence and pursue this pleasure. Hazlitt and Mr. Swinburne do not put this question, but the answer I proceed to give to it is in principle theirs.[6]

The most delightful thing to such a man would be something that gave an extreme satisfaction to his sense of power and superiority; and if it involved, secondly, the triumphant exertion of his abilities, and, thirdly, the excitement of danger, his delight would be consummated. And the moment most dangerous to such a man would be one when his sense of superiority had met with an affront, so that its habitual craving was reinforced by resentment, while at the same time he saw an opportunity of satisfying it by subjecting to his will the very persons who had affronted it. Now, this is the temptation that comes to Iago. Othello's eminence, Othello's goodness, and his own dependence on Othello, must have been a perpetual annoyance to him. At *any* time he would have enjoyed befooling and tormenting Othello. Under ordinary circumstances he was restrained, chiefly by self-interest, in some slight degree perhaps by the faint pulsations of conscience or humanity. But disappointment at the loss of the lieutenancy supplied the touch of lively resentment that was required to overcome these obstacles; and the prospect of satisfying the sense of power by mastering Othello through an intricate and hazardous intrigue now became irresistible. Iago did not clearly understand what was moving his desire; though he tried to give himself reasons for his action, even those that had some reality made but a small part of the motive force; one may almost say they were no more than the turning of the handle which admits the driving power into the machine. Only once does he appear to see something of the truth. It is when he uses the phrase 'to *plume up my will* in double knavery.'

To 'plume up the will,' to heighten the sense of power or superiority—this seems to be the unconscious motive of many acts of cruelty which evidently do not spring chiefly from ill-will, and which therefore puzzle and sometimes horrify us most. It is often this that makes a man bully the wife or children of whom he is fond. The boy who torments another boy, as we say, 'for no reason,' or who without any hatred for frogs tortures a frog, is pleased with his victim's pain, not from any disinterested love of evil or pleasure in pain, but mainly because this pain is the unmistakable proof of his own power over his victim. So it is with Iago. His thwarted sense of superiority wants satisfaction. What fuller satisfaction could it find than the consciousness that he is the master of the General who has undervalued him and of the rival who has been preferred to him; that these worthy people, who are so successful and popular and stupid, are mere puppets in his hands, but living puppets, who at the motion of his finger must contort themselves in agony, while all the time they believe that he is their one true friend and comforter? It must have been an ecstasy of bliss to him. And this, granted a most abnormal deadness of human feeling, is, however horrible, perfectly intelligible. There is no mystery in the psychology of Iago; the mystery lies in a further question, which the drama has not to answer, the question why such a being should exist.

Iago's longing to satisfy the sense of power is, I think, the strongest of the forces that drive him on. But there are two others to be noticed. One is the pleasure in an action very difficult and perilous and, therefore, intensely exciting. This action sets all his powers on the strain. He feels the delight of one who executes successfully a feat thoroughly congenial to his special aptitude, and only just within his compass; and, as he is fearless by nature, the fact that a single slip will cost him his life only increases his pleasure. His exhilaration breaks out in the ghastly words with which he greets the sunrise after the night of the drunken tumult which has led to Cassio's disgrace: 'By the mass, 'tis morning. Pleasure and action make the hours seem short.' Here, however, the joy in exciting action is quickened by other feelings. It appears more simply elsewhere in such a way as to suggest that nothing but such actions gave him happiness, and that his happiness was greater if the action was destructive as well as exciting. We find it, for instance, in his gleeful cry to Roderigo, who proposes to shout to Brabantio in order to wake him and tell him of his daughter's flight:

> Do, with like timorous[7] accent and dire yell
> As when, by night and negligence, the fire
> Is spied in populous cities.

All through that scene; again, in the scene where Cassio is attacked and Roderigo murdered; everywhere where Iago is in physical action, we catch this sound of almost feverish enjoyment. His blood, usually so cold and slow, is racing through his veins.

But Iago, finally, is not simply a man of action; he is an artist. His action is a plot, the intricate plot of a drama, and in the conception and execution of it he experiences the tension and the joy of artistic creation. 'He is,' says Hazlitt, 'an amateur of tragedy in real life; and, instead of employing his invention on imaginary characters or long-forgotten incidents, he takes the bolder and more dangerous course of getting up his plot at home, casts the principal parts among his nearest friends and connections, and rehearses it in downright earnest, with steady nerves and unabated resolution.' Mr. Swinburne lays even greater stress on this aspect of Iago's character, and even declares that 'the very subtlest and strongest component of his complex nature' is 'the instinct of what Mr. Carlyle would call an inarticulate poet.' And those to whom this idea is unfamiliar, and who may suspect it at first sight of being fanciful, will find, if they examine the play in the light of Mr. Swinburne's exposition, that it rests on a true and deep perception, will stand scrutiny, and might easily be illustrated. They may observe, to take only one point, the curious analogy between the early stages of dramatic composition and those soliloquies in which Iago broods over his plot, drawing at first only an outline, puzzled how to fix more than the main idea, and gradually seeing it develop and clarify as he works upon it or lets it work. Here at any rate Shakespeare put a good deal of himself into Iago. But the tragedian in real life was not the equal of the tragic poet. His psychology, as we shall see, was at fault at a critical point, as Shakespeare's never was. And so his catastrophe came out wrong, and his piece was ruined.

Such, then, seem to be the chief ingredients of the force which, liberated by his resentment at Cassio's promotion, drives Iago from inactivity into action, and sustains him through it. And, to pass to a new point, this force completely possesses him; it is his fate. It is like the passion with which a tragic hero wholly identifies himself, and which bears him on to his doom. It is true that, once embarked on this course, Iago *could* not turn back, even if this passion did abate; and it is also true that he is compelled, by his success in convincing Othello, to advance to conclusions of which at the outset he did not dream. He is thus caught in his own web, and could not liberate himself if he would. But, in fact, he never shows a trace of wishing to do so, not a trace of hesitation, of looking back, or of fear, any more than of remorse; there is no ebb in the tide. As the crisis approaches there passes through his mind a fleeting doubt whether the deaths of Cassio and Roderigo are indispensable; but that uncertainty, which does not concern the main issue, is dismissed, and he goes forward with undiminished zest. Not even in his sleep—as in Richard's before his final battle—does any rebellion of outraged conscience or pity, or any foreboding of despair, force itself into clear consciousness. His fate—which is himself—has completely mastered him: so that, in the later scenes, where the improbability of the entire success of a design built on so many different falsehoods forces itself on the reader, Iago appears for moments not as a consummate schemer, but as a man absolutely infatuated and delivered over to certain destruction.

V

Iago stands supreme among Shakespeare's evil characters because the greatest intensity and subtlety of imagination have gone to his making, and because he illustrates in the most perfect combination the two facts concerning evil which seem to have impressed Shakespeare most. The first of these is the fact that perfectly sane people exist in whom fellow-feeling of any kind is so weak that an almost absolute egoism becomes possible to them, and with it those hard vices—such as ingratitude and cruelty—which to Shakespeare were far the worst. The second is that such evil is compatible, and even appears to ally itself easily, with exceptional powers of will and intellect. In the latter respect Iago is nearly or quite the equal of Richard, in egoism he is the superior, and his inferiority in passion and massive force only makes him more repulsive. How is it then that we can bear to contemplate him; nay, that, if we really imagine him, we feel admiration and some kind of sympathy? Henry the Fifth tells us:

> There is some soul of goodness in things evil,
> Would men observingly distil it out;

but here, it may be said, we are shown a thing absolutely evil, and—what is more dreadful still—this absolute evil is united with supreme intellectual power. Why is the representation tolerable, and why do we not accuse its author either of untruth or of a desperate pessimism?

To these questions it might at once be replied: Iago does not stand alone; he is a factor in a whole; and we perceive him there and not in isolation, acted upon as well as acting, destroyed as well as destroying. But, although this is true and important, I pass it by and, continuing to regard him by himself, I would make three remarks in answer to the questions.

In the first place, Iago is not merely negative or evil—far from it. Those very forces that moved him and made his fate—sense of power, delight in performing a difficult and dangerous action, delight in the exercise of artistic skill—are not at all evil things. We sympathise with one or other of them almost every day of our lives. And, accordingly, though in Iago they are combined with something detestable and so contribute to evil, our perception of them is accompanied with sympathy. In the same way, Iago's insight, dexterity, quickness, address, and the like, are in themselves admirable things; the perfect man would possess them. And certainly he would possess also Iago's courage and self-control, and, like Iago, would stand above the impulses of mere feeling, lord of his inner world. All this goes to evil ends in Iago, but in itself it has a great worth; and, although in reading, of course, we do not sift it out and regard it separately, it inevitably affects us and mingles admiration with our hatred or horror.

All this, however, might apparently co-exist with absolute egoism and total want of humanity. But in the second place, it is not true that in Iago this egoism and this want are absolute, and that in this sense he is a thing of mere evil. They are frightful, but if they were absolute Iago would be a monster, not a man. The fact is, he *tries* to make them absolute and cannot succeed; and the traces of conscience, shame and humanity, though faint, are discernible. If his egoism were absolute he would be perfectly indifferent to the opinion of others; and he clearly is not so. His very irritation at goodness, again, is a sign that his faith in his creed is not entirely firm; and it is not entirely firm because he himself has a perception, however dim, of the goodness of goodness. What is the meaning of the last reason he gives himself for killing Cassio:

> He hath a daily beauty in his life
> That makes me ugly?

Does he mean that he is ugly to others? Then he is not an absolute egoist. Does he mean that he is ugly to himself? Then he makes an open confession of moral sense. And, once more, if he really possessed no moral sense, we should never have heard those soliloquies which so clearly betray his uneasiness and his unconscious desire to persuade himself that he has some excuse for the villainy he contemplates. These seem to be indubitable proofs that, against his will, Iago is a little better than his creed, and has failed to withdraw himself wholly from the human atmosphere about him. And to these proofs I would add, though with less confidence, two others. Iago's momentary doubt towards the end whether Roderigo and Cassio must be killed has always surprised me. As a mere matter of calculation it is perfectly obvious that they must; and I believe his hesitation is not merely intellectual, it is another symptom of the obscure working of conscience or humanity. Lastly, is it not significant that, when once his plot has begun to develop, Iago never seeks the presence of Desdemona; that he seems to leave her as quickly as he can (III. iv. 138); and that, when he is fetched by Emilia to see her in her distress (IV. ii. 110ff.), we fail to catch in his words any sign of the pleasure he shows in Othello's misery, and seem rather to perceive a certain discomfort, and, if one dare say it, a faint touch of shame or remorse? This interpretation of the passage, I admit, is not inevitable, but to my mind (quite apart from any theorising about Iago) it seems the natural one.[8] And if it is right, Iago's discomfort is easily understood; for Desdemona is the one person concerned against whom it is impossible for him even to imagine a ground of resentment, and so an excuse for cruelty.[9]

There remains, thirdly, the idea that Iago is a man of supreme intellect who is at the same time supremely wicked. That he is supremely wicked nobody will doubt; and I have claimed for him nothing that will interfere with his right to that title. But to say that his intellectual power is supreme is to make a great mistake. Within certain limits he has indeed extraordinary penetration, quickness, inventiveness, adaptiveness; but the limits are defined with the hardest of lines, and they are narrow limits. It would scarcely be unjust to call him simply astonishingly clever, or simply a consummate master of intrigue. But compare him with one who may perhaps be roughly called a bad man of supreme intellectual power, Napoleon, and you see how small and negative Iago's mind is, incapable of Napoleon's military achievements, and much more incapable of his political constructions. Or, to keep within the Shakespearean world, compare him with Hamlet, and you perceive how miserably close is his intellectual horizon; that such a thing as a thought beyond the reaches of his soul has never come near him; that he is prosaic through and through, deaf and blind to all but a tiny fragment of the meaning of things. Is it not quite absurd, then, to call him a man of supreme intellect?

And observe, lastly, that his failure in perception is closely connected with his badness. He was destroyed by the power that he attacked, the power of love; and he was destroyed by it because he could not understand it; and he could not understand it because it was not in him. Iago never meant his plot to be so dangerous to himself. He knew that jealousy is painful, but the jealousy of a love like Othello's he could not imagine, and he found himself involved in murders which were no part of his original design. That difficulty he surmounted, and his changed plot still seemed to prosper. Roderigo and Cassio and Desdemona once dead, all will be well. Nay, when he fails to kill Cassio, all may still be well. He will avow that he told Othello of the adultery, and persist that he told the truth, and Cassio will deny it in vain. And then, in a moment, his plot is shattered by a blow from a quarter where he never dreamt of danger. He knows his wife, he thinks. She is not over-scrupulous, she will do anything to please him, and she has learnt obedience. But one thing in her he does not know—that she *loves* her mistress and would face a hundred deaths sooner than see her fair fame darkened. There is genuine astonishment in his outburst 'What! Are you mad?' as it dawns upon him that she means to speak the truth about the handkerchief. But he might well have applied to himself the words she flings at Othello,

> O gull! O dolt!
As ignorant as dirt!

The foulness of his own soul made him so ignorant that he built into the marvellous structure of his plot a piece of crass stupidity.

To the thinking mind the divorce of unusual intellect from goodness is a thing to startle; and Shakespeare clearly felt it so. The combination of unusual intellect with extreme evil is more than startling, it is frightful. It is rare, but it exists; and Shakespeare represented it in Iago. But the alliance of evil like Iago's with *supreme* intellect is an impossible fiction; and Shakespeare's fictions were truth.

NOTES

[1] It has been held, for example, that Othello treated Iago abominably in preferring Cassio to him; that he *did* seduce Emilia; that he and Desdemona were too familiar before marriage; and that in any case his fate was a moral judgment on his sins, and Iago a righteous, if sharp, instrument of Providence.

[2] See III. iii. 201, V. i. 89f. The statements are his own, but he has no particular reason for lying. One reason of his disgust at Cassio's appointment was that Cassio was a Florentine (I. i. 20). When Cassio says (III. i. 42) 'I never knew a Florentine more kind and honest,' of course he means, not that Iago is a Florentine, but that he could not be kinder and honester if he were one.

[3] I am here merely recording a general impression. There is no specific evidence, unless we take Cassio's language in his drink (II. ii. 105f.) to imply that Iago was not a 'man of quality' like himself. I do not know if it has been observed that Iago uses more nautical phrases and metaphors than is at all usual with Shakespeare's characters. This might naturally be explained by his roving military life, but it is curious that almost all the examples occur in the earlier scenes (see e.g. I. i. 30, 153, 157; I. ii. 17, 50; I. iii. 343; II. iii. 65), so that the use of these phrases and metaphors may not be characteristic of Iago but symptomatic of a particular state of Shakespeare's mind.

[4] But it by no means follows that we are to believe his statement that there was a report abroad about an intrigue between his wife and Othello (I. iii. 393), or his statement which may be divined from IV. ii. 145) that someone had spoken to him on the subject.

[5] See, for instance, Aaron in *Titus Andronicus*, II. iii.; Richard in *3 Henry VI.*, III. ii. and V. vi., and in *Richard III.*, I. i. (twice), I. ii.; Edmund in *King Lear*, I. ii. (twice), III. iii. and v., V. i.

[6] Coleridge's view is not materially different, though less complete. When he speaks of 'the motive-hunting of a motiveless malignity,' he does not mean by the last two words that 'disinterested love of evil' or 'love of evil for evil's sake' of which I spoke just now, and which other critics attribute to Iago. He means really that Iago's malignity does not spring from the causes to which Iago himself refers it, nor from any 'motive' in the sense of an idea present to consciousness. But unfortunately his phrase suggests the theory which has been criticized above. On the question whether there is such a thing as this supposed pure malignity, the reader may refer to a discussion between Professor Bain and F. H. Bradley in *Mind*, vol. viii.

[7] I.e. terrifying.

[8] It was suggested to me by a Glasgow student.

[9] A curious proof of Iago's inability to hold by his creed that absolute egoism is the only proper attitude, and that loyalty and affection are mere stupidity or want of spirit, may be found in his one moment of real passion, where he rushes at Emilia with the cry, 'Villainous whore!' (V. ii. 229). There is more than fury in his cry, there is indignation. She has been false to him, she has betrayed him. Well, but why should she not, if his creed is true? And what a melancholy exhibition of human inconsistency is it that he should use as terms of reproach words which, according to him, should be quite neutral, if not complimentary!

Carroll Camden

IAGO ON WOMEN

When Desdemona agrees to while away the time until Othello arrives by having a contest of wit with Iago, we are introduced to a battle which lies in the main current of traditional anti-feminist literature and illustrates many common Elizabethan conceptions of women. Iago himself initiates the discussion, while Desdemona continues the contest by proposing the subject for Iago's poetical composition, and by inserting running comments which are intended to put Iago to difficulty. Iago, of course, is concerned only with the detraction of women, but Desdemona, with lively feminism, parries his cynical remarks and gets in some nice thrusts of her own. At the last she thinks to win by asking that Iago list the attributes of a perfect woman, since he has castigated the average woman as he finds her; but Desdemona loses, from Iago's point of view, when he insists that even a perfect example of womanhood is good enough only to perform the chief duties of her sex by rearing children and overseeing petty household affairs.

Iago's harangue is apparently divided into three sections.[1] He launches on his somewhat hackneyed diatribe with satirical remarks on wives in general, directed chiefly at Emilia. Next he follows with a verse composition upon a subject set by Desdemona, which is mainly a collection of witty paradoxes somewhat after the Euphuistic manner. He winds up by listing the qualities of a supposedly perfect woman, and in doing so he follows a large number of treatises which inform the cautious Benedick how to choose a good wife from a bad.

The satirical remarks just referred to have their origin in personal reasons, namely Iago's supposed jealousy of Emilia. He has seen Cassio kissing her, and says that if Emilia would give Cassio as much of her lips as she gives of her tongue to her husband, Cassio would certainly have enough. Desdemona defends Emilia by saying that at the moment, at any rate, she is properly silent in the presence of her husband, and chides him only in her thoughts. But Iago replies that Emilia talks to him constantly when he is trying to sleep. Iago is here merely giving voice to a concept frequently found in Elizabethan writers. Thomas Heywood, for example,

From *Journal of English and Germanic Philology* 48, No. 1 (January 1949): 57–71.

entitles one of his works, *A Curtaine Lecture* (i.e. a bed lecture), and relates that when the husbands "are willing to sleepe, [the wives] whisper many private lectures in their eares."[2] The nature of these lectures may be gathered from Joseph Swetnam, who says that

> Women are called night-Crowes, for that commonly in the night they will make request for such toyes as commeth in their heads in the day. Women know their time to worke their craft; for in the night they will worke a man like Waxe, and draw him like as Adamant doth Iron: and having once brought him to the bent of their Bow, then shee makes request for a Gowne of the new-fashion Stuffe, for a Petticote of the finest Stammell, or for a Hat of the newest fashion. Her husband being ouercome by her flattering speech, partly hee yeeldeth to her request, although it be a griefe to him, for that he can hardly spare it out of his stocke; yet for quietnesse sake, hee doth promise what shee demandeth, partly because he would sleepe quietly in his Bed....[3]

Because of insufficient evidence, I am unable to indicate the extent of this practice in these our pursy modern times; but well before Shakespeare similar ideas were current. The "proud wife" in her *Pater Noster* urges such action on the inexperienced newlywed,[4] and Wynkyn de Worde's printing of *The Fyftene Joyes of Maryage* offers such wifely action as one of the penalties of marriage:

> And lo maybe / his Wyfe an herte may haue
> Ryght good / desyrynge to be fresshe and gay
> For peraduenture / she this other day
> Was at a feest / where she dyde well aduyse
> Women of her degre / all other wyse
> Than she / appoynted / clothed / and arayde
> Within her mynde / than to her selfe she sayde
> That by her byrthe / she ought as well as they
> To be apparayled and in as good arey....
> But her entent to shewe / yet wyll she spare
> Tyll she with hym / at nyght be gone to bedde
> For there these Wyues trust well to be spedde
> Of suche petycyons / as they requyre.[5]

Apparently it is a custom observed by the best of wives, for interestingly enough, Desdemona herself later indicates that she indulges in it. When Cassio approaches her to request that she act as intermediary for him with Othello, Desdemona says she will assure him of his place, and continues

> If I do vow a friendship, I'll perform it
> To the last article: my lord shall never rest;
> I'll watch him tame and talk him out of patience;
> His bed shall seem a school, his board a shrift.[6]

Indeed, Thomas Nashe insists that it is the duty of good wives to discuss household affairs with their husbands when they get them in bed.[7]

After this preliminary skirmish on the age-old topic of woman's tongue, Iago, being now warmed to his subject, continues with a more complete and abusive harangue:

> Come on, Come on; you are pictures out of doors,
> Bells in your parlours, wild-cats in your kitchens,
> Saints in your injuries, devils being offended,
> Players in your housewifery, and housewives in your beds . . .
> Nay, it is true, or else I am a Turk:
> You rise to play and go to bed to work.[8]

Coleridge seems to consider Iago's remarks as thoroughly gratuitous, calling them "the sneers which a proud, bad intellect feels towards women," and going on to say that Shakespeare puts all sarcasms on women into the mouths of villains.[9] Nevertheless, these words of Iago, too, are in the long tradition of deprecations of women. Iago first calls women "pictures out of doors," referring to the somewhat inordinate figures which the Elizabethan ladies presented to the public, with particular reference to the use of cosmetics. Richard Brathwait explains what Iago has in mind:

> For what madnesse is it to change the forme of nature, and seeke beautie from a Picture? Which picture is vices posture, and the ages imposture. Neither do these affected trumperies, nor exquisite vanities become a Christian. For what is more vaine, than dying of the haire, painting of the face, laying out of breasts?[10]

Bishop Hall elaborates on the idea by suggesting that if one of an Elizabethan lady's ancestors should return, he would not recognize his offspring as a human being:

> Imagine [if] one of our fore-fathers . . . should see one of these his gay daughters walke in Cheape-side before him? What doe you thinke he would thinke it were? Here is nothing to be seene but a verdingale, a yellow ruffe, and a periwig, with perhaps some fethers waving in the top; . . . if then he should run before her, to see if by the fore-side he might ghesse what it were, when his eyes should meet with a poudred frizle, a painted hide shadowed with a fan not more painted, brests displayed, and a loose locke erring wantonly over her shoulders, betwixt a painted cloth and skinne; . . . Is this (thinks he) the flesh and blood? Is this the hayre? is this the shape of woman? or hath nature repented her work since my dayes, and begunne a new frame?[11]

Next, Iago calls the ladies "bells" when entertaining guests in the parlour. He may be contrasting their actions when displaying hospitality, with their usual behavior to the husband in the privacy of the home. Or it is possible that he is commenting on their social qualities, since "Hee that would haue fine ghests, let him haue a fine wife,"[12] and since a feminine virtue much admired is the ability to entertain by singing. "As for Musique," writes Anthony Gibson, "among women it is so familiare, as their very voyce is naturally a hermonie."[13]

When Iago accuses women of being wildcats in their kitchens, he is merely turning a virtue into a vice. After all, it is the duty of the wife to oversee the running of the household and to keep her maids busy in order to keep them out of trouble.[14] As Ludovicus Vives tells us, the kitchen is

> moore apte and conuenient for the woman than for the man, where that she in a maner doeth reygne all alone, but yet in such wise & maner, that she put to her hande to dresse her husbādes meate, and not to cōmaune it to be drest being absent.[15]

Perhaps what Iago has in mind is the use of abusive language to the kitchen maids, especially since he adds that wives become devils when they have received some real or fancied wrong. Here again, Iago is simply recording a view often expressed by anti-feminists. In an early disputation, one of William Bercher's characters argues:

> but for the women they have no spurrs that can make them go no bands that can hold them no bridle that can staye them no lawe that can subdue them no shame that can reteigne them. . . . Yf they be threpned they langwyshe. . . . And thear was never woman that cowlde pardon iniurye or acknowledge benefyte. . . . And yf any man will speake a gaynste them, they take hym for a mortall enemye.[16]

Joseph Swetnam remarks similarly,[17] and Edward Gosynhill puts the same idea into verse, as he describes women; they have

> Stomake stoute, with frowarde wyll
> And namely, when ye touche the sore
> With one bare worde, or lytle more
> They flusshe and flame, as hote as fyre
> And well as a Tode, for feruent yre.[18]

However illogical may be Iago's course of reasoning, by first accusing women of overdoing household work and in the next breath of skimping their duties, when he accuses wives of trifling in their household affairs and spending their waking hours in play, he is touching upon a serious matter. The very foundation of marriage is dependent upon a proper conception of the wifely duties, for "A woman cannot possible doe any thing that may make her Husband more in loue with her, then to play the good Huswife in her house."[19] Edmund Tilney writes that "The office of the husbande is to bring in necessaries, of the wife, to keepe them. The office of the husbande is, to go abroad in matter of profite, of the wife, to tarrye at home, and see all be well there."[20] Thus it is, as Robert Cleaver points out, that the woman of the house is called a house-wife, "not a street-wife, one that gaddeth vp and downe, like *Thamar:* nor a field wife, like *Dinah,* but a house-wife: to shew that a good wife keeps her house."[21] Besides pleasing the husband and entertaining his friends, the wife has many duties connected with the running of the household. She must not sit idle, but must make good use of her needle in mending old clothes and making new ones, and of her rock in tending to the linen.[22] Unless she is a lady, she must know well the art of cooking and be able to vary the diet according to the season: if she be a lady, she must still oversee the kitchen maids, and Ludovicus Vives insists that even the young lady of gentle birth must be trained in the preparation of food. She must be able to prescribe for her family and her servants when they are sick. And in general she must rule the household and the maids, though not the men-servants.[23] Obviously she will have little time for visiting or for outside amusements. She is to leave home so rarely that on these occasions it should seem to her than she is going on a pilgrimage.

Last of all Iago mentions the vice of eroticism as one belonging notably to women. He accuses them of being more given to sensuality than their husbands, calling them hussies in their beds, and alleging that they "'rise to play and go to bed to work." Such statements were common among those authors who wrote satirically against women. Tasso records that women are "insatiable, & vnsatisfied,"[24] and the author of *The Praise and Dispraise of Women* states:

> It seemeth that they are more borne and bredde vppon the earth, for to enterteine and nourish voluptuousnesse and Idlenesse, then for to bee trayned vp in matters of wayght and importance.[25]

Similarly, in one of John Taylor's dialogues between husband and wife, the wife contends that she never gets any rest, saying,

> I am forced as soone as I rise in the morning, to make a fire, sweepe the house, and get the childrens and your servants Breakfast; no sooner that done, and they out of the way, thinke upon Dinner; then no sooner dinner eaten, then I must make all the dishes cleane againe, and sweepe the House: Then because I would be a good Huswife, I sit me downe to spin, then thinke upon your Supper, and study what will please your dainty chops, and make it ready against you come home, when you are halfe fox't, then the children must be straight way thought upon, or else there's nothing but crying and brawling, which makes my braines ake agen. Then all being stisfied, put the children to sleepe, then to bed my selfe; and thus a womans worke is never done.

To which the husband replies,

> I doe verily thinke, when you are a bed, you doe wish that worke were never done.[26]

Puttenham sums up all of these qualities in an interesting passage:

> We limit the comely parts of a woman to consist in foure points, that is to be a shrewe in the kitchen, a saint in the Church, an Angell at the bourd, and an Ape in the bed.[27]

At this point in the discussion Desdemona asks Iago how he would praise her, but Iago rather responds with witty verses in the ornate, courtly style, in which he discusses various combinations of fair, dark and ugly, witty and foolish women.

If she be fair and wise, fairness and wit,
The one's for use, the other useth it. . . .
If she be black, and thereto have a wit,
She'll find a white that shall her blackness fit. . . .
She never yet was foolish that was fair;
For even her folly help'd her to an heir. . . .
There's none so foul and foolish thereunto
But does foul pranks which fair and wise ones do.[28]

Desdemona labels these "old fond paradoxes to make fools laugh i' the alehouse."
Rymer, in his *Short View of Tragedy*, apparently agrees with her, and berates
Shakespeare for a prostitution of his powers, and for a profanation of the tragic art.
Of this passage in *Othello*, Rymer says,

> But the ground of all this Bedlam-Buffoonery we saw in the case of the French
> Strollers, the company for acting *Christ's Passion*, or the *Old Testament*, were
> Carpenters, Cobblers, and illiterate fellows; who found that the Drolls, and
> Fooleries interlarded by them, brought in the rabble, and lengthened their
> time, so they got money by the bargain. Our Shakspeare, doubtless, was a
> great Master in his craft. These Carpenters and Cobblers were the guides he
> followed. And it is then no wonder that we find so much farce and Apocry-
> phal matter in his Tragedies. Thereby un-hallowing the Theater, profaning the
> name of Tragedy.[29]

The truth is, however, that Shakespeare was not at all following the improvised
witticisms of the mystery plays, but rather the sophisticated writings of anti-feminist
writers of various stamps. In other authors the paradoxes take various forms. In *A
Discourse of the Married and Single Life*, may be found the following paradoxes:

> If she be faire, shee wilbe proud; for pride accompanieth beauty, euen as the
> shadow doth the body. If she be foule, then will shee bee iealous: for if shee
> haue any wit, she may in her glasse espy her wāt of beauty, and knowing thee
> not to be blinde, she will soone imagine that thou seekest other company, and
> by this perswasion will perhaps procure some also for her selfe. . . . If thy wife
> which thou wilt take, be young, shee will alway be importunate for her better
> attyring. If old, her neuer-leauing to counsell thee, wilbe intolerable. . . . If shee
> be poore, then looke to haue with her vnhappinesse. If rich, then expect
> pride. . . . If thy wife be a widdow, shee will alwaies be either praising or
> praying for her first husband. If a maide, she is then vnacquainted with thy
> conditions, and vnexpert in wiues duty and businesse.[30]

Again, in *Epicoene* True-Wit warns his friend Morose of the dangers which devolve
on those who become engaged in matrimony, using language similar to that of Iago:

> If shee be faire, young, and vegetous, no sweet meats euer drew more flies;
> all the yellow doublets, and great roses i' the towne will bee there. If foule, and
> crooked shee'll bee with them, and buy those doublets, and roses, sir. If rich,

and that you marry her dowry, not her; she'll raigne in your house, as imperious as a widow. If noble, all her kindred will be your tyrannes....[31]

Likewise, Richard Brathwait delivers "A Ladies Love-Lecture," in which he says that
women "pervert the use of their five *Senses* by ingaging them to sensuall ends." He
continues:

If *old*, their rivell'd furrowes make them sullen; If *young*, their taking beauties
make them wanton. If *rich*, they are haughty; If *poore*, they turne *naughty*.[32]

Finally Desdemona, feeling rather desperate by this time, implies that there
must be some woman who would make a good wife, some "deserving woman,"
and asks Iago what sort of attributes such one would have and to list her perfec-
tions. Iago replies with the following lines:

She that was ever fair and never proud,
Had tongue at will and yet was never loud,
Never lack'd gold and yet went never gay,
Fled from her wish and yet said 'Now I may,'
She that being anger'd, her revenge being nigh
Bade her wrong stay and her displeasure fly,
She that in wisdom never was so frail
To change the cod's head for the salmon's tail,
She that could think and ne'er disclose her mind,
See suitors following and not look behind,
She was a wight, if ever such wight were,...
To suckle fools and chronicle small beer.[33]

In this passage Iago sets forth his version of what was perhaps taken seriously by
some men in search of wives. Of course Iago has not at all exhausted the list of
virtues thought necessary by such men as Swetnam, for example, who tells the
young man that before putting his foot out of doors he should inquire diligently
what the girl's reputation is, to discover if she be wise, kind, virtuous, house-wifely,
saving, contented in disposition, and disposed to wear her own hair.[34] Brathwait
recommends that the choice should include consideration of the young lady's
education, to be sure that she is qualified better in her intelligence than in her body,
and insists that the parents, too, must be scrutinized to see if they are able to give
the girl good advice.[35] In speaking generally, he says,

Chuse thou thy wife (*my Sonne*) nor *faire* nor *foule*,
Nor gay nor sluttish; silent, yet knowes when
And where it's fit to speak, one whose chaste soule
Shews modestie in blushes, and will len
No eare of desire (for such desires may bee
In purest love) by her enioying thee
                            ...let her cheeke
Be without art: *Chuse* me a bashfull *nay*
Before a quick assent....[36]

As Iago states, the lady of your choice should be fair, that is, should be of blonde complexion, even if the hair is not naturally honey-colored; beauty thus adorned will tend to induce the husband to seek his pleasures at home instead of in other places.[37] In Lyly's *Campaspe*, Appeles remarks to Alexander that the hair must have a blonde color, even if the eyebrows are black: "For now, if the haire of her eie browes be black, yet must the haire of her head be yellowe."[38] And there were many recipes for producing this required hue of the hair:

> To make haire as yellowe as gold. Take the rine or scrapings of Rubarbe, and stiepe it in white wine, or in cleere lie: and after you have washed your head with it, you shall weatte your haires with a Spoonge or some other cloth, and let them drie by the fire, or in the sunne: After this weatte them and drie them againe.[39]

The word *fair*, however, refers not only to the hair but to the whole complexion. Blondeness was seemingly preferred because it was a distinguishing feature of the idle court lady; it was the maids who were nut-brown. Of course the fact that Queen Elizabeth was a type of the blonde gave further impetus to the vogue, as did the picture of the Elizabethan beauty as portrayed in the sonnets. Anthony Gibson further attests this ideal requirement, at the same time urging that the young man's choice should not be focused upon outward beauty. He suggests that the woman who writes to her lover as follows should be considered the fairest of all:

> My Loue, I am a little blacke,
> But say that I were much more black.
> Mine eyes browne, my face like browne,
> Admit my necke and brests more browne.
> My hair and skin all black to be,
> Sauing my teeth of Iuory:....
> Must I for this my louely browne,
> Haue my Loue on me to frowne?
> Are not my eyes as piercing still,
> And able Marble hearts to kill?
> Or can my Loue be ere the lesse,
> My minde being made of gentlenesse.[40]

That the woman chosen to be a wife should avoid any tendency toward the sin of pride, is borne out by numerous writers. "A proud Woman could not loue effectually, because suspition continually attendeth her," believes the Florentine Leon Alberto.[41] Pride is a vice which has many manifestations. A prideful woman will have her breakfast in bed and spend the morning dressing her hair.[42] She will bestow too much time painting her face and using other cosmetic aids. She will give too much time to her clothes, and is very likely to beggar her husband by such unbridled vanity.[43] Even if she is wealthy (and the prospective bride should never lack gold, because the husband must have the wherewithal to live in style),[44] and need not bankrupt her husband to put finery on her back, nevertheless she should attire herself "with more *care* than *cost*."[45] Pride will lead a woman to

> haue the chamber fill'd with a succession of groomes, footmen, vshers, and other messengers; besides embroyderers, iewellers, tyre-women, sempsters, fether-men, perfumers; while shee feeles not how the land drops away; nor the acres melt; nor forsees the change, when the mercer has your woods for her veluets; neuer weighes what her pride costs.[46]

Arthur Dent sums up the qualities of a proud woman thus:

> Yet we see how proud many, especially women, be of such bables: for when they haue spent a good part of the day in tricking and trimming, pricking and pinning, pranking and pouncing, girding and lacing, and brauing vp themselues in most exquisite manner, then out they come into the streetes, with their Pedlers shop about their backe, and carie their crests very high, taking them selues to bee little Angels: or at least, somewhat more than other women; whereupon they do so exceedingly swell with pride, that it is to be feared, they will burst with it as they walke in the streetes. And truly wee may thinke the very stones in the streete, and the beames in the houses do quake, & wonder at their monstrous, intolerable, and excessiue pride: for it seemeth that they are altogether a lumpe of pride, masse of pride, euen altogether made of pride, and nothing else but pride, pride.[47]

It is no wonder, then, that he who is seeking a future wife should especially beware of a proud woman.

A woman, furthermore, as Iago insists, should be able to think without speaking, and when she does speak, it should be in a soft voice. A good wife, writes Sir Thomas Overbury, "leaves tattling to the Gossips of the Towne, and is more seene then heard."[48] She should generally be silent, "for silence and patience are the two indissoluble ties of conjugall love and piety."[49] It is only the uncontrolled woman, argues George Whetstone, who "desireth without checke to pratle, and without discretion to gouerne."[50] If a wife would only keep quiet when her husband is in a choleric and hasty mood and chides her, the meals would be much more peaceful and pleasant.[51] A man does not want a wife whose tongue sounds in his ears "like the clapper of a great bell" and whose talk is a continual torment to the whole neighborhood.[52] It is interesting to note that when Cordelia dies, the one of her virtues which Lear singles out to comment on is that "her voice was ever soft, gentle, and low, an excellent thing in woman."[53] Yet the wife should not always be silent, but should know when is the proper time to keep silence and when is the proper time to speak,[54] as Emilia does when Iago orders her to charm her tongue and she says, "I will not charm my tongue; I am bound to speak,"[55] Ludovicus Vives recommends that when a woman does speak, "let her cōmunicatiō be simple, not affectate nor ornate, for y^t declareth the vanitie of ye mind."[56]

Perhaps the virtue most difficult of achievement, which Iago includes in his list, is that of not being revengeful, even when offended and when revenge for the offence lies ready at hand. The ideal wife should be like the Patient Griselda, "patient to suffer,"[57] but few women have the ability so to conduct themselves under duress. In *The Unfortunate Traveller*, Nashe says of Diamante,

> Hir husband had abused her, and it was verie necessarie she should be reuenged. Seldome doe they prooue patient martyrs who are punisht vniustly: one waie or other they will crie quittance whatsoeuer it cost them.[58]

Edward Gosynhill expresses the idea more forcefully in verse:

> Eche other man in generall
> And namely those, that maryed be
> Gyue euydent, testimonyall
> Aferrmynge the same, yf I wolde lye
> And thus reporte, that femynye
> Ben euyll to please, and worse to truste
> Crabbed and comberous, whē them selfe luste.
> Haue tongue at large, voyce loude & shryl
> Of wordes wonderous, passynge store
> Stomake stoute, with frowarde wyll.[59]

A wife, says Iago, should be wise, especially in practical wisdom. As Barnabe Riche puts it:

> A good woman is laborious, like the marchantes ship that seeks to bring in, shee bringeth in by her good foresight, by her care, by her diligence, and by the wisdome of her gouernement.[60]

This wisdom, however, should be inherent in her, and not got by study.

> Give me next *Good*, an *understanding Wife*
> By Nature *wise*, not Learned by much Art,
> Some *Knowledge* on her side, will all my life
> More scope of conversation impart:
>   Besides her inborne vertue fortifie.
>   They are most firmly good, that best know why.[61]

Vives believes that

> Womans thought is swyfte / and for ye most parte vnstable / walkyng and wandring out from home / and sone wyl slyde / by the reason of it owne slypernes. Therfore redying were the best.[62]

A woman should be particularly careful of her demeanor in public. Iago praises that woman who can feel that suitors have their eyes on her and yet not constantly look behind to see if they are following:

Vppon no occasion [women] will crosse the streete, to haue a glaunce of some Gallant, deeming that men by one looke of them, shoulde be in loue with them.[63]

If at home the men are sitting apart from the ladies, a proper wife will not think that they are talking of her or looking at her.[64] Indeed, women should be very chary of their conduct in general: they must be careful of their speech and of their writing; they must be sure that their eyes and the expressions of their faces indicate no looseness of character; their gestures must not be gross; their language should be fashionable, but not frivolous.[65]

Iago evidently wishes to make it plain that no such paragon as he has just described exists. Here he has the company of Tasso, who writes, "It is impossible to find a shee, that hath all these good properties in her,"[66] and concludes by saying that it is therefore obvious that marriage should be entirely eschewed.

We see, moreover, that Shakespeare has been at some pains to set forth Desdemona as an example of the ideal wife; hence her conversation with her betrayer, on the subject of good women, has ironical force. Iago seems to have recognized the true quality of her whom he is to destroy, when he says of her, "And many worthy and chaste dames even thus, all guiltless, meet reproach";[67] and yet he did not hesitate. Perhaps, then, there is a slight discrepancy here in putting such conventional phrases into Iago's mouth. Cassio had previously praised Desdemona for being "a most exquisite lady," "fresh and delicate," with "an inviting eye" though "right modest," concluding that "'she is indeed perfection.'"[68] But it is Othello who gives the most complete and illustrative testament of Desdemona's praiseworthy qualities. When first tempted to jealousy by Iago, Othello calmly replies,

> 'Tis not to make me jealous
> To say my wife is fair, feeds well, loves company,
> Is free of speech, sings, plays and dances well;
> Where virtue is, these are more virtuous.[69]

And later, when Iago's insidious words have begun to work their way into Othello's gentlemanly and unsuspecting heart, the tortured husband cries out in his attempt to weigh her virtues with what he has learned:

> Hang her! I do but say what she is: so delicate with her needle: an admirable musician: O! she will sing the savageness out of a bear: of so high and plenteous wit and invention.

But Iago is afraid Othello will convince himself that Desdemona could not be lacking in chastity when she has these other requisite qualities, and inserts, the comment "She's the worse for all this." To which Othello agrees, but adds, "and then, of so gentle a condition."[70] Notice that Othello speaks particularly of her beauty, her competence as a dancer, her skill with the needle, her ability as a musician, her wisdom, her originality, and her disposition. Further, Desdemona shows by her very actions that she is an example of the perfect wife, as when she prepares for her death bed, saying, "We must not now displease him ... my love doth so approve him, that even his stubbornness, his checks, his frowns, ... have grace and favour in them";[71] or when with her dying breath she says to Emilia, "Commend me to my kind lord."[72]

NOTES

[1] II, i, 101–161.

[2] Thomas Heywood, *A Curtaine Lecture*, London, 1637, p. 145. Richard Brathwait calls one of his books *Ar't Asleepe Husband? A Boulster Lecture*, London, 1640; the engraving opposite the title page shows a wife lecturing her husband in bed.

[3] Joseph Swetnam, *The Arraignment of Lewd, Idle, Froward, and Vnconstant Women*, London, 1622, pp. 11–12. This work was very popular, ten editions of it appearing between 1615 and 1637.

[4] *The Proude Wyues Pater Noster*, London, 1560, sigs. B1–B1ᵛ.

[5] Antoine de La Sale, *The Fyftene Joyes of Maryage*, London, 1509, sig. A8ᵛ; see Thomas Dekker, *The Batchelars Banquet*, London, 1603, sigs. A3–A3ᵛ.

[6] III, iii, 21–24.

[7] "Christ's Tears over Ierusalem," *Works*, ed. McKerrow, London, 1910, vol. II, p. 144. See Lyly, "Later Love-Poems," *Works*, ed. Bond, Oxford, 1902, vol. III, p. 487; and Edmund Tilney, *A Brief and Pleasant Discourse of Duties in Mariage, Called the Flower of Friendshippe*, London, 1568, sig. E6ᵛ.

[8] II, i, 110–116.

[9] Note to line 118, Furness, Variorum edition of *Othello*.

[10] Richard Brathwait, *The English Gentleman*, London, 1630, p. 259. See Hamlet's "I have heard of your paintings too, well enough; God has given you one face, and you make yourselves another." (III, i, 148–150.)

[11] Joseph Hall, "The Righteous Mammon," (preached in 1618), *Works*, London, 1634, p. 670.

[12] Jonson, *Poetaster*, II, ii, 211–212; see Robert Snawsel, *A Looking Glasse for Maried Folkes*, London, 1610, sigs. E5–E5ᵛ.

[13] Anthony Gibson, *A Womans Woorth*, London, 1599, fol. 24. See Giovanni Michele Bruto, *The Necessaire, Fit, and Convenient Education of a Yong Gentlewoman*, London, 1598, sig. H4ᵛ; Nicholas Breton, *Pasquils Mistresse*, London, 1600, sig. C3ᵛ; Nashe, "Christ's Teares," op. cit., p. 135; Hoby's translation of *The Courtier*, ed. Lamson and Smith, *The Golden Hind*, N.Y., 1942, p. 448.

[14] Thomas Becon, *The Booke of Matrimony*, London, 1564, sig. CCC3ᵛ.

[15] Ludovicus Vives, *The Office and Dutie of an Husband*, London, 1553? sigs. U3–U3ᵛ.

[16] William Bercher, *The Nobility of Woman*, London, 1559, ed. Bond, London, 1904, pp. 128–129. See Lyly, *Sapho and Phao*, IV, iv, 21–31.

[17] Swetnam, op cit., p. 2.

[18] Edward Gosynhill, *Schole House of Women*, London, 1561, sig A1ᵛ. See Becon, op. cit., sig. BBB6ᵛ; *Everie Woman in Her Humor*, London, 1609, sig. A4.

[19] *The Court of Good Counsell*, London, 1607, sig. E2; see sig. D4. Professor John Lievsay informs me that this work is an Anglicized version of part of Guazzo's *Civil Conversations*.

[20] Tilney, op. cit., sig. C5ᵛ.

[21] Robert Cleaver, *A Godlie Forme of Householde Government*, London, 1600, p. 223. The same idea appears in Matthew Griffith, *Bethel: or A Forme for Families*, London, 1633, p. 25. See Lyly, *Euphues and His England*, Oxford, 1902, vol. II, p. 226.

[22] "A sleeke-stone to smooth hir linnen" (Lyly, *Euphues and His England*, op. cit., p. 9.)

[23] Richard Mulcaster, *Positions*, London, 1581, p. 178. See Vives, *Instructiō of a Christen womā*, London, 1529?, sig. D1ᵛ; Tilney, op. cit., sigs. E3ᵛ–E5. For the persistence of the tradition of the duties of a lady in the careful consideration of her education, see Mrs. Isabella Beeton, *the Book of Household Management*, London, n.d. (about the middle of the nineteenth century).

[24] Ercole Tasso, *Of Mariage and Wiuing*, London, 1599, sig. C4. See *The Courtier*, op. cit., p. 455.

[25] *The Praise and Dispraise of Women*, London, 1579, fol. 69.

[26] John Taylor, *A Iuniper Lecture*, London, 1639, pp. 12–14. See *Everie Woman in Her Humor, op. cit.*, sig. A4; Brathwait, *English Gentleman*, op. cit., p. 256 and Alexander Niccholes, *Of Marriage and Wiving*, London, 1615, p. 13, both of whom quote from Bacon, though not mentioning his name, that "Wiues are yong mens Mistresses," etc.

[27] *Arte of Poesie*, ed. Arber, p. 299; first noted by Steevens in his commentary on this passage, and

recorded in the Furness *Variorum*. See Samuel Rowlands, *Look to It: For, Ile Stabbe Ye*, London, 1640, sig. E1ᵛ.

[28] II, i, 130–143.

[29] Edition of 1693, p. 110; quoted in Furness *Variorum*.

[30] *A Discourse of the Married and Single Life*, London, 1621, pp. 13–14, 18, 19, 24.

[31] II, ii, 66–73.

[32] Richard Brathwait, "A Ladies Love-Lecture," *The English Gentleman*, third edition, London, 1641, p. 450.

[33] II, i, 149–161; Desdemona's words omitted at line 160.

[34] Swetnam, op. cit., pp. 46–47. Professor D. T. Starnes has called my attention to Sir Walter Raleigh's *Instructions to His Sonne* (London, 1632), chapter two of which contains careful advice on how the choice of a wife should be made.

[35] Richard Brathwait, *The Good Wife*, London, 1618, sig. B4. See Brathwait, *The English Gentlewoman*, London, 1631, sig. ¶3–¶4.

[36] Brathwait, *The Good Wife*, sig. B2ᵛ.

[37] Tasso, op. cit., sig. B2ᵛ.

[38] III, iv, 89–90.

[39] Girolamo Ruscelli (Alessio), *The Secretes of Reuerende Maister Alexis of Piemount*, London, 1568, fol. 72ᵛ.

[40] Gibson, op. cit., fols. 56ᵛ–57ᵛ.

[41] Leon Baptista Alberti, *The Arte of Loue*, London, 1598, fol. 23ᵛ.

[42] Breton, op. cit., sig. D3ᵛ.

[43] Vives, *The Office and Dutie of an Husband*, op. cit., sig. X6ᵛ. See Elizabeth Grymeston, *Miscellanea*, London, 1606?, sig. H8ᵛ; *Swetnam, the Woman-Hater . . . A New Comedie*, London, 1620, sig. F1ᵛ (Act III, Scene i); *Everie Woman*, op. cit., sig. A3ᵛ; Swetnam, op. cit., p. 7; Thomas Nashe, *Pierce Penilesse, Works*, ed. Grosart, 1883–1884, Vol. II, p. 43.

[44] Tasso, op. cit., sig. B2ᵛ.

[45] Brathwait, *Gentlewoman*, op. cit., sig. ¶4, Epistle Dedicatory.

[46] *Epicoene*, II, ii, 136–143.

[47] Arthur Dent, *The Plaine Mans Path-way to Heauen*, London, 1601, p. 43. See Thomas Carter, *Carters Christian Common V Vealth*, London, 1627, p. 81.

[48] Sir Thomas Overbury, *His Wife*, London, 1632 (6th ed.), sig. G5ᵛ.

[49] Heywood, op. cit., p. 143. See Cleaver, op. cit., p. 230; V. Herman (von Wild), *Dewty of Maried Folkes*, London, 1553?, sig. A5; Jacques Du Bosc, *The Compleat Woman*, London, 1639, p. 18; Leonard Wright, *A Display of Duty*, London, 1616, fol. 11ᵛ.

[50] George Whetstone, *An Heptameron of Ciuill Discourses*, London, 1582, sig. Q3.

[51] Robert Cleaver, *A Godlie Forme of Household Government*, London, 1598, p. 230. See Swetnam, op. cit., p. 55.

[52] Peele, *The Old Wive's Tale*, ll. 223–228.

[53] V, iii, 272–273.

[54] Sir Thomas Elyot, *The Defence of Good Women*, London, 1545, sig. D3; see Brathwait, *Good Wife*, sig. B2ᵛ.

[55] V, ii, 184.

[56] Vives, *Offices of Husband*, op. cit., sig. Q3ᵛ.

[57] Heywood, op. cit., p. 143.

[58] Thomas Nashe, *Works*, ed. McKerrow, London, 1910, vol. II, p. 263.

[59] Gosynhill, op. cit., sig. A1ᵛ.

[60] Barnabe Riche, *The Excellency of Good Women*, London, 1613, p. 11. See Alberti, op. cit., fol. 13ᵛ.

[61] Overbury, op. cit., sig. D5.

[62] Vives, *Instructiō*, op. cit., sigs. C3ᵛ–C4.

[63] Thomas Nashe, *The Anatomie of Absurditie*, London, 1589, sig. B1.

[64] Vives, *Instructiō*, op. cit., sig. N4ᵛ.

[65] Heywood, op. cit., pp. 46–47.

[66] Tasso, op. cit., sig. B2ᵛ.

[67] IV, i, 47–48.

[68] II, iii, 18–28.

[69] III, iii, 183–186.

[70] IV, i, 189–204.

[71] IV, iii, 17–21.

[72] V, ii, 125.

Marvin Rosenberg

IN DEFENSE OF IAGO

I would like first to defend Iago against the charge that he was a decent man—a man, that is, who injured others only after he was provoked to do so. This libel against Iago's wickedness, first made in the late eighteenth century,[1] has been advanced on the grounds that the Ancient was unfairly deprived of promotion, that he was really cuckolded by Othello, or that he found it necessary to act as if one or both of these possibilities were true, and somehow found himself doing wrong in spite of himself. In modern times, Iago's apologists have become so tender that one described the rascal as "an honest, charming soldier, a man of honesty and innate kindliness";[2] another felt "he might almost serve as an example of the Aristotelian hero, a good man brought, like Oedipus, to commit enormities unforeseen";[3] and a third, "Iago . . . is a pitiful plaything of circumstance; there is, after all, something pitiful in this man's final doom."[4] I can't agree; Iago was not that good a man.

On the other hand, I want also to defend the Ancient against the more frequent charge that he was a creature of subhuman evil, malignant without any motivation, an embodiment of Satan himself. By one modern he has been called "a black angel . . . the Spirit of Evil . . . with no passions and no habitation . . .";[5] by another, ". . . a monster, whose wickedness should lie far deeper than anything that could be explained by a motive . . .";[6] by still another, "a devil in the flesh . . . a fiend."[7] Again I cannot agree; Iago was not that bad a man.

A variant of the interpretation equating Iago with evil has come from symbolist critics. One student of imagery finds serpent and devil references that identify Iago "with the devil himself", and make his implicit diabolism explicit;[8] another, more Freudian-minded, sees Iago as an abstraction of the base side of Othello: "Othello's is the human soul as it strives to be, and Iago is that which corrodes and subverts it from within";[9] still another Freudian sees Iago as all this and homosexual too;[10] while an allegorist feels that Iago represents ". . . unlimited, formless villainy . . . the spirit of denial . . . undefined, devisualized, inhuman. . . ."[11] The impressionists are entitled to their impressions; but it seems to me that they fail to do justice to Iago's

From *Shakespeare Quarterly* 6, No. 2 (Spring 1955): 145–58.

flesh and blood qualities in seeing him as a symbol; he is a better dramatic character than that.

This last is an important point. Some modern critics, seeing neither essential humanity nor significant symbolism in Iago, conclude that he is simply badly made: stupid and dull,[12] one calls him; a poor and implausible character,[13] says another; because of his stationary, toneless character, says a third, *Othello* cannot stand beside *Macbeth, Hamlet,* and *Lear.*[14] This I agree with least of all. What I hope to show, after exonerating the rascal of charges of outraged decency and Satanic or abstract evil, is that he was wonderfully shaped by Shakespeare into a first-rate dramatic character, as well as a clearly recognizable type of human being, with passions and frustrations—and even physical symptoms—characteristic of a type of troubled humanity common enough so that psychologists in our time regularly encounter it. Shakespeare was not content, in Iago, to load his play with yet another stock Machiavel, another version of an old Morality figure,[15] nor even one of the newer-fangled malcontents;[16] he was building much more than a "necessary piece of dramatic mechanism";[17] with a great playwright's searching insight, he was prob-ing into the roots of human wickedness to find—and show in the theater—how it was that a man really could smile and smile and smile and be a villain.

Iago's first apologist, an eighteenth-century Exeter gentleman, argued that the Ancient was respectable at the beginning of the play, but was badly treated by Othello, suspected his wife of affairs with Othello and Cassio, and largely for these reasons revenged himself. The apologist wrote: ". . . if vengeance can be vindicated by an accumulation of injuries, Iago's, though exorbitant, was just."[18]

In the next century, Iago's right to suspect Othello's relations with Emilia was affirmed. To one critic, Iago was really the jealous one—and he had a right to be jealous. The unsuspected infidelity was a fact; Othello's part in it explained why Othello himself should have been so ready to suspect his own wife of adultery.[19] In the twentieth century, the attitude toward Iago as a wronged individual with a double motivation has been refined: he was at least a relatively decent man, his character flaws not emergent, until he was passed over for promotion and his suspicion of the adultery was aroused; then only did he plunge into a sea of iniquity, going in deeper at last than he would at first have liked to do.[20]

Massive arguments have been summoned to prove both his motivations. Of Othello's adultery with Emilia, we have been reminded that: 1. Othello is a fully sexed veteran soldier with a bent for erotic satisfaction, 2. Iago has no reason to rationalize his suspicion, 3. Emilia is portrayed as a "lewd and filthy-speaking harlot" who, in talking with Desdemona, does not indignantly repudiate the idea of cuck-olding of her husband, and 4. Othello's conversation with Emilia indicates his per-sonal acquaintance with her as a subtle whore who will kneel and pray.[21]

In connection with Iago's other suggested motivation, that he is a soldier wrongfully passed over, some research has been made into the Elizabethan popular attitudes toward the military. It has been deduced that Iago was a frontline soldier passed over for an example of the less popular type of book-soldier, and that Othello's action in this appointment, and in his otherwise "lovesick" attitude, would suggest to the Elizabethans that he is at fault as a general and is inviting the disaster that comes.[22]

At the extreme of these apologist attitudes an almost lovable Iago emerges. Thus one modern writes: "It is evident, I think, that Shakespeare imagined Iago a man of warm, sympathetic qualities," a kind of Falstaff who, through no real fault of his own, goes wrong.[23] This critic feels the Elizabethans would find Iago distinctly attractive, and so does another, who argues that Iago would be regarded as a kind of central figure in a thesis play on the military code of martial honor, that he would rouse more interest and sympathy than Othello in many of Shakespeare's spectators because they could identify with him as one of their own class.[24]

This is the crux of the extreme apologists' case. If an injured Iago has been given due cause for vengeance, if he is a wronged man, then he must almost certainly arouse some sympathy in an audience. Was he wronged? Does he arouse sympathy? We cannot answer this simply by hunting the text for bits and scraps of lines from which to deduce the nature of the characters. The lines give us only one of the character's dimensions. For depth, to get an adequate test of a character's implications in the round, we must examine the possibilities of the play as it comes to performance in the theater. Meanings that cannot be made apparent in some way through words, voice, and action on the stage are unlikely to have been intended by the playwright. For instance if Othello had an affair with Emilia before the play opened, or after, this must be communicable in a theater. Now it is not in the lines, as such; true, Emilia is cynical about marital fidelity, true, Othello throws harsh words at her, but there is no evidence of an illicit connection between them. To establish such a connection, we would have to see the Moor engage in some sort of by-play with her—or perhaps refuse to, now that he is married. But there is no remote suggestion of this in the lines, and it is difficult to conceive of it integrated into any consistent Othello characterization. By the measure of totality of effect—of the unity of poetry, speech, and action in living drama—such an interpretation seems impossible.

The same seems true of Iago's complaint about being unfairly treated in his military position by Othello. If he was, there must be more than his word to show it; but nowhere in the lines or implied action is it suggested that Othello, either consciously or unconsciously, is less than fair to his ensign. In fact, the dramatization of the play demands that he go out of his way to show his respect and friendship for Iago.

Again, the interpretation of Iago as suddenly turning from decency to unpleasantness seems incompatible with a theater performance of the role. His cruel exploiting of Roderigo is clearly a habitual thing with this Ancient; thus does he *ever* make his fool his purse, and the butt of his angry witt. Even more significant, though not adequately recognized in criticism, is Iago's attitude toward his wife. Before others, he treats her at best with sadistic humor; alone with her, as when he tears the handkerchief from her hand and sends her about her business, he snarls orders at her as if she were an inferior being. It seems meant to be clear, in the theater, that Emilia's is no happy marriage; she resents Iago's sharp tongue, as on the Cyprus quay, she has had painfully to bear his suspicion of her adultery with Othello, she has been made by this time very cynical about loyalty to husbands, as is obvious from her conversation with Desdemona in the "willow song" scene. So Iago has long been vicious by habit, and the audience seems meant to sense this in his appearance with subordinates on the stage.

Finally, is it at all possible that Iago, on the stage, might draw compassion as a wronged or erring man? However Shakespeare mixed frailty into the character of Othello and Desdemona—and Cassio and Emilia—surely they are unmistakably the ones meant to capture audience sympathy. Could Iago, on the stage, possibly draw the good will of a normal audience—when almost his every line with its implied action is an invitation to hate and fear him? An apologist who believes Shakespeare was trying to ". . . raise an element of sympathy in the audience for this 'villain' " sees Iago as not meaning to rouse Othello to such a fury, and as hesitating after he sees the storm he has caused;[25] another view finds Iago recoiling from his villainy after the scene when Emilia, in Desdemona's chamber, voices her suspicion that "some eternal villain, some cogging, cozening slave" has made Othello jealous.[26] Considering the subsequent wickedness Iago initiates, a considerable exercise of the imagination is required to accept the conception of a conscience-stricken villain. It seems utterly incompatible with any stage performance, where Iago appears clearly intended to plunge steadily deeper into crime. And surely class has nothing to do with this villain's character as has been suggested; Iago was no George a Greene; he was, as the Folio unmistakably identifies him, a "Villaine."

To go on—was he more than this? Was he the devil himself? Was he evil incarnate? Or perhaps the symbolic representation of what the devil stands for—of destructiveness, of nothingness, of the baser side of Othello himself?

The outright Satanists, who see Iago as indeed the foul fiend, have two large problems to face: one theoretical, one practical. The theoretical difficulty is this: if Iago is the Prince of Darkness, why does he seek, in his soliloquies, human motives for his evil? Why does he not sail straight ahead, passionless, doing his worst? The only answer, if there is one, is that he is making up his humanity, hunting about for motives. It is not a good answer, and the Satanists tend to talk around the point.[27] Of course they have the right, on the theoretical level, to count on the validity of their own impressions; if, reading the text, they visualize Iago as a demon, then a true demon he is to them. On the practical level, however, we must question interpretations of character that do not fit the artistic medium in which the playwright functioned. Shakespeare wrote for the theater. His effects are the effects that could be communicated from a stage. Given this play, the most recognizably domestic of all his tragedies, if the playwright intended to develop as a central figure a cloven-foot devil, would he not have made his intention effective in terms of language and action? Can Iago be presented on the stage as a fiend in human form?

I have seen something of the sort tried in a performance wherein Iago appeared as an ugly, twisted, gnomelike creature, clinging like a dirty shadow to Othello. Visually the thing was interesting; but there was no humanity in it, no sense of friendship betrayed; Iago's own claims of frustration and hate sounded meaningless in a devil's mouth, and the lines about his honesty and friendliness seemed to belong to another play. The performance did not stir the pulse by a flicker.

In the better performances of Iago I have seen, it seemed unquestionable to me that the closer the actor came to a projection of Iago as a thwarted human being, the more powerful was the total impression of tragic life being played out. A great tragedy might certainly be written on the betrayal of a noble man by a devil—a devil real or symbolic, Satan himself or the personified expression of the evil in the hero's character; but *Othello* is not that play as it must be done in the theater for which Shakespeare designed it. If it is something different in the limitless imagination of a critic, it is only because the critic disregards the conditions which determined the mode of expression of Shakespeare's creative fantasy. The critic is then, in effect, transmuting Shakespeare's work into a different art form, and his judgments may be only obliquely relevant to the original play.

Perhaps the best evidence of this comes from the experience of one of the most imaginative of the symbolic interpreters of the tragedy, Wilson Knight. In a first study of the play, Knight describes the characters in this manner: ". . . on the plane of personification, we see that Othello and Desdemona are concrete, moulded of flesh and blood, warm. Iago contrasts with them metaphysically as well as morally: he is unlimited, formless villainy. He is the spirit of denial, wholly negative. He never has visual reality . . . (he) is undefined, devisualized, inhuman."

It is instructive to turn from this estimate to the critic's next book. Sometime after his first study, Wilson Knight produced and acted in *Othello*—a procedure strongly recommended to any who would discuss critically a Shakespearian play. Knight's experience changed his attitude toward the tragedy. There is a considerable softening of the impressions he had first reported, of "ugliness, hellishness, idiocy, negation";[28] and though the critic again spoke of another level of meaning: "Othello, Desdemona, and Iago are Man, the Divine, and the Devil . . ."[29] he followed this with a most significant *but.* "The symbolic effects," Knight wrote, "'are all in the poetry. Iago knows he is in league with hell's forces and often says so, while Desdemona is clearly equated imagistically with Divinity. *But* [the italics are mine] *the moment any of this is allowed to interfere with the expressly domestic and human qualities of the drama, you get disaster.*"

This makes splendid sense. The symbolism of the devil, of denial, of the alter ego, or whatever, *is* in the poetry—for those who find it there; and indeed the body of Shakespearian criticism has been enriched by much stimulating subjective interpretation by the symbolists. But the symbolism is often essentially private; it does not have a natural place on the stage Shakespeare wrote for; to repeat the words of the critic, "the moment any of this is allowed to interfere with the expressly domestic and human qualities of the drama, you get disaster." You get disaster because, as far as we can tell objectively, Shakespeare was not creating personifications, but people—the people of drama—people communicated with such reality within the limits of the art form that their troubled emotions would deeply involve watching audiences. We would not spare much pity for the troubles of Divinity; but we weep for the frail and lovely woman who was Desdemona; and in the same way we are strangely stirred by the wickedness of the man Iago.

For there is some curiously compelling fascination in Iago, something that brings us back to him, and that results in the wide range of criticism I have reviewed. What it is, I think, is the wonderfully contrived projection, in him, of emotional drives that run deep in humanity generally. In Iago the playwright was showing these drives as they may be deformed in personality under the pressures of life.

To test this suggestion, let us try to examine Iago afresh, forgetting previous attitudes toward him. Shakespeare needed a wicked man for a play he wanted to do involving the betrayal of one man by another. I think it is quite possible that Shakespeare was drawn to this story because it was one of betrayal; the theme was one of his favorites, and at the point when he was ready to write *Othello* I believe he had a particularly personal motivation toward it. However this may be, he needed a wicked man, a betrayer, a villain. He needed one because his borrowed story called for one; but it was this plot function only that he borrowed for Iago. The rest is Shakespeare's.

What we know about Shakespeare's Iago appears in two aspects: his external appearance, as he reacts with others, and his inner life, as revealed by the soliloquies. If we neglect what we learn from the soliloquies for a moment, and examine only the face that Iago turns to others during the play, we observe a clever, ambitious man coolly manipulating others for his own ends. In conversation with his confidant he is outspoken about his overt philosophy; he denies the reality of loving feelings—they are only a lust of the blood, a permission of the will; he asserts the supremacy of the will and intelligence, and their power to efface emotions so that desired ends may be achieved; he idealizes the self-sufficient man—the one who knows how to love himself. In Iago's actions with others this philosophy has obviously long since hardened into expert practice, as already observed. Toward those he can exploit openly, he is domineering and brutal. But in accordance with his ideal of supremacy of the self-seeking intellect, when he is with his superiors in station, his true emotions are almost always pushed down below the surface, his actions seem guided by the working of a cool, calculating will. He makes a near-perfect pretence of being a pleasant, decent fellow during most of his time on stage with others; almost his only show of passion is when he is so sad about Cassio's drunkenness, or when he is matching Othello's honest rage with what seems sympathetic anger of his own. So complete is his control that only in momentary slips do we see his hate of the people about him. Without the soliloquies, we get in Iago a picture of a villain who moves almost passionlessly from crime to crime; and as far as it goes, the picture is complete.

Now this brings up a point worth dwelling on. Read the play through omitting the soliloquies and you discover that the soliloquies are actually not necessary to the dramatic action at all, that without them, in fact, there is an increased suspense and tightness of plot. The plans Iago reveals in his discussion with Roderigo are enough to make the lurking menace clear; the apprehension is whetted by the uncertainty of what is to come, and the surprise executions of the villainy are received with more of a jolt. For instance, when Iago first gets the handkerchief, if he did not tell us how he was going to use it, the subsequent revelations of his villainy with it, as they come out in the action, would have even more impact. And the whole play moves faster.

The playwright must have been aware of this. He knew long before the dramatic value of planting a bare hint of villainy and letting the audience imagination work; recall, for instance, Aaron hiding the bag of gold without explanation and the shock value of the trick he plays with it; or remember Richard III, after only an intimation of his intention, manipulating Hastings' doom. For that matter, how effective it is when Iago himself, in the fifth act, improvises so brilliantly to throw the blame on Bianca for Cassio's brawl. On the stage the threat of a hidden villainy that may break out in a new form without preparation is a powerful dramatic weapon.

Yet Shakespeare was content to lose some of the effect of surprise by introducing Iago's soliloquies. Probably one reason he did this was that it was the tradition of the art form he had grown up in, and inevitably there are traces of the conventional villain in Iago. However, if a repetition of the conventional had been Shakespeare's only purpose, he could have let Iago, as a devil or man, merely outline the villainy to come and gloat over it. But the conventional was not enough for Shakespeare. If it had been, we should not be so interested in him today. That he understood and dramatized the hidden working of the soul hardly needs to be said; generation after generation has been helped to understand its own behavior through Shakespeare's poetry. Surely he was not doing this accidentally, or by tacking pieces of convention together; nor, surely was he a kind of innocent genius who had brilliant insights without knowing what he was doing. He was too good a craftsman, too adept at getting the most out of his human and dramatic materials, so much more than his contemporaries. When he made Iago he was at one of the peaks of his art, he was dealing with a wicked man—a kind of humanity in which he had considerable interest—and he seems to have made deliberate use of the soliloquies to show what went on behind the surface of this kind of man.

So we come to the soliloquies. What do they tell us about Iago's inner being that is different from what his exterior told us? Remember that the outer man seemed a cool, controlled villain, usually the complete master of his feelings, and indeed he boasted of his power to control emotion. If we were left with only this side of him, we might be content with the classic estimate of Bradley and Granville-Barker,[30] inherited from the nineteenth century, of Iago, the cold, passionless designer of tragedy in real life; or we might see him, with the Satanists, a devil who of course needs no passion.[31] But there is another aspect to Iago, his inner life; a look into this, and we know how little, actually, he is what he is. The moment he is alone and the mask comes off, all the passions hidden behind the smooth, subordinate surface suddenly boil up. Far from being passionless, this inner Iago is one great fury of passion, the more furious because so much of his passion is smothered when he is with people. Anyone on whom his thought lingers becomes an object of some spurt of passion—hate, envy, jealousy, lust, fear. His superior, his superior's wife, his military companions, his gull, his wife—in the existence of all of them he finds some torment, some threat to his own ego. His wife and his gull take up relatively little of his imaginative fury, because he exploits them with satisfying sadism in actual life; but the others, Othello, Cassio, and Desdemona, to whom he must outwardly turn a pleasant, social face, are, for their real or imagined superiority, intolerable to him, and he needs to crush them in his mind. When the thought of their decent or noble qualities forces itself into his awareness, it automatically evokes a counter-thought of hostility—the Moor, of a free and open nature, must be led by the nose; fruitful Desdemona must have her virtue turned into pitch; Cassio, a proper man, must be overthrown. The contempt Iago shows for others is fierce and tireless; but we learn at last that behind it is a searing contempt for his own self, when the thought rises to his consciousness that Cassio

> ... hath a daily beauty in his life
> That makes me ugly. ...

Mostly be defends himself from the awareness of this self-contempt by transferring his hostility into furious fantasies of his great power: he is clever, very very clever, indeed he has superhuman cunning, he is above—or below—the common sentiment and morality of those he resents and needs to despise. It is not any single need that frustrates Iago—the passed-over lieutenancy, the fantasied passion for Desdemona, the imagined cuckolding by Othello; it would do him no good to be satisfied on all these points—indeed, when he does get the lieutenancy, it does nothing to satisfy his fury. What we are shown in the inner Iago is a bottomless, consuming passion that feeds on all life around it.

Let me sum up, briefly, the inner and the overt manifestations of Iago's personality. On the surface he gives this impression:

> He believes in the omnipotence of will, of intelligence, and reason, while denying the power of emotional forces and showing contempt for them; he has an essential disrespect for others, their dignity, and their feelings, his only concern being his subordination of them; he thinks of them as people to be exploited, he is proud of his ability to exploit them, by hook or by crook, working with anything at hand—money, sexuality, feelings.[32]

This fairly well describes Iago from the observable actions Shakespeare has provided. Is this the picture of a kind of human being? It is; not a pleasant one, certainly, but one so common in society that in psychological writing we may find it charted as a type. In fact, the preceding paragraph about Iago is an abstract; almost word-for-word, of the description by a distinguished modern medical psychologist of a familiar neurotic pattern. Iago might have been a model for the study. And the pattern of Iago's overt activity is matched by the recognizable drives of his inner life. Here is another abstract, almost verbatim, from a description of the motivations of such a neurotic type:

> His main motivating force in life is his need for vindictive triumph ... he cannot tolerate anybody who knows or achieves more than he does, wields more power, or in any way questions his superiority. Compulsively he has to drag his rival down or defeat him. Even if he subordinates himself for the sake

of his career, he is scheming for ultimate triumph. Not being tied by feelings of loyalty, he easily can become treacherous . . . the drive for a triumphant mastery of life . . . with the unsatiable pride that accompanies it, becomes a monster, more and more swallowing all feelings . . . [and covering] the self-hate and self-contempt that are appalling in their dimensions. Love, compassion, considerateness—all human ties—are felt as restraints on the path to sinister glory . . . he must prove his own worth to himself. And he can prove it to his satisfaction only by arrogating to himself extraordinary attributes, the special qualities of which are determined by his particular needs. . . . Having smothered positive feelings, he can rely upon only his intellect for the mastery of life. Hence his pride in his intellectual powers reaches unusual dimensions, pride in vigilance, in outwitting everybody, in foresight, in planning. . . . [A] frequent outcome of [his] tendency to deprive or exploit is an anxiety that he will be cheated or exploited by others. . . . He gives free range, at least in his mind, to his ample supply of bitter resentment . . . [though the outward] expressions of vindictiveness may be checked by the considerations of prudence or expediency. . . . In order to understand why his process of crushing feelings persists . . . we have to take a look . . . at his imagination and his vision of the future. He is and will be infinitely better than "they" [the others] are. He will become great and put them to shame. He will show them how they have misjudged and wronged him. He will become the great hero . . . or (the great) persecutor. . . . Driven by . . . a need for vindication, revenge, and triumph, these are not idle fantasies. They determine the course of his life. Driving himself from victory to victory, in large or small matters, he lives for the "day of reckoning."[33]

It is not necessary here, as it was for the psychologist, to explain the early stresses that twist the normal human drives into these vindictive channels, to find in a man's childhood the conditions that make him fearful of emotion and drive him to seek omnipotence in fantasy. For us, Iago had no childhood; he exists only as a more or less valid reflection of life in the dramatic art form. What is important here is that Shakespeare saw and worked out dramatically, as the psychologist did in textbook observation, how these things could be—how intimately related were the need for vindictive triumph and the need to deny positive feelings, how pervasive and powerful was the resulting misdirected hostility, how dangerously and poisonously the hostility fumed beneath the surface when it was further compressed by the outward need to appear pleasant and subordinate.

It is no longer surprising to us that Shakespeare sensed complexities of human motivation that psychologists are still trying to explain. Freud long ago paid tribute to him for that. But it is interesting to see how deep his insight could go, as in the case of Iago. For having shaped the true mental and emotional qualities of his vindictive man, the playwright added a distinctive physical illness that unmistakably belongs to Iago. It was an illness that plagued Iago savagely, and one that, in his revenge fantasies, he hoped to fasten onto Othello.

The illness is common today—it is almost expected to occur among those individuals who burn with resentment and hostility that they try to suppress. It feeds on internalized rage. In Iago it occurs when, out of the deep well of his self-contempt, he dredges up a fantasy upon which to center his furious resentment—specifically when he tortures himself with the thought that Othello had sexual relations with Emilia.

> ... The thought whereof
> Doth, like a poisonous mineral, gnaw my inwards. ...

Iago does, that is, burn inwardly from a familiar, severe functional disorder, a disorder that eats a man away within when his nerves flay his stomach. Modern medical studies show that emotionally Iago is curiously like the type that suffers from the psychosomatic stress which abrades the "inwards" and frequently leads to the painful, persistent ulcer. The ulcer "type", as these studies show, can be from any field of activity, but however diverse the occupations and environment he is likely to be a person who was driven, to quote one study, to evolve "... a life pattern of being self-sufficient, independent, or the 'lone-wolf.'" This pattern was "... commonly accompanied by feelings of resentment and hostility."[34]

The case studies show that ulcer patients frequently take out some of their aggressions on exploitable underlings; this was an accompaniment to the smothered resentment and hostility fantasies they suffered in their relations with persons they could not manipulate.

Iago, who is ceaselessly on fire with suppressed hostility against those he cannot openly exploit, represents excellently the typical host for this gnawing, poisonous mineral of an illness; and if he mistakes its physiological nature, he knows well enough what causes it in him. A thought, a conceit, like his suspicion of Emilia's infidelity, is enough to set the sharp teeth biting at his gut; and it is precisely such a conceit that he hopes to feed Othello, for

> Dangerous conceits are in their nature poisons ...
> which ...
> ... with a little act upon the blood
> Burn like the mines of sulphur.

Iago knew the feeling well. The imagery is so sharp that one wonders how well Shakespeare himself might have been acquainted with the problem. Certainly Renaissance psychologists knew the signs of it, little as they understood its location or its causes in detail; thus, a late sixteenth-century treatise explained: "But the envious body is constrained to bite on his bridle, to chew and to devoure his envy within himselfe and to lock up his owne miserie in the bottome of his heart, to the end it breaks not foorth and show itself...."[35] Iago indeed chewed and devoured his envy within himself, and locked up his misery in the bottom of his heart—or in that approximate location.

If this characterization I have proposed is consistent with Shakespeare's intention, it should be able to stand the same test I applied to the other interpretations: is it communicable in the theater? I believe it is. Indeed, in my view its value for criticism would be seriously limited unless it *did* have meaning in terms of the art form in which Shakespeare worked. This does not mean a belief that Iago—or any complex Shakespearian character—can or should be presented in any rigidity patterned way from the stage. One of Shakespeare's greatnesses as a dramatist was his sense of the flexibility of the art in which he worked, and particularly its demands for language and characterization that could fit, like a loose but always shapely garment, the widely varying creative approaches inevitable when different actors play the same role. Actors of many sizes, shapes, temperaments, and cultural backgrounds have shown, and will show, Iagos with different surfaces: one more brooding, another more mercurial, or more genial, or more sardonic. But the character is most powerfully communicated on the stage, it seems to me, when its nucleus is the conception of humanity I have outlined.

The two sharply contrasting, yet complementary sides of Iago give a suspenseful unity to the role on the stage. A constant tension surrounds the Ancient in his outward seeming; it emerges from the impression not only of his cynical hypocrisy but also of his continuously holding his emotions down. When he smothers his deep hostility, and appears, without any show of hypocrisy—even to the audience—the true friend and subordinate of Othello, we know he is more than a coolly calculating pretender; he is a dangerous high explosive. We get a glimpse of his passion when he is exploiting Roderigo, and a hint of its heat in his treatment of Emilia. Probably Shakespeare meant the mask to slip momentarily in other company, too: as when Cassio kisses Emilia on the Cyprus quay, and Iago, after a flashing look of hate, covers with the line of sadistic humor aimed at his wife; or when the Ancient is talking to Roderigo a bit later about the plot to ruin Cassio, and in his furious envy lets his passion get away from him, and he runs on and on: "Besides, the knave is handsome, young, and hath all those requisites in him that folly and green minds look after; a pestilent complete knave, and the woman hath found him already."

When Iago is in the very midst of lecturing Roderigo on the philosophy of the supremacy of reason and will, his suppressed emotion seems meant to show, as when he dwells more than he needs to on erotic love. Probably there is not a scene where the rumble of Iago's inner passion is not meant to be sensed beneath the controlled surface.

Then, the moment Iago is left alone, we look into the volcano itself: the resentment wells up, and he rages down the stage, fantasying revenge and triumph. The sudden contrast is first rate theater, and it adds the necessary deep shadows to the characterization of the surface man. Each soliloquy sharpens the audience sense of the controlled hostility that must be so carefully hidden at other times, and makes more dramatic the moment when the hostility shows. The better Iagos I have watched have seemed to sense, whether consciously or not, the constant emotional smoldering of the character, and have deliberately damped the fire during Iago's scenes with others, and masked it with biting humor, to let it blaze out in the soliloquies. There the diffuse character of Iago's pervasive hostility is emphasized. No one passion is seen to dominate him, but all that can crowd in, jealousy, envy, pride, fear, humiliation, hate, self-contempt.

These are no made-up emotions, either; they shake Iago fiercely; yet as he moves through his stormy theater life it is clear, from the fair treatment he is seen to get from others, that the source of his torment is not outside him. It is seen in perspective to be within, where the denial of positive feelings has diverted his emotions into a fountain of hostility that must release itself in all the furious fantasies he can manufacture. To the end he tries to deceive the outer world about his inner life, just as he is himself obviously deceived about his power to subdue his own emotions. Finally, when all is lost, when the others have lifted the curtain on his secret world, and he murders his wife in a sudden release of hostility, he immediately re-asserts the strenuous rein on his rebellious emotions, and tries for the last time to seal off his feelings from the sight of others. These mortals cannot make him speak, though his heart were in their hand.

What is compelling about this kind of Iago in the theater is his unmistakable humanity. He does not draw our sympathy, because he is a very wicked man; but he evokes our fear, because we know wicked men do exist, and here is a shockingly real reflection of how their twisted emotions work; and he evokes some other nameless kind of terror, a terror of recognition, for he is compounded of deep human motives that run through all of us. I believe it is this uncanny echo in Iago—uncanny in the Freudian sense—that has made him so fascinating and puzzling to so many audiences and critics.

The critics who have sought to explain Iago's humanity were certainly on the right track; if their studies were incomplete—as this one may similarly be—it was perhaps because they did not go far enough behind Iago's jealousy, or pride, or envy, or other manifestations to his broad-based affinity with mankind. The apologists have generally sought an outside provocation for Iago's wickedness because they felt that only this could justify his humanity; and perhaps this feeling also prompts those who find Iago a veritable devil because they cannot bring themselves to accept as human the flood of hostility that pours from him. The devil has for a long, long time, either as a figure of reality or as a symbol, taken the blame for human wickedness. I think we understand by now the impulse to unload human evil on spiritual and allegorical scapegoats.

This impulse may have lain in Shakespeare's unconscious, and if so the symbolists have made a discovery for us; but there is no sound evidence that Shakespeare meant consciously to find responsibility for the evil that men do anywhere but in men themselves. Largely his greatness as a dramatist for times beyond his own lay in his recognizing and revealing the purely mortal forces that move people to action—or inaction. In Iago, he went deep into the nature of thwarted humanity; we can try to go no less far in confirming the accuracy of his portrait.

The aggressive drives we have learned to recognize as a badge of humanity are twisted and magnified in Iago, but we cannot disown them. Even in people we call normal, those who learn to channel their forces into socially useful releases, resentment rises at real and fancied wrongs, hostilities sometimes build up at obstacles in the life path. Decent persons living under the inner tension this kind of life produces find flitting through their thoughts momentary wishes that harm, disease, or death will come to rivals or enemies, while they fantasy triumph for themselves. In the neurotic, hopelessly unsatisfied with reality, the hostile wishes and glory fantasies take on more and more importance, as they are charged with the full force of the repressed libido, and sometimes the fantasies are even translated recklessly into action. It is this kind of human being, when he is driven to change the form of reality to fit his vision of omnipotence, who makes tragedy, in life or in the drama; I believe it is this kind of human being, with his uncanny attraction for endless audiences and readers, that Shakespeare with surpassing technical skill and insight reflected in Iago.

NOTES

[1] "An Apology for the Character and Conduct of Iago," in *Essays, by a Society of Gentlemen* (1796), pp. 395–409. See the Variorum *Othello*, pp. 408–409, and *Monthly Review*, NS (1796), XXII, 7.
[2] Tucker Brooke, "The Romantic Iago," *Yale Review*, VII (Jan., 1918), 3–59.
[3] J. W. Draper, "*Othello* and Elizabethan Army Life," *Review Ang.-Am.*, IX (April, 1932), 324.
[4] Allardyce Nicoll, *Studies in Shakespeare* (1927), pp. 94, 103.
[5] John Jay Chapman, *A Glance toward Shakespeare* (Boston, 1922), p. 47.
[6] Lytton Strachey, *Characters and Commentaries* (New York, 1935), pp. 295–296.
[7] E. E. Stoll, *Shakespeare and Other Masters* (Cambridge, 1940), pp. 231, 246.
[8] Robert Heilman, "Dr. Iago and His Potions," *Virginia Quarterly Review*, XXVIII (Autumn, 1952), 568–584. (Heilman has a curiously different imagistic approach to the same problem in "The economics of Iago and Others," *PMLA*, LXVIII (June, 1953), 555–571.) S. L. Bethell ("Shakespeare's Imagery: The Diabolic Images in *Othello*," in *Shakespeare Survey* (Cambridge, 1952), pp. 62–80) comes to pretty much the same conclusion on the basis of the "devil" images.
[9] J. I. M. Stewart, *Character and Motive in Shakespeare* (London, 1949), p. 108. The split-ego conception of Shakespearian heroes was first suggested as applying to Macbeth by Freud, after a hint by Jekels (Sigmund Freud, *Collected Papers* (London, 1925), IV, 332. For Jekel's expansion of the idea, see L. Jekels, "Shakespeare's Macbeth," *Imago*, V (1917–19), 170–195). It has been applied several times to Othello. See also Derek Traversi, "*Othello*," *The Wind and the Rain*, VI (Spring, 1950), 268–269, Bodkin (see note 11), Leavis (see note 17), T. F. Connolly, "Shakespeare and the Double Man," *Shakespeare Quarterly*, I (Jan., 1950), 30–35, and Feldman, below. Burke (Kenneth Burke, "*Othello*: An Essay to Illustrate a Method," *Hudson Rev.*, IV (Summer, 1951), 166–168) seems, in his curious and complex study of the play, to go one further and find that Othello, Iago, and Desdemona are all expressions of one "inseparable integer".
[10] A. B. Feldman, "Othello's Obsession," *Am. Imago*, IX (June, 1952), 151–152, 156.
[11] G. W. Knight, *Wheel of Fire* (London, 1930), pp. 127, 131. Maud Bodkin (*Archetypal Patterns in Poetry* (London, 1934), pp. 220–221) follows Knight's imagery, although she also considers the possibility of the split ego conception, of ". . . Iago as a projected image of forces present in Othello. . . ."
[12] John R. Moore, "The Character of Iago," *U. of Missouri Studies*, XXI, i, 39–46.
[13] Robert Bridges, *The Influence of the Audience on Shakespeare's Drama* (London, 1927), p. 23.
[14] J. W. Abernethy, "Honest Iago," *Sewanee Review*, XXX (July, 1922), 336–344.
[15] P. A. Jorgensen, "'Honesty' in *Othello*," *Studies in Philology*, XLVII (Oct., 1950), 557–568, sees Iago as a knave posing as the morality Honesty.
[16] Theodore Spencer, "The Elizabethan Malcontent," in *Joseph Quincy Adams Memorial Studies* (Washington, 1948), p. 530, suggests that Iago had some qualities in common with Marston's Malevole, and—for the convenience of classification—lists him as a "malcontent".
[17] F. R. Leavis ("Diabolic Intellect and the Noble Hero: A Note on *Othello*," *Scrutiny*, VI (December, 1937) 261, 264), calls him this, partly in reaction to the impression the critic had from Bradley that Othello was merely Iago's foil. Leavis makes Iago the auxiliary, and even suggests (264) the split-ego conception noted above (see note 9).
[18] *Essays*, op. cit. (Note 1), p. 409.
[19] D. J. Snider, *System of Shakespeare's Drama* (St. Louis, 1877), II, 97. J. A. Heraud (*Shakespeare, His Inner Life* (1865), p. 270), says the adultery was "not impossible". Interestingly enough, S. A. Tannenbaum ("The Wronged Iago," *Shakespeare Association Bulletin*, XII (Jan., 1937), 57) in expanding this argument, noted that most critics were too squeamish to discuss the adultery issue, and added "From nineteenth century critics nothing else could have been expected."

The Snider-Heraud interpretation of Iago as a deeply jealous personality was, it seems to me, a step in the right direction. It has been elaborated effectively by modern critics: John W. Draper, "The Jealousy of Iago," *Neophilologus*, XXV (1939), 50–60; F. P. Rand, "The Over-Garrulous Iago," *Shakespeare Quarterly* (July, 1950), 155–161; and Kenneth Muir, "The Jealousy of Iago," in *English Miscellany*, II (Rome, 1951), 65–83. Muir emphatically denies the possibility of a relationship between Emilia and Othello; Draper and Rand are not certain.

[20] Rand (p. 158) sees Iago's treachery as perhaps the sudden outbreak of what may have been a predisposition: ". . . he could hardly have been the Iago we know when Emilia married him, or during the years when he was becoming the 'honest Iago' to the Venetians." Jordan (H. H. Jordan, "Dramatic Illusion in *Othello*," *Shakespeare Quarterly* (July, 1950), 146–152) also finds Iago, a brooding egoist, at loose ends between wars, moved by his intelligence to desert a life of honesty to plunge into treachery for the first time when he seems unfairly treated. Here Jordan follows Nicoll (pp. 94–97). Rand, Jordan, and Nicoll take for granted, as do—among others—Kittredge (*Othello*, ed. G. L. Kittredge (New York, 1941), p. x), Hallett (W. H. Hallett, "Honest, Honest Iago," *Fortn. Rev.*, NS, LXXIX, 275–286), Praz (Mario Praz in *Proceedings of the British Academy*, XIV (1928), p. 76), Lewis (Wyndham Lewis, *The Lion and the Fox* (New York, n.d.), p. 197), Bowman (Thomas D. Bowman, "A Further Study in the Characterization and Motivation of Iago," *College English*, IV (May, 1943), 460–469). Shackford (John B. Shackford, "The Motivation of Iago," *Shakespeare Newsletter* (Sept., 1953), 30), and Tannenbaum, Draper, Webb and Brooke agree (see following notes) that Iago was definitely motivated to revenge by his loss of the appointment and/or the suspicion of Emilia's infidelity with Othello. Miller (Donald C. Miller, "Iago and the Problem of Time," *Eng. Stud.* (June, 1940), 97–115) argues that Othello had made a secret "contract marriage" with Desdemona well before the play opened, and that Iago suddenly realized, with the overt elopement, that he had been superseded by a man (Cassio) merely better able to act as an assistant in the courtship.

[21] Tannenbaum (pp. 58–60) catalogues the arguments. He adds a fifth point that contributes nothing to the case.

[22] H. J. Webb, "The Military Background in *Othello*," *Philological Quarterly*, XXX (Jan., 1951), 40–51. For more on the title subject, see J. R. Moore's answer to Webb, "Othello, Iago, and Cassio as Soldiers," *Philological Quarterly*, XXXI (April, 1952), 189–195; and J. W. Draper, "Honest Iago," *PMLA*, XLVI (Sept., 1931), 724–737. "Captain General Othello," *Ang. Zeit. für Eng. Phil.*, LV (Halle, 1931), 296–310, and Shackford. (See note 24 below.)

[23] Brooke, pp. 351–359. See also Nicoll (p. 103) for the "conception of Iago as a character to be pitied."

[24] Draper, "Othello and Elizabethan Army Life," pp. 324–326.

[25] Nicoll (p. 102) finds that Iago evinces, after setting Othello aflame, ". . . a hesitation which betrays a certain fear . . . that he has gone too far. . . ." But in performance Iago seems to gain assurance as he goes along. It is Iago after all who urges Othello on to "strangle her in her bed", and who brings the Moor back to the murderous purpose when he wavers momentarily (IV. i), remembering Desdemona's gentle qualities.

[26] Brooke (p. 358). Goddard (H. C. Goddard, *The Meaning of Shakespeare* (Chicago, 1951), pp. 481–485), also suggests that after this scene, and Desdemona's pathetic appeal to him, Iago, profoundly disturbed, his power sapped, goes haltingly to his end. Goddard cites as his chief support the scene following with Roderigo, where ". . . we see Iago for the first time at his wit's end, unable to devise anything by way of answer to Roderigo's importunities." As customarily staged, the scene points in the other direction. Iago is more disdainful than ever of Roderigo, until the gull threatens to go to Desdemona, whereupon Iago promptly—and with some humor—flatters him again into temporary submission. Surely Iago is shown as never more resourceful and purposeful than in the opening scene of the fifth act, where, pressed at last to take a hand in the violence he has initiated, he almost kills Cassio, does kill Roderigo, and blames the whole thing on Bianca with hardly a stop for thought.

[27] See, for instance, John Palmer, *Studies in the Contemporary Theatre* (1927), p. 78.

[28] Wheel, p. 129.

[29] G. W. Knight, *Principles of Shakespearean Production* (1936), p. 57.

[30] Bradley (A. C. Bradley, *Shakespearean Tragedy* (1929), p. 224) is frankly bewildered to find that Iago ". . . has *less* passion than the ordinary man, and yet he does these frightful things." Bradley accepts in principle the suggestions of Hazlitt and Swinburne (p. 228), and he accepts Coleridge's "motive-hunting" figure too (p. 226); Bradley's point is that Coleridge's estimate does not equate with "evil for evil's sake." Barker (H. Granville-Barker, *Prefaces* (Princeton, 1947), pp. 98ff.) allows Iago the emotion of hate, but even this is seen as cold.

[31] For the Satanist view of Iago's lack of passion, see Chapman, Stoll, p. 247, and Palmer.

[32] Karen Horney, *Self-Analysis* (New York, 1942), pp. 56ff. See also, by the same author, "The Quest for Power, Prestige, and Possession," and "Neurotic Competitiveness," in *The Neurotic Personality of Our Time* (New York, 1937), pp. 162–206.

The neurotic personality manifests itself in various ways, some marked by withdrawal, some by aggression. In this abstraction from Horney, and in the following one, I have brought to focus, from many pages, the psychologist's descriptions of one "expansive" manifestation.

[33] Karen Horney, *Neurosis and Human Growth* (New York, 1950), pp. 197–213. Bradley, I think, was reaching for some such explanation for Iago's humanity in his emphasis on the Ancient's urge to "plume up my will" (Bradley, pp. 229 ff.), Bradley saw, too, that Iago did not understand the power of love; but the critic stopped short of the further insight that it was some repression of the passion all humans share, and not the utter lack of it, that accounted for the power of Iago's characterization. Perhaps a greater tolerance for seeing *Othello* in the theater would have helped Bradley here. Kittredge, though he tended to justify Iago's actions on the basis of external provocation, sensed more acutely the "raging torment" within the Ancient.

[34] B. Mittelman, H. G. Wolff, and M. Scharf, "Emotions and Gastroduodenal Functions," *Psychosomatic Medicine*, IV (1942), 5, 16.

[35] Peter de la Primaudaye, *The French Academy*, trans. T. B(owes) (1586), quoted in Lily B. Campbell, *Shakespeare's Tragic Heroes—Slaves of Passion* (Cambridge, 1930), p. 153.

W. H. Auden

THE JOKER IN THE PACK

Reason is God's gift; but so are the passions.
Reason is as guilty as passion.

—J. H. NEWMAN

I

Any consideration of the Tragedy of Othello must be primarily occupied, not with its official hero but with its villain. I cannot think of any other play in which only one character performs personal actions—all the *deeds* are Iago's—and all the others without exception only exhibit behavior. In marrying each other, Othello and Desdemona have performed a deed, but this took place before the play begins. Nor can I think of another play in which the villain is so completely triumphant: everything Iago sets out to do, he accomplishes—(among his goals, I include his self-destruction). Even Cassio, who survives, is maimed for life.

If *Othello* is a tragedy—and one certainly cannot call it a comedy—it is tragic in a peculiar way. In most tragedies the fall of the hero from glory to misery and death is the work, either of the gods, or of his own freely chosen acts, or, more commonly, a mixture of both. But the fall of Othello is the work of another human being; nothing he says or does originates with himself. In consequence we feel pity for him but no respect; our aesthetic respect is reserved for Iago.

Iago is a wicked man. The wicked man, the stage villain, as a subject of serious dramatic interest does not, so far as I know, appear in the drama of Western Europe before the Elizabethans. In the mystery plays, the wicked characters, like Satan or Herod, are treated comically, but the theme of the triumphant villain cannot be treated comically because the suffering he inflicts is real.

A distinction must be made between the villainous character—figures like

From *The Dyer's Hand and Other Essays* (New York: Random House, 1962), pp. 246–72. First published in *Encounter*, August 1961.

Don John in *Much Ado,* Richard III, Edmund in *Lear,* Iachimo in *Cymbeline*—and
the merely criminal character—figures like Duke Antonio in *The Tempest,* Angelo
in *Measure for Measure,* Macbeth or Claudius in *Hamlet.* The criminal is a person
who finds himself in a situation where he is tempted to break the law and succumbs
to the temptation: he ought, of course, to have resisted the temptation, but everybody, both on stage and in the audience, must admit that, had they been placed in
the same situation, they, too, would have been tempted. The opportunities are
exceptional—Prospero, immersed in his books, has left the government of Milan to
his brother, Angelo is in a position of absolute authority, Claudius is the Queen's
lover, Macbeth is egged on by prophecies and heaven-sent opportunities, but the
desire for a dukedom or a crown or a chaste and beautiful girl are desires which
all can imagine themselves feeling.

The villain, on the other hand, is shown from the beginning as being a malcontent, a person with a general grudge against life and society. In most cases this
is comprehensible because the villain has, in fact, been wronged by Nature or
Society: Richard III is a hunchback, Don John and Edmund are bastards. What
distinguishes their actions from those of the criminal is that, even when they have
something tangible to gain, this is a secondary satisfaction; their primary satisfaction
is the infliction of suffering on others, or the exercise of power over others against
their will. Richard does not really desire Anne; what he enjoys is successfully wooing
a lady whose husband and father-in-law he has killed. Since he has persuaded
Gloucester that Edgar is a would-be parricide, Edmund does not need to betray his
father to Cornwall and Regan in order to inherit. Don John has nothing personally
to gain from ruining the happiness of Claudio and Hero except the pleasure of
seeing them unhappy. Iachimo is a doubtful case of villainy. When he and Posthumus make their wager, the latter warns him:

> If she remain unseduced, you not making it appear otherwise, for your ill
> opinion and th'assault you have made on her chastity you shall answer me with
> your sword.

To the degree that his motive in deceiving Posthumus is simply physical fear of
losing his life in a duel, he is a coward, not a villain; he is only a villain to the degree
that his motive is the pleasure of making and seeing the innocent suffer. Coleridge's
description of Iago's actions as "motiveless malignancy" applies in some degree to
all the Shakespearian villains. The adjective *motiveless* means, firstly, that the tangible gains, if any, are clearly not the principal motive and, secondly, that the motive
is not the desire for personal revenge upon another for a personal injury. Iago
himself proffers two reasons for wishing to injure Othello and Cassio. He tells
Roderigo that, in appointing Cassio to be his lieutenant, Othello has treated him
unjustly, in which conversation he talks like the conventional Elizabethan malcontent. In his soliloquies with himself, he refers to his suspicion that both Othello and
Cassio have made him a cuckold, and here he talks like the conventional jealous
husband who desires revenge. But there are, I believe, insuperable objections to
taking these reasons, as some critics have done, at their face value. If one of Iago's

goals is to supplant Cassio in the lieutenancy, one can only say that his plot fails for, when Cassio is cashiered, Othello does not appoint Iago in his place. It is true that, in Act III, Scene 3, when they swear blood-brotherhood in revenge, Othello concludes with the words

. . . now thou are my lieutenant

to which Iago replies:

I am your own for ever

but the use of the word *lieutenant* in this context refers, surely, not to a public military rank, but to a private and illegal delegation of authority—the job delegated to Iago is the secret murder of Cassio, and Iago's reply, which is a mocking echo of an earlier line of Othello's, refers to a relation which can never become public. The ambiguity of the word is confirmed by its use in the first line of the scene which immediately follows. Desdemona says

Do you know, sirrah, where the Lieutenant Cassio lies?

(One should beware of attaching too much significance to Elizabethan typography, but it is worth noting that Othello's lieutenant is in lower case and Desdemona's in upper). As for Iago's jealousy, one cannot believe that a seriously jealous man could behave towards his wife as Iago behaves towards Emilia, for the wife of a jealous husband is the first person to suffer. Not only is the relation of Iago and Emilia, as we see it on stage, without emotional tension, but also Emilia openly refers to a rumor of her infidelity as something already disposed of.

> Some such squire it was
> That turned your wit, the seamy side without
> And made you to suspect me with the Moor.

At one point Iago states that, in order to revenge himself on Othello, he will not rest till he is even with him, wife for wife, but, in the play, no attempt at Desdemona's seduction is made. Iago does not make an assault on her virtue himself, he does not encourage Cassio to make one, and he even prevents Roderigo from getting anywhere near her.

Finally, one who seriously desires personal revenge desires to reveal himself. The revenger's greatest satisfaction is to be able to tell his victim to his face—"You thought you were all-powerful and untouchable and could injure me with impunity. Now you see that you were wrong. Perhaps you have forgotten what you did; let me have the pleasure of reminding you."

When at the end of the play, Othello asks Iago in bewilderment why he has thus ensnared his soul and body, if his real motive were revenge for having been cuckolded or unjustly denied promotion, he could have said so, instead of refusing to explain.

In Act II, Scene I, occur seven lines which, taken in isolation, seem to make Iago a seriously jealous man.

> Now I do love her too,
> Not out of absolute lust (though peradventure
> I stand accountant for as great a sin)
> But partly led to diet my revenge
> For that I do suspect the lusty Moor
> Hath leaped into my seat; the thought whereof
> Doth like a poisonous mineral gnaw my vitals.

But if spoken by an actor with serious passion, these lines are completely at variance with the rest of the play, including Iago's other lines on the same subject.

> And it is thought abroad, that twixt my sheets
> He's done my office: I know not if't be true
> Yet I, for mere suspicion in that kind,
> Will do, as if for surety.

It is not inconceivable, given the speed at which he wrote, that, at some point in the composition of *Othello*, Shakespeare considered making Iago seriously jealous and, like his prototype in Cinthio, a would-be seducer of Desdemona, and that, when he arrived at his final conception of Iago, he overlooked the incompatibility of the *poisonous mineral* and the *wife-for-wife* passages with the rest.

In trying to understand Iago's character one should begin, I believe, by asking why Shakespeare should have gone to the trouble of inventing Roderigo, a character who has no prototype in Cinthio. From a stage director's point of view, Roderigo is a headache. In the first act we learn that Brabantio had forbidden him the house, from which we must conclude that Desdemona had met him and disliked him as much as her father. In the second act, in order that the audience shall know that he has come to Cyrpus, Roderigo has to arrive on the same ship as Desdemona, yet she shows no embarrassment in his presence. Indeed, she and everybody else, except Iago, seem unaware of his existence, for Iago is the only person who ever speaks a word to him. Presumably, he has some official position in the army, but we are never told what it is. His entrances and exits are those of a puppet: whenever Iago has company, he obligingly disappears, and whenever Iago is alone and wishes to speak to him, he comes in again immediately.

Moreover, so far as Iago's plot is concerned, there is nothing Roderigo does which Iago could not do better without him. He could easily have found another means, like an anonymous letter, of informing Brabantio of Desdemona's elopement and, for picking a quarrel with a drunken Cassio, he has, on his own admission, other means handy.

> Three lads of Cyprus, noble swelling spirits
> That hold their honours in a wary distance,
> The very elements of this warlike isle
> Have I to-night flustered with flowing cups.

Since Othello has expressly ordered him to kill Cassio; Iago could have murdered him without fear of legal investigation. Instead, he not only chooses as an accomplice a man whom he is cheating and whose suspicions he has constantly to allay, but also a man who is plainly inefficient as a murderer and also holds incriminating evidence against him.

A man who is seriously bent on revenge does not take unnecessary risks nor confide in anyone whom he cannot trust or do without. Emilia is not, as in Cinthio, Iago's willing accomplice, so that, in asking her to steal the handkerchief, Iago is running a risk, but it is a risk he has to take. By involving Roderigo in his plot, he makes discovery and his own ruin almost certain. It is a law of drama that, by the final curtain, all secrets, guilty or innocent, shall have been revealed so that all, on both sides of the footlights, know who did or did not do what, but usually the guilty are exposed either because, like Edmund, they repent and confess or because of events which they could not reasonably have foreseen. Don John could not have foreseen that Dogberry and Verges would overhear Borachio's conversation, nor Iachimo that Pisanio would disobey Posthumus' order to kill Imogen, nor King Claudius the intervention of a ghost.

Had he wished, Shakespeare could easily have contrived a similar kind of exposure for Iago. Instead, by giving Roderigo the role he does, he makes Iago as a plotter someone devoid of ordinary worldly common sense.

One of Shakespeare's intentions was, I believe, to indicate that Iago desires self-destruction as much as he desires the destruction of others but, before elaborating on this, let us consider Iago's treatment of Roderigo, against whom he has no grievance—it is he who is injuring Roderigo—as a clue to his treatment of Othello and Cassio.

When we first see Iago and Roderigo together, the situation is like that in a Ben Johnson comedy—a clever rascal is gulling a rich fool who deserves to be gulled because his desire is no more moral than that of the more intelligent avowed rogue who cheats him out of his money. Were the play a comedy, Roderigo would finally realize that he had been cheated but would not dare appeal to the law because, if the whole truth were made public, he would cut a ridiculous or shameful figure. But, as the play proceeds, it becomes clear that Iago is not simply after Roderigo's money, a rational motive, but that his main game is Roderigo's moral corruption, which is irrational because Roderigo has given him no cause to desire his moral ruin. When the play opens, Roderigo is shown as a spoiled weakling, but no worse. It may be foolish of him to hope to win Desdemona's affection by gifts and to employ a go-between, but his conduct is not in itself immoral. Nor is he, like Cloten in *Cymbeline*, a brute who regards women as mere objects of lust. He is genuinely shocked as well as disappointed when he learns of Desdemona's marriage, but continues to admire her as a woman full of most blessed condition. Left to himself, he would have had a good bawl, and given her up. But Iago will not let him alone. By insisting that Desdemona is seducible and that his real rival is not Othello but Cassio, he brings Roderigo to entertain the idea, originally foreign to him, of becoming a seducer and of helping Iago to ruin Cassio. Iago had had the pleasure of making a timid conventional man become aggressive and criminal. Cassio beats up Roderigo. Again, at this point, had he been left to himself, he would have gone no further, but Iago will not let him alone until he consents to murder Cassio, a deed which is contrary to his nature, for he is not only timid but also incapable of passionate hatred.

> I have no great devotion to the deed:
> And yet he has given me satisfying reasons.
> 'Tis but a man gone.

Why should Iago want to do this to Roderigo? To me, the clue to this and to all Iago's conduct is to be found in Emilia's comment when she picks up the handkerchief.

> My wayward husband hath a hundred times
> Wooed me to steal it . . .
> > what he'll do with it
> Heaven knows, not I,
> I nothing but to please his fantasy.

As his wife, Emilia must know Iago better than anybody else does. She does not know, any more than the others, that he is malevolent, but she does know that her husband is addicted to practical jokes. What Shakespeare gives us in Iago is a portrait of a practical joker of a peculiarly appalling kind, and perhaps the best way of approaching the play is by a general consideration of the Practical Joker.

II

Social relations, as distinct from the brotherhood of a community, are only possible if there is a common social agreement as to which actions or words are to be regarded as serious means to a rational end and which are to be regarded as play, as ends in themselves. In our culture, for example, a policeman must be able to distinguish between a murderous street fight and a boxing match, or a listener between a radio play in which war is declared and a radio news-broadcast announcing a declaration of war.

Social life also presupposes that we may believe what we are told unless we have reason to suppose, either that our informant has a serious motive for deceiving us, or that he is mad and incapable himself of distinguishing between truth and falsehood. If a stranger tries to sell me shares in a gold mine, I shall be a fool if I do not check up on his statements before parting with my money, and if another tells me that he has talked with little men who came out of a flying saucer, I shall assume that he is crazy. But if I ask a stranger the way to the station, I shall assume that his answer is truthful to the best of his knowledge, because I cannot imagine what motive he could have for misdirecting me.

Practical jokes are a demonstration that the distinction between seriousness and play is not a law of nature but a social convention which can be broken, and that a man does not always require a serious motive for deceiving another.

Two men, dressed as city employees, block off a busy street and start digging it up. The traffic cop, motorists and pedestrians assume that this familiar scene has a practical explanation—a water main or an electric cable is being repaired—and make no attempt to use the street. In fact, however, the two diggers are private citizens in disguise who have no business there.

All practical jokes are anti-social acts, but this does not necessarily mean that all practical jokes are immoral. A moral practical joke exposes some flaw in society which is a hindrance to a real community or brotherhood. That it should be possible for two private individuals to dig up a street without being stopped is a just criticism of the impersonal life of a large city where most people are strangers to each other, not brothers; in a village where all the inhabitants know each other personally, the deception would be impossible.

A real community, as distinct from social life, is only possible between persons whose idea of themselves and others is real, not fantastic. There is, therefore, another class of practical jokes which is aimed at particular individuals with the reformatory intent of de-intoxicating them from their illusions. This kind of joke is one of the stock devices of comedy. The deceptions practiced on Falstaff by Mistress page, Mistress Ford and Dame Quickly, or by Octavian on Baron Ochs are possible because these two gentlemen have a fantastic idea of themselves as lady-charmers; the result of the jokes played upon them is that they are brought to a state of self-knowledge and this brings mutual forgiveness and true brotherhood. Similarly, the mock deaths of Hero and of Hermione are ways of bringing home to Claudio and to Leontes how badly they have behaved and of testing the genuineness of their repentance.

All practical jokes, friendly, harmless or malevolent, involve deception, but not all deceptions are practical jokes. The two men digging up the street, for example, might have been two burglars who wished to recover some swag which they knew to be buried there. But, in that case, having found what they were looking for, they would have departed quietly and never been heard of again, whereas, if they are practical jokers, they must reveal afterwards what they have done or the joke will be lost. The practical joker must not only deceive but also, when he has succeeded, unmask and reveal the truth to his victims. The satisfaction of the practical joker is the look of astonishment on the faces of others when they learn that all the time they were convinced that they were thinking and acting on their own initiative, they were actually the puppets of another's will. Thus, though his jokes may be harmless in themselves and extremely funny, there is something slightly sinister about every practical joker, for they betray him as someone who likes to play God behind the scenes. Unlike the ordinary ambitious man who strives for a dominant position in public and enjoys giving orders and seeing others obey them, the practical joker desires to make others obey him without being aware of his existence until the moment of his theophany when he says: "Behold the God whose puppets you have been and behold, he does not look like a god but is a human being just like yourselves." The success of a practical joker depends upon his accurate estimate of the weaknesses of others, their ignorances, their social reflexes, their unquestioned presuppositions, their obsessive desires, and even the most harmless practical joke is an expression of the joker's contempt for those he deceives.

But, in most cases, behind the joker's contempt for others lies something else, a feeling of self-insufficiency, of a self lacking in authentic feelings and desires of its own. The normal human being may have a fantastic notion of himself, but he believes in it; he thinks he knows who he is and what he wants so that he demands recognition by others of the value he puts upon himself and must inform others of what he desires if they are to satisfy them.

But the self of the practical joker is unrelated to his joke. He manipulates others but, when he finally reveals his identity, his victims learn nothing about his nature, only something about their own; they know how it was possible for them to be deceived but only why he chose to deceive them. The only answer that any practical joker can give to the question: "Why did you do this?" is Iago's: "Demand me nothing. What you know, you know."

In fooling others, it cannot be said that the practical joker satisfies any concrete desire of his nature; he has only demonstrated the weaknesses of others and all he can now do, once he has revealed his existence, is to bow and retire from the stage. He is only related to others, that is, so long as they are unaware of his existence; once they are made aware of it, he cannot fool them again, and the relation is broken off.

The practical joker despises his victims, but at the same time he envies them because their desires, however childish and mistaken, are real to them, whereas he has no desire which he can call his own. His goal, to make game of others, makes his existence absolutely dependent upon theirs; when he is alone, he is a nullity. Iago's self-description, *I am not what I am,* is correct and the negation of the Divine *I am that I am.* If the word motive is given its normal meaning of a positive purpose of the self like sex, money, glory, etc., then the practical joker is without motive. Yet the professional practical joker is certainly driven, like a gambler, to his activity, but the drive is negative, a fear of lacking a concrete self, of being nobody. In any practical joker to whom playing such jokes is a passion, there is always an element of malice, a projection of his self-hatred onto others, and in the ultimate case of the absolute practical joker, this is projected onto all created things. Iago's statement, "I am not what I am," is given its proper explanation in the *Credo* which Boito wrote for him in his libretto for Verdi's opera.

> Credo in un Dio crudel che m'ha creato
> Simile a se, e che nell'ira io nomo.
> Dall viltà d'un germe e d'un atomo
> Vile son nato,
> Son scellerto
> Perchè son uomo:
> E sento il fango originario in me
> E credo l'uom gioco d'iniqua sorte
> Dal germe della culla
> Al verme dell'avel.

Vien dopo tanto irrision la Morte
E poi? La Morte e il Nulla.

Equally applicable to Iago is Valéry's "Ebauche d'un serpent." The serpent speaks to
God the Creatur thus

O Vanité! Cause Première
Celui qui règne dans les Cieux
D'une voix qui fut la lumière
Ouvrit l'univers spacieux.
Comme las de son pur spectacle
Dieu lui-même a rompu l'obstacle
De sa parfaite éternité;
Il se fit Celui qui dissipe
En conséquences son Principe,
En étoiles son Unité.

And of himself thus

Je suis Celui qui modifie

the ideal motto, surely, for Iago's coat of arms.

Since the ultimate goal of Iago is nothingness, he must not only destroy others,
but himself as well. Once Othello and Desdemona are dead his "occupation's
gone."

To convey this to an audience demands of the actor who plays the role the
most violent contrast in the way he acts when Iago is with others and the way he
acts when he is left alone. With others, he must display every virtuoso trick of
dramatic technique for which great actors are praised, perfect control of movement, gesture, expression, diction, melody and timing, and the ability to play every
kind of role, for there are as many "honest" Iagos as there are characters with
whom he speaks, a Roderigo Iago, a Cassio Iago, an Othello Iago, a Desdemona
Iago, etc. When he is alone, on the other hand, the actor must display every
technical fault for which bad actors are criticized. He must deprive himself of all
stage presence, and he must deliver the lines of his soliloquies in such a way that he
makes nonsense of them. His voice must lack expression, his delivery must be
atrocious, he must pause where the verse calls for no pauses, accentuate unimportant words, etc.

III

If Iago is so alienated from nature and society that he has no relation to time
and place—he could turn up anywhere at any time—his victims are citizens of
Shakespeare's Venice. To be of dramatic interest, a character must to some degree
be at odds with the society of which he is a member, but his estrangement is
normally an estrangement from a specific social situation.

Shakespeare's Venice is a mercantile society, the purpose of which is not
military glory but the acquisition of wealth. However, human nature being what it
is, like any other society, it has enemies, trade rivals, pirates, etc., against whom it

must defend itself, if necessary by force. Since a mercantile society regards warfare as a disagreeable, but unfortunately sometimes unavoidable, activity and not, like a feudal aristocracy, as a form of play, it replaces the old feudal levy by a paid professional army, nonpolitical employees of the State, to whom fighting is their specialized job.

In a professional army, a soldier's military rank is not determined by his social status as a civilian, but by his military efficiency. Unlike the feudal knight who has a civilian home from which he is absent from time to time but to which, between campaigns, he regularly returns, the home of the professional soldier is an army camp and he must go wherever the State sends him. Othello's account of his life as a soldier, passed in exotic landscapes and climates, would have struck Hotspur as unnatural, unchivalrous and no fun.

A professional army has its own experiences and its own code of values which are different from those of civilians. In *Othello*, we are shown two societies, that of the city of Venice proper and that of the Venetian army. The only character who, because he is equally estranged from both, can simulate being equally at home in both, is Iago. With army folk he can play the blunt soldier, but in his first scene with Desdemona upon their arrival in Cyprus, he speaks like a character out of *Love's Labour's Lost*. Cassio's comment

Madam, you may relish him more in the soldier than the scholar

is provoked by envy. Iago has excelled him in the euphuistic flirtatious style of conversation which he considers his forte. Roderigo does not feel at home, either with civilians or with soldiers. He lacks the charm which makes a man a success with the ladies, and the physical courage and heartiness which make a man popular in an army mess. The sympathetic aspect of his character, until Iago destroys it, is a certain humility; he knows that he is a person of no consequence. But for Iago, he would have remained a sort of Bertie Wooster, and one suspects that the notion that Desdemona's heart might be softened by expensive presents was not his own but suggested to him by Iago.

In deceiving Roderigo, Iago has to overcome his consciousness of his inadequacy, to persuade him that he could be what he knows he is not, charming, brave, successful. Consequently, to Roderigo and, I think, to Roderigo only, Iago tells direct lies. The lie may be on a point of fact, as when he tells Roderigo that Othello and Desdemona are not returning to Venice but going to Mauritania, or a lie about the future, for it is obvious that, even if Desdemona is seducible, Roderigo will never be the man. I am inclined to think that the story Iago tells Roderigo about his disappointment over the lieutenancy is a deliberate fabrication. One notices, for example, that he contradicts himself. At first he claims that Othello had appointed Cassio in spite of the request of three great ones of the city who had recommended Iago, but then a few lines later, he says

Preferment goes by letter and affection,
Not by the old gradation where each second
Stood heir to the first.

In deceiving Cassio and Othello, on the other hand, Iago has to deal with characters who consciously think well of themselves but are unconsciously insecure. With them, therefore, his tactics are different; what he says to them is always possibly true.

Cassio is a ladies' man, that is to say, a man who feels most at home in feminine company where his looks and good manners make him popular, but is ill at ease in the company of his own sex because he is unsure of his masculinity. In civilian life he would be perfectly happy, but circumstances have made him a soldier and he has been forced by his profession into a society which is predominantly male. Had he been born a generation earlier, he would never have found himself in the army at all, but changes in the technique of warfare demand of soldiers, not only the physical courage and aggressiveness which the warrior has always needed, but also intellectual gifts. The Venetian army now needs mathematicians, experts in the science of gunnery. But in all ages, the typical military mentality is conservative and resents the intellectual expert.

> A fellow
> That never set a squadron in the field
> Nor the division of a battle knows
> More than a spinster ... mere prattle without practise
> Is all his soldiership

is a criticism which has been heard in every army mess in every war. Like so many people who cannot bear to feel unpopular and therefore repress their knowledge that they are, Cassio becomes quarrelsome when drunk, for alcohol releases his suppressed resentment at not being admired by his comrades in arms and his wish to prove that he is what he is not, as "manly" as they are. It is significant that, when he sobers up, his regret is not that he has behaved badly by his own standards but that he has lost his reputation. The advice which Iago then gives him, to get Desdemona to plead for him with Othello, is good advice in itself, for Desdemona obviously likes him, but it is also exactly the advice a character-type like Cassio will be most willing to listen to, for feminine society is where he feels most at home.

Emilia informs Cassio that, on her own initiative, Desdemona has already spoken on his behalf and that Othello has said he will take the safest occasion by the front to restore him to his post. Hearing this, many men would have been content to leave matters as they were, but Cassio persists: the pleasure of a heart-to-heart talk with a lady about his fascinating self is too tempting.

While he is talking to Desdemona, Othello is seen approaching and she says:

Stay and hear me speak.

Again, many men would have done so, but Cassio's uneasiness with his own sex, particularly when he is in disgrace, is too strong and he sneaks away, thus providing Iago with his first opportunity to make an insinuation.

Cassio is a ladies' man, not a seducer. With women of his own class, what he enjoys is socialized eroticism; he would be frightened of serious personal passion.

For physical sex he goes to prostitutes and when, unexpectedly, Bianca falls in love with him, like many of his kind, he behaves like a cad and brags of his conquest to others. Though he does not know who the owner of the handkerchief actually is, he certainly knows that Bianca will think that it belongs to another woman, and to ask her to copy it is gratuitous cruelty. His smiles, gestures and remarks about Bianca to Iago are insufferable in themselves; to Othello, who knows that he is talking about a woman, though he is mistaken as to her identity, they are an insult which only Cassio's death can avenge.

In Cinthio nothing is said about the Moor's color or religion, but Shakespeare has made Othello a black Negro who has been baptized.

No doubt there are differences between color prejudice in the twentieth century and color prejudice in the seventeenth and probably few of Shakespeare's audience had ever seen a Negro, but the slave trade was already flourishing and the Elizabethans were certainly no innocents to whom a Negro was simply a comic exotic. Lines like

> ... an old black ram

is tupping your white ewe ...
The gross clasps of a lascivious Moor ...
What delight shall she have to look on the devil

are evidence that the paranoid fantasies of the white man in which the Negro appears as someone who is at one and the same time less capable of self-control and more sexually potent than himself, fantasies with which, alas, we are only too familiar, already were rampant in Shakespeare's time.

The Venice of both *The Merchant of Venice* and *Othello* is a cosmopolitan society in which there are two kinds of social bond between its members, the bond of economic interest and the bond of personal friendship, which may coincide, run parallel with each other or conflict, and both plays are concerned with an extreme case of conflict.

Venice needs financiers to provide capital and it needs the best general it can hire to defend it; it so happens that the most skillful financier it can find is a Jew and the best general a Negro, neither of whom the majority are willing to accept as a brother.

Though both are regarded as outsiders by the Venetian community, Othello's relation to it differs from Shylock's. In the first play, Shylock rejects the Gentile community as firmly as the Gentile community rejects him; he is just as angry when he hears that Jessica has married Lorenzo as Brabantio is about Desdemona's elopement with Othello. In the second place, while the profession of usurer, however socially useful, is regarded as ignoble, the military profession, even though the goal of a mercantile society is not military glory, is still highly admired and, in addition, for the sedentary civilians who govern the city, it has a romantic exotic glamour which it cannot have in a feudal society in which fighting is a familiar shared experience.

Thus no Venetian would dream of spitting on Othello and, so long as there is no question of his marrying into the family, Brabantio is delighted to entertain the famous general and listen to his stories of military life. In the army, Othello is accustomed to being obeyed and treated with the respect due to his rank and, on his rare visits to the city, he is treated by the white aristocracy as someone important and interesting. Outwardly, nobody treats him as an outsider as they treat Shylock. Consequently, it is easy for him to persuade himself that he is accepted as a brother and when Desdemona accepts him as a husband, he seems to have proof of this.

It is painful to hear him say

But that I love the gentle Desdemona
I would not my unhoused free condition
Put into circumscription or confine
For the sea's worth

for the condition of the outsider is always unhoused and free. He does not or will not recognize that Brabantio's view of the match

If such actions may have passage free,
Bond-slaves and pagans shall our statesmen be

is shared by all his fellow senators, and the arrival of news about the Turkish fleet prevents their saying so because their need of Othello's military skill is too urgent for them to risk offending him.

If one compares *Othello* with the other plays in which Shakespeare treats the subject of male jealousy, *The Winter's Tale* and *Cymbeline*, one notices that Othello's jealousy is of a peculiar kind.

Leontes is a classical case of paranoid sexual jealousy due to repressed homosexual feelings. He has absolutely no evidence that Hermione and Polixenes have committed adultery and his entire court are convinced of their innocence, but he is utterly possessed by his fantasy. As he says to Hermione: "Your actions are my dreams." But, mad as he is, "the twice-nine changes of the Watery Starre" which Polixenes has spent at the Bohemian court, make the act of adultery physically possible so that, once the notion has entered his head, neither Hermione nor Polixenes nor the court can prove that it is false. Hence the appeal to the Oracle.

Posthumus is perfectly sane and is convinced against his will that Imogen has been unfaithful because Iachimo offers him apparently irrefutable evidence that adultery has taken place.

But both the mad Leontes and the sane Posthumus react in the same way: "My wife has been unfaithful; therefore she must be killed and forgotten." That is to say, it is only as husbands that their lives are affected. As king of Bohemia, as a warrior, they function as if nothing has happened.

In *Othello*, thanks to Iago's manipulations, Cassio and Desdemona behave in a way which would make it not altogether unreasonable for Othello to suspect that they were in love with each other, but the time factor rules out the possibility of adultery having been actually committed. Some critics have taken the double time in the play to be merely a dramaturgical device for speeding the action which the audience in the theatre will never notice. I believe, however, that Shakespeare meant the audience to notice it as, in *The Merchant of Venice,* he meant them to notice the discrepancy between Belmont time and Venice time.

If Othello had simply been jealous of the feelings for Cassio he imagined Desdemona to have, he would have been sane enough, guilty at worst of a lack of trust in his wife. But Othello is not merely jealous of feelings which might exist; he demands proof of an act which could not have taken place, and the effect on him of believing in this physical impossibility goes far beyond wishing to kill her: it is not only his wife who has betrayed him but the whole universe; life has become meaningless, his occupation is gone.

This reaction might be expected if Othello and Desdemona were a pair like Romeo and Juliet or Antony and Cleopatra whose love was an all-absorbing Tristan-Isolde kind of passion, but Shakespeare takes care to inform us that it was not.

When Othello asks leave to take Desdemona with him to Cyprus, he stresses the spiritual element in his love.

> I therefore beg it not
> To please the palate of my appetite
> Nor to comply with heat, the young affects
> In me defunct, and proper satisfaction,
> But to be free and bounteous to her mind.

Though the imagery in which he expresses his jealously is sexual—what other kind of images could he use?—Othello's marriage is important to him less as a sexual relationship than as a symbol of being loved and accepted as a person, a brother in the Venetian community. The monster in his own mind too hideous to be shown is the fear he has so far repressed that he is only valued for his social usefulness to the City. But for his occupation, he would be treated as a black barbarian.

The overcredulous, overgood-natured character which, as Iago tells us, Othello had always displayed is a telltale symptom. He had *had* to be overcredulous in order to compensate for his repressed suspicions. Both in his happiness at the beginning of the play and in his cosmic despair later, Othello reminds one more of Timon of Athens than of Leontes.

Since what really matters to Othello is that Desdemona should love him as the person he really is, Iago has only to get him to suspect that she does not, to release the repressed fears and resentments of a lifetime, and the question of what she has done or not done is irrelevant.

Iago treats Othello as an analyst treats a patient except that, of course, his intention is to kill not to cure. Everything he says is designed to bring to Othello's consciousness what he has already guessed is there. Accordingly, he has no need to tell lies. Even his speech, "I lay with Cassio lately," can be a truthful account of something which actually happened: from what we know of Cassio, he might very well have such a dream as Iago reports. Even when he has worked Othello up to a degree of passion where he would risk nothing by telling a direct lie, his answer is equivocal and its interpretation is left to Othello.

> OTHELLO: What hath he said?
> IAGO: Faith that he did—I know not what he did.
> OTHELLO: But what?
> IAGO: Lie—
> OTHELLO: With her?
> IAGO: With her, on her, what you will.

Nobody can offer Leontes absolute proof that his jealousy is baseless; similarly, as Iago is careful to point out, Othello can have no proof that Desdemona really is the person she seems to be.

Iago makes his first decisive impression when, speaking as a Venetian with firsthand knowledge of civilian life, he draws attention to Desdemona's hoodwinking of her father.

> IAGO: I would not have your free and noble nature
> Out of self-bounty be abused, look to't:
> I know our country disposition well:
> In Venice they do let God see the pranks
> They dare not show their husbands: their best conscience
> Is not to leave't undone but keep't unknown.
> OTHELLO: Dost thou say so?
> IAGO: She did deceive her father, marrying you:
> And when she seemed to shake and fear your looks,
> She loved them most.
> OTHELLO: And so she did.
> IAGO: Why, go to then!
> She that so young could give out such a seeming
> To seal her father's eyes up, close as oak.
> He thought 'twas witchcraft.

And a few lines later, he refers directly to the color difference.

> Not to affect many proposed matches,
> Of her own clime, complexion, and degree,
> Whereto we see in all things nature tends,
> Foh! one may smell in such a will most rank,
> Foul disproportions, thoughts unnatural.
> But pardon me: I do not in position
> Distinctly speak of her, though I may fear
> Her will, recoiling to her better judgment
> May fall to match you with her country-forms,
> And happily repent.

Once Othello allows himself to suspect that Desdemona may not be the person she seems, she cannot allay the suspicion by speaking the truth but she can appear to confirm it by telling a lie. Hence the catastrophic effect when she denies having lost the handkerchief.

If Othello cannot trust her, then he can trust nobody and nothing, and precisely what she has done is not important. In the scene where he pretends that the Castle is a brothel of which Emilia is the Madam, he accuses Desdemona, not of adultery with Cassio, but of nameless orgies.

> DESDEMONA: Alas, what ignorant sin have I committed?
> OTHELLO: Was this fair paper, this most goodly book
> Made to write whore upon. What committed?
> Committed? O thou public commoner,
> I should make very forges of my cheeks
> That would to cinders burn up modesty
> Did I but speak thy deeds.

And, as Mr. Eliot has pointed out, in his farewell speech his thoughts are not on Desdemona at all but upon his relation to Venice, and he ends by identifying himself with another outsider, the Moslem Turk who beat a Venetian and traduced the state.

Everybody must pity Desdemona, but I cannot bring myself to like her. Her determination to marry Othello—it was she who virtually did the proposing— seems the romantic crush of a silly schoolgirl rather than a mature affection; it is Othello's adventures, so unlike the civilian life she knows, which captivate her rather than Othello as a person. He may not have practiced witchcraft, but, in fact, she is spellbound. And despite all Brabantio's prejudices, her deception of her own father makes an unpleasant impression: Shakespeare does not allow us to forget that the shock of the marriage kills him.

Then, she seems more aware than is agreeable of the honor she has done Othello by becoming his wife. When Iago tells Cassio that "our General's wife is now the General" and, soon afterwards, soliloquizes

> His soul is so enfettered to her love
> That she may make, unmake, do what she list
> Even as her appetite shall play the god
> With his weak function

he is, no doubt, exaggerating, but there is much truth in what he says. Before Cassio speaks to her, she has already discussed him with her husband and learned that he is to be reinstated as soon as is opportune. A sensible wife would have told Cassio this and left matters alone. In continuing to badger Othello, she betrays a desire to prove to herself and to Cassio that she can make her husband do as she pleases.

is frightened because she is suddenly confronted with a man whose sensibility and superstitions are alien to her.

Though her relation with Cassio is perfectly innocent, one cannot but share Iago's doubts as to the durability of the marriage. It is worth noting that, in the willow-song scene with Emilia, she speaks with admiration of Lodovico and then turns to the topic of adultery. Of course, she discusses this in general terms and is shocked by Emilia's attitude, but she does discuss the subject and she does listen to what Emilia has to say about husbands and wives. It is as if she had suddenly realized that she had made a *mésalliance* and that the sort of man she ought to have married was someone of her own class and color like Lodovico. Given a few more years of Othello and of Emilia's influence and she might well, one feels, have taken a lover.

IV

And so one comes back to where one started, to Iago, the sole agent in the play. A play, as Shakespeare said, is a mirror held up to nature. This particular mirror bears the date 1604, but, when we look into it, the face that confronts us is our own in the middle of the twentieth century. We hear Iago say the same words and see him do the same things as an Elizabethan audience heard and saw, but what they mean to us cannot be exactly the same. To his first audience and even, maybe, to his creator, Iago appeared to be just another Machiavellian villain who might exist in real life but with whom one would never dream of identifying oneself. To us, I think, he is a much more alarming figure; we cannot hiss at him when he appears as we can hiss at the villain in a Western movie because none of us can honestly say that he does not understand how such a wicked person can exist. For is not Iago, the practical joker, a parabolic figure for the autonomous pursuit of scientific knowledge through experiment which we all, whether we are scientists or not, take for granted as natural and right?

As Nietzsche said, experimental science is the last flower of asceticism. The investigator must discard all his feelings, hopes and fears as a human person and reduce himself to a disembodied observer of events upon which he passes no value judgment. Iago is an ascetic. "Love" he says, "is merely a lust of the blood, and a permission of the will."

The knowledge sought by science is only one kind of knowledge. Another kind is that implied by the Biblical phrase, "Then Adam knew Eve, his wife," and it is this kind I still mean when I say, "I know John Smith very well." I cannot know in this sense without being known in return. If I know John Smith well, he must also know me well.

But, in the scientific sense of knowledge, I can only know that which does not and cannot know me. Feeling unwell, I go to my doctor who examines me, says "You have Asian flu," and gives me an injection. The Asian virus is as unaware of my doctor's existence as his victims are of a practical joker.

Further, to-know in the scientific sense means, ultimately, to-have-power-over. To the degree that human beings are authentic persons, unique and self-creating, they cannot be scientifically known. But human beings are not pure persons like angels; they are also biological organisms, almost identical in their functioning, and, to a greater or lesser degree, they are neurotic, that is to say, less free than they imagine because of fears and desires of which they have no personal knowledge but could and ought to have. Hence, it is always possible to reduce human beings to the status of things which are completely scientifically knowable and completely controllable.

This can be done by direct action on their bodies with drugs, lobotomies, deprivation of sleep, etc. The difficulty about this method is that your victims will know that you are trying to enslave them and, since nobody wishes to be a slave, they will object, so that it can only be practiced upon minorities like prisoners and lunatics who are physically incapable of resisting.

The other method is to play on the fears and desires of which you are aware and they are not until they enslave themselves. In this case, concealment of your real intention is not only possible but essential for, if people know they are being played upon, they will not believe what you say or do what you suggest. An advertisement based on snob appeal, for example, can only succeed with people who are unaware that they are snobs and that their snobbish feelings are being appealed to and to whom, therefore, your advertisement seems as honest as Iago seems to Othello.

Iago's treatment of Othello conforms to Bacon's definition of scientific enquiry as putting Nature to the Question. If a member of the audience were to interrupt the play and ask him: "What are you doing?" could not Iago answer with a boyish giggle, "Nothing. I'm only trying to find out what Othello is really like"? And we must admit that his experiment is highly successful. By the end of the play he does know the scientific truth about the object to which he has reduced Othello. That is what makes his parting shot, "What you know, you know," so terrifying for, by then, Othello has become a thing, incapable of knowing anything.

And why shouldn't Iago do this? After all, he has certainly acquired knowledge. What makes it impossible for us to condemn him self-righteously is that, in our culture, we have all accepted the notion that the right to know is absolute and unlimited. The gossip column is one side of the medal; the cobalt bomb the other. We are quite prepared to admit that, while food and sex are good in themselves, an uncontrolled pursuit of either is not, but it is difficult for us to believe that intellectual curiosity is a desire like any other, and to realize that correct knowledge and truth are not identical. To apply a categorical imperative to knowing, so that, instead of asking, "What can I know?" we ask, "What, at this moment, am I meant to know?"—to entertain the possibility that the only knowledge which can be true for us is the knowledge we can live up to—that seems to all of us crazy and almost immoral. But, in that case, who are we to say to Iago—"No, you mustn't."

Madeleine Doran
IAGO'S ''IF''

Very soon after the opening of what is often called the temptation scene in *Othello*, Cassio, who has been talking with Desdemona, walks away as Othello and Iago enter, and this interchange takes place:

> IAGO: Ha! I like not that.
> OTH.:   What dost thou say?
> IAGO: Nothing, my lord; or if—I know not what.
> OTH.: Was not that Cassio parted from my wife?
> IAGO: Cassio, my lord? No, sure, I cannot think it . . .   [III.iii.35–38][1]

Iago's "if" is the great central *if* in the play. It is vague and incomplete, with neither condition nor conclusion stated. It is the small hole in the dike which, persistently widened by Iago, will let in the destroying flood. If Cassio's stealing away from Desdemona means something sinister, if Desdemona is not a faithful wife, if Cassio is not a true friend, if certainties are not certainties, chaos is come again. For Othello cannot entertain *if*s. He cannot live as Hamlet does, weighing possibilities, holding hypotheses, thinking of consequences. To be once in doubt is once to be resolved. This casual but calculated "if" has been prepared for by others in the play, and will be followed by others. Indeed, if we look closely, as I propose we do, we see that conditional sentences (by no means all Iago's) mark the stages of the action. When they express doubt they are disruptive of the assurance expressed in Othello's unqualified declarative sentences. Under Iago's *if*s, Othello's verse turns to prose and even his syntax goes momentarily to pieces. The conditionals of possibility are verticals coming up from below, first touching, then penetrating, the horizontal movement, distorting and disrupting it. They are like molten rock which, thrusting itself up from below into old sedimentary beds, heaves up, twists, cracks, and dislimns their level planes.

I propose to look at the syntax of *Othello*, for it is in the interplay of assertion

From *The Drama of the Renaissance: Essays for Leicester Bradner*, edited by Elmer M. Blistein (Providence: Brown University Press, 1970), pp. 69–99.

and negation that the bare bones of a fable are given dramatic life and sensibility. Syntax is the most intimate way to show movement of mind; it is the dramatist's most refined tool in shaping monologue or dialogue. Revelation of character may or may not be in question; always important is the dramatic structure which the syntax helps to shape. In *Othello,* as in every one of his plays, Shakespeare uses syntax to create special effects appropriate to particular situations—as, for instance, in the dominant syntax of exclamation, command, and question in the three scenes of public disturbance begun by Iago (I.i and ii; II.iii; V.i). But in this play (as in *Lear* and perhaps others), Shakespeare does something more: he uses syntax, I believe, to inform in a subtle way his larger dramatic structure. It is with this second use that I shall be principally concerned.

There are two large syntactical patterns, I would say, which operate in the drama as a whole. These are chiefly sentences expressive of possibility in varying degrees (that is, conditional sentences of varying structure and mood) and operative within a framework of sentences expressive of certainty (mainly declarative sentences, not greatly complicated, in the indicative mood). The conditional sentences function in the way they do because they are intimately allied with the way in which action in the play is motivated and understood. The nonconditional declarative pattern must be looked at first, because it is the ground which the conditional pattern partly supports, partly disturbs.

The dominant voices in the play are Othello's and Iago's. If one takes Othello's love of Desdemona as the primary theme of the play in a major key, one may perhaps call Othello's directness and simplicity the tonic chord. His normal sentences are declarative, in the indicative mood, often simple in construction; if compound or complex, they are not greatly extended or involved. This is the way he is introduced to us when Iago rushes to him to warn him that Brabantio and his kin are coming to arrest him: " 'Tis better as it is"; "I fetch my life and being / From men of royal siege"; "Not I. I must be found" (I.ii.6, 21–22, 30). The assertions which help establish Othello's ethos[2] are not hedged with concessions and doubts. They are candid but brief, not emphatic because they need not be; they imply a natural confidence in himself, a confidence born of an innate self-respect and based on experience in the tented field: "The world is thus and so; I am thus and thus; I shall do what I need to do." He moves with quiet authority into the military man's imperatives when necessary: "Keep up your bright swords, for the dew will rust them.... Hold your hands, / Both you of my inclining and the rest" (I.ii.59, 81–82). Or, more sharply when disorder is threatened, as in the tumult on Cyprus: "Hold for your lives!"; "Silence that dreadful bell! ... What's the matter?"; "Give me answer to't" (II.iii.165, 175–76, 196).

At the beginning, Othello has the same confidence in his love for Desdemona and in hers for him as in his profession; and his affirmations are as simple and frank:

> That I have ta'en away this old man's daughter,
> It is most true; true I have married her.   [I.iii.78–79]

> She lov'd me for the dangers I had pass'd,
> And I lov'd her that she did pity them.   [I.iii.167–68]

It is a confidence truly placed. Desdemona's declarations of love are as direct and as unqualified as his.

I am hitherto your daughter. But here's my husband.   [I.iii.185]

> My heart's subdu'd
> Even to the very quality of my lord.
> I saw Othello's visage in his mind,
> And to his honours and his valiant parts
> Did I my soul and fortunes consecrate.   [I.iii.251–55]

There are, of course, normal variations of sentence pattern in Othello's speech, which is always sensitively responsive to any immediate situation. But we may take the uncomplicated sentences in the indicative mode, sometimes re-enforced by the imperative of wish or command, as the warp of his speech. To change the figure, it is in these that we hear the characteristic and distinctive notes of his speech.

His style is not always what one would call plain. But even when it is marked, as it often is, by courtly diction, richness of imagery, and beauty of rhythm, it rests on a base of directness of apprehension and simplicity of structure. The images are uncomplicated, given in similes or metaphors not greatly extended, certainly always lucid, rarely in mixed or knotted tropes.

The counterstatement to Othello's love, Iago's malicious hatred of Othello, also opens in a major key and is also simply declarative in form. The hatred is stated at the outset in plain terms, first in Iago's racy circumstantial narrative to Roderigo about Othello's promotion of Cassio to the lieutenancy—

ROD.: Thou told'st me thou didst hold him in thy hate.
IAGO: Despise me if I do not. . . .   [I.i.7–8]

and then in his promise to get even: "I follow him to serve my turn upon him" (I.i.42). The assertion of hate made to Roderigo is insisted upon ("I have told thee often, and I retell thee again and again, I hate the Moor" [I.iii.372–73]) and it is repeated in soliloquy (I.iii.392). Iago's mind seen straight into, when he is talking to himself (hence to us) or to Roderigo, is always vulgar and obscene. His plainness, therefore, quite as direct in assertion as Othello's, is in a wholly different key. Plain also is the mask of blunt soldier he wears to meet the world. The interesting thing is that the mask is remarkably like his own face. There are only shadings of difference in the language (to Othello it is cleaned up a little), or none at all (as in his obscenities to Brabantio about the Barbary horse and the old black ram). The essential difference is in the intent. His opening statement to Roderigo, true as we find it to be, is yet less candid than it seems, since he uses it to manipulate this stupid cat's-paw. His natural cynicism (the ethos Shakespeare invents for him) need hardly change its tone; or if it does, only enough to seem, in the context of its directed use, a healthy realism. Iago often assumes the style of the homely moralist. He states general moral truths (or seeming truths) in aphorisms or sentences ("Poor and content is rich . . ." [III.iii.172]), gives examples and analogies, draws plausible but subtly false conclusions, or misapplies the lesson, as in his homily to Roderigo on the hoary text that our bodies are our gardens to cultivate as we will (I.iii.322 ff.). The differences in style, whether in prose or verse, are governed by the decorum of the person or of the scene as a whole; the verse to Othello is as plain, if not as vulgar, as the prose to Roderigo. The rhetoric of simplicity is a subtle mask, and he wears it with pleasure.

Iago's pattern of declarative sentences, therefore, differs from Othello's in two fundamental ways—in quality and in relation to the truth. Iago's prosy, if lively, vulgarity is counterpointed against Othello's poetic grace. Othello's assertions match the truth of himself and the truth he sees; up to the point of his deception they mirror reality. Iago's do not. His "honest" statements—sometimes true, sometimes false, sometimes partly one, partly the other, always devious in intent—do not reflect the world as it is. In fact, the truth of love Desdemona and Othello know Iago does not even recognize. To him love would appear to be, as he defines it to Roderigo, "merely a lust of the blood and a permission of the will" (I.iii.339–40).

Iago's method of operation is to introduce doubt into Othello's confidence. The conditional sentence expressing a condition assumed to be possible is the subtlest of his grammatical and logical tools.

We might consider the conditional sentence itself for a moment. It expresses relations in the world of contingent possibilities. Take the form in which the relation between condition and conclusion is assumed to be necessary: If *this* is true, then *that* is; if *this* should happen, then *that* would. The question in such a sentence is not about the conclusion, but about the condition on which the conclusion or consequence is, or seems to be, contingent. (In the alternative "seems" there is a trap, for even if *this* is true, *that* only may be. It is a trap Iago knows very well how to set.) The probability of the condition's existing or occurring has to be assessed on a scale of degrees. Probability amounting to certainty is at one end—what may be and is; improbability, also amounting to certainty, is at the other—what might conceivably be, but is not. Uncertainty lies in an indeterminate middle zone between. When the condition is assumed to be only possible, it has obviously less predictive force than when it is assumed to be fact. There is room, however, in nice distinctions of mood and tense, to suggest variations of relation (or rather, feeling about the relation) between condition and conclusion. Shakespeare uses such distinctions with more subtlety than we are accustomed to in modern English, in which the indicative mood so often usurps the prerogative of the subjunctive in conditional sentences of possibility. The condition contrary to fact has many uses. Suppose we say that if *this* were true (believing it not to be), *that* would happen; this carries us by implication to an assertion in the indicative. But *this* is not true; therefore *that* will not happen. By using the conditional form, however, we can do something we cannot in a simple assertion. We may intend a relieved "Thank goodness it is not true!" or a wistful "If only it were!" Condition contrary to fact offers subtle possibilities of variation (which we shall find illustrated in *Othello*). It is a form capable of the most delicate nuances in expressing our responses to the contingencies among which we live. For excluded possibilities may affect us as much as open ones.

They remind us of limits beyond which we cannot go, but sometimes, too, of our incredible escapes. And only to imagine the exclusion of the possibilities we live by may make either our worst fears or our strongest certainties. Possibilities still unrealized hold the door open to the future, hopefully or fearfully. But we do not put contemplation of them aside because they are over—when they have lived in act, died forever, or never come into being. These make our thankful deliverances, our regrets, or our frustrations. What if it had not happened! If only it had not! If only it had!

One way in which Shakespeare establishes Othello's ethos is to make him rarely speak in *if*s. He quickly creates for us an illusion of a full and adventurous past for Othello, a past in which the possibilities appear to have been always successfully dealt with or successfully escaped from. Here he is now, assured and serene, taking what comes, asking few questions, not worrying about contingencies, not thinking too precisely on the event. He uses few conditional sentences in the first two acts—that is to say, before Iago disturbs him. Most are in forms nearest improbability; they imply his confidence that the world will not be upset. One sort is the condition contrary to fact in the subjunctive: "Were it my cue to fight, I should have known it / Without a prompter" (I.ii.83–84). The other form has the condition in the indicative or subjunctive and the consequence in the imperative or optative subjunctive:

> when light-wing'd toys
> Of feather'd Cupid seel with wanton dullness
> My speculative and offic'd instruments,
> That my disports corrupt and taint my business,
> Let housewives make a skillet of my helm,
> And all indign and base adversities
> Make head against my estimation!   [I.iii.269–75]

This is a strong form of asseveration, having almost the force of an oath. It calls for an unwished consequence to follow upon an incredible condition: If I am not what I am, then let this shame fall on my head. Conditions contrary to fact, subtly varied in form, often asseverative, recur in Othello's speech to the end of the play. How they are placed at strategic points in the action, usually as forewarnings, we shall see as we go along.

Iago, on the other hand, is continually holding the door open to hitherto unthought-of possibilities. To Roderigo it is the door to the enjoyment of Desdemona; to Othello it is the door to the unbounded darkness of nightmare. He keeps it open by a dexterous game of rhetoric that includes a game of false logic. He manipulates events so that his conclusions seem to follow on the conditions he has pointed to. The "seem" is important, because there is never a necessary relation between Iago's arranged and predicted condition, and the conclusion supplied. He works by false enthymemes, arguing from a sign that seems a true one but is not.[3] He traps Othello by the fallacy of multiple cause and can do it because, having suggested the cause he wants believed, he can then bring off the effect he has foreseen. Interestingly enough, Iago does not think too precisely on the event either. The conditional possibilities he phrases for himself are simply the confident opportunist's, with only an immediate consequence seen: If I can do this, so much will be done; then we'll see what next. He moves easily up the stairs, one at a time, in a *gradatio* of achieved possibilities: "If this poor trash of Venice . . . stand the putting on"; "If I can fasten but one cup upon him"; "If consequence do but approve my dream" (II.i.312–13; iii.50, 64). It always does—or almost.

The two fundamental conditions of the story, the given ones with which we start, are Iago's revengeful hatred of Othello, and Othello's and Desdemona's love of each other. The drama is to be built out of the drive of the hatred to destroy the love, beginning with the antagonist's cry of "poison his delight" (I.i.68), and ending with the agonist's destruction of his wife and of himself.[4] Two other conditions are also given in the story, and it is with the leverage they give the villain that he operates against the hero. The first of these complicating conditions is the disparity between Othello and Desdemona—in race, nation, age, social background, and experience: between Othello the black Moor, in middle years, a soldier of fortune with an adventurous, far-traveled past, an "extravagant and wheeling stranger," and Desdemona the fair Venetian, "a maiden never bold," young, home-keeping, and innocent. The second complicating condition is the position and character of Cassio, the handsome and gracious young Florentine whom Othello trusts, whom he has promoted over Iago to the vacant lieutenancy, and who, we later learn, was an intermediary between him and Desdemona in his wooing. Iago's game begins by opening up the possibilities of doubt which would seem to lie in the disparity between Othello and Desdemona—doubt, that is, of the quality and permanence of their love. His first move against Othello, by slander and through Desdemona's father, does not work. But then, by bringing in the second condition, the attractiveness and familiar manners of the youthful Cassio, and by linking it with the doubts already raised about the strangeness of the marriage, he wakens a destructive jealousy in Othello and successfully makes him the agent of his own ruin.

Conditional sentences in asseverative form, set as they are in the frame of unqualified declarative sentences, mark with strong emphasis at the beginning of the play the given conditions of love and hate. Then, in varying forms, conditional sentences mark the entry and manipulation throughout the play of the complicating conditions. We shall examine the most crucial ones to observe how they operate with the movement of the action[5]—with Iago's undermining thrusts at Othello's peace and with the movement of Othello's mind from certainty to doubt of Desdemona's love, next, to certainty of her disloyalty (the false certainty which leads to murder), then back quickly through doubt of his cause to the final certainty of her love and of his irretrievable mistake. Every move to the catastrophe is marked by a condition—an *if*, a *when*, a *but that*.

The play falls into three major movements, to which we may give the old grammarians' terms of *protasis, epitasis,* and *catastrophe*.[6] The protasis, or presentation, comprising the first act, lays down the initial circumstances of the story, introduces the principal characters, emphasizes the opposition of Iago to Othello out of which the drama will grow, and prepares the ground for Iago's future operations. The epitasis, or intensifying of the action, comprising the second, third, and fourth acts, ties the knot of complication, with Iago breaking Cassio and moving Othello to the point of murder. The catastrophe, or overturn, comprising the last act, brings the tragic consequence in the murder of Desdemona, the recognition by Othello of what he has done, and his suicide.

You will recall how boldly the play opens, not with the hero, but with the villain—the hatred before the love, the Serpent before Adam and Eve. Shakespeare starts the run toward tragedy swiftly and at once. All in the first scene, Iago makes the necessary exposition of circumstances (the promotion of Cassio, the marriage of Othello); states his feeling (hatred), his motive (disappointed ambition), his intent (revenge); adumbrates his future methods of operation (his use of Roderigo as a tool, his initiation of a public disturbance to cause fear and confusion, his rhetoric of innuendo, slander, and affected honesty); and makes his first move against Othello's peace. The two conditional sentences of Iago's which we must not miss are the two in his speech of self-declaration, defining him for us unequivocally:

> It is as sure as you are Roderigo,
> Were I the Moor, I would not be Iago.
> In following him, I follow but myself;
> Heaven is my judge, not I for love and duty,
> But seeming so, for my peculiar end;
> For when my outward action doth demonstrate
> The native act and figure of my heart
> In compliment extern, 'tis not long after
> But I will wear my heart upon my sleeve
> For daws to peck at. I am not what I am.   [I.i.56–65]

Taken together, the obvious condition contrary to fact ("Were I the Moor") and the imagined condition ("when my outward action . . .") with its preposterous conclusion serve to announce his role as antagonist, emphasize his absolute difference from the agonist, and declare in essence what his mode of operation against him will be. The conditionals are two forms of excluding possibilities; hence they work to establish certainties. They are emphatic ways of telling us, the audience, to keep our eyes open to Iago's covert operations.

In the second scene, when Othello first appears, he also is given a speech of self-declaration, which may be set against Iago's. Before we see Othello, Iago has blackened his name in gross obscenities to Brabantio and has roused a hue and cry after him for his elopement with Desdemona. Before we have witnessed for ourselves the quality of the love, Iago has obscured it in a murky cloud of ugliness and doubt. When the outcry moves to Othello's door, it is quieted by his calm and assured authority: "Keep up your bright swords, for the dew will rust them"; "Hold your hands, / Both you of my inclining and the rest" (I.ii.59, 81–82). In the magic of a few brief sentences Shakespeare creates a figure which, in its simplicity and dignity, expunges the memory of the leering preface. The sun shines all the brighter for the clouds which have stained it. In the same way as his character, the love appears for the first time in its true and proper light. Iago's speech of self-declaration, for the audience's sake, is now matched by Othello's:

> 'Tis yet to know—
> Which, when I know that boasting is an honour,
> I shall promulgate—I fetch my life and being
> From men of royal siege; and my demerits
> May speak (unbonneted) to as proud a fortune
> As this that I have reach'd. For know, Iago,
> But that I love the gentle Desdemona,
> I would not my unhoused free condition
> Put into circumscription and confine
> For the sea's worth.   [I.ii.19–28]

Othello's parenthesis, ironic in its condition contrary to fact, sets the decent reticence of the man conscious of his own worth against the practical concealment of the double-tongued. Iago, in his busy duplicity, says, "I am not what I am." Othello says that he is what he is.

In the second conditional sentence, the love is affirmed *simpliciter,* without need of description, but in a form which leaves no doubt of its worth. Here is the love and the cost, the choice and the consequence. The expected form of such a condition contrary to fact would be: "If I did not love Desdemona, I would not . . ." But putting the conditional verb in the positive rather than in the negative quite alters the emphasis, places it on the true condition, not the untrue one, marks its acceptance with no undertone of regret, makes the statement imply: "This is the only condition for which I would have paid such a price." The value of both the love and the free life is enhanced. Yet Othello's first words spoken of his love sound, unknown to him, with the dark undertone of prophecy. The cost will be more than anything Othello can imagine.

In this speech, Shakespeare has put for us in other terms than Iago's the unusualness of the marriage. Iago's way of looking at it—as lust on Othello's part, unnaturalness on Desdemona's—is the only one, however, which Desdemona's father can credit. Since his gentle daughter's voluntary part in such a union is unimaginable to him, Brabantio has found a way out in the only condition he can understand: the use of charms or drugs. He enters soon after Othello's speech to confront him and order his arrest:

> O thou foul thief, where hast thou stow'd my daughter?
> Damn'd as thou art, thou has enchanted her!
> For I'll refer me to all things of sense,
> If she in chains of magic were not bound,
> Whether a maid so tender, fair, and happy,
> So opposite to marriage . . .
> . . . .

Would ever have (t' incur a general mock)
Run from her guardage to the sooty bosom
Of such a thing as thou—to fear, not to delight.
Judge me the world if 'tis not gross in sense
That thou hast practis'd on her with foul charms,
Abus'd her delicate youth with drugs or minerals
That weaken motion.

                                                    [I.ii.62–75]

Othello is willing to answer, at the proper time.

Brabantio makes his charge formally in an *ad hoc* trial of Othello before the Duke and Senate of Venice. The episode has, in brief form, most of the features of a trial: charge, questioning of the defendant, defendant's reply (including a narrative of his past), questioning of a witness, dismissal of charges. The syntax is partly interrogative, but mainly assertive on both sides.

At one point, Othello, requesting that Desdemona be called to speak for him, solemnly sets his condition against Brabantio's:

If you do find me foul in her report,
The trust, the office, I do hold of you
Not only take away, but let your sentence
Even fall upon my life.

                                                    [I.iii.117–20]

Desdemona's testimony, as candid and unqualified as Othello's in his account of his wooing, settles the matter, and Brabantio must perforce dismiss his charge.

Come hither, Moor.
I here do give thee that with all my heart
Which, but thou hast already, with all my heart
I would keep from thee.

                                                    [I.iii.192–95]

Do we hear an echo of Othello's acceptance of the same condition: "But that I love the gentle Desdemona, I would not . . ."? The same phrasing, but in another key. The same unalterable condition, but with all the difference of meaning, to father and husband, between separation and union. Brabantio's last word also carries a condition: "Look to her, Moor, if thou hast eyes to see. / She has deceiv'd her father, and may thee" (I.iii.293–94). Othello sees the truth now with unaided vision; but Iago will help him readily enough to false glasses. Again, there lies in the condition, unperceived of the speaker, a prodigious irony which time will bring to birth. Othello rightly replies, "My life upon her faith!" (I.iii.295).

This forensic episode is of great importance. Othello has been tried for a supposed crime, and the case has been dismissed for want of evidence. Before the self-evident truth of the love, the charge of unnaturalness has melted like snow in June. The very strangeness between the conditions of Othello and Desdemona which has called the love in question is, given the transparent honesty of the two, the best guarantee of its truth, as, later on, Othello's first, unprompted response to Iago's doubts is to tell him: "She had eyes, and chose me" (III.iii.189).

It does not matter to Iago that he has failed in his first attempt to bring Othello into disrepute. He promises Roderigo to find a way to succeed another time: "If sanctimony and a frail vow betwixt an erring barbarian and a supersubtle Venetian be not too hard for my wits and all the tribe of hell, thou shalt enjoy her" (I.iii.363–65). These are the terms of the marriage he has seen, or chosen to see, from the beginning. In the soliloquy which ends the act he hits on a hopeful way to break the union apart, by making something of Cassio's charming person and "smooth dispose." The act ends as it began, in an affirmation of Iago's hate, but now with a promise as well: "Hell and night / Must bring this monstrous birth to the world's light" (I.iii.409–10).

Bringing the monstrous birth to light is the business of the epitasis, or second movement of the play, in which Iago moves Othello to a jealous and murderous rage. This long movement is broken into smaller movements, each marking a stage of Iago's maneuverings or of Othello's passion or of both together. But first there is a prelude to the whole. The "high-wrought" tempest which we hear of as the second act opens serves double duty, for it is both a fortunate dismissal of the Turkish threat and an omen of a more dreadful tempest to come in the mind and life of Othello. It is disorder of a huge kind, like the storm in Lear. Yet, the elements "As having sense of beauty, do omit / Their mortal natures, letting go safely by / The divine Desdemona" (II.i.71–73). That we should not miss the portent, Shakespeare makes Othello say, on his finding Desdemona safely landed ahead of him:

> O my soul's joy!
> If after every tempest come such calms,
> May the winds blow till they have waken'd death!
> And let the labouring bark climb hills of seas
> Olympus-high, and duck again as low
> As hell's from heaven!   [II.i.186–91]

For Othello, who knows that after tempests such calms do not always come, the wish is a way of emphasizing the relief of this escape, this happy reunion, the feeling that any hardship or fear would be worth this conclusion. The condition might almost be true. For us, who see Iago standing by, weaving his spider's web for Cassio out of the young man's courtesies to Desdemona, the contrariness to fact is absolute, the wish for another tempest like a defiance of the omens. Another prophetic conditional comes immediately:

> If it were now to die,
> 'Twere now to be most happy; for I fear
> My soul hath her content so absolute
> That not another comfort like to this
> Succeeds in unknown fate.   [II.i.191–95]

This clearly improbable condition with its conclusion in the superlative is a way of acknowledging the joy, the perfection of such a moment—and its rarity, too, for *happy* also means "fortunate." The joy and the fear are complementary. We must take the speech as something like the classical tragic hero's fear of too much good fortune and meant primarily as a warning to us. It is not, as the interchange between him and Desdemona makes clear (II.i.195–201), a pessimistic expectation on his part. It is only Iago and we who must perceive the full truth of the conclusion. As Othello kisses his wife, with the prayer, "And this, and this, the greatest discords be/That e'er our hearts shall make!" Iago promises,

> O, you are well tun'd now!
> But I'll set down the pegs that make this music,
> As honest as I am.
>
> [II.i.201–3]

The first discord Iago creates is another tumult—the drunken fight in the court of guard on the night of their arrival in Cyprus (II.iii). This oblique move, against Cassio, is of course preparatory to the direct move against Othello yet to be made. As Iago considers how to use to his advantage the evening of celebration Othello has allowed the garrison, he states the condition on which he will operate, Cassio's weak head for liquor:

> If I can fasten but one cup upon him
> With that which he hath drunk to-night already,
> He'll be as full of quarrel and offence
> As my young mistress' dog.
>
> [II.iii.50–53]

He can and does, and the consequences follow: Cassio enmeshed in a brawl, Montano the Cypriot governor seriously wounded, Othello scandalized and angry, Cassio dismissed in disgrace from his lieutenancy. In this maneuver Iago has also satisfied a second and larger condition he had mused upon: "If consequence do but approve my dream, / My boat sails freely, both with wind and stream" (II.iii.64–65). Consequences have approved his dream, and Iago's boat is well launched, on course for the larger prize.

Before the scene ends, Iago has arranged, out of the young officer's desperate need to be reinstated, a new condition, that Cassio will ask Desdemona to intercede with Othello for him. Iago's game is to work the condition two ways. To Cassio the argument that if Desdemona speaks for him he will have a better chance with Othello, must be made to seem compelling, and under Iago's persuasion it does. In point of fact, intercession would not have been necessary, for Othello has said, according to Emilia, that he "needs no other suitor but his likings" to reinstate Cassio when he can expediently do so (III.i.50–53). Still, Desdemona's word would have done no harm—far from it. "Let him come when he will!" Othello replies to her first importunings, "I will deny thee nothing" (III.iii.75–76). But of course Iago intends it to do great harm. To Othello the condition "If Desdemona speaks for Cassio" must be made to seem to require the conclusion "she is false to me." The spurious enthymeme must not seem so. Iago's method will be to predict the possibility he knows will happen and at the same time prepare Othello's response to it by supplying ahead of time a false interpretation. Unlike the brawl, the outcome of which had to depend on a certain amount of luck, the new condition he has arranged he can take wholly into his own hands.

The temptation scene opens with Desdemona's promise to help Cassio, a promise assured by the conditions of her integrity: "If I do vow a friendship, I'll perform it / To the last article" (III.iii.21–22). Iago, entering with Othello in time to see Cassio leave, can now bring out his most cunning tools to work an upheaval in Othello's mind. Recall once again the exchange between the two:

> IAGO: Ha! I like not that.
> OTH.:   What dost thou say?
> IAGO: Nothing, my lord; or if—I know not what.
> OTH.: Was not that Cassio parted from my wife?
> IAGO: Cassio, my lord? No, sure, I cannot think it . . .

The exclamation of surprise, the strong assertion of disapproval, the tentative "if" begin a long and intense dialogue between himself and Othello, a dialogue which occupies more than one scene and which does not end for 672 lines (III.iii.35–IV.i.227). The dialogue is broken by short episodes in which Desdemona's insistent suit for Cassio is renewed and in which the business of the handkerchief is introduced and continued. Each of these episodes supplies Iago with new "evidence" to work with, so that after each interruption the dialogue is resumed with a bolder line and with increased suffering and disorder in the mind of Othello. The whole has three parts: the movement to doubt, the movement to conviction, the movement to proof.

How this whole long movement toward "proof" will end is foretold in Othello's lines of unconscious prophecy, spoken, soon after Iago's "if," as Desdemona leaves with her husband's consent to see Cassio:

> Perdition catch my soul
> But I do love thee! and when I love thee not,
> Chaos is come again.   [III.iii.90–92]

His love of Desdemona, the condition of his life, is twice affirmed in the imagined consequences of its unimaginable negation. Trembling with the burden of our superior awareness, we watch Iago make his nothing into a seeming something, shape his formless *if* into a credible phantasm, flesh it out with seeming substance. The first stage is to awaken an uncertainty Othello cannot stand, to hint at something monstrous without saying what it is, yet to prepare for the revelation by little cautionary lectures on reputation and jealousy. Othello's rising impatience, expressed in a series of conditions truer than he knows—"By heaven, he echoes me, / As if there were some monster in his thought / Too hideous to be shown" (III.iii.106–8); "As if thou then hadst shut up in thy brain / Some horrible conceit" (III.iii.114–15)—comes to a climax as he tries to break out of the maddening phantasmagoria:

> Why, why is this?
> Think'st thou I'ld make a life of jealousy,
> To follow still the changes of the moon
> With fresh suspicions? No! To be once in doubt
> Is once to be resolv'd....
>
> . . . .
>
>   . . . No, Iago;
> I'll see before I doubt; when I doubt, prove;
> And on the proof there is no more but this—
> Away at once with love or jealousy!   [III.iii.176–80, 189–92]

But Iago's reminders of the differences between him and his wife and of Brabantio's warning dash his spirits. This is Iago's moment to bring out his prediction with its false conclusion:

> Yet, if you please to hold him [Cassio] off awhile,
> You shall by that perceive him and his means.
> Note if your lady strain his entertainment
> With any strong or vehement importunity.
> Much will be seen in that.   [III.iii.248–52]

The condition of Desdemona's love, the very thing that confirmed it, is being made to seem the negation of it; her innocence and her earlier reluctance to marry are being turned into Venetian subtlety. Othello, feeling himself a stranger in such a world, is at the mercy of Iago's evidently superior knowledge. He promises his own condition of future action:

>   If I do prove her haggard,
> Though that her jesses were my dear heartstrings,
> I'ld whistle her off and let her down the wind
> To prey at fortune.   [III.iii.260–63]

With the "If" at the beginning of the dialogue, Iago's muddy stream entered Othello's clear one. The two currents at first ran side by side, not mingling. But now the discoloring has begun and will not end until pollution is complete. Desdemona is later to say, with true observation of the state if not the cause of her husband's troubled mind: "Something sure of state . . . Hath puddled his clear spirit" (III.iv.140–43). Iago puts it differently: "The Moor already changes with my poison" (III.iii.325).

  The first half of the temptation scene has brought Othello to doubt. The next brings him to certainty and decision. At the first interruption of the dialogue the sight of Desdemona as she enters clears his mind, and his right impulse makes him say: "If she be false, O, then heaven mocks itself!/I'll not believe't" (III.iii.278–79). For a breathing space things are stood upright again. But it is the last time they will be. For now Desdemona drops her handkerchief; and Emilia, who finds it, gives it to Iago, with an upside-down condition of fearful import to us:

EMIL.: What will you do with't, that you have been so earnest
To have me filch it?
IAGO: Why, what's that to you?
EMIL.: If it be not for some purpose of import,
Give't me again.   [III.iii.314–17]

Now Iago, with the handkerchief in his pocket, begins to shape his obscene phantasm with free and bold invention.

This second half of the scene, the movement to certainty, is different in tone from the first. It is prefaced by Iago's great cue lines for Othello's re-entrance:

Look where he comes! Not poppy nor mandragora,
Nor all the drowsy syrups of the world,
Shall ever medicine thee to that sweet sleep
Which thou ow'dst yesterday.   [III.iii.330–33]

Othello has crossed a bridge into another country. He has begun to inhabit the realm of perdition he spoke of so innocently at the beginning of the scene, and he now looks back to the place he knows forever beyond recovery:

                    O, now for ever
Farewell the tranquil mind! farewell content!
Farewell the plumed troop, and the big wars
That make ambition virtue! . . .

. . . .
Farewell! Othello's occupation's gone!   [III.iii.347–50, 357]

The price of his marriage, once so gladly accepted, is being exacted. While Iago's busy brain continues to invent more ingenious traps and more refined tortures, Othello's moves out into great imaginative reaches of perception and feeling. At one point of intense dramatic irony, he turns on Iago with a possibility that is a true description of Iago's *modus operandi:*

If thou dost slander her and torture me,
Never pray more; abandon all remorse;
On horror's head horrors accumulate;
Do deeds to make heaven weep, all earth amaz'd;
For nothing canst thou to damnation add
Greater than that.   [III.iii.368–73]

But it is a truth he must not be allowed to recognize. With Iago's offended protest that "To be direct and honest is not safe" (III.iii.378), the moment of insight has passed, and Othello, tortured by a divided mind, calls for proof:

I think my wife be honest, and think she is not;
I think that thou art just, and think thou art not.
I'll have some proof. . . .

. . . .

> ... If there be cords, or knives,
> Poison, or fire, or suffocating streams,
> I'll not endure it. Would I were satisfied! [III.iii.384–86, 388–90]

The time has come for another of Iago's false enthymemes. He prepares the way for its psychological reception:

> If imputation and strong circumstances
> Which lead directly to the door of truth
> Will give you satisfaction, you may have't. [III.iii.406–8]

The imputation and strong circumstances he supplies at once in the form of two lies, one the vivid and lewd narrative of Cassio's dream, the other a statement that he has today seen Cassio wipe his beard with the handkerchief Othello had given his wife. "If 't be that—," Othello begins. Iago widens the condition and supplies the plausible but false conclusion: "If it be that, or any that was hers, / It speaks against her, with the other proofs" (III.iii.440–41). Convinced by emotion and false logic, Othello cannot even wait on the possibility: "O, blood, blood, blood!" (III.iii.451). Othello's current must run, if not to love, then to vengeance:

> Like to the Pontic Sea,
> Whose icy current and compulsive course
> Ne'er feels retiring ebb, but keeps due on
> To the Propontic and the Hellespont;
> Even so my bloody thoughts, with violent pace,
> Shall ne'er look back, ne'er ebb to humble love,
> Till that a capable and wide revenge
> Swallow them up. [III.iii.453–60]

He kneels to make a solemn vow of revenge. This is the moment of decision, from which there is no turning back.

The third stage in this long dialogue is the movement to visible "proof"—that is, to the exhibition of the handkerchief in Cassio's hand. In Othello's mind it is the final movement to chaos. It is preceded by another interlude, this time a discordant antiphony between Desdemona's insistence to Othello that he keep his promise to hear Cassio's appeal and Othello's to her that she fetch the handkerchief. Othello's demand is accompanied by his story of the handkerchief and the grave conditions which possession of it imposes on the owner. The Egyptian who gave it to his mother had told her:

> while she kept it,
> 'Twould make her amiable and subdue my father
> Entirely to her love; but if she lost it
> Or made a gift of it, my father's eye
> Should hold her loathly. . . .
> . . . .
> To lose't or give't away were such perdition
> As nothing else could match. [III.iv.58–68]

What wonder that the frightened Desdemona lies, "It is not lost. But what an if it were?" (III.iv.83). What indeed! The rest of the interlude keeps us aware of Iago's legerdemain with the handkerchief, for we see Cassio, who has found it in his room, giving it to Bianca to have the pattern copied.

The dialogue between tormentor and tormented is resumed in a new scene, which is chaos enacted. Under the pressure of Iago's indecent suggestions and perverse *ifs*—"So they do nothing, 'tis a venial slip. / But if I give my wife a handkerchief—"; "What / If I had said I had seen him do you wrong?"—Othello's sentences break down and he falls in a fit: "Lie with her? lie on her? . . . It is not words that shakes me thus.—Pish! Noses, ears, and lips? Is't possible?—Confess?—handkerchief?—O devil!" (IV.i.9–10, 23–24, 35–44). A successful period is put to Iago's manipulation when his condition "If 't be that . . ." is fulfilled and he can point out the handkerchief passing between Bianca and Cassio (IV.i.150–67). Othello is torn almost to incoherence with the conflict between what his own experience of Desdemona tells him and what Iago has led him to see.

> Ay, let her rot, and perish, and be damn'd tonight; for she shall not live. . . . O, the world hath not a sweeter creature! She might lie by an emperor's side and command him tasks.
>
> IAGO: Nay, that's not your way.
>
> OTH.: Hang her! I do but say what she is. . . . But yet the pity
> of it, Iago! O Iago, the pity of it, Iago!   [IV.i.191–207]

Iago proposes strangling in the bed she has contaminated, he offers to be "undertaker" for Cassio, and the long dialogue is over. A trumpet announces the emissary from Venice, come to call Othello home.

This epilogue to the scene provides Iago with his moment of triumph. After the shocked Lodovico has seen Othello strike Desdemona, Iago hints at Othello's ruin in the fine duplicity of a pious wish:

> He's that he is. I may not breathe my censure.
> What he might be—if what he might he is not—
> I would to heaven he were!   [IV.i.281–83]

This is surely the masterpiece of all conditional sentences.

Although the stage leading to proof has ended, one more scene rounds it out. It is the "gate of hell" scene in which Othello, having viewed with his own eyes the evidence of guilt, interrogates the supposed criminal. It is forensic, like the scene which ended the protasis, although more loosely so. This time the legal procedure of question and answer, statement and denial, is distorted in purpose and operation, for the prosecuting attorney is also the plaintiff and he has no ears to hear the truth. The defendant rests her oath of denial on the condition of a true definition:

> No, as I am a Christian!
> If to preserve this vessel for my lord

From any other foul unlawful touch
Be not to be a strumpet, I am none.

[IV.ii.82–85]

In the midst of this cruel process, Othello expresses another of his great poetic insights into experience, yet one dreadfully ironic in the untruth on which it is founded:

Had it pleas'd heaven
To try me with affliction, had they rain'd
All kinds of sores and shames on my bare head,
. . . .
I should have found in some place of my soul
A drop of patience. . . .

. . . .
But there where I have garner'd up my heart,
Where either I must live or bear no life,
The fountain from the which my current runs
Or else dries up—to be discarded thence. . . .

[IV.ii.47–60]

He weighs excluded possibilities against the one which seems to have come into being: If only it had been that, not this!

Emilia has "the office opposite to Saint Peter" and keeps the gate of hell. Part of the dramatic irony with which the scene is saturated comes from her clear-eyed perception and downright statement of the true relations between conditions and conclusions. This logical sequence, spoken in answer to Othello's questioning before the interview with Desdemona, has everything which Iago's *ifs* do not:

I durst, my lord, to wager she is honest,
Lay down my soul at stake. If you think other,
Remove your thought; it doth abuse your bosom.
If any wretch have put this in your head,
Let heaven requite it with the serpent's curse!
For if she be not honest, chaste, and true,
There's no man happy; the purest of their wives
Is foul as slander.

[IV.ii.12–19]

And when Othello has left and Iago himself is present, Emilia in a strong asseverative conditional hits the truth precisely:

I will be hang'd if some eternal villain,
Some busy and insinuating rogue,
Some cogging, cozening slave, to get some office,
Have not devis'd this slander. I'll be hang'd else.
IAGO: Fie, there is no such man! It is impossible.
DES.: If any such there be, heaven pardon him!

[IV.ii.130–35]

Desdemona's optative subjunctive is counterpointed by Emilia's: "A halter pardon him! and hell gnaw his bones!" Desdemona's own solemn asseveration, in a pitiful appeal to the author of her ruin, follows:

> Here I kneel.
> If e'er my will did trespass 'gainst his love,
> Either in discourse of thought or actual deed,
> . . . .
> Or that I do not yet, and ever did,
> And ever will . . .
>   . . . love him dearly,
> Comfort forswear me!   [IV.ii.151–53, 156–59]

The catastrophe occupies the last long scene of the play. It is foreshadowed poetically by the bedchamber scene: "If I do die before thee," Desdemona says to Emilia, "prithee shroud me / In one of those same sheets" (IV.iii.24–25). Emilia has laid the wedding sheets on the bed, Desdemona sings her forlorn Willow Song, and they talk of the conditions under which women betray their husbands. Emilia would do it if the world were the price; Desdemona, not for the world.

The ground for the catastrophe is cleared by Iago's last maneuverings: his scheming to get Cassio and Roderigo killed (IV.ii.172 ff.)—his last promise to Roderigo ("If thou the next night following enjoy not Desdemona . . ." [IV.ii.219–20])—his last conditions of operation ("If you will watch his going thence . . ." [IV.ii.241–42])—his assessment of alternative possibilities ("Now whether he kills Cassio, / Or Cassio kills him, or each do kill the other, / Every way makes my game" [V.i.12–14])—his recognition that his own fate hangs on the success of this last act of violence ("If Cassio do remain, / He hath a daily beauty in his life / That makes me ugly; and besides, the Moor / May unfold me to him; there stand I in much peril. / . . . This is the night / That either makes me or fordoes me quite" [V.i.18–21, 128–29]). The scene is another one of tumult, of swords clashing in the dark, of outcries and arrests, like those beginning the protasis and epitasis; but this time it is a huggermugger. Cassio, though seriously wounded, escapes with the "daily beauty" of his loyalty unimpaired to make Iago ugly.

The long last scene falls into three parts: the deed of violence, the discovery or recognition, and the suicide. The first part opens with Othello's illuminated awareness of the finality of his act of execution on Desdemona:

> Put out the light, and then put out the light.
> If I quench thee, thou flaming minister,
> I can again thy former light restore,
> Should I repent me; but once put out thy light,
> Thou cunning'st pattern of excelling nature,
> I know not where is that Promethean heat
> That can thy light relume.   [V.ii.7–13]

This is awareness only in idea, clothed in the beauty of metaphor. When the deed is done—not as it was meant to be, sternly and in justice, but in rage and violence—it is followed by an anticlimax of bewilderment about the merely practical question of what to do next. At this moment, with Emilia's cry, the immediate world is at the door; reality strikes in the homeliest of ways and is inexpressible: "If she come in,

she'll sure speak to my wife. / My wife! my wife! what wife? I have no wife"
(V.ii.96–97).

Recognition, or discovery, begins with Emilia's insistence on Desdemona's
fidelity (V.ii.125 ff.). The recognition Othello has to make is that the monster Iago
has shown him, the monster at whose prompting he has killed his wife, has never
been anything but a monstrous fantasy, housed in his own mind. The recognition is
so bewildering and so damning that he must resist it:

> O, I were damn'd beneath all depth in hell
> But that I did proceed upon just grounds
> To this extremity.   [V.ii.137–39]

This is one of his old forms of asseveration, based on a condition he believes
contrary to fact; only now the affirmation is not a promise for the future but a
justification of the past. Another follows:

> Nay, had she been true,
> If heaven would make me such another world
> Of one entire and perfect chrysolite,
> I'ld not have sold her for it.   [V.ii.143–46]

The lines are heavy with the nearly unbearable irony that the condition is most true.
Do we hear Desdemona's voice saying, as she prepared to lie down on her
wedding sheets, "Beshrew me if I would do such a wrong / For the whole world"
(IV.iii.80–81)?

But when, with Emilia's testimony about the handkerchief, Othello's awakening
is complete, the recognition of the truth is so dreadful that he can imagine only
damnation:

> Now, how dost thou look now? O ill-starr'd wench!
> Pale as thy smock! When we shall meet at compt,
> This look of thine will hurl my soul from heaven,
> And fiends will snatch at it.   [V.ii.272–75]

The conjunction is temporal, not an *if* but a *when*. An *if* follows as he makes a
wounding, but not fatal, thrust at Iago: "If that thou be'st a devil, I cannot kill thee."
The consequence seems to approve the condition.

The *ifs* are over. We are again in a world of fact, monstrous but true. At last
a crime has been committed, and it is Othello's. Were he tried, he must this time be
found guilty. In place of a trial, we have his last formal speech. It is cast fittingly in the
hortatory imperative to express a plea in the strongest possible way: "I pray you, . . .
Speak of me as I am. . . . Set you down this; . . . say besides that in Aleppo once, . . ."
(V.ii.340–52). Notice that the form of his plea, though imperative, implies a condition:
if you tell the truth impartially, without a bias either extenuating or malicious, you will
be bound to say these things about me. His hearers must then speak:

> Of one that lov'd not wisely, but too well;
> Of one not easily jealous, but, being wrought,

Perplex'd in the extreme; of one whose hand
(Like the base Indian) threw a pearl away
Richer than all his tribe; of one whose subdu'd eyes,

. . . .

Drop tears as fast as the Arabian trees
Their med'cinable gum.   [V.ii.344–51]

The obligation is placed on us to understand the speech precisely. The relation
of the condition to its conclusion is necessary. The truth is this and no other. To
read the speech otherwise, with reservations about Othello's motives or the psychology of jealousy, is not to have attended to the syntax of the play in its dramatic
functioning. From beginning to end there has been a precise discrimination between
the true and false relations of a condition to its conclusion. Iago's monster was
created from the false relation. The imperative form of this last speech is an
adjuration to Othello's hearers (and to us) to speak of him truly and justly.

But notice that Othello is also declaring something. What his hearers are
bound to report are his final affirmations—of his love, his jealousy, his folly, and his
remorse. They are the only declarations he can make; the old simple truth cannot
be had again. The final declaration in the speech—a report of the act of justice he
did on a turbaned Turk—is, with the utmost economy, caught up in the final
adjuration that they report the act of justice he does at this instant on himself.

Othello's last sentence is nevertheless simply declarative:

I kiss'd thee ere I kill'd thee. No way but this—
Killing myself, to die upon a kiss.   [V.ii.358–59]

Simple as it is, it goes beyond the kiss before the murder and ties the end to the
beginning. The tragedy lies all between.

NOTES

[1] The Kittredge edition of *Othello* (Boston, 1941) has been used for reference.

[2] I am not attempting character interpretation for its own sake; my position is that of Stoll in putting
dramatic necessity before completeness or consistency of character. What Shakespeare does is to
create within the dramatic framework an illusion of credible action, convincing as long as one abides by
his terms. My study of the movement of the syntax is meant to account in part for this credibility.

[3] For an excellent example of this, see in Roderigo's speech to Brabantio (I.i.120–38) a logical sequence
of conditional sentences ending in a false conclusion based on the argument from sign; dramatically at
this moment Iago and Roderigo are acting as one. On the use of the enthymeme in rhetoric, see
Aristotle's *Rhetoric*, in *Rhetoric and Poetics*, ed. Friedrich Solmsen (New York: Modern Library, 1954),
esp. 1355^a6ff., 1356^b1ff. (definition), 1357^a14ff. (basis in the contingent), 1357^b1ff. (type based on sign),
1394^a26ff. (relation to maxims), 1397^a7ff. (examples in conditional form), 1400^b35ff. (spurious kinds,
esp. 6, arguments from consequence; 7, causes which are not causes).

[4] On Iago's destructive role put in other terms (i.e., as slanderer) see the present writer's "Good Name
in Othello," *Studies in English Literature*, VII (Spring 1967), 195–217.

[5] Many others, reinforcing or varying these, are left as riches for the exploring reader.

[6] In Evanthius, iv. 5, and Donatus, vii. 1–4 (*Comicorum Graecorum Fragmenta*, ed. G. Kaibel [Berlin,
1899], vol. I, fasc. I, pp. 67, 69), familiar through Renaissance editions of Terence and commentaries on
him; see especially Erasmus's school edition (Basel: Froben, 1532, 1534).

Jane Adamson

"PLUMING UP THE WILL": IAGO'S PLACE IN THE PLAY

> let me see now;
> To get his place and to plume up my will
> In double knavery. How? How? Let's see.   (I, iii, 386–8)

So many critics over the years have made so much sense (not to mention nonsense) of Iago that one naturally hesitates to dig over the plot again.[1] Yet much of the debate about his 'character' and about his 'symbolic' status has tended less to clarify than to obscure his place in the dramatic design, and it still seems worth insisting on what by now ought to be a commonplace—that Iago's intrigue and what prompts him to undertake and persist in it, are imagined and judged in the same terms as apply to everyone else in the play. His speeches and actions continually illuminate and are themselves illuminated by those of all the other characters. As Bradley rightly pointed out, Iago is not arbitrarily introduced into the play to represent inexplicable evil or Evil. Certainly, his behaviour cannot be accounted for by any or all of his own declared motives for it, nor did Shakespeare see fit to explain how Iago *came to be* as he is; but—and it is a 'but' whose force we cannot afford to ignore—the way Iago thinks and speaks is dramatically conceived and dramatically 'placed' in relation to everything else in *Othello*. At times knowingly and at times unwittingly, Iago reveals—or rather Shakespeare gives him speeches that reveal to *us*—aspects of his nature that strike us as significantly (and often dismayingly) akin to those of his 'victims', especially Othello, even while in other more obvious respects he is shown to differ from them.

Iago's dramatic function in the play is certainly complex. Clearly he is an interesting and significant figure in himself—though not, I would argue, one that warrants the kind of exclusive attention he has often been given.[2] For he does not merely act in and upon the world the play dramatizes; he is himself a defining aspect

From Othello *as Tragedy: Some Problems of Judgment and Feeling* (Cambridge: Cambridge University Press, 1980), pp. 64–106.

of it. More specifically—though this point too has not commonly been recognized, still less understood—Iago serves as a crucial *limit case* in the play, a man whose life and being vividly demonstrate, in extreme form, certain habits of feeling, certain ways of viewing and responding to the world, that the drama gradually makes us recognize as to some extent characteristic of everyone in it (and of us watching it), each in his own particular (and definitive) form and degree. In short, no less than Desdemona, or Emilia, or Roderigo, Iago embodies an essential part of Shakespeare's integrated thinking in *Othello:* his life, his mode of being and of responding to his world, demonstrate one basic human premise, as it were, in the play's unfolding logic.

To put the point another way, I think that Bradley and others have not only exaggerated Iago's importance, but have thereby distorted it as well. Iago needs to be demythologized. But in trying to do just that, Leavis and other anti-Bradleyan critics have again, as it seems to me, pushed too hard, and so distorted the facts in an opposite way. Iago is too distinctive a dramatic figure, too forcefully real, to be reducible to a mere theatrical device—the conventional Villain—or to a (luridly coloured) 'mechanism' necessary to the plot. This is not to say that he does not fulfil any technical function. Obviously he does—but only because he is dramatically realized *as* a dramatic character inhabiting the same world as the others.

For example (as has often been remarked), he is the main means by which Shakespeare affords us—one might almost say inflicts on us—an unrelievedly ironic perspective on the action as it takes place before us. His soliloquies obviously affect how we view him, but they also condition how we see, and how we cannot see, everyone else. The way Shakespeare presents him robs *us,* totally and forever, of any chance to remain innocent of the snares we see others in the play innocently falling into. Hence, even in the early scenes we can never share the relatively simple clarity of Desdemona's view of the world, say, or Emilia's, or Othello's own, not only because our view of a drama is always larger than that of any of the characters in it, but because in this case Iago makes us sharply aware, right from the start, that there is a particular *kind* of moral fact in the dramatic world, which the other main characters are somehow too innocent, too unsuspicious, or too unperceptive—too 'honest'—to reckon on. 'Innocence' may be comfortable, but it is a comfort we are never allowed. But neither, of course, are we allowed the comfort of being able to do anything about the malignity we witness. Iago's disclosures leave us, as mere onlookers, with no option but to remain silent with him as if in forced complicity, excruciatingly bound to him by the knowledge we cannot share with those who (if we only could speak) might avert the disasters which will otherwise befall them.

This is surely one reason why *Othello* is so continuously painful. Having to watch, we are in no way free to act on the crucial information Iago reveals to us, even though it urgently excites our natural wish to tell what we know and so forestall calamity. This kind of helplessness is a necessary function of all play-watching, of course; indeed, some people would argue that part of our interest in drama is always an unacknowledged wish to witness 'disaster' whilst being free of responsibility for causing or failing to avert it. But although the sustained dramatic

irony of *Othello* is by no means peculiar to it among Shakespeare's plays—
Cymbeline and *Twelfth Night,* for example, are only two among many other
cases—it is arguable that only in some of the late plays, and not in the other great
tragedies immediately following *Othello,* did Shakespeare again rely so much on this
pervasively ironic mode of presentation which *Othello* shares with the earlier
comedies. Certainly, in no other Shakespearean tragedy, and perhaps in no other
Shakespearean play, is our foreknowledge of what the protagonists are ignorant of
so deeply and so *unrelievedly* burdensome. More importantly, this prolonged
anxiety—this lurching between the extremes (as Bradley put it) of 'sickening hope
and dreadful expectation'[3]—which we experience because of what we know but
cannot forestall or 'amend' is comparable with and so brings us more fully to
understand the unrelieved tension Othello himself experiences because of what (so
he thinks) he 'knows' yet cannot change, ignore or bear.

It is Iago whose speeches force that burden of 'knowing' upon us. Nevertheless, like the main protagonists, we know even more—in particular, various moral
and emotional realities—that Iago himself is ignorant of. He is like anybody else in
that the terms as well as the spirit in which he views the world delimit what he sees
and fails to see in it. As Marlowe put it in *Hero and Leander* (Sestiad I, 174), 'What
we behold is censur'd by our eyes'—an insight that, for Shakespeare, became a
basic assumption and working-principle of his art (as it was to become a basic
assumption of writers like Blake and Lawrence after him). What a man sees or does
not see reflects what he values; what he values reflects what he is; and no less than
in Shakespeare's other tragedies (perhaps most especially in *Antony and Cleopatra*), this is both the basis on which all the characters in *Othello* are dramatically
realized, and also partly what the tragedy is about.

All through the play, the presence of Iago brings this home to us with particular force. In the first two acts we may notice for example how often particular
characters recognize in others, or project onto others, qualities which in fact they
themselves possess, though often without their being conscious that this is so.
When Iago appears, we can hardly miss the point. When he declares that Emilia is
like all women—'saints in your injuries, devils being offended' (II, i, 110), these
phrases immediately strike us as far more suggestive of Iago's own self-righteous
vindictiveness than of Emilia. When in the same scene Desdemona asks Iago, 'what
praise couldst thou bestow on a deserving woman indeed?', the very terms of her
question reveal her own qualities. The terms of Iago's reply reveal his scorn for
fairness even more vividly: 'She that was ever fair . . . was a wight, if ever such wight
were . . . to suckle fools and chronicle small beer'. In the same scene again, the
qualities Othello recognizes and praises in the master of his ship are precisely
those—for example, the 'authority of merit'—he values in himself: 'He is a good
one, and his worthiness / Does challenge much respect.' But we cannot fail to notice
the point when, at the end of the scene, Iago speaks to Roderigo of Cassio:

a knave very voluble; no further conscionable than in putting on the mere
form of civil and humane seeming for the better compassing of his salt and

most hidden loose affection ... a slipper and subtle knave, a finder out of
occasions; that has an eye can stamp and counterfeit advantages, though
true advantage never present itself; a devilish knave ... a pestilent complete
knave.   (II, i, 231–40)

Clearly, all these judgments of other people reveal as much (or more) about
the judge as about the judged; and I think it was to underline the significance of this
that Shakespeare included in the scene I have been quoting from (II, i) the otherwise
rather odd game of praise and censure played by Iago and Desdemona—an
incident that has no parallel at all in Cinthio.

The point of it is usually overlooked, perhaps because the game seems so
clumsily imposed on the story. Certainly, Desdemona's excuse for amusing herself at this time ('I am not merry, but I do beguile / The thing I am by seeming
otherwise') is pretty weak, whichever way we look at it: it obliges us to take at
face value the sort of 'I am not what I am' explanation that on Iago's lips would
be most suspect, and so it distracts us into wondering (even while we sense it
is beside the point to do so) why, if she isn't merry, she should feel obliged to
pretend she is, and further, why she proves so *able* here to 'give out such a
seeming'. In trying to account for her part in the game it hardly seems adequate
to speak (as Coleridge did, for example) about her courtesy and consideration for others' feelings here: after all, these would seem a pretty thin reason
for (even dissembled) frivolity in a newly wed wife whose husband may be
drowning while she thus chatters on to cheer up his friends. Besides, her 'counterfeit' merriness doesn't exactly strike one as an effortful disguise of anxiety.
Perhaps a more convincing line of argument would link this quay-side discussion
with Othello's later speech where he denies that Desdemona's gregariousness
(the fact that she 'loves company, / Is free of speech') is a cue for jealousy, and
thus take the game as illustrating her easy sociableness; her aside ('I am not
merry ...') could then be regarded as a sign of her slight shame or embarrassment in catching herself at being so playful—and even a bit coarse-grained—
when she ought to be reserved or worried. The trouble with that explanation
however, is that it leaves us with a Desdemona whose taste for superficial
chat is evidently stronger than her love (why is she *not* worried?) and who is
able to fool or 'beguile' herself simply by declaring 'I am not merry' when obviously she *is*.

But Shakespeare challenges, he doesn't need protection from, our critical
scrutiny; and surely the truth of the matter here is simple enough: finding himself
unable, or unwilling, to invent any very convincing motivation for Desdemona's
behaviour at this point, he perfunctorily put in her aside as at least a plausible
explanation of it. Indeed, though he never troubled to improve it, the dialogue hints
perhaps at his own faintly sheepish but amused sense that the game-scene is all
rather laboured and clumsily managed. Iago's remarks about *his* difficulty in inventing witty repartee are dramatically apt to his character and thus repellent in the
casual brutality of his images (so out of place in the chit-chat situation); but in a more

relaxed and good-humoured sense they could also apply to the self-conscious dramatist himself at this point:

> invention
> Comes from my pate as birdlime does from frieze—
> It plucks out brains and all. But my Muse labours,
> And thus she is delivered.
>
> (II, i, 124–7)

In any case, there seems little need to fuss over the laboured and clumsy delivery of the game: the important thing is that Shakespeare felt he needed such a dialogue between Desdemona (not anyone else) and Iago, and the main question to concentrate on is, why?

The answer lies in its general import and effect. While the game makes us realize how self-revealing are particular people's views of others, it also shows us, in an apparently frivolous context, the collision of two radically different moral outlooks. Desdemona's, which—like Cassio's—generously inclines to see and affirm 'true merit' in others (as was so beautifully attested by her language in the previous scene, for instance, when she spoke of how 'I saw Othello's visage in his mind / And to his honours and his valiant parts / Did I my soul and fortunes consecrate'), here collides with Iago's fundamentally different outlook or disposition—that of a natural defiler and desecrator, for whom the notion of 'consecrating' oneself to anyone else is romantic claptrap ('A fig!'), and who thus always 'profanely' denies any merit besides his own. 'Profane' here is Desdemona's word for Iago's attitude (II, i, 160), and in using it, however light-heartedly, she implicitly appeals to the moral standards she herself lives by, which are once again emphasized by Iago's characteristic perversion of the same language of moral sanctity. Her word may remind us of Iago's own perverse use of it in an earlier soliloquy:

> For I mine own gained knowledge should profane
> If I would time expend with such a snipe
> But for my sport and profit.
>
> (I, iii, 378–80)

Of course the clash between Desdemona's and Iago's moral styles in this quay-side scene is minor, polite, ostensibly joking and cast in hypothetical terms ('O, fie upon thee, slanderer!', Desdemona blithely cries). Only later, amid Iago's more gross slanders and Othello's wild delusion that she must be foul, do we grasp just how revealing, indeed how paradigmatic, this strange little game actually was. Even at the time, however, we feel quite sharply that Iago's habits of mind are no laughing matter. We notice, for example, that Emilia is well aware of his unwillingness to recognize any real worth in others. She seems to speak from bitter experience in remarking to Iago, 'You shall not write my praise.' She implies (and hence makes us aware) that his judgment of her would be merely a sour product of his own sour disposition. And we begin to grasp the darker implications of this fact about Iago when we also notice—or rather deduce— Emilia's pragmatic assumption that it would therefore be utterly futile to challenge him or to try to persuade him to see things her way. Though provoked, she refuses to take an active part in the game. She withdraws and lapses into silence. But we also notice that unlike Emilia and despite her comments, Desdemona entirely misses the point about Iago (just as she later fails to see it about Othello). She naïvely presses him with the question, 'What wouldst thou write of me, if thou shouldst praise me?'; and despite his wry warning—'do not put me to't, / For I am nothing if not critical'—she childishly persists: 'Come on, assay . . .'; 'Come, how wouldst thou praise me?'

Flippant as they are, Iago's comments in this scene make very plain to us that, for a mind as warped as his, terms like 'fair' and 'foul' do not answer to anything objectively real. They are merely labels he applies or withholds as it happens to suit him. Indeed, he treats them as interchangeable. In slick little couplets he applies them in handy-dandy fashion, inverting them in accordance with his own personal whim, his own 'pride and purposes'. Of course, he is teasing Desdemona here, but the fact that his teasing takes this form betrays a good deal about him. (We can't readily imagine Desdemona or Cassio, for instance, trotting out these cynical generalizations.) There is always a virulent sting in the tail of Iago's 'praise'. He is nevertheless not the kind of man who would ever raise even to himself a philosophic question like that Troilus asks, in II, ii, of *Troilus and Cressida*, for instance: 'What's aught but as 'tis valued?' Iago's cast of mind is much rougher than that, much more meanly pragmatic, much less self-reflexively intelligent. He simply assumes that everything depends on his own valuation of it, and sees himself as the sole accurate judge in a world that is wholly manipulable. His personal 'vouchings' are his 'proof' that merit comprises nothing more than a ridiculous fitness 'to suckle fools'. In short, the main thing about Iago that emerges from the quay-side game confirms what we had glimpsed in the opening scenes of Act I: for all his air of coolly detached objectivity, Iago's judgments are not shaped by objective realities at all, but by subjective feelings as hot as any that Brabantio or Othello exhibit in their blackest moments of panic or rage. And, like Emilia, we begin to see that such a man could never be persuaded that the world is other than he 'judges' it to be. That is what Desdemona fails to grasp during the course of the game, and what makes rather frighteningly ominous her innocent inability to realize it. Iago's mind is not one to produce what she calls 'old fond paradoxes', simply 'to make fools laugh i'th' alehouse'.

As I see it, Shakespeare's main interest in Iago from beginning to end of the play centres on the various forms of *imperviousness* Iago cultivates in himself. The action continually makes us scrutinize the nature and source of these attempts to make a shell around himself, the degree to which they work or fail, and the relationship between this impulse in him and his destructiveness.

The first two acts strongly reveal the sort of moral stupidity that is Iago's way of remaining *morally* impervious to life. All his early speeches show what the quayside-scene confirms: that his 'thoughts' are composed of 'certainties' which swing with his current feelings and which he hugs to himself too tightly for them to be ever assailed by conscious doubts. It never occurs to him to wonder whether they might not be open to question. And it is this terrible blind fixity of Iago's moral outlook which makes him often seem to us—to borrow some phrases from Ted Hughes's poem, 'Thrushes'—'more coiled steel than living': he acts always with 'bullet and automatic / Purpose' to size up everyone (or size them down), with a sudden devouring 'efficiency which / Strikes too streamlined for any doubt to pluck at it / Or obstruction deflect'.

His very first speech evinces clearly enough his mental habit of rigidly categorizing people into two kinds—those foolish enough to get used and abused, and those (like himself) clever enough to do the using and abusing themselves. For him, people are starkly polarized into victims and victimizers. Yet he himself, as we notice right from the start of the play, exploits the practical advantages of both. When it suits him to do so, he likes to claim that others have criminally stabbed him in the vitals. At the same time, he likes to think of himself as having absolute governance over himself and his world. He understands human relationships solely in predatory terms. His assumption that life consists either in hurting others or getting hurt oneself is reflected in his every speech and action—his most characteristic verbs (and actions) being those such as 'gyve', 'ensnare', 'enfetter', 'enmesh' and the like. If we refrain from sharing his fascination with his own cleverness and really observe him, we notice that his sense of his cunning and his manipulative skills is grossly inflated. Increasingly clearly, we realize that his power as a hunter and 'poisoner' derives, not from any splendid intellect, but far more from the particular constitutions of his chosen victims. This is true not only in his relations with Othello, but equally with Roderigo and with Cassio, with Brabantio, even (in a rather different way) with Emilia and Desdemona. In each case Iago is more a catalyst that precipitates destruction than a devil that causes it: without his victims' infirmities—including their propensity to trust him—he is in fact utterly impotent.

Iago's self-conceit, impervious to reality, rests on his alacrity in seizing not just on the practical but also the emotional—especially the self-aggrandizing—advantages of *both* views of his relations with his world: he congratulates himself on what he considers his potent ingenuity in snaring others, whom at the same time he swaggeringly despises for being so easily snared. He sees it as his special prerogative to victimize whomever he pleases—usually by inducing people to injure one another for his own 'peculiar end'. Equally, he coolly assumes that for him—though of course not for others—it is fair rather than foul play to trap people in their own infirmities, to poison them with the distilled essence of what they are at their weakest or worst. He views everyone (except himself) as he views Cassio, of whom he declares that his (Cassio's) 'vice' is 'to his virtue the just equinox'. To Iago's mind, in short, personal qualities are mutually cancelling, good and bad merely 'the just equinox' of each other; and since, like 'fair' and 'foul', 'vice' and 'virtue' are (for him) interchangeable, he finds it just as easy to make others' 'virtues' instruments to plague them as he does to capitalize on their 'vices', 'playing the god' with their 'weak function'. Virtually anything serves as fodder for his consuming appetite to negate (for the appetite is to feed and affirm the only 'self' he can acknowledge);

and this is his deliberate policy with everyone on whom he preys—not least, Desdemona:

> For 'tis most easy
> Th'inclining Desdemona to subdue
> In any honest suit. She's framed as fruitful
> As the free elements . . .
> . . . .
> And by how much she strives to do [Cassio] good,
> She shall undo her credit with the Moor.
> So will I turn her virtue into pitch,
> And out of her own goodness make the net
> That shall enmesh them all.   (II, iii, 329–32, 348–52)

Desdemona's earlier reference to such 'merit' as would 'justly put on the vouch of very malice itself' emerges—in the light of Iago's soliloquies—as an attractive but dangerously sentimental illusion, comparable with Cassio's remarks about the storm's readiness to '[let] go safely by the divine Desdemona'. Clearly, nothing would ever 'put on the vouch' of Iago's malice. His soliloquies blast any budding hopes or illusions *we* may have that moral virtue makes a moral universe.

Iago's, then, is an essentially simple mind, for whom life is correspondingly simple. He reduces everything to his own terms, his own labels, his own certainties. Nothing in life as he sees it can't be pigeon-holed. And this outlook—this apparent imperviousness to any moral stress or perplexity—naturally attracts not only men like the callow, vacillating Roderigo, who is a fool any knave could handle, but men like Cassio and Othello too. The kind of 'honesty' Iago cultivates is that of the simple soldier-man—a 'realistic', or rather cynical, blunt man-of-the-world, unimpressed by fine emotions and super-subtle manners, a 'man's man', who cuts through to the nub of a matter, and preserves a firm self-sufficiency.[4] (At least, so it appears.) Nor is this sort of 'honesty' merely a façade, as Iago's very last words in the play demonstrate so clearly: 'Demand me nothing; what you know, you know:/From this time forth I never will speak word.' This exhibits the real potency of his moral outlook: the pragmatic, simplistic, reductive habit of mind that makes his attitudes and schemes so plausible and so attractive to men caught in complex emotions and situations. What they do not reckon on, of course, is Iago's positive need—in Lawrence's phrase—to 'do the dirty' on life; in as much as they are drawn to or sucked in by his defiling view of things, however, they nevertheless share it themselves.

In some ways the simplicity (or the sheer crudeness) of Iago's mind, his complacency, his assumption that the world is at his disposal, are very like Lady Macbeth's.[5] The similarities remind us that in *Macbeth* (as well as in *Lear*) Shakespeare is still pondering the strong allurement, and the crippling cost, of various kinds of moral and emotional insusceptibility. Like Lady Macbeth's, Iago's superficial 'wittiness' turns out to be mere knowingness: for instance, his knowing speech about love as a 'mere permission of the will' is comparable with Lady Macbeth's characteristic tone, as for instance in her speech (I, V, 58ff.) about reading the 'book' of Macbeth's face. Lawrence's remark about her in his poem 'When I Read Shakespeare'—'such suburban ambition'—applies just as well to Iago too. Like her, he makes murder or injury to others sound quite rational, even conventional: both of them speak, not of 'murder', but of sensible self-advancement. No wonder then that Iago finds it as easy as Lady Macbeth does to put others in a state of moral stupefaction, and for much the same reason: moral simplicity is always seductive to those whose lives are complicated and anguished. For Iago, as for Lady Macbeth, nothing is easier than coping with emotions and moral complexities (they even suppose they cope with their own), since they assume it needs only a mere act of will to eradicate feelings and (as Iago puts it) 'turn virtue into pitch'.

Thus Iago assumes and argues that anybody with a proper sense of his own 'pride' and 'place' can readily tell the difference between an advantage and a handicap, and can readily 'stamp and counterfeit advantages, though true advantage never presents itself' (II, i, 236–7). To meet frustration, hurts and disappointments, a man need only—as he says to Roderigo—'know how to love himself':

> If thou wilt needs damn thyself, do it a more delicate way than drowning. Make all the money thou canst. If sanctimony and a frail vow betwixt an erring barbarian and a super-subtle Venetian be not too hard for my wits and all the tribe of hell, thou shalt enjoy her—therefore make money. A pox of drowning thyself! It is clean out of the way. Seek thou rather to be hanged in compassing thy joy than to be drowned and go without her.
>
> (I, iii, 348–55)

For Iago, people—other people, that is—are such knaves that one can easily toy with them for 'sport and profit', as he does with Roderigo here. He has the same attitude to everyone, and exploits them each in exactly the same way. Despite his own (and Bradley's) vast admiration for his cunning, his 'wit' is in fact remarkably stereotyped and inflexible. One after another, he scoffs at people for not showing due self-regard and proper forwardness in discerning and battening onto whatever works for their 'good'. To exactly the extent that he intends to abuse each, he advertises his own disinterested generosity and usefulness in indicating and promoting his 'friend's' best self-interest. The admonitory speech to Roderigo just quoted, for instance, is recognizably a parallel and extended version of an earlier speech to Brabantio, advising him likewise to look sharp and distinguish between benefits and injuries:

> Zounds, sir, you are one of those that will not serve God if the devil bid you. Because we come to do you service, and you think we are ruffians, you'll have your daughter covered with a Barbary horse; you'll have your nephews neigh to you, you'll have coursers for cousins, and gennets for germans.
>
> (I, i, 109–14)

In another situation, and in a different tone, this might strike us as a comically creative fantasy. But here, as always in Iago's accent, relish is so hotly mated with scorn and revulsion that the product is obscene as well as grotesque. To put this speech and others like it beside, say, those of Falstaff in *Henry IV* (especially Part 1) is to see at once that for all the apparent vitality and earthiness of his speech at times, Iago's methods of converting others' benefits to injuries are far less various and far less inventive, as well as more malignant. His stature as a 'wit' and an adroit manipulator of circumstance is barely ankle-high beside Falstaff's capacity to 'turn diseases to commodity': indeed that very Falstaffian word 'commodity' is itself far more comic, droll and genial than any of Iago's terms or euphemisms for self-profit—terms in fact much closer to the less imaginative Hal's, whose method of gaining 'respectability' consists, not in turning 'diseases to commodity', but rather (as Warwick predicts) in 'turning past evils to advantages'.[6] But Iago's talent as 'ingener' (to use Cassio's word) is cruder still—and practically as minimal as that of another sterile malcontent, Thersites in *Troilus and Cressida*. Like his, Iago's *tone* varies hardly at all throughout the play (compare Emilia's), and his 'invention' likewise twists everything into the same contorted shape, and by the same means.

The paucity of his 'inventiveness' plainly reflects the spiritual bankruptcy that prompts it. He merely repeats with Cassio, for example, what he does to Brabantio and Roderigo, being predictably the first to offer (hypocritical) sympathy for the 'hurt' he has in fact engineered, the first to draw attention to his generosity in offering help, and in advising Cassio to change the facts of his situation by changing his attitude to it: after all, he says, 'you have lost no reputation unless you repute yourself a loser'. And he goes on to point out, in what *we* realize are appallingly ambiguous terms, the easiest steps by which Cassio might 'remedy' his pain and 'mend it for your own good':

> Our General's wife is now the General . . . This broken joint between you and her husband, entreat her to splinter; and my fortunes against any lay worth naming, this crack of your love shall grow stronger than it was before.
>
> (II, iii, 306, 312–17)

And once again we find him at the end of the scene coaxing Roderigo out of his misery (at having been hurt in the brawl) by urging him likewise to look on his injury as a benefit consisting of an injury to Cassio:

> How poor are they that have not patience!
> What wound did ever heal but by degrees?
> Thou know'st we work by wit, and not by witchcraft,
> And wit depends on dilatory time.
> Does't not go well? Cassio hath beaten thee,
> And thou by that small hurt hath cashiered Cassio.   (II, iii, 359–64)

It is perfectly simple for Iago thus to play off against one another the self-despising Cassio and the naïvely optimistic Roderigo, cajoling each to undertake the course of remedial action that, unbeknown to themselves, must necessarily cost them most dear. And we already begin to suspect that his advice and procedure with Othello in the following acts will be exactly the same.

*   *   *

It is part of Iago's dramatic function to illuminate the behaviour and attitudes of other characters in the play by comparison as well as by contrast. He is, for example, by no means the only one who self-interestedly exploits or abuses others, and who cannot or will not acknowledge as real anything that clashes with his own wishes or needs. Roderigo and Brabantio are obvious cases in point. Each heatedly tries to deny or refuses to acknowledge that Desdemona might really be in love (and stay in love) with Othello. They do so, we see, because each of them wants or needs not to believe it. Not only does Iago of course deny this too, but even Othello himself in Act III—because of *his* peculiar needs—also comes to assert that it 'cannot be'. Nor is Iago the only one prepared to tread on people's necks or manipulate or exploit them to get what he wants. All through the Venetian world, social and political aims as well as personal ones are often implicitly thought to justify—even, indeed, to necessitate—some form of what we might call 'practised imperviousness' to others' feelings. Iago's comments in I, i about the power and mastery to be got from 'service', for instance, are immediately echoed by Othello himself in the next scene, when he calmly declares that 'My services, which I have done the signory, / Shall out-tongue [Brabantio's] complaints.'

In the following scene, the political version of the same sort of attitude is revealed in the behaviour of the Duke and Senators. Brabantio had asserted that 'if such actions [as Othello's] may have passage free, / Bondslaves and pagans shall our statesmen be'—by which he seems to mean that the lower classes will marry into the aristocracy and thereby assume power in matters of state. But to us his words suggest something else as well, something confirmed when Othello's actions do have passage free—not because they are proved guiltless but because his past and more especially his future services can so readily 'out-tongue' and 'non-suit' Brabantio's challenge.[7] Venice's statesmen are to that extent already surreptitious 'bondslaves' to their political ends.

The details make their point with a nice irony. When the aggrieved Brabantio bursts into the Senate chamber, we notice that, despite the First Senator's clear announcement, 'Here comes Brabantio and the valiant Moor' (in that order), the Duke is so engrossed in thinking about the Turks' attack and Othello's consequent usefulness to the state that he greets Othello first and Brabantio second, and then justifies this rudeness with a placatory white lie:

> DUKE: Valiant Othello, we must straight employ you . . . [*To Brabantio*] I did not
> see you: welcome, gentle signor.

With more pressing matters to deal with than Brabantio's domestic disaster, the Duke first of all swiftly assures Brabantio that 'whoe'er' has done 'this foul pro-ceeding' will be duly punished; and he then, when the invaluable General is alleged to be the criminal, sweeps this promise quietly under the mat. Although he now quite properly (if somewhat tardily) insists that Brabantio's allegations must undergo a wider and more objective test, the Duke proves quite prepared to accept Othello's 'vouchings' as proof—even before Desdemona arrives to confirm them.

Othello has only to announce his version of the courtship, a version which for all its eloquence merely gainsays Brabantio's, and the Duke at once urges Brabantio to back down. We cannot help noticing the double shuffles, I think; and even if they seem reasonable enough in the circumstances (given that we know how irrational Brabantio's tale about 'witchcraft' is), we also cannot help noticing how peremptory the Duke is. Indeed, throughout the scene, the ducal imperatives reveal both his lack of interest in anything not in accord with his own concerns, and his habit of ignoring or overriding everything that conflicts with his will: 'we must straight employ you'; 'take up this mangled matter at the best'; 'you must therefore be content to slubber the gloss of your new fortunes'; 'you must hence tonight'.

Of course, the Duke's concerns are those of the state, not merely private ones; and since his public responsibilities are so evident, neither we nor anyone in the play judges it wrong in him to treat the current international crisis as more important than a domestic complaint. But the very fact that we mentally make these qualifications is interesting. (In fact we tend to speak as though the Duke's public office not only explained his attitude but automatically absolved him from any personal responsibility for the cost his imperatives exact from those he overrides.) For it suggests that we—like the characters in the play—quite happily assume that a strong element of heartlessness (or, as we might say less bluntly, a high degree of human imperviousness) is a necessary and therefore self-justifying condition of political wisdom and success. One effect of the Senate scene is simply to make us aware of the ease with which, when it suits us, we too assume that personal morality and political morality are somehow separate and distinct. And that, in turn, reminds us that in *Othello* Shakespeare is interested in the close relationships between the two, even though this interest is clearly less central here than in those plays more explicitly concerned with politics.

One effect of the whole business about the Turks, I am suggesting, is to make us realize that Iago is not the only person in the play who unthinkingly assumes that his own ends are paramount and self-justifying, and acts accordingly. It would be comforting to be able to hive him off into a special category labelled 'villainous' and treat him as a wholly unique phenomenon in the drama. But the Turkish affair makes it very plain that the same Venetian world that is later (like us) to censure Iago's personal opportunism as the fell morality of a 'Spartan dog' allows free and approved passage to *political* opportunism of a comparably ruthless kind. Shakespeare's wish to suggest this irony is presumably one of the main reasons he includes such details as he does about the Venetians' attitude to the Turks, and (by implication) the Turks' attitude to Venice: both sides take it for granted that, in this sort of struggle for power, self-interest is the sole consideration. Thus everyone (including us) tacitly accepts that as head of state the Duke *has* to think in terms of the same political calculus the First Senator imputes to the Turks. Yet, watching the drama, we also realize what those taking part in it cannot. Even though it is necessary (if the Venetians are to survive the Turks' aggression), their cool reckoning of profit and loss is not essentially very different from the computations of personal self-interest Iago practises and preaches and which we so detest in him:

When we consider
Th'importancy of Cyprus to the Turk,
And let ourselves again but understand
That as it more concerns the Turk than Rhodes,
So may he with more facile question bear it,
For that it stands not in such warlike brace,
But altogether lacks th'abilities
That Rhodes is dressed in. If we make thought of this,
We must not think the Turk is so unskilful
To leave that latest which concerns him first,
Neglecting an attempt of ease and gain
To wake and wage a danger profitless.   (I, iii, 19–30)

Of course it is because the Venetians are themselves so adept at such calculations that they are not taken in by the Turks' deceptive tactics. They see at once that the Rhodes expedition is a mere front, 'a pageant / To keep us in false gaze'—a phrase admirably suitable for Iago's characteristic tactics. So too are the messenger's phrases when he reports that the Turks now 'restem / Their backward course, bearing with frank appearance / Their purposes towards Cyprus'.[8]

However, in suggesting that Shakespeare makes us aware of such affinities as these I do not at all mean to imply that Iago finds 'just' external corroboration in the Turks' or Venetians' political behaviour for the kind of power-game he likes to play in the realm of personal relationships. The drama makes us see very clearly that there is *not* that sort of corroboration in Iago's world. Hence the significance of the fact that Iago likes to suppose there is. On the whole, the world of *Othello* is a trusting one—as Desdemona's, Cassio's and Roderigo's behaviour, for example, keeps reminding us; and even in the political sphere there is a considerable degree of dignity, courtesy and trust amongst the Venetians. And since it is thus not a Marlovian, cynical, stab-in-the-back world that we are shown in *Othello*, we are not inclined to say of Iago (as we might of, say, Barabas, in *The Jew of Malta*) that he's a 'nasty chap, yes, but in a world such as this, how else could one survive?' That is not my point, therefore. Rather, it is that such similarities as we do observe between Iago's personal style and others' actions whether in the public or the private sphere give us cause to think more deeply about the ways in which certain moral assumptions, if given 'passage free', can easily harden into Iago-like extreme destructiveness. Iago's vicious egotism is not corroborated, but neither is he a total freak in the play's dramatic world—and it is this that we begin to realize when we notice, for example, that in the political sphere of Acts I and II nobody hesitates to hope for others' disasters, or to treat them when they occur as their own merited gains. Cassio, for example, 'speak[s] of comfort touching the Turkish loss', and, later on, 'Othello's pleasure' is that every man should 'put himself into triumph' upon certain 'beneficial news' 'importing the mere perdition of the Turkish fleet' (II, ii, 1–6).

It is just this kind of equation of others' injuries or perdition with merited benefits for oneself that the play dramatizes in one way or another not only in Iago but in Roderigo, Brabantio and, later on, Othello as well. Every one of the main characters at some point in some way disregards or uses or abuses others' lives or feelings; and we ourselves become partisan in just this way as well, of course. Which of us does not icily discountenance Iago's wounded feelings for example? Which of us is not prepared mentally to cashier or eradicate him to get what we want? Our willingness to consider him as a beastly 'thing' in our road (to use Brabantio's word for Othello) is not made less dangerous or more admirable by the fact that it is on others' behalf that we 'want' his removal. He is the thorn in the side of our own feelings and these are what make us yearn to 'remedy' the situation by lashing out at him. Indeed—for reasons I shall come to later—part of Iago's dramatic function is precisely to arouse our intolerant loathing, and to make us realize how extreme our own intolerance can be. (Whatever grains of truth there may be in a remark like Johnson's, 'I like a good hater', such an attitude to Iago is possible only if we remain far more detached than the play's action and poetry really allow or enable us to be.)[9] We would love to make him pay in kind for the damage he does to others' lives; we too, in other words, are not above equating another's ill with our own good; and it is the dangerous implications of just this tendency that the play makes so painfully visible, especially in its last three acts. The upshot of Shakespeare's exploration of it, however, as we realize during Desdemona and Emilia's highly pertinent discussion of these issues in the willow scene in Act IV, is not simply to make us condemn it. The play presses us not towards any new, bright-eyed programme of moral reform or re-armament, but towards a fuller understanding of how and why people respond to unhappiness, whether others' or their own. We are brought gradually to recognize (in the characters and in ourselves as we watch them live their lives) the unacknowledged fears and desires and needs that impel people to see the world in this way: the psychological states whose twists and turns reveal or disguise themselves in this sort of moral outlook.

Iago's is the extreme case; and in him as in all the other characters those twists and turns are revealed most clearly in his most energetic efforts to disguise them—in the various ways in which he seeks to justify himself, to cheer himself up and protect or fortify himself against real or imagined threats. In fact, Iago busies himself with self-justification more continuously, obsessively, than any other person in the play. He is always dictating to others how they are to think of him. Of course, most of these self-images are designed to deceive others; but the 'frank' revelations of his nature and aims in his soliloquies are different only in being designed (and managing) to deceive himself. Actually, it is the very urge to justify himself, which is there right from the beginning (and which he never seems to notice), that is most significant. Even in the first scene of Act I, for instance, before we really know he is exploiting Roderigo, his 'honest' self-revelations strike us as remarkably over-insistent—almost as though he were trying to convince himself as well as Roderigo of the truth and justice of his claims. Thus from the very moment he first appears, with his swaggering air of being an 'all-in-all sufficient' man, we are pressed to query the real nature and extent of his self-sufficiency. From the beginning, we cannot help suspecting a large dose of self-consoling fiction in the bits and pieces of autobiography he so eagerly and superfluously recites to Roderigo. His protestations are indignantly self-righteous, repeatedly appealing to external guarantees, external testimony and sanctions: 'be judge yourself'; 'by the faith of man'; 'I, of whom his eyes had seen the proof'; 'Heaven is my judge'. This last comes in an extraordinary speech in which, by way of asserting and congratulating himself on his own total autonomy, Iago calls on (of all things) 'Heaven' to judge, attest, underwrite and sanction his falseness to others and his truth to himself:

> In following him, I follow but myself.
> Heaven is my judge, not I for love and duty,
> But seeming so for my peculiar end:
> For when my outward action doth demonstrate
> The native act and figure of my heart
> In complement extern, 'tis not long after,
> But I will wear my heart upon my sleeve
> For daws to peck at—I am not what I am.   (I, i, 59–66)

This is a highly revealing speech in many respects, and one that makes it clear that Shakespeare knew exactly what he was about right from the very beginning. With consummate precision and control he here alerts us both to the particular propriety and significance of this speech as *Iago's*, and also, more widely, to his own essential subject and dramatic procedure for the whole play. The play's 'outward action', comprising what all its people do and say, dramatically 'demonstrates' to us, 'in complement extern', the 'native act and figure' of Shakespeare's vital concerns as he imagines and projects this particular total dramatic action. And likewise— despite Iago's point about concealment and hypocrisy in real life—each individual dramatic character's 'outward actions' (including his silences and failures to act) are the means by which his inner being is revealed to us. Iago's act here, for example, in making this very speech, demonstrates to us what he is—more clearly than it does either to Roderigo or even to himself. The speech itself, and more especially his impulse or need to make it, all too clearly reveal to us 'in complement extern' the native act and figure of the heart whose power to be hurt it is so busily trying to deny. Despite his claims that his power to wound others cleverly manages to prevent them from injuring him, Iago's images, his tone, his characteristic, watchful sense of all life as predatory, betray a man who feels deeply threatened by others but is totally unable to acknowledge his fear, and who therefore has to reassure himself by scorning 'daws' and cheering himself up with his cleverness in outwitting their power to 'peck at' him.

Charles Lamb once praised a particular actor's performance as Iago because, as he put it, Iago's speeches were rightly delivered in a triumphant tone natural to his general consciousness of power. Many others too have followed Iago's own lead in supposing he gloats because he is so powerful. Yet once we notice how intensely Iago loathes and fears any form of subordination to others (the play's careful emphasis on military rank is not just ornamental),[11] and notice how much he loathes and fears any *in*subordination from others (for instance, Emilia at the end), we are hardly struck by a 'consciousness of power' in him. What appears is rather the reverse—a scorching need to dominate whatever might dominate him.

In this respect, Iago's fleeting, late-in-the-day acknowledgment of Cassio's fineness is as rare as it is revealing:

> He hath a daily beauty in his life
> That makes me ugly . . .[12]   (V, i, 19–20)

It betrays the vestiges in him of a lurking 'sense of beauty' which he everywhere suppresses by transforming it into a 'certainty' that 'fair' really means 'foul' and 'foul' (himself) is 'fair'. As Sen Gupta remarks, Iago's 'allergy to the daily beauty' of others' lives clearly springs from something much more radical than (as Bradley claimed) a mere 'itching for superiority'.[13] The 'itching' is simply part of a remedial endeavour. All through, Iago is eaten up by the suspicion that others are more worthy of respect than he and so make him 'ugly'—a suspicion which Othello comes frightfully to duplicate, and which in Iago is so corrosive that he usually cannot admit it at all. But he is a clear enough example of the general truth of Bacon's dictum about riches: 'they despise them that despair of them'. As with Edmund in *King Lear,* for instance, the very extremity of Iago's compensatory devices reveals to us the raw nerve in him they attempt to cauterize.

Thus, surely, we should interpret his sour contempt for those who 'dote' on 'obsequious bondage', and his mocking pretence of obsequious bondage to Othello and Cassio (whom he gloatingly terms 'Lieutenant' only when he himself has practically robbed him of the job). Hence, too, we should interpret as a mark of impotence rather than power his habit of always taking the benefit and giving others the injury of any doubt, his incessant need to besmirch, belittle and take down, his need to cut the world back to manipulable size and shape so as to immunize himself to every possible threat it might contain. Not surprisingly his own scorn for 'this counter-caster' (Cassio) is what first alerts us to the fact that he himself is the most obsessive scoreboard-keeper or counter-caster in the play. His scheming 'debitor and creditor' economy, his itchy-fingered calculations of how, at least cost to himself, he might turn others' profits to losses and his own losses to gains, are precisely what show him as irrecoverably self-impoverished. The man who so busily promotes disease in others' lives, so busily preaches the moral hygiene of self-interest, so busily hawks about poisonous medicines for others' woes, is powerless to cure his own ills. His only balm is to spread his sickness, to watch others suffer what he cannot admit he suffers himself.

Like others in the play (and probably like most of us who watch it too), Iago's most 'heart'-felt acts are not those in which he edits the version of himself he wants others to read, but those in which he edits the version of himself he needs for his own consciousness. He is extraordinary only in the vast liberties he takes as an editor. As Shakespeare dramatizes Iago's self-justifications and self-explanations, he exposes to our gaze, very clearly indeed, the inner realities they are designed to dissolve, deny or hide. In his speech to Roderigo about 'daws' for instance (I, i, 59–66), we realize the obvious sense in which Iago's claims are valid: we see that, for the unwitting Roderigo, Iago is indeed not what he seems to be. But I think we also begin to realize what is further confirmed every time Iago opens his mouth: that the false 'forms and visages' he puts on to mask from others what he takes to be his real self also serve in a different but equally successful way to mask his real self from what he himself takes it to be.

The major thing that Iago cannot admit into his picture of himself is his own capacity to be hurt—his capacity, that is, for feeling. His will is always prompted by the need to guard against or neutralize wounded feelings (especially self-disgust), precisely as he urges the same remedy on others. In a much-quoted speech to Roderigo in I, iii, he explains his contempt for people who allow themselves to be overwhelmed by emotions. When Roderigo confesses that 'it is my shame to be so fond [of Desdemona], but it is not in my virtue to amend it', Iago's retort comes pat. Brusquely sweeping aside the emotional reality of 'fond', he treats it as merely a synonym for 'foolish', and sweeping aside the moral implications of 'virtue', he converts the issue into a simple matter of manly strength and power. As always, he overrides others' feelings and doubts by jeering at them—'O villainous!'; 'Blessed fig's end!':

> Virtue? A fig! 'Tis in ourselves that we are thus, or thus. Our bodies are our gardens, to the which our wills are gardeners. So that if we will plant nettles or sow lettuce, set hyssop and weed up thyme, supply it with one gender of herbs or distract it with many, either to have it sterile with idleness or manured with industry, why the power and corrigible authority of this lies in our wills.[14]
>
> (I, iii, 316–23)

This is a speech crucial both to our sense of Iago and our understanding of his place in the total action. Of course, he has an ulterior motive here—to stampede Roderigo into complying with his (Iago's) will, by persuading him that he can and ought to exercise his own. But his speech also expresses an attitude he really believes in and likes to think he acts upon. Just as he likes to think the external world is entirely malleable, disposable according to his personal predilections, so he refuses (or is unable) to acknowledge anything in his inner experience that might prove intractable to his will. This is why his admonition to Roderigo comes so easily and with such slick plausibility. Every turn of phrase is revealing. The oppositions slide out neatly, one after another—human lives are seen as passive 'gardens' to be acted upon by 'gardeners' who can simply arrange, as they see fit, to have the garden 'sterile with idleness' or 'manured with industry', and who have the 'power and corrigible authority' to 'plant' or 'weed up' whatever they please, whether this be 'nettles' or 'lettuce'. We can hardly miss how well, in some respects at least, his terms here accord with his own relations with other people, whom he always likes to treat as objects to be cultivated or rooted up ('displanted') at will. But his claim that *inner* experience can be pruned, weeded and fertilized by the will is another matter—one which the whole play is quite centrally directed to exploring.

What Iago asserts to Roderigo is just what he everywhere needs and is pleased to suppose applies to himself—that any man has the right, and (more to the point) the power, to control his inner life so that, because he can simply choose what to feel, he *does not have to suffer anything*. No wonder that this argument cheers Roderigo up. It would cheer anyone up—if (as Iago assumes) it were really as easy as that. The consolations of Iago's philosophy are as obvious as they are large, and it takes in not only Roderigo and (in a more fundamental way) Iago himself, but also many of the play's critics. For it is relatively easy to exonerate Othello of guilt by taking this speech of Iago's at face value, and regarding Iago's will as an irresistible power. After all, did he not succeed in his schemes? This is precisely Iago's view of it. He elevates his will to the status of an irresistible cosmic power: events 'in the womb of time'—that is, the events he wishes to occur—'will be delivered'; nature 'must bring this monstrous birth to the world's light'. To Roderigo he peddles the same kind of story about Desdemona's will. She too, he says, having planted love must inevitably wish to weed it up; everyone has 'reason to cool our raging motions', and love is nothing but a 'scion' of our 'unbitted lusts'. When the love-sick Roderigo demurs, 'It cannot be', Iago echoes and contradicts him, repeating that love is merely 'a permission of the will':

> It cannot be that Desdemona should long continue her love to the Moor . . .
> She must change for youth: when she is sated with his body she will find the
> error of her choice.   (I, iii, 338–9, 345–7)

He comes back to the same point later on:

> Now for want of these required conveniences [sympathy in years, manners,
> beauties], her delicate tenderness will find itself abused, begin to heave the
> gorge, disrelish and abhor the Moor. Very nature will instruct her in it and
> compel her to some second choice. Now, sir, this granted—as it is a most
> pregnant and unforced position. . .   (II, i, 224–8)

Whether or not Iago believes this of Desdemona is dramatically far less important here than his characteristic logic. He assumes that to lack any 'required conveniences' is to find oneself 'abused'; nature's instructions inevitably become compulsions which 'must' be obeyed; desire is equated with necessity: a 'want' automatically 'compels'. Anyone—in particular, himself—can justly have, do, become, or feel whatever he fancies.

Yet what deludes Iago and others in the play ought not to delude us quite so readily. A moment's thought should make it obvious that Iago's actual behaviour everywhere gives the lie to his claims about his power and right to master the world. If, as he likes to think, he can simply determine what to feel and what not to feel, how does the thought of anything come to 'gnaw [his] inwards / Like a poisonous mineral'? Why is his life so full of nettles instead of lettuces? Why does he not simply root up his envy and plant satisfaction in its place? If his will is indeed so omnipotent as he claims, why does he need to plot and plan so elaborately to plume it up? The more we watch him in action the more his much-vaunted powers of 'will' seem as mythical as his much-vaunted powers of 'wit'. Indeed, it is precisely because his 'wit' and 'will' are so impotent that he needs so energetically to plume them up. He is not nearly so much the master of himself and others as a man enslaved by the need to think himself that. His self-bolstering and self-fortifying postures, his assertions of limitless personal power, betray an emotional suscepti- bility he masks from his own consciousness by the iron screen of cynical 'realism'. In short, his conviction of power is revealed to us as a last-ditch defensive strata- gem: his whole mind's endeavour is rigidly and permanently geared to prevent him from having to see his own vulnerability.

The play's concern with the human need for insurance against and remedies for hurt or rejection is obviously not confined to Iago alone.[15] It is significant in a number of ways, for instance, that Iago's first major statement about the will's power to rule the heart is placed where it is, as early as I, iii. It is in this same scene—the dramatic juxtaposition is highly revealing—that the Duke pontificates to Brabantio in a way remarkably similar to (if more pompous than) the way Iago then explains to Roderigo that his grief and distress are an unnecessary waste of time and energy. Roderigo lacks the gumption to point out, as Brabantio does to the Duke, how almost totally impracticable this philosophy is. Nevertheless, Brabantio's reply to the Duke is fresh in our minds as Iago speaks, and Iago's insistence that the will has sovereignty over feelings is thereby immediately set in dynamic opposition to Brabantio's reply to the same idea. Brabantio at least can see and insist that no bruised or broken heart was ever mended by the power of mere exhortatory words, that human feelings are *not* subject to the dictates of the will and have to be suffered in order to be alleviated, and that the only effective way to 'pay grief' is to borrow patience and bear one's pain until it heals—or (as we later learn has been the case with Brabantio) until it kills.

This same opposition is sustained throughout the play: between, on the one hand, assertions like Iago's that one can just *choose* not to suffer, and on the other hand the actual experience of people like Brabantio when they find themselves abruptly discarded or shut out. In Act II, for example, when Iago argues to Cassio what he had earlier argued to Roderigo, Cassio is sufficiently honest with himself to see and say at once what he is later to realize more painfully still: that one cannot just decide not to feel emotions—self-contempt, for instance—and that it involves more than a simple act of will to change one's nature: 'I will ask him for my place again; he shall tell me I am a drunkard. Had I as many mouths as Hydra, such an answer would stop them all.'

Paradoxically, therefore, a crucial part of Iago's dramatic significance in the play is to underline both the need and the cost of *having* to feel rejection, bewilderment, grief and even shame and guilt. Eventually, as we see in the last three acts, it is within Iago himself that the two ways of responding to this fact (that one *has* to feel) collide most terribly: on the one hand, Iago's method of denying one's deepest feelings and trying to substitute other, more tolerable ones in their place, and, on the other hand, the kind of response Desdemona is brought to make: recognizing (as Marlowe's famous couplet so succinctly puts it) that 'It lies not in our power [to choose whether] to love or hate', that one cannot just plant and root up feelings in oneself, for 'will in us is over-rul'd by fate'—by those parts of one's nature that lie beyond the will's reach. In the end, it emerges, one is fated to be the self one is: for all the possibilities of growth and change, one has to live within the limits and potentialities of one's own individual being. And since this includes far more than the conscious will, the will cannot really preserve the self intact—except, of course, by killing it.

Iago's significance, I am suggesting, centres on his unremitting efforts to deny or suppress the feelings that consume him, and to transform them into other feelings that might at once allow and justify a course of retributive action, instead of his having impotently to suffer fear, loss and self-disgust and negation. As we see it, Iago deals with what he is afraid of partly by denying that he fears anything at all, and partly by turning himself into it, becoming the monster who fills him with monstrous dread: he represents the very destructiveness and malignancy he so perpetually, so anxiously, expects from others. Watching him, we are faced with the fact that, like storms, people are indeed capable of wrecking others' lives. Thus, another part of his dramatic function is, in being so persistently present and active in the play's world, to prohibit *us* from dismissing as merely absurd or mad such suspicions, such fearful wariness, as Iago's own or Othello's. His very existence formidably demonstrates that life can indeed be fraught with dangers even more terrible than those one feared, dangers which are real precisely because they can lurk in the quarter where one least suspects them—in one's own self, for instance, or in the person of one's trusted 'friend'. Fears of being destroyed can turn out to have been totally justified—yet the very harbouring of them can destroy the self they were meant to preserve.

Iago's lust for imperviousness perverts his whole life and being, and, paradoxically, it is this that both sets the limit on our capacity to care for him as a fellow human being, yet forces us to acknowledge him as such. The need to protect and preserve oneself, to make oneself psychologically less vulnerable to the injuries life can inflict, is one we recognize in various forms in everyone else and in ourselves, and recognize as naturally and definitively human. But the problem with Iago—which aggravates our need totally to deny our kinship with him—is the extent to which, on the face of it at least, he actually succeeds in making himself morally and emotionally impervious to life. As John Bayley puts it, 'Iago maintains to the end the dreadful integrity of his own ignorance.'[16]

The extremity of Iago's self-preservative arts and the degree to which they succeed are what most clearly mark him off as a limit case in the play: his permanent and absolute *impatience* of life, his insistence on the supremacy of his will, his incapacity ever to be driven to admit (even to himself) the indomitable actuality of anything in his self or his world. He makes himself incapable of any form of conscious self-recrimination, self-doubt or guilt—utterly incapable, that is, of really risking anything of himself. But his entire life is consumed in the perpetual obsession with keeping up all his life-assurance policies. To make himself able to lose nothing, he inevitably (and unawares) makes himself capable only of negative and self-negating gains. When at the end Othello insists that Iago is an honest man 'who hates the slime that sticks on filthy deeds', even though we fully recognize the absurdity of the claim we cannot think that, on the contrary, Iago 'loves' slime. He enjoys sliming and begriming, gets a deep, cheap thrill of fascinated revulsion as he vicariously savours others' (imagined) bestiality—as we discover very early on from the excited insistent rhythms of 'Even now, now, very now, an old black ram / Is tupping your white ewe'. Yet for all that, what we have seen in him is not only that (as Albany puts it in *King Lear*) 'filths savour but themselves', but further that even Iago's 'savouring' is very short-lived—dull and finally unsatisfying to him. Hence the double irony of his taunts at Othello in Act IV, for instance—'Satisfied? . . . How satisfied? . . . Where's satisfaction?' Even after he has got Othello to request and authorize Cassio's assassination, for example, he cannot rest content for a moment but can keep his relish simmering only by keeping on tormenting Othello about the handkerchief. And even in V, i, when he finds himself at the crisis-point he has engineered for others—'it makes us or mars us', 'it makes me or foredoes me quite'—the 'peril' of the situation turns out to have no real piquancy for him at all. In fact, there is nothing in him to 'make' or 'foredo', nothing he will allow to be open to benefit or injury. This becomes unmistakable in the very last scene, when he is finally cornered. He refuses to yield an inch: 'Demand me nothing'—for what *could* he yield? Othello speaks more truly than he knows when he declares 'If that thou be'st a devil, I cannot kill thee.' He cannot, nor could anyone else, kill Iago's heart, not because Iago is a 'devil' but because he—alone of the central figures—is incapable of committing himself to another, and is therefore not open to serious, even fatal injury at anyone else's hand.

In this respect his is a peculiarly significant case, because throughout the play Shakespeare is exploring the capacity of the human heart to break or be broken, and of men to die of grief or, in Emilia's words, 'Kill [themselves] for grief' (and of course for guilt too). Whereas no one other than himself can ever seriously hurt Iago, Cassio finds that the loss of his honour and Othello's love 'e'en kills me'. Even Roderigo is almost fatally wounded because in his own inimitable fashion he loves Desdemona.[17] The last scene presents many deaths, each of which symbolically reinforces the play's stress on the necessary link between loving and vulnerability: Brabantio, Emilia, Desdemona, Othello—they are all killed, emotionally and physically, solely because they were willing to love.

Iago's absolute unlovingness, absolute unforgiveness—his commitment to the supreme safety of *non*-commitment—underline the fact that we come to care about the other characters in the play in direct proportion as they do dare risk themselves, do dare to care about others. For him no one is ever in any real sense *'you'* (though of course he uses that word), but always an object—'she' or 'him'; and his cool competence in dealing with 'problems' is obviously continuous with his cool brutality in dealing with people. But, to compare him again with two not dissimilar characters in other plays, whereas Lady Macbeth's defences eventually collapse, and Goneril is prepared to die because in her own way she loves Edmund—facts which convince us that neither woman has entirely (in Iago's phrase) changed her 'humanity with a baboon'—Iago, who never loses his conviction that his will can protect him from any and every human susceptibility, seems so far gone that it is hard indeed for us to acknowledge his membership of our own species, our own human 'tribe'.

That very difficulty is highly significant. For Shakespeare's presentation of Iago challenges us to dare *not* to shield ourselves from what the drama shows: that Iago's inhumaneness is itself the clearest sign of his humanity. It cannot be safely fenced off into a category labelled 'devilish', 'unhuman'. Despite its best (or its worst) efforts, Iago's will cannot enclose itself totally and permanently in protective armour-plating. Its rapacious need to try to do so betrays the hidden existence of a somewhere-vulnerable self that needs protection, just as the insatiable need to justify his destructiveness makes us see him as destructible—capable, not of being destroyed by another, but of destroying himself in his very craving to make that impossible.

What I am trying to get at here is Iago's dramatic effect on *us*, what his life brings us to see. Bradley remarked of Iago's 'egotism' and 'want of humanity' that Iago 'tries to make them absolute and cannot succeed'. But, as I have tried to suggest about all the other characters, our response to Iago is significantly modified by the considerable degree of success as well as the ultimate (and by him unacknowledged) failure of his self-preservative stratagems. What we find most loathsome is not his unscrupulousness *per se* but his success in continuing to delude himself that it is justified. Somehow, we feel, it would be deeply satisfying to us to make him face the immitigable horror of his own vileness. What hurts us most (and so makes us yearn for the 'comfort' of being rid of him) is just this fact that he retains the comfort of self-delusion.

If we pause to reflect on the emotional logic of that response, we soon realize—with whatever degree of dismay—that Iago's dangerous, gnawing resentment of others' 'benefits' and 'comforts' is exactly mirrored in our potent resentment at *his*. He is so vigilant in protecting himself that it is impossible for us to feel any 'inwardness' with him in the usual sense of that term, since he alienates our sympathies as successfully as he alienates himself from any possible sympathies in his own being. But that very sense of total alienation from him is precisely what makes us bound to him for ever. Our 'inwardness' with him, we might say, is mediated by—indeed, it consists in—our violent antipathy to him. Our hatred and fear of him is commensurate with and duplicates his hatred and fear of life. The multiple 'cause' we so quickly find to 'do justice' on him, the scorching need for retributive action that burns in us and, because frustrated, grows more acute as we watch, corresponds and is equivalent to the same arts of self-preservation, the very destructiveness we abhor in him. It is a chilling thought. But in a play that presses us so hard to realize the implications of all our habits of feeling it is one we can evade only if, Iago-like, we successfully delude ourselves.

Like his towards the world, our inhumaneness towards him is a symptom of our humanity, though a part we normally like to deny the existence of in ourselves. Just as his aggressiveness and his real or imagined vulnerability go hand in hand, so do ours. Yet for us to recognize this is not to find any ready way to sever the connection. And this too is an important truth the play pushes us to see: that our natural impulse to shun or lessen our emotional vulnerability to such a person as Iago is not in itself necessarily culpable, but our every attempt to translate it into action (for example, by wishing for some dire fate to befall him) is bound to be destructive, bound to resemble the behaviour we judge criminal in him.

It is perhaps useful to add here two further obvious but important points. The first is that the old adage, 'tout comprendre c'est tout pardonner' does not—and I believe cannot—apply to our response to Iago. For one thing, we do not really comprehend 'all', and for another it is probably true that the more we understand him the *less* we are inclined to forgive. We blame him because he will not or cannot love or forgive others, but to recognize in ourselves a corresponding refusal or incapacity to love or forgive him does not dissolve or diminish it—or even make us believe we ought to try to muster more charity.

The second point is a related one. If it is a sentimental falsification to suppose that the play makes mercy and love flow warm and tender in all our veins, it is no less sentimental to suppose that the resemblance to Iago's behaviour that we find in our own response to him is tantamount to identification with him. Whilst our reaction to him is in significant ways like his own to others, our response to others is in equally significant ways unlike anything Iago is capable of. Although I have stressed his dramatic function in objectifying our own potential destructiveness, a linked and certainly no less crucial part of his function in the play is to underscore how much we *do* care about those whose joy he plots to annihilate.

Most critics would of course agree that Iago is quite crucial in the dramatic design. What I have been trying to suggest, however, is that this is true in a sense rather different from those usually meant. The basic contradictions in Iago as Shakespeare conceived him are the essence both of his dramatic 'character' and therefore of his dramatic importance—so essential, in fact, that it is perhaps useful to summarize them before turning to consider Othello, who has so much in common with his 'friend' and yet who differs so vitally from him.

From beginning to end of the play, Iago represents, in an extreme form, the urge to shield oneself from hurt and injury by the exercise of sheer will (on others and on oneself) and the effect of doing so: a ruthless *maiming* of life both inside and outside the self. Iago's contempt for others is significant because it is so clearly the other side of an unacknowledgeable self-contempt—a sense of injury and resent-ment aroused by feeling disregarded and therefore denigrated by others, but masking itself from conscious recognition by a conscious 'philosophy' of cynicism and a readiness to find 'causes' for injuring everyone else. Indeed, some of his phrases to Roderigo concerning will-power are also strikingly apt to the manifold motives or 'causes' he offers himself for his own behaviour: according to his whim or 'necessity' of the moment, he 'sets' or 'weeds up' any suitable rationale that springs to mind, his policy being simply to 'supply [his mind] with one, or distract it with many'. No one cultivates his motive-garden more assiduously than Iago does. Nor does it take us long to see that (to use the Duke's words in Act I) 'there is no composition' (consistency) in Iago's claims about himself 'that gives them credit'.

The inconsistencies are strongly emphasized. To act as he does, Iago needs to think of himself as a persecuted and wounded victim, even while pluming up his will by asserting and seeking to prove that he is too tough and clever to be woundable. On the one hand, identifying himself with what he claims is his autonomous will, he sees himself as free, omnipotent and thus invulnerable because moved only by self-chosen emotions; on the other hand, he identifies himself as the scandalously victimized object of *other* people's malignant wills, thus justifying his chosen methods for remedying the 'injuries' allegedly done to him. This sense of himself as both victim and agent allows him a wonderfully flexible sense of his own freedom. It enables him not to recognize how much he is bound by emotions and fears he cannot choose either to have or to discard; at the same time, it enables him to absolve himself of any sense of culpability by supposing that everyone behaves (or ought to) in the same way:

> And what's he then that says I play the villain,
> When this advice is free I give, and honest,
> Probal to thinking . . .
>
> . . . .
>
>   How am I then a villain
> To counsel Cassio to this parallel course
> Directly to his good? Divinity of hell!   (II, iii, 326–8, 338–40)

In Iago, the need of sheer will-power, and the contradictions it betrays, are more deep-seated and thus more extreme than in any of the other characters; but in varying forms and degrees all the others exhibit these as well. Roderigo, Brabantio and Cassio all veer on occasion between a sense of being unfairly victimized and a sense of being a free agent rationally justified in injuring others. In the last three acts of the play, as we shall see, even Emilia and Desdemona (each in her own fashion) veer between assertions of their autonomy and a sense of being helplessly negated by others. Similarly, but most terribly of all, Othello careers wildly from one sense of himself to another, or tries to entertain both simultaneously in a frantic effort to avert total self-distintegration. Yet in each case the drama is concerned with more than the mere fact of such habitual contradictions in people. It probes the underlying causes why they think of themselves in these ways, and further, the reasons why people often, in times of real or imagined crisis, *must* do so in order to survive at all. Again and again *Othello* shows how, in the face of potential or actual threats from others or from one's own feelings, the only comfort or consolation an individual can sometimes find, and which he instinctively clutches at or even invents, is some or any relatively clear-cut sense of himself and of his place in the world. When external conditions in one's life prove (or seem to prove) intolerably refractory, a fluctuating—or, better, an ever-adaptable—sense of *one-*

self is often the only means of 'coping', though (as Shakespeare makes crystal clear in this as in virtually every play he wrote) to 'cope' with a problem is always costly and not at all necessarily the same as 'solving' it. In Iago's case, the gymnastic leaps from one sense of himself to another are revealed as gratuitous, glibly opportunistic, usually a simple function of 'required convenience'. But at the other extreme from Iago we find Desdemona also striving to find some steady foothold, some steady sense of herself, amid the changing current of her life, and struggling the more desperately to retain it as her experience grows more and more turbulent. For her and for Othello alike, the maintenance of any clear, true and yet still bearable, still livable, sense of themselves and of each other not only becomes more difficult as the action develops, but becomes in the end a tragic impossibility, grounded in their love itself.

As it progresses, the play explores and brings home to us the ways in which each of the lovers' attempted defences against shock and grief differ from, resemble or combine the defensive stratagems employed instinctively by each of the other characters. Of these, the most revealing cases are perhaps Cassio's, where the stratagems are the most frankly self-acknowledged, and Iago's, where they are the most fixed, far-gone and indissoluble. Iago is the only one of all the main characters who cannot be crushed by grief; the defences of each of the others become eroded and broken at last by the engulfing tide of their experience. This seems to me another reason why the play is so deeply disturbing. In showing us how *all* its people seek at times to evade, deflect or master their insurgent feelings, and in showing us how and why they all (except Iago) ultimately fail, it shakes the ground beneath our own habitual props and shelters. It makes us realize both the naturalness of the human need for self-consolation, and the delusions involved in such necessary efforts to cheer ourselves up. Iago's case reveals to us the essential human hollowness of one who can never recognize what every other character is eventually, at vast emotional cost, forced and able to see: that one's freedom begins only in realizing how far one is necessarily bound by the feelings that grow in and around commitments one can neither ignore nor change; that the 'will' is therefore subject to the core in human beings that makes them susceptible to pain as well as being capable of inflicting pain on others—that it cannot be autonomous any more than it can make one impregnable. More clearly than any other character, Iago exhibits why human life ultimately cannot, for all its need to, insulate and defend itself in mere will, or find any citadel worth defending that is stronger than its own power to hurt and to be hurt.

NOTES

[1] Marvin Rosenberg, 'In Defense of Iago', *Shakespeare Quarterly*, 6 (1955), pp. 145–58, offers a convenient summary of some of the main views.
[2] Cf. for example, W. H. Auden's assertion that 'any consideration of the Tragedy of Othello must be primarily occupied, not with its official hero, but with its villain'; *The Dyer's Hand* (London, 1962 [1948]), p. 246. Perhaps the most ambitious example is Stanley Edgar Hyman's *Iago: Some Approaches to the*

Illusion of His Motivation (New York, 1970). This is offered as 'a display of pluralistic literary criticism' (p. 3), but the result seems only 'perplexed in the extreme'.

[3] *Shakespearean Tragedy*, p. 143; see also his rather Johnsonian remark on p. 146: 'Nowhere else in Shakespeare do we hold our breath in such anxiety, and for such a long time as in the later Acts of *Othello*.' In observations like these Bradley seems to me much truer to our actual dramatic experience than the cooly analytic distance most anti-*Othello* critics suggest we can and should maintain.

[4] A pertinent study of the play's critique of the 'male ego-ideal' is John Fraser, '*Othello* and Honour', *The Critical Review*, 8 (1965), pp. 59–70.

[5] On this point, and for a number of other insights about *Macbeth*, I am gratefully indebted to an unpublished study of that play by Jillian Redner (Melbourne).

[6] Falstaff's characteristic phrase comes at the close of Part 2, I, ii; Warwick's narrowly pragmatic one (symptomatic of the play's imaginative contraction during Part 2) comes in IV, iv, 78.

[7] Cf. Iago's phrases in I, i, 12ff.: 'But he [Othello] . . . / Evades [my supporters] with a bombast circumstance . . . / Non-suits my mediators'.

[8] Iago's 'frank appearances' disguise his 'purposes' as heavily as do his 'backward courses'—see for example III, iii, 191ff., when he begins his grossest deception by declaring, 'now I shall have reason / To show the love and duty I bear to you / With franker spirit'.

[9] For a very different view of our relationship with Iago, see for example E. A. J. Honigmann's discussion of *Othello* in his *Shakespeare's Seven Tragedies: The Dramatist's Manipulation of Response* (London and New York, 1976). (Honigmann's opening chapters set out some of the same general issues I am also concerned with, though his discussions of particular plays do not seem to develop his opening suggestions as far as they deserve.)

[10] Muir follows Rowe's second (1714) edition in giving 'compliment' at line 64; but because it catches the more far-reaching meaning of the pun, I have substituted the spelling of the Folios and Quartos, 'complement'.

[11] See John Robert Moore, '*Othello*, Iago and Cassio as Soldiers', *Philological Quarterly*, 31 (1952), pp. 189–94.

[12] There are some interesting comments on this in William Empson's essay on *Othello*: see *The Structure of Complex Words* (London, 1951), p. 234.

[13] S. C. Sen Gupta, *Aspects of Shakespearian Tragedy* (Calcutta, 1972), p. 17.

[14] For reasons which I hope will be plain from my argument about the play's examination of 'will-power', it does not seem to me in the least worth while to enter into the interminable debate about the relationship of this speech to Christian doctrine, as conducted by, for example, Bernard Spivack, *Shakespeare and the Allegory of Evil* (New York, 1958), pp. 423–4; J. V. Cunningham, *Tradition and Poetic Structure: Essays in Literary History and Criticism* (Denver, 1960), pp. 150–3; Roland Mushat Frye, *Shakespeare and Christian Doctrine* (Princeton, 1963), pp. 159–60; Daniel Stempel, 'The Silence of Iago', *Publications of the Modern Language Association of America*, 84 (1969), pp. 252–63; Ruth Levitsky, 'All-in-All Sufficiency in *Othello*', *Shakespeare Studies*, 6 (1970), pp. 209–21. The real significance of this speech surely lies in its *dramatic* context and implications.

[15] A fascinating study could be made of how words such as 'sure', 'assured', 'satisfied', 'secure', 'safe', operate throughout the play.

[16] *The Characters of Love* (London, 1960), p. 146.

[17] Roderigo is usually said by critics to be 'killed' at the end, but Shakespeare is careful to qualify Lodovico's phrase 'the slain Roderigo' (V, ii, 306) with Cassio's 'and even but now he spake / After long seeming dead—Iago hurt him, / Iago set him on' (V, ii, 323–5). His severe yet *un*mortal injury symbolically confirms our sense of Roderigo's genuine yet relatively shallow and accidental love for Desdemona. Despite his assertions in I, iii, he doesn't (unlike Othello) have to call on death as his only 'physician'. Less radical 'surgery' will do.

Randolph Splitter

LANGUAGE, SEXUAL CONFLICT AND ''SYMBIOSIS ANXIETY'' IN *OTHELLO*

A s Stephen Dedalus says in Joyce's *Ulysses,* Iago and Othello seem like two parts of one mind, Shakespeare's: "in *Othello* he is bawd and cuckold. He acts and is acted on. . . . His unremitting intellect is the hornmad Iago ceaselessly willing that the moor in him shall suffer."[1] Iago appears as Othello's alter ego, his evil demon, who "infects" him with (his own) morbid suspicion and jealousy, so that Othello comes to share some of Iago's attitudes and to reveal, in himself, some of the same fundamental fears and desires.[2] Indeed, the problem of relationships in the play—between men and women, men and men—leads to the seductive but frightening possibility that the boundaries between people might be breached, destroying the separate, autonomous identity of each individual self. As Iago says (rather ambiguously) in the opening scene of the play: "Were I the Moor, I would not be Iago. / In following him, I follow but myself. / . . . I am not what I am" (I, i, 54–55, 62).[3] The passionate, paranoid, contradictory feelings about human relations in this play reflect not only an ambivalence about sex and the sexual role of women but—and this is the subject of my essay—a fundamental, "preoedipal" uncertainty about (sexual) identity, the boundaries of the self, the interpenetration of inner and outer worlds.[4] Moreover if the boundaries of the self can be transgressed and violated, the dangerous pathogenic agents that penetrate these boundaries turn out, in *Othello,* to be thoughts, images or simply words. Thus uncertainties about personal relations, in the play, correspond to uncertainties about the relation between words and "things," between language and reality.

Iago has his reasons for acting the way he does—he gives several of them—but these reasons are unconvincing, partly because there are too many of them.[5] He resents the fact that Othello has made Cassio his lieutenant instead of himself, but he also wonders, in a soliloquy, if Othello has committed adultery with his wife: "I hate the Moor, / And it is thought abroad that 'twixt my sheets / H'as done my office. I know not if't be true, / But I, for mere suspicion in that kind, / Will do, as if for surety" (I, iii, 377–81). He does not know if the rumor is true; the mere

From *Mosaic* 15, No. 3 (September 1982): 17–26.

suspicion is enough for him. Indeed, he does not hate the Moor *because* he has gone to bed with his wife: the rumor (if in fact there is a rumor) is only an excuse, a pretext, for hating Othello. There is no evidence for this suspicion in the play and no indication of it in the scenes between Othello and Emilia. In a later soliloquy Iago insists that the thought of this adultery, "Doth, like a poisonous mineral, gnaw my inwards; / And nothing can or shall content my soul / Till I am evened with him, wife for wife" (II, i, 297–99). Although he immediately backs down from this resolution— deciding to make Othello jealous instead—he claims that he wants to pay Othello back by committing adultery with *his* wife: "Now I do love her too; / Not out of absolute lust" (II, i, 291–92) but because he wishes to feed ("diet") his desire for revenge. Besides, Iago, who seems to believe that adultery is universal, wonders if Cassio, the man he puts in the role of illicit lover, has also cuckolded *him*: "For I fear Cassio with my nightcap too" (II, i, 307).

This paranoid multiplication of lovers suggests that sexual betrayal is simply Iago's (as it is Othello's) favorite form of persecution. In fact, these ambiguous reasons raise more questions than they answer. Does Iago hate Othello because of Cassio's preferment or because of his wife's supposed adultery (with Othello)? Does he imagine going to bed with Desdemona merely because he wants to hurt Othello or because he does in fact desire her, out of "absolute lust" or not? Or does he desire Desdemona because she is Othello's wife, not only for the sake of revenge but because he identifies himself with Othello?: "In following him, I follow but myself" (I, i, 55). Is it for this reason that he imagines Othello in bed with *his* wife, because he wishes to share his bed (and his wife) with Othello?

At the very beginning of the play Iago has to protest to Roderigo that he does not love Othello: "If ever I did dream / Of such a matter, abhor me" (I, i, 4–5). Later, after kneeling together with Othello to seal the "sacred vow," he pretends to swear loyalty to him in words that suggest amorous devotion more than military duty: "I am your own forever" (III, iii, 458, 476). Moreover, Iago recounts to Othello a surprising episode which he (presumably) invents in order to make Othello jealous: "I lay with Cassio lately, / And being troubled with a raging tooth, / I could not sleep" (III, iii, 410–12). That Iago is lying in bed with Cassio, even if the influx of soldiers has created a shortage of beds on Cyprus, is already surprising, but Iago goes on to say that Cassio, in a dream, mistook him for Desdemona:

> In sleep I heard him say, "Sweet Desdemona,
> Let us be wary, let us hide our loves!"
> And then, sir, would he gripe and wring my hand,
> Cry "O sweet creature!" Then kiss me hard,
> As if he plucked up kisses by the roots
> That grew upon my lips; laid his leg o'er my thigh,
> And sigh, and kiss, and then cry, "Cursèd fate
> That gave thee to the Moor!"   (III, iii, 416–23)

Of course the "manifest content" of his dream is Cassio's alleged desire for Desdemona, but Cassio's dream is actually part of Iago's waking "dream"—his made-up story—of lying in bed with Cassio. In this story, Iago himself plays the part of Desdemona while Cassio makes sexual advances to him. Ironically, when Cassio cries, "Cursèd fate / That gave thee to the Moor!" he is speaking to Iago. But fate has given Cassio, not Iago, to the Moor, and Iago could just as well have given this line (which he has "written") to himself: Iago curses the fate that gave thee (Cassio) or thee (Desdemona) to the Moor, not only because he wants Cassio or Desdemona for himself but because he wishes that *he* instead of they had been given to Othello ("I am your own forever"). The interpretation of dreams—particularly ones that are, like this one, not dreams at all but conscious, deliberate inventions, whether Iago's or Shakespeare's—is a tricky business, but let us recall Iago's line at the opening of the play, when we do not yet know what he and Roderigo are talking about: "If ever I did dream / Of such a matter, abhor me." The word *abhor* is used again, by Desdemona: "I cannot say 'whore.' / It does abhor me now I speak the word" (IV, ii, 160–61). The pun on *whore* in *abhor* implies that if Iago ever did dream of "loving" Othello, this love would not be an innocent figure of speech, a rhetorical display of devotion, but would make him whorelike and effeminate.

Needless to say, Iago's "love" for Othello, Cassio, Desdemona or anyone else is buried in a general mistrust of human relations. For the most part, he views men as enemies who would like to cuckold him, and women as whores who are always cuckolding their husbands. He accuses women of being "Players in your housewif-ery, and housewives in your beds. . . . You rise to play, and go to bed to work" (II, i, 111, 114). Thus they play the wrong roles in the wrong situations, confusing work and pleasure, fun and profit, either because they are too cold and practical in bed or because they work as "housewives" in the special sense of prostitutes: as Iago says of Bianca, "A huswife that by selling her desires / Buys herself bread and cloth" (IV, i, 96–97). Although Bianca is genuinely concerned about Cassio and cares more for him than he does for her, Iago attempts to pin the blame for Cassio's murder on her: "I do suspect this trash / To be a party in this injury": "This is the fruits of whoring" (V, i, 85–86, 116).

Bianca claims that she leads an honest life, and this word *honest,* the ironic epithet which Othello repeatedly applies to the deceitful, dishonest Iago as if to assure himself that it is true, is a crucial word in the play.[6] Emilia assures Othello that Desdemona is "honest, chaste, and true" (IV, ii, 17), with honest meaning virtuous and faithful in love, as in the phrase "an honest woman"—which does not mean quite the same thing as "an honest man." Iago tells Othello that a woman may give up—to another man—anything that belongs to her, even if it is a gift that her husband has given her, even a handkerchief. Othello says, "She is protectress of her honor too. / May she give that?" and Iago replies that honor (from the same Latin word as *honest*) is not a tangible possession: "Her honor is an essence that's not seen; / They have it very oft that have it not" (IV, i, 14–17). In other words, a woman's honor is an idea, a moral virtue, perhaps even an unattainable ideal, which—because it is not visible and tangible—may be feigned by those who do not really possess it. This honor is an idealized essence with no ultimate reality, a mere word, as in Falstaff's soliloquies in *Henry IV, Part One:* "What is honor? A word. What is in that word honor? What is that honor? Air" (V, i, 134–35).

In a more specific sense, however, the unseen essence that a woman can give away is her sexual favors, the "property rights" to her "private parts," which (Othello implies) are a possession that a woman should *not* be able to give away because they ultimately belong to her husband, like the magical, symbolic hand-kerchief which a husband (receiving it from his mother) bestows upon his wife. The context refers to married women, but in the most literal sense, the unseen, invis-ible, hidden sign of chastity—which a woman "owes" to her husband and is not supposed to give to any other man—is her virginity. Of course virginity has a certain literal reality, but it also seems to be a kind of magical quality which virgins possess and "fallen women," unfaithful wives and prostitutes do not. Married women, even faithful ones, are in an ambiguous position, because they lose their virginity but are supposed to retain their chastity, their virtue. In short, a woman's honor may be "an essence that's not seen" (1) because it is so insubstantial, so hard to be sure of; (2) because it is literally kept hidden, by those who are chaste and by those who deceive their husbands; (3) because it does not really exist, a woman's sexual organs being (in Iago's mind) only an empty space rather than a visible, tangible possession; and (4) because it *does* exist, because it is (again, in Iago's mind) so valuable, so desirable and so dangerous a possession that it *must* be kept hidden.

In an earlier scene "honest Iago" tells Othello that a person's "good name" is likewise an "unseen essence" that is worth more to him than mere money:

"Good name in man and woman, dear my lord,
Is the immediate jewel of their souls.
Who steals my purse steals trash; 'tis something, nothing;
'Twas mine, 'tis his, and has been slave to thousands;
But he that filches from me my good name
Robs me of that which not enriches him
And makes me poor indeed."   (III, iii, 155–61)

Although Iago does not really believe that his purse is trash, he knows the value of an honest reputation, whether or not the reputation is deserved. And at least in this speech, he claims that money is worthless because it passes through so many hands that it never really belongs to anyone: since it has been "slave to thousands," it is in a sense worn-out and tarnished, soiled by so much handling, and since it has only a "symbolic" exchange-value, it is intrinsically, in itself, worthless. Ironically, in this argument, the tangible, material money in one's purse is "something, nothing," while one's good name—an abstract idea or simply a word like the name "honest Iago," like Falstaff's "word honor"—is a valuable jewel.

Indeed, the phrase "good name in man and woman" makes it seem very close to the idea of a woman's reputation or honor, which is conventionally compared to a jewel (Othello's "threw a pearl away" [V, ii, 343]). A man who robs a woman of her virtue, her virginity, takes something which (under the prevailing social code) is valuable to her but does not enrich him, at least not permanently. Moreover, virginity is "something" while it lasts but then it is "nothing." Of some women's virtue, as of Iago's purse, it may be said: " 'Twas mine, 'tis his, and has been slave to thousands." This is precisely what Iago argues and what Othello fears. In fact, if Iago calls his purse "trash," he also calls Bianca, the prostitute who sells her favors for money, by this name, as if she were worthless trash because she too had become shopworn and soiled. In the very act of saying it Desdemona says she cannot say the word "whore," as if the word itself would tarnish her lips (IV, ii, 160).

DES.: Am I that name, Iago?
IAGO: What name, fair lady?
DES.: Such as she said my lord did say I was.   (IV, ii, 117–18)

Othello asks, "Was this fair paper, this most goodly book, / Made to write 'whore' upon?" (IV, ii, 70–71), as if writing or naming were the same as making it so, as if having (adulterous) sexual relations with a woman were the same as writing the (foul) word whore upon her fair body. Is virtue (honor, honesty) only a word, a name, or does it really exist? If it does exist, can it be seen or touched? How can one tell if it is there? Can one find it by looking at a woman's naked body, or will one find nothing? And can one conjure it into existence simply by naming it, by writing it down, by writing a play about it?

"Thieves! Thieves! / Look to your house, your daughter, and your bags!" (I, i, 76–77), Iago cries to Brabantio—echoing Shylock's "My daughter! O my ducats! O my daughter!" in *The Merchant of Venice* (II, viii, 15)—as if a daughter were merely an economic possession, a commodity to be traded on the marketplace like a prostitute. Near the end of the play, Othello, treating Desdemona as if she were a whore in a brothel, throws some money to the "madam" Emilia. In his harangue against Roderigo for not continuing to pursue Desdemona (I, iii), Iago repeats the phrase "Put money in thy purse" like an obsessive, ritualistic, slightly insane incantation, belying his later claim that one's purse is trash. (Preserving one's good name, the bourgeois version of honor, while at the same time putting money in one's purse is classic middle-class morality.) In giving this advice to Roderigo, Iago is trying to fatten his own purse: "Thus do I ever make my fool my purse" (I, iii, 374) or, in Roderigo's words, Iago "hast had my purse / As if the strings were thine" (I, i, 2–3). But Iago is also implying that one needs money in order to woo women, as if (once again) they were commodities to be bought and sold. Indeed, if purse and prostitute (both "trash") are identified in Iago's mind, perhaps the ultimate meaning of "putting money in a purse" is giving money to a prostitute and putting something else inside her, in that empty pocket where her "good name" should be written. For Iago, who believes that all women are whores, putting money in a purse is an economic, bourgeois metaphor for sexual intercourse, an elaboration upon the metaphor of "spending" (Shakespeare's "expense of spirit in a waste of shame").[7] In fact, the question arises whether putting-money-in-a-purse is spending or saving, should put "money" in one's own purse—should keep it for oneself—rather than spending or expending it on women.

When Cassio, having gotten into a drunken brawl, bemoans the loss of his reputation (his good name), Iago, always ready with practical, hard-headed, realistic advice, replies: "I had thought you had received some bodily wound. There is more sense in that than in reputation. Reputation is an idle and most false imposition, oft got without merit and lost without deserving. You have lost no reputation at all unless you repute yourself such a loser" (II, iii, 265–70). As of honor, "They have it very oft that have it not." But Cassio feels that in losing his reputation he has "lost the immortal part of [him]self"—his spiritual essence—"and what remains is bestial" (II, iii, 262–63). And Iago's comparison to a bodily wound hints that the loss of reputation—at least in a woman's case—is like a bodily wound: as if, in a bloody intercourse, a virgin lost that elusive, fetishistic possession—her virginity—and became, in effect, "castrated." Even men fight "in terms like bride and groom/ Devesting them for bed ... tilting one at other's breasts/In opposition bloody" (II, iii, 179–83). And Iago's description of Cassio plucking up kisses by the roots implies that something—such as Iago's raging "tooth"—is being torn out.

In short, violent passions cause people to lose their reason—the body acting without the mind—and sex itself, which transforms human beings into the "beast with two backs" (I, i, 114), is a violent, bloody struggle in which women lose their virtue and men lose their manhood. When Roderigo is grief-stricken in his love for Desdemona, Iago urges him to "be a man" (I, iii, 331) and, criticizing Othello for a "passion most unsuiting such a man," Iago advises him to be patient: "Or I shall say you're all in all in spleen,/And nothing of a man" (IV, i, 79, 90–91). As in *Hamlet* and *King Lear,* passion—the loss of rationality, of self-control—is considered effeminate. Even sexual passion, which would seem to corroborate one's manliness, may cause one to lose one's manhood, to become, in Iago's fantasy of sexual violence, castrated. In this version of the battle between the sexes, both sides risk losing the ambiguous, possibly even imaginary possession that gives them their sexual value.

The violence that contaminates sexuality in *Othello* is made manifest in the last scene of the play, where murder becomes a substitute for sex. "Thy bed, lust-stained, shall with lust's blood be spotted" (V, i, 36), says Othello, confusing the different fluids that may be spilled in sexual relations and confusing as well the different ways blood may be spilled, as if he were murdering a virgin by sexual means. Othello and Desdemona, whose wedding night is interrupted by the voyage to Cyprus and the threat of war, seem to spend the rest of the play trying to consummate their marriage; whether they ever do is not absolutely clear. Although Iago imagines Othello as the adulterous, "lusty Moor," the Moor himself claims that "the young affects" are "defunct" in him and he is in no great hurry to go to bed with Desdemona (I, iii, 256–59). On her last night alive Desdemona asks Emilia to put her wedding sheets on her bed, as if the marriage were not yet consummated. Othello realizes that a dead Desdemona would be lost to him forever—"When I have plucked the rose,/I cannot give it vital growth again;/It needs must wither"

(V, ii, 13–15)—but his words have another meaning: when he has robbed her of her virginity, "deflowered" her, the "flower" will not grow back again. She is desirable only if she remains a virgin, and this belief coexists in Othello's mind with the contradictory belief that she is a "whore" who has lost her virginity many times over. He tries to preserve her virginity, in effect, by killing her: "Be thus when thou art dead, and I will kill thee,/And love thee after" (V, ii, 18–19). But killing—and killing himself along with her—is also a substitute for sex, whereby he can punish her for betraying him, punish himself for punishing her, and at the same time make sure that she will be his forever: "I kissed thee ere I killed thee. No way but this,/Killing myself, to die upon a kiss" (V, ii, 354–55).

A woman's honor is an intangible possession, perhaps merely a word, but throughout the play words, thoughts and mental images are represented as real, literal and potentially dangerous "things." Early in the play Brabantio, mourning the loss of his daughter, says, "These sentences, to sugar, or to gall,/Being strong on both sides, are equivocal./But words are words. I never yet did hear/That the bruisèd heart was piercèd through the ear" (I, iii, 213–16). But this is a minority opinion. The very thought of Othello's reputed adultery inflames Iago's passions and invades his body: "the thought whereof/Doth, like a poisonous mineral, gnaw my inwards" (II, i, 296–97). Turning his own paranoid fears against Othello, Iago frames a plan "to abuse Othello's ears" (I, iii, 386) with the information that Cassio is too familiar with his wife. Feeding him the lies, doubts and suspicions that will infect him with morbid jealousy as if it were an almost physical disease, Iago will "pour this pestilence into his ear" (II, iii, 356), in exactly the same way that Claudius poisons his brother in *Hamlet*. Iago's poisonous words, poured into Othello's ear, may well reach the "bruisèd heart" or brain, and, according to the metaphor, they are the pathogenic agents that will bruise, contaminate and infect it. As Iago himself says, "The Moor already changes with my poison:/Dangerous conceits are in their natures poisons" (II, iii, 322–23).[8]

At the turning-point of the play Othello complains that Iago is hiding from him "some monster in thy thought/Too hideous to be shown. . . . As if thou then hadst shut up in thy brain/Some horrible conceit. If thou dost love me,/Show me thy thought" (III, iii, 107–08, 114–16). Leading Othello on, Iago says that everyone's imagination sometimes harbors "foul things" even if they are "vile and false" (III, iii, 136–38): "As I confess it is my nature's plague/To spy into abuses, and of my jealousy/Shape faults that are not" (III, iii, 146–48). The "abuses" that he spies into are also the dangerous, horrible or monstrous conceits with which he poisons ("abuses") Othello's ears. If Iago's poisonous words embody the information that Desdemona is committing adultery with Cassio, it is the visible image of this relation that Othello wants Iago to provide for him. Iago arranges for Othello to eavesdrop while he gets Cassio to discuss his love life, Othello mistakenly thinking that they are talking about Desdemona rather than the prostitute Bianca. In his verbal report of Cassio's alleged dream, Iago gives Othello an imaginary vision of Cassio in bed with his wife, which is, on closer inspection, a vision (also imaginary) of Cassio in bed with Iago. But Othello sees what he wants to see and remains blind to the existence of

Iago in the bed. This vision, which Othello calls "monstrous," is the horrible conceit, the monster in Iago's thought too hideous to be shown.

But the monster is, equally, in Othello's thought, and it is hard to say whether Iago put it there or simply found it, latent, potential, unconscious, waiting to be made conscious. Demanding "ocular proof" that his wife is a whore (III, iii, 356–57), Othello is in the position of a child wishing to observe the disturbing, confusing and sexually exciting "primal scene" of his parents making love; the "beast with two backs" is a child's view of sex. He even says that he would have been happy if all the soldiers in the camp "had tasted her sweet body" (III, iii, 343), as long as he had not known about it. In effect, Iago "impregnates" Othello—"It is engendered!... this monstrous birth" (I, iii, 394–95)—with the poisonous image of a primal scene, an image of two people of indeterminate sex doing something passionate, violent and bloody to each other. As Lodovico says at the end of the play, "Look on the tragic loading of this bed./... The object poisons sight;/ Let it be hid" (V, ii, 359–61).

The idea of disturbing thoughts penetrating one's mind from the outside suggests that the boundaries of the self are dangerously vulnerable. This psychological poisoning, the primal-scene image of sexual relations as *one* beast with two backs, and the subtle confusion of identity between Iago and Othello—"Were I the Moor, I would not be Iago./... I am not what I am"—all reflect an underlying uncertainty about the autonomy of the self, a kind of "symbiosis anxiety" which may originate in the early, preoedipal dependence of an infant on its mother. Indeed, both Iago and Emilia describe sexual attraction in oral terms which suggest that one lover "swallows" the other, making him a part of herself or vice versa, like a baby feeding at his mother's breast or imagining his mother eating him up in return. But they are cynical enough to feel that this merger is only temporary and that eventually the infant lover vomits up his sweet love (or the mother her child). Iago says that Desdemona's "eye must be fed" with ever-new objects of visual pleasure: "her delicate tenderness will find itself abused, begin to heave the gorge, disrelish and abhor the Moor" (II, i, 224, 230–32). And Emilia characterizes men, in turn, as hungry babies: "They are all but stomachs, and we all but food;/ They eat us hungerly, and when they are full,/ They belch us" (III, iv, 104–06). More subtly, Iago feeds Othello lies and poisons his mind.

In "La Pharmacie de Platon," Jacques Derrida investigates the conception of language (in Plato's *Phaedrus*) as *pharmakon,* a drug or medicine or magic potion, whether poisonous or life-sustaining, harmful or beneficial.[9] As *pharmakon,* language may be either "good" or "bad," "true" or "false," either an interior presence or an alien, invading foreign substance, and it is impossible to resolve these dichotomies in the meaning of the term. This *pharmakon,* a homeopathic agent that may turn out to be poisonous, a foreign substance that penetrates the body's defenses, is also identified with the fertilizing, lifegiving substance that enters the body in sexual (in the *Phaedrus,* homosexual) relations. In *Othello,* the "unseen essence" signified by the word *honor*—the secret, perhaps invisible, perhaps nonexistent "possession" of women, analogous (in a bourgeois society) to a man's "honest" reputation or even to the money in his purse—becomes, for Othello, for men, for the society as a whole, a magically powerful and valuable *pharmakon*. Iago's poisonous (verbal) images of sexual violence, in which the fetishistic *pharmakon* is lost and destroyed, are, in effect, substitute *pharmaka* which replace what one has lost but also break down the integrity of the self. Does Othello possess these fantasies (what he calls "ocular proof") or is he "possessed" by them?

When, at the end of the play, Othello and Desdemona become (on their marriage bed) a bloody image of quasi-sexual union like the beast with two backs, Lodovico orders the poisonous "object" of sight hidden from view as if this sign of sexual violence revealed too much. However, the really poisonous, corrupting, destructive *pharmaka* are not visual "objects" at all but rather the false "conceits" of female honor and purity, the whole social code of masculinity and femininity, which reinforces and revives early childhood fears of betrayal, loss and contamination. Ironically, the fear of losing a woman's love—of losing the ideal, virginal, maternal purity she represents—may cause a man to be overly dependent on someone else, so that his mind is poisoned and his "self" is no longer his own. The polarization of the sexes, in this play, helps to create an unwitting and irrational interdependence between two men, in which (as in early childhood) one can no longer tell the difference between inner and outer worlds, between fantasy and reality.

NOTES

[1] James Joyce, *Ulysses* (New York, 1961), p. 212.

[2] See Robert Rogers, "Endopsychic Drama in *Othello*," *Shakespeare Quarterly*, XX, 2 (Spring 1969), 205–15; Martin Wangh, "*Othello*: The Tragedy of Iago," and Gordon Ross Smith, "Iago the Paranoiac," in *The Design Within: Psychoanalytic Approaches to Shakespeare*, ed. M. D. Faber (New York, 1970), pp. 155–82.

[3] All references to *Othello* (and Shakespeare's other plays) are to the *Signet Classic Shakespeare* editions, ed. Alvin Kernan (general ed. Sylvan Barnet) (New York, 1963).

[4] On sexual conflict in *Othello* see Carol Thomas Neely, "Women and Men in *Othello*: 'What Should Such a Fool / Do with So Good a Woman?,'" *Shakespeare Studies*, X (New York, 1977), pp. 133–58; Arthur Kirsch, "The Polarization of Erotic Love in *Othello*," *Modern Language Review*, 73, Part 4 (October 1978), 721–40; and Edward A. Snow, "Sexual Anxiety and the Male Order of Things in *Othello*," *English Literary Renaissance*, 10, 3 (Autumn 1980), 384–412. My shift in emphasis to early, preoedipal issues of dependency and autonomy follows what I consider to be one of the most fruitful post-Freudian developments in psychoanalytic theory: the "object relations" approach of British analysts such as D. W. Winnicott (in, for example, *Through Paediatrics to Psycho-Analysis* [New York, 1975], esp. "Transitional Objects and Transitional Phenomena," pp. 229–42) and the accompanying focus on mother-infant relations in the work of John Bowlby (*Attachment and Loss*, 3 vols. [New York, 1969, 1973, 1980]). A good summary of object relations theory—in contrast to Freud's own quasi-biological emphasis on libidinal drives and autoerotic bodily zones—may be found in Nancy Chodorow, *The Reproduction of Mothering: Psychoanalysis and the Sociology of Gender* (Berkeley, 1978), pp. 57–73. Chodorow's book stresses the connection between early childhood experience, especially dependence on a mother, and adult sexual relationships. On this question see also Robert J. Stoller, "Symbiosis Anxiety and the Development of Masculinity," in *Perversion: The Erotic Form of Hatred* (New York, 1975), pp. 135–62. Two recent psychoanalytic studies of Shakespeare show a similar emphasis upon issues of autonomy and identity: Coppélia Kahn, *Man's Estate: Masculine Identity in Shakespeare* (Berkeley, 1981) and Richard Wheeler, *Shakespeare's Development and the Problem Comedies: Turn and Counter-Turn* (Berkeley, 1981).

[5] See Robert B. Heilman, *Magic in the Web: Action and Language in* Othello (Lexington, 1956), pp. 30–34.

[6] See William Empson, "Honest in *Othello,*" in *The Structure of Complex Words* (London, 1951), pp. 218–49 and also pp. 185–217.

[7] On the obsessive fantasy of sexual "spending" in the Victorian era, see G. J. Barker-Benfield, "The Spermatic Economy and Proto-Sublimation," in *The Horrors of the Half-Known Life: Male Attitudes toward Women and Sexuality in Nineteenth-Century America* (New York, 1976), pp. 175–88; Steven Marcus, *The Other Victorians* (New York, 1967), pp. 21ff.; and Peter Cominos, "Late Victorian Sexual Respectability and the Social System," *International Review of Social History,* VIII (1963), 18–48, 216–50.

[8] See Ernest Jones, "The Madonna's Conception through the Ear," in *Essays in Applied Psycho-Analysis* (London, 1923), pp. 261–359.

[9] Jacques Derrida, "La Pharmacie de Platon," in *La Dissémination* (Paris, 1972), pp. 69–197.

Michael Neill

CHANGING PLACES IN *OTHELLO*

Iago's notion of himself is as a man whose expectations are properly governed not merely by his personal worth, but also by his being native to the place called Venice. This, in his estimate, properly raises him above such outsiders as Othello and Cassio. From Iago's point of view (as to Brabantio's prejudiced eyes) Othello is a man without any true place, 'an extravagant and wheeling stranger / Of here and everywhere' (1.1.137–8), a man whose undeserved office can be tossed aside with that dismissive mock-honorific, 'his Moorship' (1.1.33). He discovers a special bitterness, therefore, in the fact that it should be this contemptible alien who has conspired to keep him from his own rightful place—and that in favour of yet another stranger, 'One Michael Cassio, a Florentine' (1.1.20). The heavy metrical stress on the first syllable of 'Florentine' exactly catches the force of Iago's scorn, the curl of his lip. In his own estimate he is a man doubly displaced; and this is the theme of his tirades in the opening scene:

> Three great ones of the city,
> In personal suit to make me his Lieutenant,
> Off-capped to him: and by the faith of man,
> I know my price, I am worth no worse a place.
>
> (1.1.8–11)

Iago's sense of self, as this speech already suggests, is founded upon the treacherous relativities of comparison. For such a man to be bilked of the place which answers to his conviction of his own market price is to be cheated of identity, since the very centre of his being is to be found in that obsessive concern for what is 'wholesome to my place' (1.1.146).

Iago is possessed by comparison: it is hardly too much to say that he has *become* comparison. For him nothing (and no one) has a value in and of itself, but only as a measure or object of comparison—hence his overriding faith in money, that ultimate agent of comparison which offers to place everything within a comprehensive taxonomy of price. Such a construction of the world does, however,

---

From *Shakespeare Survey* 37 (1984): 118–26.

invoke its own nemesis, for it commits one to a devouring torment of self-comparison that has, in principle, no end. In act I Iago presents himself to Roderigo as a model of rational self-love (1.3.311), one of those who know how to 'Do themselves homage' (1.1.54); he is thus a free man, liberated from those bonds of service, affection and duty which, by putting a man comprehensively in his place, serve as constant provocations of unwelcome comparison, stinging reminders of the price that others put upon one. Yet ironically enough the very speeches in which this claim is most fiercely advanced are full of nagging self-comparison—both with those whose servitude he despises and those whose superior authority he resents:

> We cannot all be masters, nor all masters
> Cannot be truly followed. You shall mark
> Many a duteous and knee-crooking knave
> That, doting on his own obsequious bondage,
> Wears out his time, much like his master's ass,
> For naught but provender, and when he's old—cashiered!
> Whip me such honest knaves. Others there are
> Who, trimmed in forms and visages of duty,
> Keep yet their hearts attending on themselves ...
> It is as sure as you are Roderigo,
> Were I the Moor, I would not be Iago:
> In following him, I follow but myself.   (1.1.43–59)

Iago dreams of a world without comparison, a bureaucratic Utopia in which place is determined by the 'old gradation, where each second / Stood heir to th'first' (1.1.37–8); yet this ideal of egalitarian succession is contradicted by his wounded sense of superiority to both the braggart Moor, with his 'bombast circumstance / Horribly stuffed with epithets of war', and to the desk-soldier, Cassio, that 'counter-caster' with his 'bookish theoric' (ll. 13–31). The true accountant, endlessly poring over his ledger of 'debitor and creditor', is, needless to say, Iago himself. For Iago is a kind of moral mercantilist: there is only a certain stock of virtue in the world, and by that rule one man's credit must necessarily be another's debit:

>   If Cassio do remain
> He hath a daily beauty in his life
> That makes me ugly.   (5.1.18–20)

Cassio's charm, Desdemona's goodness, Othello's nobility—none of these can be granted an intrinsic worth or independent significance; each is comprehensible only as an implicit criticism of Iago's life. Intolerable objects of comparison whose very existence challenges his place in the order of things, they must be eliminated.

The villain's preoccupation with displacement is, interestingly enough, one of Shakespeare's principal additions to the story. In Giraldi Cinthio's *Hecatommithi*, Iago's equivalent, the Ensign, is motivated not by thwarted ambition, but by lust; it is not his rival's rank that the Ensign covets, but his favour with Disdemona. It is worth asking why Shakespeare, who seems to have worked with a version of Giraldi beside him and who otherwise seldom departs from his original without good reason, should have chosen to make 'place' the point at issue in this way.[1] Kenneth Muir's explanation (fairly representative of those critics who have troubled to pose the question) is that it is merely a device to complicate the villain's motives. The loss of promotion is one of three stings of envy which have lodged in Iago: it combines with 'pathological jealousy of his wife' and 'a jealous love of Desdemona' to arouse his hatred of the Moor; but in Muir's estimate it is the least important of the three because it 'is not directly mentioned after the start of the play, except once'.[2] I should argue that the sheer dramatic prominence given to the lost lieu-tenancy by the opening dialogue establishes it as so much an essential *donnée* of the action that it scarcely needs reiteration—particularly since Iago's nagging conscious-ness of the slight is registered in a self-lacerating punctilio over Cassio's title of rank. He uses the word 'lieutenant' more often than all the other characters of the play together: fifteen of its twenty-five occurrences are from his mouth, where it increasingly sounds like a kind of sarcastic caress. Just as tellingly it is Othello's 'Now art thou my Lieutenant' (3.3.475)—perhaps the weightiest half-line in the tragedy—which announces Iago's moment of supreme triumph. Far from being a mere aggravation of the villain's envious disposition, the question of place lies at the very heart of the play: properly understood it is the only begetter of that 'monstrous birth' which issues from the fertile womb of Iago's resentment.

At the same time as he made the question of promotion the focus of Iago's bitterness, Shakespeare also elected to change his rival's rank. In Giraldi, Cassio's counterpart is called 'the Captain'. The alteration may, at first sight, seem trivial, but its inherent improbability makes it virtually certain that it was done with deliberate purpose: for while captain was a long-established military rank, lieutenant was still something of a novelty; in Shakespeare's own plays where 'captain' is common-place, 'lieutenant' is relatively rare, occurring only nine times in the rest of the canon. In six of these cases it appears to denote a specific grade of officer, more or less equivalent to the modern rank, in the others it carries its older, more general sense of 'deputy' or 'substitute'; only in *Othello* does it seem to describe a rank imme-diately below that of general, corresponding to the modern lieutenant-general. Clearly, then, the word had not yet stabilized to its modern meaning and still carried a good deal of its original French sense, 'one holding [another's] place' (*lieu tenant*); and in a play so ferociously preoccupied with place it inevitably develops the force of a peculiarly bitter pun.[3] For Iago in particular it acts as a constant reminder that Cassio is not merely the man appointed to deputize in the general's place, but the one who is standing in his own. While Cassio is in the ascendant, Iago probes the word as one might an aching tooth, goading the pain of his own deprivation: and then, as his rival's star begins to wane, 'lieutenant' becomes a term of contempt, a covert sarcasm anticipating their change of places. Thus the high point of Iago's vindictive pleasure in the drinking scene is reached with Cassio's stumbling recognition that he is behaving in a fashion 'unworthy of his place' (2.3.96), and registered in Iago's softly crowing response, 'It's true, good Lieutenant' (l. 100). His triumph is confirmed by Montano's sober expression of disappointment.

> 'tis great pity that the noble Moor
> Should hazard such a place as his own second
> With one of an ingraft infirmity.   (2.3.133–5)

When Othello enters to check the ensuing brawl, Iago is ready with a rebuke that uses the terms of rank to hint successfully at cashierment while maintaining an air of honest and properly deferential concern: 'Hold, ho, Lieutenant, sir . . . Have you forgot all sense of place and duty' (ll. 160–1). Once the cashierment is achieved Cassio's place must surely follow the old gradation and fall to Iago; and Othello's promise at the end of the temptation scene, 'Now art thou my Lieutenant', sounds almost like a formal commissioning. Iago, characteristically, registers his richly ironic satisfaction at this change of places by continuing to dignify his rival with his lost rank, a joke which develops a special relish in his last veiled jeer at the wounded Cassio (as Q1 prints it): 'O *my lieutenant,* what villains have done this?' (5.1.56).[4] The plot to kill Cassio, after all, has stemmed not (as is commonly assumed) from the desire to get rid of an inconvenient potential witness ('the Moor / May unfold me to him', 5.1.20–1), but from Iago's bitter spite at the discovery that 'there is especial commission come from Venice to depute Cassio in Othello's place' (4.2.219–20). This is lieutenantry with a vengeance!—by a kind of cheating pun it mockingly fulfils the very libel he has put on Cassio, whilst robbing Iago of the coveted place he has just obtained with so much labour. With that final 'my Lieutenant' Iago means to say good night to one who has never done more than hold his own rightful place and is now about to surrender it for ever.

Since Coleridge first accused him of 'motiveless malignity', there has been much debate over the allegedly confused and contradictory nature of Iago's motives. But the problem exists only if one makes the doubtful assumption that, to be psychologically plausible, motivation need be coherent, systematic and rational. What is significant about Iago's various self-explanations is not so much their apparent factual inconsistencies as their deadly consistency of tone and attitude. It hardly matters that the alleged reasons for his behaviour are changeable or even incompatible, since they are, in the last analysis, only stimuli to the expression of that underlying resentment which is the principal defining trait of his personality: they are all, to this degree, rationalizations for an attitude towards the world whose real origins lie much deeper, within the impregnable fortress of silence into which Iago withdraws at the end of the play. Indeed I take it to be profoundly true of emotions like resentment, envy, and jealousy that they are in some sense *their own motive.* As Emilia puts it, in response to Desdemona's baffled reaching for a 'cause', the jealous

> are not ever jealous for the cause,
> But jealous for they're jealous. It is a monster
> Begot upon itself, born on itself.   (3.4.156–8)[5]

Resentment dreams of usurpation as jealousy dreams of cuckoldry, but is itself the cuckoo of displacement: '*it* is the cause'—at once motive, justification and purpose in a system as hermetically closed as the enigmatic syntax of Othello's great soliloquy.

Psychologically speaking, then, there is no conflict between Iago's professional envy and his sexual jealousy: one indeed follows naturally from the other, since both are symptomatic expressions of his core of resentment, the cancer of comparison at the heart of his being. Displacement from one office can seem almost tantamount to replacement in the other; the only doubt concerns the question of who is to be held responsible—the man who has put him out of his place, or the one who has taken it? To begin with it is Othello who is the single object of a suspicion which seems to grow spontaneously from those fantasies of sexual athleticism which Iago concocts for Brabantio:

> Your heart is burst, you have lost half your soul.
> Even now, now, very now, an old black ram
> Is tupping your white ewe.   (1.1.88–90)

The striking thing about this speech is that it presents the abduction of a daughter as though it were an act of adultery—an adultery conceived (like Desdemona's later) in terms of both physical and psychological displacement. The elopement is said to rob Brabantio of half his own soul: it is almost, as the quibble promoted by the relentless hammered stresses on 'your white *ewe*' suggests, as though the rape were on Brabantio's own person. The imaginative intensity of Iago's vision far exceeds what is required by the mere theatre of the occasion: in the 'old black ram', the 'Barbary horse', and the heaving 'beast with two backs', are projected Iago's own loathing and fear of Othello as sexual rival. The imposture works upon Brabantio as effectively as it does only because of the degree of Iago's own emotional engagement with the scene he invents; but equally it is only through the excitement of this invention that he discovers his own sexual insecurity and with it a new torment of comparison to which his soliloquy in scene 3 gives voice:

> I hate the Moor,
> And it is thought abroad that 'twixt my sheets
> He's done *my office*.   (1.3.380–2)

The point of promoting Cassio to Othello as a rival for Desdemona is not merely to 'get his place', but to turn the tables on the cuckold-maker by exposing him to the shame of cuckoldry. The wounding comparison to which Iago has been subject by Othello's sexual prowess will be cancelled by subjecting the Moor to a similar denigration. Ironically however the logic of Iago's temperament ensures that his leering recollection of Cassio's 'person...framed to make women false' (ll. 391–2) plants a further seed of resentment and suspicion which matures in the following scene. By now he has convinced himself that the adultery is a matter of simple fact:

That Cassio loves her, I do well believe't:
That she loves him, 'tis apt and of great credit.   (2.1.277–8)

Resentment typically tends to reduce everything to its own level; and the fantasy is
flattering because, by putting Cassio in Othello's place, it puts Othello in Iago's
own.[6] Beyond that, it appeals to the perverse eroticism which is a paradoxical
constituent of all jealousy;[7] and it is this that produces the parallel fantasy by which
Iago in turn takes Cassio's place in Desdemona's bed:

            Now, I do love her too;
Not out of absolute lust—though peradventure
I stand accountant for as great a sin—
But partly led to diet my revenge
For that I do suspect the lusty Moor
Hath leaped into my seat, the thought whereof
Doth, like a poisonous mineral, gnaw my inwards,
And nothing can, or shall, content my soul
Till I am evened with him, wife for wife.   (2.1.282–90)

The shocking way in which the metaphors of eating here ('diet ... gnaw') confuse
sexual appetite with the devouring emotions of jealousy and revenge,[8] emphasizes
the dangerously volatile interrelation of these apparently opposite drives; but Iago
is able to protect himself against the frenzy into which a similar welter of feelings
will drive Othello by retreating into the reassuringly objective language of moral
accounting ('evened with him, wife for wife'). The calculus, however, leads to its
own disturbance, for insofar as Cassio seems a likely usurper of Othello's seat, he
may just as well have pilfered Iago's cap of matrimonial office: 'I fear Cassio with my
night-cap too' (l. 298). It is a suspicion which, at a casual glance, may seem to
disappear as suddenly and arbitrarily as it grips him; but in fact it is another of those
extraordinary flashes which fitfully illuminate the dark night of Iago's inner self,
making him seem a figure of infinitely greater complexity than the stage devil or
vice he is sometimes mistaken for. It is possible to trace his painfully self-wounding
fascination with Cassio's sexual potency through the elaborate dream-fantasy of the
temptation scene: just as his sexual envy of the Moor was first apparent in
the bestial pornography of the 'black ram' speech, so here his jealous hatred of the
Lieutenant surfaces through the ambiguous sexual excitements of his concocted
night with Cassio:

In sleep I heard him say: 'Sweet Desdemona,
Let us be wary, let us hide our loves';
And then, sir, would he gripe and wring my hand,
Cry 'O sweet creature!' and then kiss me hard,
As if he plucked up kisses by the roots,
That grew upon my lips; then laid his leg
Over my thigh, and sighed and kissed, and then
Cried 'Cursèd fate that gave thee to the Moor!'   (3.3.416–23)

As in the earlier episode with Brabantio, the calumny can lodge its sting so effectually only because of Iago's own intense identification with the sexual humiliation
he describes. In this context it is tempting to see his attempt on Cassio's life, his
determination to make him 'uncapable of Othello's place' (4.2.228), as constituting
in part an act of sexual revenge. The political murder he envisages, as the sardonic
pun on 'uncapable' suggests, and as that mysteriously emphasized wound 'in the leg'
tends to confirm, is also a physical emasculation, a final and absolute displacement
of the hated usurper.[9]

From the very opening of the play, it should be clear, Iago's imagination feeds
upon (as it is eaten by) fantasies of displacement—public, domestic, and sexual:
such is the self-devouring nature of that 'green-eyed monster' whose habit he
understands so well. But there is another side to his scheming, revealed in the glee
with which he contemplates the ingenious symmetries of his vengeful design. In act
1, scene 3 the inculpation of Cassio holds out the prospect of a 'double knavery'
(l. 338): setting out 'To get [Cassio's] place' (l. 387), he will achieve it by making
Cassio appear to have taken Othello's. Cassio's crime against himself will be
matched by the Lieutenant's imagined crime against his general—the usurpation of
one rightful place being balanced against the usurpation of another; and the effect
will be to link Cassio and Desdemona in Othello's mind as seconds who have
proved unworthy of their office. The growing conviction that both Othello and
Cassio have usurped his own place with Emilia gives a further ironic aptness to the
scheme by making Othello his own surrogate as both cuckold-victim and potential
revenger. For a time he even dreams of crowning this elaborately witty contrivance
by himself taking the Moor's place with Desdemona; but that is perhaps too
commonplace a solution: his last and most perfect usurpation, as we shall see, will
be to take Desdemona's place with Othello. Such refinements help one to remember how much Iago owes to the earlier villain-heroes of the Elizabethan stage like
Barabas and Richard III. Like them he is a conscious and self-delighting artist in evil
(much more than the detached Baconian scientist of Auden's famous essay);[10] and
his pleasure in the aesthetic cunning of his creations is matched by a delight in verbal
ingenuity, in puns, *double entendres* and ironic equivoques. Like Richard's tutor-
Vice, Iniquity, he has learned to 'moralise two meanings in one word'; and he
weaves his net for Cassio, Othello, and Desdemona from the threads of ambiguous
hint and ambivalent suggestion. But this verbal duplicity also operates at a deeper
and more vicious emotional level. When, for instance, the mechanism of Iago's
revenge first begins to move in the drinking scene, his satisfaction at the smoothness
of its functioning finds play in a passage of intensely private innuendo. He steers the
Lieutenant towards Desdemona in a speech whose apparently innocent language is
full of gloating sexual suggestiveness:

Confess yourself freely to her; importune her help to *put you in your place*
again. She is so *free*, so *kind*, so *apt*, so blessed a disposition, that she holds it
a vice in her goodness not to *do* more than she is requested.

(2.3.309–12)

'Place' here (though Cassio cannot hear it) has begun to carry that obscene sense which Iago will deploy to such deadly effect in the temptation scene:

> Although 'tis fit that Cassio have his place,
> For sure he *fills it up* with great *ability,*
> Yet, if you please to hold him off awhile,
> You shall by that perceive him and his means;
> Note if your lady *strain* his *entertainment*
> With any strong or vehement importunity—
> Much will be seen in that.   (3.3.244–50)[11]

Even the concluding appeal to 'hold her free' (l. 253) seems to involve, beneath its frank concession of Desdemona's probable innocence, a dark suggestion of licentiousness. That these *double entendres* have found their mark is suggested by Othello's tight-lipped response, 'Fear not my government' (l. 254), tersely asserting his claim not merely to stoical self-control, but to domestic and sexual rule.[12] Othello, as we shall see, has always felt his political 'government' to be in some sense dependent on the private office of his love; now he is being lured into the demented conflation of the two which first appeared in Iago's diseased imagination.

By its wanton insistence on arbitrary associations the pun is a perfect instrument of emotions such as jealousy and resentment which thrive on paranoid connection. It is characteristic of jealousy, with its obsessional reaching after certainties which it at once needs yet cannot bear to face, that it should track the paths of suspicion with the doubtful clews of pun and equivoque; and it is no accident that word-play should be of special significance both in *Othello* and in Shakespeare's other drama of jealousy, *The Winter's Tale.* In each case the action can be seen to hang upon the fatal doubleness of certain words, the ambiguity of certain signs. There is a kind of awful decorum about this, that jealousy with its compulsive dreams of adulterous substitution should discover a self-lacerating pleasure in what is essentially a form of semantic displacement, in which one meaning surreptitiously, adulterously even, takes the place of another. The pun is a kind of verbal bedtrick—as essential to the process of inner displacement by which an Othello or a Leontes collaborates in his own destruction as to Iago's sleight-of-hand. The very triviality of the device (which Shakespeare seems reflexively to acknowledge in Leontes's murderous teasing of meaning from the innocence of 'play'[13]) corresponds to that ultimate triviality of motive so characteristic of jealousy; it is what carries the drama of jealousy uncomfortably close to the border of black comedy which *The Winter's Tale* often crosses, and helps to make the action of *Othello* the most meanly degrading—in some respects, therefore, the cruellest—of all the tragedies.

It was this aspect of *Othello* which excited Thomas Rymer's notorious indignation. The focus of his scorn was the handkerchief device: the handkerchief provides Othello with the certainty he both craves and fears, it is the pivot of the entire tragic design; and yet, as Rymer saw, there is a kind of desperate frivolity about it.[14] The whole embroidery which Iago weaves about this patch of cloth, culminating in the carefully mounted 'ocular proof' of act 4, scene 1 and Cassio's contemptuous account of 'Desdemona's' infatuation with him, amounts to nothing more than an elaborate *double entendre,* a piece of perspective juggling, a theatrical *trompe l'oeil,* a kind of enacted pun. What is perhaps less obvious is the way in which the handkerchief develops its grip on Othello's jealous mind through a chain of verbal associations which convert it to a material substitute for the love between himself and Desdemona. The Moor's first encounter with his wife after the temptation scene finds its emotional course through a series of feverish quibbles: 'Give me your hand,' he demands (3.4.36), as if seeking reassurance in the familiar gesture of affection; but hardly is her hand in his than it becomes an object of furious scrutiny, as though the simple flesh itself concealed some treacherous meaning. 'This hand is moist . . . This argues fruitfulness and liberal heart. . . . This hand of yours requires / A sequester from liberty . . . 'Tis a good hand, / A frank one. . . . A liberal hand! The hearts of old gave hands; / But our new heraldry is hands, not hearts' (3.4.36–47). If the hand will not give up its secret, the words do: 'hand' leads by habitual association to 'heart'; and the condition of the heart in turn is disclosed by those maddening equivoques on 'liberal', 'liberty', and 'frank'; at the same time, by a curious semantic alchemy, hand and heart combine to remind him of that *'hand*kerchief . . . dyed in mummy . . . Conserved of maidens' *hearts'* (ll. 55–75).[15] Thus the handkerchief becomes for Othello both heart and hand together; it not merely stands for but, imaginatively speaking, *is* all that he has ever given Desdemona, all that she owes to him:

> *That handkerchief which I so loved* and gave thee,
> Thou gav'st to Cassio. . . .
> By heaven I saw my *handkerchief* in's *hand!*
> O perjured woman! Thou dost stone my *heart,* . . .
> I saw the handkerchief.   (5.2.48–66)

Once the poison of suspicion has been planted in Othello, language becomes for him a fabric of mocking duplicities as the world seems a tissue of deceiving appearances; so that by act 4, scene 1, when Iago's medicine has already thoroughly done its work, the most innocent remark can inspire a frenzy of jealous rage: he is like Wycherley's Pinchwife surrounded by that 'power of brave signs' each one of which carries its secret message of cuckoldom. Desdemona's harmless reference to 'the love I bear to Cassio' (l. 231) is heard as an outrageously public declaration of infidelity, provoking his enraged 'Fire and brimstone!'; and her pleasure in Lodovico's ill-timed announcement of the order 'Deputing Cassio in his government' (l. 237) only seems to redouble the public insult. To Othello's ear the order itself sounds as a covert taunt, gratuitous and cruel; and on the sexual *double entendre* lurking in 'government' depends the equally wounding ambivalence of Lodovico's soothing praise of Desdemona as 'an obedient lady' (l. 248), a compliment which Othello instantly converts to the mocking description of a compliant whore:

> Sir, she can turn, and turn, and yet go on,
> And turn again. And she can weep, sir, weep.

And she's obedient; as you say, obedient,
Very obedient.   (4.1.255–8)

Othello here is close to breakdown; he arrests the collapse briefly by turning away
from this seeming travesty of domestic duty to the larger world of political obli-
gations ('I *obey* the mandate', I. 261) only to confront once again the grotesque
confusion of the two: language now begins to break upon the rack of
equivocation—

Cassio shall have my place. And sir, tonight
I do entreat that we may sup together.
You are welcome, sir, to Cyprus. Goats and monkeys!
                                     Exit.   (4.1.263–5)

Just beneath the surface of this speech there is a thread of frightful association
('Cassio . . . my place . . . tonight . . . sup together . . . welcome . . . to Cyprus') which
runs like a subterranean fuse towards the explosion of disgust and rage in 'Goats
and monkeys'. It is as Iago has warned: Cassio has usurped his function; and by that
fact Othello now seems to occupy precisely Iago's position at the beginning of the
play, forced to surrender his military rank to one he suspects of having stolen his
domestic office. To the baffled Lodovico it is as though the Moor's very self had
been displaced: 'Is this the nature / Whom passion could not shake?' (ll. 267–8). He
is not altogether mistaken: the deliberately muddy ambiguity of Iago's reaction
exposes for the audience his satisfaction at the ironic perfection of Othello's apparent metamorphosis—'He's that he is . . . If what he might he is not / I would to
heaven he were' (ll. 272–4). The riddling patter takes us back to the beginning of
the play and to Iago's 'I am not what I am'; now it is Othello who is not what he
might be. As his sudden collapse into Iago's characteristic language of bestiality
confirms, they two have changed places.

NOTES

[1] See M. R. Ridley (ed.), *Othello*, the Arden Shakespeare, paperback edn. (1965), Appendix 1, p. 238.
[2] See the introduction to his New Penguin edition, pp. 20, 15.
[3] It is just possible that the pun was emphasized by Shakespeare's preferred pronunciation of the word,
since the alternative spelling 'lieftenant', which is thought to represent the usual seventeenth-century
pronunciation, occurs only once in the canon (in the Quarto text of *2 Henry IV*, 5.5.95). That Shakespeare was thinking of his titles of rank in this way is given some independent confirmation by the
apparent play on Iago's rank (ancient/ensign) at 1.1.157–8: 'I must show out a flag and sign of love, /
Which is indeed but sign'.
[4] In this and all other quotations from the play the italicized emphases are my own.
[5] The idea of jealousy as a kind of 'monstrous birth' seems to have been a potent one for Shakespeare:
it lies behind Othello's 'strong conception / That I do groan withal' (5.2.55–6), and is built into the
structure of *The Winter's Tale* where a clear parallel is developed between the corrupted 'issue' of
Leontes's suspicious mind and the supposedly corrupt 'issue' of Hermione's womb. The self-generating
nature of jealousy is noted by Freud in 'Some Neurotic Mechanisms in Jealousy, Paranoia and Homo-
sexuality' (*Works*, vol. 18, p. 223), and is discussed by the American psychologist Leslie H. Farber in 'On
Jealousy', *Lying, Despair, Jealousy, Envy, Sex, Suicide, Drugs and the Good Life* (New York, 1976),
pp. 188, 193–9; for Farber jealousy is the expression of a personality which has taken refuge from its

own felt inadequacy in an excessive dependence on the love and esteem of another—in this sense 'the crucial source of [the jealous person's] pain *is* his corruption' (p. 196); jealousy therefore 'is self-confirming: it breeds itself' (p. 188).

[6] For an account of resentment which makes it seem a much more exact description of Iago's ruling passion than the traditional 'envy', see Robert C. Solomon, *The Passions: The Myth and Nature of Human Emotion* (New York, 1976), pp. 350–5.

[7] See Freud, pp. 223–4; and Farber, pp. 190–1. The same pornographic excitement can be sensed in the excesses of Othello's imagination—'I had been happy if the general camp, / Pioners and all, had tasted her sweet body …' (3.3.342–3); and he attempts to give these fantasies a hideous reality in 'the brothel scene (4.2).

[8] Cf. Iago's description of jealousy as 'mock[ing]/The meat it feeds on' (3.3.165–6), where 'meat' includes *both* the psyche on which the monster battens and (at a further remove) the object of sexual appetite itself.

[9] A wound in the thigh is, of course, a traditional euphemism for gelding; and the emphasis on the place of the wound seems to gather a special significance from the obscene imagery of Iago's dream-fantasy ('then laid his leg/Over my thigh, and sighed and kissed', 3.3.421–2).

[10] W. H. Auden, 'The Joker in the Pack', in *The Dyer's Hand* (1937).

[11] For the bawdy meanings of the italicized words in this and the previous quotation, see the relevant entries in Eric Partridge, *Shakespeare's Bawdy* (1969). T. G. A. Nelson and Charles Haines, 'Othello's Unconsummated Marriage', *Essays in Criticism*, 23 (1983), 15–16, also notice the importance of bitter sexual punning as a sign of Othello's gathering dementia.

[12] For an equivalent use of 'government', see, for instance, Middleton's *Women Beware Women*, 1.3.45.

[13] *The Winter's Tale*, 1.2.187–90. For a discussion of word-play in *The Winter's Tale* see Molly Mahood's brilliant essay in *Shakespeare's Wordplay* (1957).

[14] See Curt A. Zimansky (ed.), *The Critical Works of Thomas Rymer* (New Haven, 1956), p. 163.

[15] For the suggestion that the handkerchief with its strawberry spots constitutes a kind of visual pun on the wedding sheets, see Edward A. Snow, 'Sexual Anxiety and the Male Order of Things in *Othello*', *English Literary Renaissance*, 10 (1980), pp. 390–2, Nelson and Haines, 'Unconsummated Marriage', pp. 8–10, and Lynda E. Boose, 'Othello's Handkerchief: "The Recognizance and Pledge of Love"', *English Literary Renaissance*, 5 (1975), 360–74. In the Nelson and Haines reading the pun becomes especially cruel because Othello's wedding sheets remain unstained with virgin blood until the murder.

Garry Gray

IAGO'S METAMORPHOSIS

In "Freedom and Freud's Theory of Instincts," Herbert Marcuse asserts that the individual psyche derives from the social totality, and that goals, motivations, and behavior are socially predetermined. Marcuse calls societal control of individual psyche social domination, which "is in effect, whenever the individual's goals and purposes and the means of striving for and attaining them are prescribed...."[1] Therefore, it would seem that society does not allow or encourage personal individualization. It prevents one's leading his life in his own way and without conforming to prevailing patterns. Thus, Marcuse concludes that "freedom becomes an impossible concept, for there is nothing that is not prescribed for the individual in some way or other."[2]

William Shakespeare's *Othello* is concerned with the issue of social domination and psychic freedom. In Act I, Scene ii, of the expository act, Iago undergoes a psychological reversal away from his initial state of being "socially dominated" to a state of psychological freedom. Such a reversal gives Iago an opportunity to victimize and exploit others.

Shakespeare demonstrates how individual freedom is suppressed by the way a person adopts a socially accepted behavior in order to attain a personal goal when he has Iago adjust his behavior to fit society's definition of what constitutes a "good," faithful soldier. The original Iago, who is introduced at the beginning of the play, is a victim of social domination. He has rationalized that faithful service will enhance his chances of becoming a lieutenant. However, like other members of society, he feels disappointment after he is not promoted:

> Why, there's no remedy; 'tis the curse of service,
> Preferment goes by letter and affection,
> And not by old gradation, where each second
> Stood heir to the first.   (I.i.35–38)[3]

Although the route for social mobility has been prescribed, Iago is dismayed and disheartened when he fails to realize his goal. Hardin Craig offers the following

From *CLA Journal* 28, No. 4 (June 1985): 393–403.

explanation for Iago's attitude: "He [Iago] has worked hard, or at least has kept his service record unspotted, in order that he may achieve promotion, and it has been denied on what to him are contemptible and infuriating terms."[4]

The *disappointment* Iago experiences changes into frustration. The situation prompts him to ruminate over the numerous instances in which other individuals, who also have adopted similarly appropriate behaviors, have been "rewarded." He identifies with their experience:

> You shall mark
> Many a duteous and knee-crooking knave,
> That, doting on his own obsequious bondage,
> Wears out his time, much like his master's ass,
> For nought but provender, and when he's old, cashier'd.   (I.i.44–48)

The lesson that Iago learns is that the identification, utilization, and mastery of prescribed societal behaviors and values do not necessarily result in social mobility. He concludes that promotion comes through private recommendation and favoritism and not by order of seniority. The outcome of such a realization is that he no longer desires to abide by the societal constraints of being a dutiful soldier, and resolves that "Heaven is my judge, *not I for love and duty,* / But seeming so, for my peculiar end" (I.i.58–60; emphasis mine). From these lines, one can note not only the negative view that Iago has attached to the concept of social domination but also the fact that Iago's failure to receive a promotion has made him become self-absorbed. Such a morbid state is similar to that negative level of self-absorption described by Thomas Carlyle, in which "all that the young heart might desire and pray for has been denied: nay . . . *offered* and then snatched away" that "the poison-drop of bitterness . . . runs over and hisses in a deluge of foam"[5]

Thus, it is possible to claim that bitterness and disappointment produce Iago's psychological reversal. He moves from being socially dominated to being psychologically free of restraint. Unlike the original Iago, who has underestimated the need to understand the nature of social mobility and, as mentioned earlier, believes that faithful service determines one's promotion, the "new" Iago is committed only to himself. He is independent of societal restraints. His thoughts and actions have become totally individualized, or as he asserts in his own words, *"I follow but myself"* (I.i.58; emphasis mine).

The man who becomes psychologically free creates a new reality that conforms to his own definitions. Hence, the path of psychological freedom that Iago follows resembles the definition of the process offered by Angela Davis. In "Lectures on Liberation," she offers an existentialist explanation of freedom: "The first phase of liberation is the decision to reject the image of [one's] self which [society] has painted, to reject the conditions which society has created, to reject [one's] own existence. . . ."[6] Unencumbered, Iago rejects the initial prescribed definition, and he resolves, "I am not what I am" (I.i.65).

Iago creates a two-sided, web-like structure which is cleverly fashioned. On the one side, others note only the manner in which his values and opinions coincide with their own. Therefore, he is better able to entice and ensnare his victims. On the other side, Iago's reality is a structure controlled by the imposition of his own thoughts. Note, Iago's synthetic structure is in retaliation to the self-imposed ostracism that he adapts after not being promoted. Moreover, as sole manipulator, he is able to control, judge, and even punish others within the confines of this structure. It is a dynamic phenomenon which surreptitiously surrounds and engulfs its victim like a hungry amoeba. It is always undergoing change; thus, it appears totally chaotic, when, in fact, the reality is structured around three constituent parts: frankness, license, and indeterminism.

Psychologically free, Iago, the individual, embodies what Jean-Paul Sartre calls "the possibility of choice."[7] Hence, he chooses frankness to be a major feature in his reality. For instance, he uses candor, or a willingness to tell others what he feels, as a device to demonstrate his sensitivity to others' problems, as well as to denote honesty. He divulges truths in his initial contacts with those who people his reality. For example, Roderigo frantically informs him that so final is Desdemona's resolve to reject his (Roderigo's) love that his only recourse is suicide. Thus, Roderigo's belief demonstrates his sense of unworthiness of love now or in the future. Yet, without equivocation, Iago makes the following admission to Roderigo:

> O villainous! I have looked upon the world for four times seven years; and since I could distinguish betwixt a benefit and an injury, I never found man that knew how to love himself.   (I.iii.312–15)

Amazed at Iago's comments, Roderigo becomes ensnared; Roderigo seeks further advice: "What should I do?" (I.iii.320). Iago assesses Roderigo's disappointment and offers the following comments:

> If the balance of our lives had not one scale of reason to poise another of sensuality, the blood and baseness of our natures would conduct us to most preposterous conclusions: but we have reason to cool our raging motions, our carnal stings, our unbitted lusts, whereof I take this that you call love to be a sect or scion.   (I.iii.331–37)

Roderigo's reply, "It cannot be," is answered by another one of Iago's candid comments, "It is merely a lust of the blood and a permission of the will" (I.iii.339).

Roderigo's collective responses prompt Iago to resolve that Roderigo, too, is attempting to perform a prescribed role. Iago uses Roderigo's plight as confirmation of the rightness of his (Iago's) stealthy actions. Roderigo follows the route of the courtly gentleman who loves and pursues the noble lady, Desdemona, only to fail.

On another occasion, when Cassio castigates himself for being caught drunk, Iago offers the following encouragement, "You or any man living may be drunk at some time, man" (II.iii.318). Later, Othello, who is outraged at Cassio's behavior, commands Iago to admit his "candid" thoughts about the situation: "By heaven, I'll know thy thoughts" (III.iii.162). In the opening lines in an otherwise frank admission, Iago makes a confession about the creditable nature of his assessments of others:

Though I perchance am vicious in my guess,
As, I confess, it is my nature's plague
To spy into abuses, and oft my jealousy
Shapes faults that are not. . . .   (III.iii.144–48; emphasis mine)

Iago openly admits that his view of life is informed only by the negative aspects of life. For the first time in the play, such a candid admission exposes Othello to the negative perspective from which Iago views life.

Several lines later, Iago cautions Othello about how one's emotions can govern one's perspective. According to Iago, jealousy—the jealousy Iago believes can engulf Othello's vision—is capable of reducing a person to a state of frenzy; Iago warns:

O *beware*, my lord, of jealousy:
It is the green-eyed monster which doth mock
The meat it feeds on: that cockold lives in bliss
Who, certain of his fate, loves not his wronger;
But, O, what damned minutes tells he o'er
Who dotes, yet doubts, suspects, yet strongly loves!
                                                      (III.iii.166–71; emphasis mine)

Several lines later, Iago concludes his warning by saying, "Good heaven, the soul of all my tribe defend / From jealousy!" (III.iii.175–76). As one can see, Iago's frank admissions speak to Othello's and Roderigo's respective problems. Yet, in each instance, both Othello and Roderigo repress Iago's truths because these truths do not appear directly related to their own conceptions of their respective problems. According to Thomas Vellilamthadam, Marcusean "repression" derives from the Freudian concept of this psychological mechanism in which "undesirable instinctual demands are expelled and are kept away from the conscious mind. When the mind cannot do this directly, it uses various means to allay or repress them."[8]

Just as Iago is self-ostracized in *Othello*, Edmund, in *King Lear*, is ostracized. The ostracism of which Edmund is victim stems from his illegitimacy. As illegitimacy negates the validity of title, it negates Edmund's ever receiving social stature or inheritance. Note, while he becomes self-absorbed—like Iago—and shouts the following commitment: "Now, gods, stand up for bastards!" (I.ii.22),[9] he, too, makes frank comments to those individuals whom he ensnares. For example, while Edmund reads aloud a forged letter supposedly written by Edgar to Gloucester, the nature of the letter causes Gloucester to doubt his son's (Edgar's) loyalty. Such doubts distort Gloucester's ability to hear the frank warning uttered by Edmund:

If it shall please you to suspend your indignation against my brother till you can derive from him better testimony of his intent, you shall run a certain course; *where, if you violently proceed against him, mistaking his purpose, it would make a great gap in your own honour, and shake in pieces the heart of his obedience.*
                                                      (I.ii.84–90; emphasis mine)

Indeed, Edmund's comments are etched with wisdom. As he reveals, the nature of one's true character can be discerned from the way a person handles a given situation. Thus, the solution rendered by the thoughtless, hasty person will differ from that of the conscientious, thoughtful person.

The bitterness and disappointment that Iago has experienced are central to the formation and sustenance of his reality. Therefore, Iago's past is solely responsible for the reality that he imposes upon others. The nature of such a responsibility is manifest in the definition offered by Jean-Paul Sartre in his *Existentialism and Humanism;* he contends, "I am thus responsible for myself and for all men, and I am creating a certain image of man as I would have him to be."[10] When one is no longer a victim of social domination, one's psychological freedom allows him not only to be responsible for his image but responsible for the image of other men as well. Such is the basis upon which the second stage of Iago's reality lies.

License, the second stage of Iago's reality, gives him the latitude to deviate from strict facts or forms without the fear of experiencing any guilt. One liberty that license avails him with is the freedom to judge and mete out the punishments and/or rewards he deems appropriate for the respective predicaments of his victims. For instance, the nature of the judicial review that Iago compels his victims to experience is one etched with his own subjective evaluations. However, Iago's judgments are always changing; he believes that justice lies in the eyes of the beholder, himself. Hence, the explanation arising from Iago's belief that his own judgments as well as the judgments of mankind are determined by personal bias can be discerned from the following rhetorical question:

> Who has a breast so pure
> But some uncleanly apprehensions
> Keep leets and law days, and in session sit
> With mediations lawful?   (III.iii.138–41)

G. B. Harrison offers the following interpretation of these lines in his marginal notes: "Whose heart is so pure but that some foul suggestion will sit on the bench alongside lawful thoughts; i.e., *foul thoughts will rise even on the most respectable occasions*"[11] (emphasis mine). Such subjective thinking is instructive when one is considering the cavalier way that Iago decides suddenly to disengage himself from Roderigo. Iago's decisive comments are as follows:

> Thus do I ever make my fool my purse;
> For I mine own gained knowledge should profane
> If I would time expend with such a snipe
> But for my sport and profit.   (I.iii.389–92)

It is apparent that thievery and deceit are valid features in the second stage. Features such as these obtain their validity from the disrespect that accrues from Iago's success in ensnaring his victims. Surely, Roderigo's unimaginative nature does not sufficiently stimulate Iago; instead, it tires, as well as displeases him. The incident, however, does serve as a catalyst; it causes Iago to suppress Roderigo from his mind and directs Iago's attention toward other intrigue.

A more engrossing point of intrigue for Iago is Cassio. As Iago has not been able to coordinate all essentials to devise a challenging, yet demonic plot, his recall of an earlier incident with Cassio stimulates his thoughts. Summarily the opportune moment arises when Iago inadvertently observes Cassio's kiss of Desdemona's palm. Surreptitiously, Iago remarks, "with as little a web as this will I/Ensnare as great a fly as Cassio" (II.i.168–69). Hence, the profundity of Iago's nature becomes even more intense in the second stage of his reality. To be sure, Iago's self-removal from his original, dominated state enhances his level of pleasure. Herbert Marcuse addresses the level of pleasure the freed man obtains once he removes himself from his original environment and creates his own in the following manner:

> [I]t is only this traumatic transformation, which is an "alienation" of man from nature in the authentic sense, an alienation from his own nature, that makes man capable of enjoyment; only the instinct that has been restrained and mastered raises the merely natural satisfaction of need to pleasure that is experienced and comprehended—to happiness.[12]

Iago's resolve is that once he finds the central thread that will crystalize his web of illusion, he will be better able to demolish all of his victims. Iago reveals the quintessence of his creative, yet demonic plot in the following extended comment:

> Divinity of hell!
> When devils will the blackest sins put on,
> They do suggest at first with heavenly shows,
> As I do now: for whiles this honest fool
> Plies Desdemona to repair his fortunes
> And she for him pleads strongly to the Moor,
> I'll pour this pestilence into his ear,
> That she repeals him for her body's lust;
> And by how much she strives to do him good,
> She shall undo her credit with the Moor.
> So will I turn her virtue into pitch,
> And out of her own goodness make the net
> That shall enmesh them all.
> (II.iii.356–68)

Iago derives his greatest pleasure from what Sartre calls "the possibility of choice" in that Iago relies upon his primacy of choice in identifying Desdemona's virtue as the catalyst to spur other intrigue. He reveals his decision when he decides to "turn her [Desdemona's] virtue into pitch" (II.iii.366). Interestingly enough, the diabolical nature, which Hardin Craig offered earlier as a description of Iago's character, is now released to its greatest proportions. Within his self-fashioned environment, Iago is able to attain satisfaction because he knows that Othello and others misinterpret his kindness and collectively they wrongfully respect him, for "this advice is free I give and honest" (II.iii.343).

Free of internal constraints, as well as constraints from others, Iago is able to direct/misdirect others in accordance with his personal design. Such is the background upon which indeterminism, stage three, exists. Here, Iago's will is free and his deliberate choices or acts are not always determined by or predictable from antecedent causes. Stage three differs from the second stage in a primary way. Just as Marcuse infers that social domination denotes the constancy of form and/or structure—the attitudes and roles of individuals are prescribed—indeterminism precludes constant form.

The liberality Iago accords himself in stage three of his reality is manifest, for example, in the way he uses his native birth as a Venetian to add credence to his estimation of the salient features of Venetian culture. What better way to challenge Othello's selfhood than to remind him of his foreignness. Iago well understands that the ethos of a country can be discerned from the customs and folkways practiced by its citizens. Thus, in his cynical verve, as only a native of Venetian society could offer, Iago's comments to Othello are etched with personal warning:

> I know our country disposition well;
> In Venice they do let heaven see the pranks
> They dare not show their husbands; their best conscience
> Is not to leave 't undone, but keep 't unknown.   (III.iii.201–04)

Iago continues in the same vein:

> She did deceive her father, marrying you
> And when she seem'd to shake and fear your looks,
> She loved them most.   (III.iii.206–08)

As an outsider, Othello is made to feel insecure in his lack of knowledge about the intimacies of Venetian romance and courtship. In fact, Iago's Venetian citizenship does not make him privy to any special yet secret information about Venetian culture, especially love. Iago's comfort again stems from his freedom to convert the insignificant item into that which can be used as a device to control others.

Repeatedly, one notes how Iago mocks social conventions in the third stage of his reality. In his reality, the smallest trifle, Desdemona's handkerchief, is transformed into an important item. Thus, Iago is able to exploit a situation in which an otherwise misplaced handkerchief is used to reduce Desdemona's loyalty as a wife to the lascivious level of an adulteress.

The dynamic reality that Iago establishes in retaliation to his self-imposed ostracism has its limitations. True, freedom allows him a chance to introduce a "new" reality but it lacks any system of checks and balances; only the creator is privy to its future course. The hate, trickery, subterfuge and pleasure that are manifest in all three stages of this dynamic reality offer nothing of substance to its victims but destruction. Thus, as such a reality precludes growth, one may better understand the need for the tragic end of its creator, Iago.

NOTES

[1] Herbert Marcuse, *Five Lectures; Psychoanalysis, Politics, and Utopia,* trans. Jeremy J. Shapiro and Shierry M. Weber (Boston: Beacon Press, 1970), p. 1.

[2] Marcuse, p. 2.

[3] William Shakespeare, *The Complete Works of Shakespeare*, ed. Hardin Craig (Glenview, Illinois: Scott, Foresman, 1961), p. 947. Subsequent references to *Othello* noted in the body of this paper will refer to this text.

[4] Craig, p. 946.

[5] Thomas Carlyle, *Sartor Resartus* (1836; rpt. New York: Fawcett World Library, 1939), p. 245.

[6] Angela Davis, "Lectures on Liberation" (n.p.: Committee to Free Angela Davis, 1969), p. 12.

[7] Jean-Paul Sartre, *Existentialism and Humanism*, trans. Philip Mairet (London: Methuen, 1948), p. 32.

[8] Thomas Vellilamthadam, *Tomorrow's Society: Marcuse and Freud on Civilization* (Kollayam: Oriental Institute of Religious Studies, 1978), p. 44.

[9] Craig, p. 986.

[10] Sartre, p. 32.

[11] G. B. Harrison, ed., *Shakespeare: The Complete Works* (New York: Harcourt, Brace, 1952), p. 1070.

[12] Marcuse, p. 28.

Kenneth Palmer

IAGO'S
QUESTIONABLE SHAPES

In the last scene of *Othello*, Lodovico, returning to the stage, asks

> Where is this rash and most unfortunate man?

to be answered by Othello himself

> That's he that was Othello: here I am.[1]

The reply is significant. It contrasts sharply with those hasty evaluations, the formulae otherwise used to allude to persons present ('Where is that viper?'; 'If that thou be'st a devil'; 'a damned slave'; 'This wretch'; 'that demi-devil'), all of which belong with the hurried trussing-up of a play's action. On the other hand, it sorts well enough with the penultimate line given to Iago:

> Demand me nothing; what you know, you know. (V.ii.300)

Iago's words represent one of his most characteristic pieces of syntax; Othello's, the last example of the language which he derived from Iago; and I point to these two lines because they begin to tell us a good deal about the ways in which Iago's language operates throughout the play.

It is Iago's business (when he is not giving instructions, or playing the blunt good fellow) to isolate other characters from what they know. In *Othello*, characters (and I hope that I may be forgiven this innocent usage) show us little by little that they have pasts—pasts which represent, as they must do in a play, the sum of experience and knowledge which we, the audience, must attribute to those characters. But Iago is different. What we believe that we know of his past is much more largely reflected in the attitudes of other characters towards him. He is twenty-eight years old, married, well-thought-of, an experienced soldier recently disappointed in hopes of promotion; apart from that, we know his present; and, for most persons of the play that is all. His past has become distilled (as it were) into

---

From *"Fanned and Winnowed Opinions": Shakespearean Essays Presented to Harold Jenkins*, edited by John W. Mahon and Thomas A. Pendleton (London: Methuen, 1987), pp. 184–201.

a convenient formula. Othello fought, and travelled, and spoke of it; even Cassio went to Staff College, and helped in Othello's wooing; but Iago is reduced to the mere essence of what has been known of him: he loves people (according to his own account, e.g., II.iii.126, 282–3, 297; III.iii.118, 196, 215, 218–19, 381, 413), and he is 'honest'. Any other past experience for which he gives us warrant we know to be fiction. More than most men who help to open the action of a play, he is anonymous. It is not until I.i.57–8 that he can be said to identify himself, and then it is in riddling and conditional terms:

> It is as sure as you are Roderigo,
> Were I the Moor, I would not be Iago.

Eight lines later, he produces the first of his paradoxes: 'I am not what I am.' And that formula, paradox in form, is yet more characteristic of him; for, quite apart from its parody of Exodus 3:14, it depends upon that kind of ellipsis which strict reliance on grammar will permit.

To look a little further into that first scene would be to find most of the other devices that Iago uses: his habit of defining and categorizing; his way of imposing his own style and syntax upon another man's speech, even to the point of interruption; his insistence on the present moment; and his way of translating or redefining (usually with a change of register). These devices interact; but I should like first to suggest how it is that Iago can even begin the process of isolating other characters from their knowledge and from their modes of knowing. The process involves control of men's movements, emphasis upon his own terminology, and the use of misleading syntax.

(1) Physical control of others is essential to Iago's purposes. Throughout the play, he separates people, tries to prevent them from meeting lest they should exchange information (even to the point of attempting murder: e.g., setting Roderigo to kill Cassio, in V.i), or at least contrives to manage their movements. He leaves Roderigo to face Brabantio alone (I.i.143f.); manages the brawl (II.iii), and causes the alarm bell to be rung; forces Othello to allow him to join in the ritual vow (III.iii); keeps Cassio from Othello (IV.i); places Othello to overhear Cassio (IV.i); and even instructs Othello in the best way to kill his wife. Of some twenty examples of the imperative *go* in the play, Iago uses fifteen. It is indeed small wonder that his part is the longest in the play: the length does not derive from his soliloquies, but from the simple fact that he is engaged for much of the time in dialogue merely. Provided that he can, to a sufficient degree, control each conversation, then the isolation of the other character, in terms of space and time, can be developed further by linguistic means.

(2) Whenever Iago is involved with any other character for a short time, he adapts his style of speech with some precision to that character. The form of adaptation varies: sometimes Iago tries to tempt a man to act, or speak, in a given way; sometimes he tries to persuade people to have confidence in himself; and sometimes he encourages a specific attitude or emotional response. He is not always successful. At I.ii.50–1, in talking to Cassio, he uses an obscure metaphor in

reference to Desdemona ('a land carrack'), and Cassio apparently affects incomprehension. Again, at II.iii.15–16, 18, 20–1, 23, and 25, he tries to involve Cassio in what seems to be his own view of Desdemona's sexuality, and is discreetly snubbed. On the other hand, the contemptuous phrases which he uses before Roderigo, in disabling both Desdemona and Othello, seem to have their effect (II.i.212–62), and the prose of the passage contrives to be at once knowing and weighty, marked especially by the repeated formula of adjective + adjective + noun; e.g. pregnant and unforced position; salt and most hidden loose affection; slipper and subtle knave; master and main exercise (224, 228, 229, 247—this formula is by no means peculiar to Iago, but it is one of his linguistic disguises).

(3) There is, however, one linguistic device which Iago uses when with a variety of other speakers, and it serves not to control or to persuade them, as with (1) or (2), but rather to dissociate them from their normal and native responses. It takes two forms.

(i) The most obvious case is found at I.i.76–8, where Roderigo, agreeing to rouse Brabantio, is immediately told how to do it, in a lengthy simile which is pure stage direction:

> Do, with like timorous accent and dire yell,
> As when, by night and negligence, the fire
> Is spied in populous cities.

But this is more than simile: it elaborates the details of what is compared; so that what matters is less the mode of utterance, and much more the contextual details—the modifiers. Iago wants to emphasize *timorous, dire, by night and negligence, in populous cities*—all, indeed, that is common to both the real and the postulated context, without need for translation. He goes to work in the same way at II.iii.160–2:

> Friends all, but now, even now,
> In quarter and in terms like bride and groom,
> Devesting them for bed;

where the simile refers directly to Othello's own condition.

(ii) The other device occurs whenever Iago uses a syntax lending itself to complex subordination. The number of main clauses is not very important: what matters is the weight which the speaker contrives to give the subordinate clauses and phrases. Consider Iago's first long speech: despite the logical primacy of the main clauses (which, after all, sustain the narrative), those clauses serve chiefly to articulate the phrases which are subordinate to them ('as loving his own pride and purposes, / . . . with a bombast circumstance / Horribly stuffed with epithets of war'). Something similar occurs even at I.i.28–30, where there is but one subordinate clause:

> of whom his eyes had seen the proof
> At Rhodes, at Cyprus, and on other grounds
> Christian and heathen,

but its length is considerable; and within the main clauses the word order is so rhetorically disjointed, and the nouns, pronouns and verbs so far modified, or translated into metaphor (lee'd and calmed: debitor and creditor: countercaster), that it is the modifiers—those devices which affect emphasis and evaluation—which dominate the sentence. The same tendency can be seen in the satirical account of the 'duteous and knee-crooking knave' (I.i.44–8). But the chief use is of course to be found in III.iii.145–52, where the syntax appears almost to have broken down. Iago's preceding speech had offered, in question form, arguments for his silence; now, he begs Othello to ignore his comments, in a syntax and phrasing that exploits to the full the ambiguity of the situation:

> I do beseech you,
> Though I perchance am vicious in my guess—

[Now? Habitually? Is the vice in the guesser, or in the matter of the guess?]

> As I confess it is my nature's plague
> To spy into abuses,

[Real abuses? or matters of suspicion?]

> and oft my jealousy

[= critical enquiry, but the sexual context is already there, to weight the word]

> Shapes faults that are not

[But *faults* is not cancelled by *are not*]

> I entreat you then

[Q reading—anacoluthon]

> From one that so imperfectly conjects,

[*imperfectly* = (a) incompletely (b) faultily (c) viciously; *conjects* (Q only) = (a) conjectures (b) supposes (c) prognosticates (d) (perhaps) devises (but not noted after 1552)]

> Would take no notice, nor build yourself a trouble
> Out of [my] scattering and unsure observance.

[i.e., Othello may see more clearly than Iago]

The whole effect is to render untrustworthy the very language in which Othello might examine his possible cause of suspicion. Each sentence speaks doubtfully of reason, but persuasively of feelings. In old-fashioned terms, tone and attitude dominate sense. Logic is subordinate to rhetoric.

Iago's definitions and categories take a variety of forms, of which the simplest and most obvious are his 'old fond paradoxes' in II.ii. In them, as in Jaques's Seven Ages of Man, the neatness is misleading, for what in each case looks like a complete statement is in fact only partial: not all 'fair and wise ones', for example, commit foul pranks, nor should charity and humility and chastity be lumped together with 'small beer'. But all of that belongs to the Iago who is known to be blunt and sceptical, and who classifies foreigners by their facility in drinking: more important is what pertains to the Iago who appears to think in the forms of grammatical relationships, or in terms of dramatic function. We have already noticed the former of these two ('I would not be Iago.... I am not what I am'), and another example occurs at IV.i.261–3, where Iago says

> He's that he is; I may not breathe my censure
> What he might be. If what he might, he is not,
> I would to heaven he were!

It is a puzzling riddle: it seems at first to shrug off the difficulty of answering Lodovico's 'Are his wits safe?' To say 'He's that he is' is almost to say 'you may see for yourself', yet it is also a kind of tautology—it asserts the obvious in a pleonastic form, which nevertheless may derive more significance from context (as is true also of circumstantial evidence, such as handkerchiefs). To continue

> I may not breathe my censure
> What he might be

grows more ambiguous: it seems to imply that 'He's that he is' means 'Othello is badly disturbed, though not yet crazed' by saying in its turn 'I hardly dare admit how bad he could become' (if 'What he might be' bears that sense). But, in that case, the speech then turns back on itself, for the remainder of it makes 'What he might be' refer to the sanity and self-command that Othello should show. Any hint that Iago has committed himself here to an opinion is of course withdrawn by his final speech (IV.i.267–72), which compels Lodovico to make his own observations.

The alternative form of definition is a very different matter, and it is found in the first scene of the play. Here, Iago overrides Roderigo's ineffectual formality, to impose his own disrespectful assertiveness: the more insulting of these two speakers in the dark street tells Brabantio that he is

> one of those that will not serve God if the devil bid you.   (I.i.109–10)

and five lines later, in reply to an indignant question, answers

> I am one, sir, that comes to tell you your daughter and the Moor are now
> making the beast with two backs.   (I.i.115–16)

The shocked 'Thou art a villain' provokes the pregnant retort 'You are a senator.' At one level, of course, it is broad comedy, and must always have got its laugh; but its real, and lasting, effect is not comic at all. Iago is insisting, by imposing his own linguistic terms upon this encounter in the dark, that the only thing that matters is function, and not identity. To be known, as Roderigo is known, is to have one's testimony ruled out of court; but to have scored one's point—to have put Desdemona's absence in the lewdest form—is to have established uncertainty in Brabantio without making testimony depend upon the probity of the witness.

(Roderigo's next speech, we may notice, is heard out, and believed.) Iago has hit upon an essential fact in his own kind of drama: that a known man brings with him his strengths or weaknesses, his truth or falsehood, but the unknown, provided he may have a hearing, can speak from a void—he has no past or origin, but only a function; and his hearer, the more he listens to him, partakes of his condition.

I have laid myself open to the riposte that this is not the method by which Iago really operates, for his manipulation of Othello succeeds precisely because he *is* known and trusted. But the objection is apparent, not real. What Iago does, in the main action of the play, is to translate himself into a function that might have been Othello's: he becomes, that is, the alternative attitude to experience, the other way of thinking, that Othello hardly realized was there to be used. And, lest I be supposed to be rewording the doctrine that Iago 'is' the dark side of Othello, it must be made clear that the danger which Iago manifests does not lie within the heart and mind of Othello; it lies much rather in the nature of language itself—in that other way of articulating experience which belongs to Iago's dialect, and not to that of Othello.

For Iago to offer, as in effect he does, the possibility of a new language is really to dissociate other speakers from what they know most intimately. Our 'world', our experience, is not wholly comprehended by the language that we use, but we feel most nearly in control of it when that language is commensurate with it; and the language must be trusted and trustworthy. At crises, it may prove inadequate: Othello finds it so at IV.i.40–1 (where incoherence leads on to a fit), and almost so at II.i.188–9; but for the most part we know, and we control, by what we say, in the way in which we habitually speak. Another man's speech is not ours: his experience is not congruent with ours. If we speak with his speech, we know inwardly the strangeness of his experience. And if his mode of speech should begin to open rifts in language—to discover doubt where we expected none—then we are doubly estranged from what we thought we knew. The ambiguity we derive from another man may cause a flaw in our own metaphysical system.

The most obvious way in which Iago can impose his own mode of speech upon another man is the most blatant and theatrical: it is to take control of tone and tempo by interruption. Iago does it to Roderigo most of all, taking over the assault on Brabantio's house, and insisting upon not only his shocking news but his shocking style, in defiance of time, place, and dignity. With Roderigo, again, he talks his opponent down (I.iii) with a variety of techniques: iteration ('our raging motions, our carnal stings, our unbitted lusts'); repeated command ('Put money in thy purse'); consistent scepticism (love is a sub-division of lust; a woman is a guinea-hen; no marriage lasts); copious and familiar allegory ('Our bodies are our gardens'); paradox (no man can love himself; virtue is irrelevant or non-existent); exotic vocabulary ('acerb as the coloquintida')—as typical of Iago as of Othello, despite the common opinion. But with Roderigo he can afford to be blatant, for the man is a fool, and lacks the wit to retain an argument.

Negation is not, in its most simple form, Iago's favourite weapon, for although he tells the lie direct in both negative and affirmative forms, he seldom uses the negative form in order to suggest what he formally denies. Indeed, while many of his other devices depend upon such indirect allusion, negation is usually a little more devious, and is found with a variety of phrasing; that is, Iago employs the simple formula of *not a* verb, but he also makes play with the related forms *none, never, nothing,* together with the occasional use of the derived form with prefix (*imper-fectly, un*sure). Whatever method he may choose, the negative is almost always supported by other devices. For example, in II.iii, when called upon to explain the brawl, he begins with two straightforward negatives ('I do *not* know' [160]; 'I *cannot* speak' [165]), defends himself against Montano's imputation with another ('Touch me *not* so near' [201]), uses three different negatives ('*nothing* wrong him' [205]; 'I *ne'er* might say' [217]; 'More ... can I *not* report' [221]), and names Cassio six times (so that very iteration makes the name suspect). The full naming, at II.iii.202–3,

> I had rather have this tongue cut from my mouth
> Than it should do offence to Michael Cassio.

does more damage still, for its hypothesis is allowed to work in two ways: it implies that offence might easily be done, while the following lines, turning grudgingly on 'Yet', insist that the truth could readily wrong the man:

> Yet, I persuade myself, to speak the truth
> Shall nothing wrong him.

But this is uncomplicated. Much more telling are the two formulae used in III.iii:

> I speak not yet of proof   (198)

>   I do not in position
> Distinctly speak of her   (236–7)

each of which uses a term from formal argument, and the former of which is combined with the adverbial *yet* (which contrives at once to suggest more potent testimony to come, while allowing Iago an escape if he should fail to provide it). The most powerful uses are those which operate in set; besides a pair at 164–5 ('You cannot, if my heart were in your hand, / Nor shall not, while 'tis in my custody') there are such sets at 200 / 201–2 / 204–6 / 220–2 / 224–5:

> *not* jealous, *nor* secure.

> I would *not* have your free and noble nature,
> Out of self-bounty, be abused.

>   they do let God see the pranks
> They dare *not* show their husbands. Their best conscience
> Is *not* to leave't *un*done, but keep't *un*known.

I am to pray you *not* to strain my speech
To grosser issues *nor* to larger reach
Than to suspicion.

My speech should fall into such vile success
As my thoughts aimed *not* at.

The effect of these is primarily to establish a growing but undefined sense of uncertainty: doubt is cast not only on what Othello might know of Venetian customs, but also on the 'right' degree of suspicion that he should show, as well as the firmness of Iago's judgement of his own words. The most subtle group of negatives occurs earlier in the same scene, where 'I like *not* that'; '*Nothing*'; 'I know *not*'; '*No*'; 'I *cannot* think it' follow in rapid succession, and draw attention away from the factual context, so that Othello may focus instead upon liking, thinking and knowing.

Questions achieve an effect akin to that of negation: grammatically, neither forms an assertion, but logically each presupposes what is then left open, or negated. If Keats says: 'I cannot see what flowers are at my feet', we concede the effect of dusk upon human vision, but we concur in believing, with him, that at his feet there are flowers. When Iago says,

Would you, the supervisor, grossly gape on?
Behold her topped?   (III.iii.396–7)

we know that direct witness would be needed to prove adultery, and that Iago must so express the matter; but his question, asked in order to show the impossibility of providing that witness, nevertheless implies what it says it cannot demonstrate. Of themselves, of course, questions may be innocent or even playful (as with Desdemona's 'What? Michael Cassio, / That came a-wooing with you . . . ?' [III.iii.70–1]), and one may set aside as merely neutral most questions asked by men in authority. Othello's first question to Iago (I.ii.32) serves only to have confirmed what was offered as a guess, and is promptly withdrawn: 'Is it they?' virtually expects the answer no, and, following as it does an assertion of patience and confidence, it comes perhaps as close to indifference as a question can do. Indeed, it is the assurance that comes from birth and rank that determines the tone of another of Othello's questions: in the brief scene III.ii, his enquiry, 'This fortification, gentlemen, shall we see't?' is at once an invitation ('Perhaps you would care to accompany me?') and a concealed command ('Show me the fortification'). It is a question only in form; and its effect is to reinforce an authority that is so natural as to be almost unconscious. Even during the brawl in II.iii, his questions are modified by the commands which flank them: 'Are we turn'd Turks . . . ?' is meant to reduce, and not stir up, excitement, and stands between 'From whence arises this?' (a typical search for fact and causation) and a series of orders, so that the ensuing 'What is the matter, masters? . . . / Speak. Who began this?' grow less urgent, and more judicious, than they might otherwise be. Significantly, when the culprits can be identified in the darkness and addressed directly, Othello's questions set action against reputation, and invite each man to pass judgement upon himself:

> How comes it, Michael, you are thus forgot?
> . . . .
> Worthy Montano, you were wont be civil:
> The gravity and stillness of your youth
> The world hath noted; and your name is great
> In mouths of wisest censure. What's the matter
> That you unlace your reputation thus,
> And spend your rich opinion for the name
> Of a night-brawler? Give me answer to it.   (II.iii.169–77)

The effect overall is to make questions part of a process by which stability is reasserted: they restore the *status quo ante*. Like the commands, they refer to a known system of order, to which other men also subscribe. They do not try to negate that order, or to suggest any other, not yet otherwise defined.

But if Othello's questions attempt, by determining facts, to establish order, Iago's go clean contrary. He opens his temptation scene with a question which appears to have no real motive, and which provokes questions from Othello, serving to produce imperfect utterance in Iago: 'Indeed?'; 'Honest, my lord?'; 'Think, my lord?' (III.iii.100, 103, 106). This is already a minor victory, for it allows Iago to revert to questioning; but it also moves attention from circumstances to language, and begins to cast doubt on those words and phrases which determine thought and evaluation (*think: thought: honest: know*) so that 'I dare presume, I think that he is honest' follows quite naturally.

Iago's questions, therefore, operate in two ways. With the first kind, questions interrogate while keeping in our minds the form of the assertion from which they derive. With the second kind, which Iago uses in the latter part of the play, the question is highly elliptical, as we find it to be at IV.i.1f.:

> IAGO: Will you think so?
> OTH.:   Think so, Iago?
> IAGO: What,
> To kiss in private?
> OTH.:   An unauthorised kiss?
> IAGO: Or to be naked with her friend in bed
> An hour or more, not meaning any harm?
> OTH.: Naked in bed, Iago, and not mean harm?

It tends to provoke questions in reply (as here, with Othello). It can be linked to the conditional or concessive mood:

> But if I give my wife a handkerchief—   (IV.i.10)

and naturally employs an aposiopesis—as it does again at IV.i.18; indeed, as the interrogative gives way to the conditional, the aposiopesis takes over (IV.i.28, 32,

34). The two forms, from Iago's point of view, go together: the question or the conditional form opens up the latent possibilities of the sentence, and the aposiopesis then serves a double purpose, saving Iago from the need to complete the syntactical pattern, and forcing Othello to find the answer for himself.

The effect of such questions is twofold. The first is to demonstrate that, despite his apparent reliance on rhetoric, Iago has in fact practised as a logician. For Iago is a Ramist, and it is Ramism that offers us a hint of Iago's method.

To see anything in a predicament is, for Ramus, to argue; and from that follows Iago's habit of shifting the object of discussion from its normal context, and seeing it under a different aspect. (Such a notion explains Iago's willingness to be seen by function [as in I.i] rather than by identity.) But more important is the Ramist alteration of the nature of proof. For Ramus, proofs need not be syllogistic: they need merely to derive from the nature of man's reason, and follow the natural order of the operation of the understanding. This is why Iago's ordering of the affair is so persuasive, and why he can refer so casually (but so confidently) to 'the other proofs', for 'proof' in the Ramist sense is precisely what his evidence has become. There is the further point that Ramist logic deals (as with the enthymeme) with probability, and not with absolute proof: but in the circumstances of Othello's case nothing could be more suitable.[2]

The purpose of Iago's rhetoric is to create a situation in which Othello is to perceive enthymemes, and complete them. Cassio receives every excuse from Iago for his drunken brawl, in *rhetorical* enthymemes (if Cassio drew his sword, he probably had good reason) as well as a *logical* enthymeme ('But men are men; the best sometimes forget'); but it is left to Othello to find the true form of argument: it is criminal to be drunk and quarrelsome on guard; Cassio was drunk and quarrelsome on guard; (suppressed conclusion) therefore Cassio was criminal. A similar pattern arises from Iago's gnomic verses at III.iii.169–72, which leave Othello to deduce the alternative courses of action open to him (jealous misery, or hatred of Desdemona) while tacitly accepting the premise that he is a cuckold.

The second general effect of questions like Iago's is that they do not only divide habitual significance from language but also habitual significance from visual images; hence, Iago is able to make Cassio mime a lie without Cassio knowing it. Indeed, IV.i demonstrates both aurally and visually Iago's disjunctive techniques and their effects. They are, to list them briefly:

(1) disjointed utterance (35f.) in Othello;
(2) Othello's fit (because consciousness cannot bear coexistent contradictions);
(3) a series of aposiopeses from Iago (10, 18, 29, 32);
(4) assertions by Iago, coupled with negations (16, 30–2);
(5) interruptive speech (215, 222, 228);
(6) violence: Othello strikes Desdemona, because language no longer suffices his purposes;
(7) two syntactical patterns simultaneously (248–54).

By contrast, IV.ii shows Othello adopting one of the characteristics of Iago's speech. Unable to make sense of language once more by forcing Desdemona to take an oath, he tries to express the situation, not by stating the case but by *exclaiming*, in an attempt to utter his inward anguish by metaphor, or by comparing the actual with the hypothetical. He expresses, that is, effects alone, and never facts or opinion of facts. This response to a cause never named is something that Desdemona cannot understand at first, and when she begins to see his drift, Othello refuses to give an explicit answer to her question (70–80). He deals only with the consequences of an act which he cannot name, and which nothing natural can bear to hear of. It is not until he breaks out with 'Impudent strumpet!' that his meaning becomes clear to her.

How far Iago succeeds in making Othello adopt some of his ways of speaking may be seen in the use of the conjunction *yet*. Iago is very fond of it at the beginning of the play, using it four times in the first two scenes, and three times again in his satirical rhymes (II.i) as well as twice in describing Cassio's brawl (II.iii). The danger of the word (as Iago uses it) is that it purports to maintain a balance, but in effect makes a concession, and even appears at times to issue a warning. The more judicious and temperate Iago seems to be, the more ominous is the warning tone (cf. Othello's comment on Iago's hesitation at III.iii.119–21). The effect can be observed at III.iii.250 ('Yet if you please to hold him off awhile') and again at IV.i.90 ('But yet keep time in all'), and it persists even when *yet* might be adverb rather than conjunction ('Yet be content', III.iii.451). After IV.ii.203, where he speaks to Roderigo, Iago dispenses with the conjunction; but Othello, who had hitherto used it rarely, and then in speculation ('And yet how nature erring from itself', III.iii.229), now makes it habitual. His usual practice applies it in making judgements on people—as for example on Emilia ('yet she's a simple bawd / that cannot say as much . . . / And yet she'll kneel; and pray', IV.ii.19–22) or in condemning Desdemona before Lodovico ('Sir, she can turn, and turn, and yet go on', IV.i.244), although these may be evidence of his uncertainty about observed fact. More significant is the way he uses it in coming to terms with his divided feelings ('but yet the pity of it, Iago!', IV.i.184), or maintaining his equivocal position in V.ii ('It is the cause. Yet I'll not shed her blood'; 'Yet she must die, else she'll betray more men'; 'I that am cruel am yet merciful').[3]

From IV.i onwards, Othello and Iago do not meet until, in V.ii, Desdemona is dead. During the interim, Iago's language undergoes a change. His tentative consolation of Desdemona appears natural enough, and so does his conversation with Roderigo; but after the attempted assassination of Cassio his manner grows melodramatic, and indeed almost self-parodic. He can risk this before Gratiano and Lodovico because they know him chiefly by repute ('This is Othello's ancient . . . a very valiant fellow', V.i.51–2), and because they fear to expose themselves to unknown danger in the darkness ('These may be counterfeits: let's think't unsafe / To come in to the cry', V.i.43–4), so that for *them* his language corresponds to what they believe the situation to be. For the audience, by contrast, Iago's language is exaggerated and false:

Lend me a light. Know we this face or no?
Alas, my friend and my dear countryman!
Roderigo? No—yes, sure—O, heaven, Roderigo!   (V.i.88–90)

This passage is known for what it is—namely, play-acting, with stage-directions for
the benefit of the audience on stage; the effect of black comedy is comparable with
that in IV.i, when Othello watches, but cannot overhear, Iago and Cassio.[4] Evidently,
Iago feels that he can risk broad effects in the darkness of the scene, as he did in
the opening of the play; and his questions and exclamations, although apparently
natural enough, serve as a grimly comic commentary on the scene in which he has
just played, and acted as prompter and producer.

And this is the last time that Iago can play both actor and dramatist, for in V.ii
he is forced once more to rely upon action ('Fie!/Your sword upon a woman!',
221–2) in trying to silence hostile witnesses. He answers questions, or tries to stop
Emilia from talking; but at no point does he seem to speak to Othello (since 'I bleed,
sir, but not killed' must surely be addressed to Lodovico), unless it be to Othello
that he speaks his question-begging brag ('what you know, you know') and his final
determination upon silence. Both language and action (despite his attempt on
Cassio, and his successful killing of Emilia and Roderigo) betray him in the end.

Othello's case is different. He hardly appears in IV.iii or V.i—like other
Shakespearean protagonists, he is 'rested' before the climax[5]—and when he enters
at the beginning of V.ii, his language represents something quite unexpected: an
attempt to restore an order which he had formerly destroyed. The opening of the
scene is a noble failure to find a symbol or ritual which will enable him to speak of
Desdemona's death without thinking of himself as a revenger (as he had at III.iii.448,
452, and as he does again at V.ii.64–5, 75–6, 116–17): it is Desdemona's natural
reaction of fear toward physical danger which breaks down his precarious control.
His difficulty lies in the nature of the balance which he tries to hold. Ever since IV.i,
he has been liable to sustain two incompatible attitudes at once ('Ay, let her rot and
perish. . . . She might lie by an emperor's side and command him tasks.' IV.i.172–5);
now, he recognizes that the moment of the present before killing Desdemona, and
the moment of the present after killing her, will satisfactorily bear up the notion of
a sacrificial action. Only the action itself is something that he cannot, in calmness,
contemplate; and he is able to refer to it only in metaphor ('Put out the light'; 'If I
quench thee, thou flaming minister'; 'When I have plucked the rose'). His purpose
here is to maintain the stasis of the moment when the killing is merely potential:
Desdemona asleep is as if Desdemona dead; and Othello can contemplate both
cases indifferently:

Be thus when thou art dead, and I will kill thee
And love thee after.   (V.ii.18–19)

Indeed, his purpose—perhaps unconfessed—is to transform Desdemona to
an object: something which he could love because it would not change, and could
not betray. It would be an object effectually existing out of time, something be-

longing to a changeless present. Othello has already been able to see himself in the third person as early as III.iii.358 ('Othello's occupation's gone'), again at IV.ii.88–9 ('that cunning whore of Venice / That married with Othello'), and after at V.ii.268, 269, 281 ('a rush against Othello's breast'; 'Where should Othello go?'; 'That's he that was Othello'); and that is halfway to seeing himself as an object. The first sign that another attitude is possible to him is made clear at V.ii.98: 'My wife, my wife! What wife? I have no wife.' The exchanges with Emilia proceed almost stichomythically:

> OTH.: You heard her say herself it was not I.
> EMIL.: She said so; I must needs report the truth.   (128–9)
>
> OTH.: She turned to folly, and she was a whore.
> EMIL.: Thou dost belie her, and thou art a devil.
> OTH.: She was false as water.
> EMIL.:   Thou art rash as fire   (133–5)

as two opposed opinions confront one another. Othello's next concession comes as he asserts that he proceeded justly (139), and is backed by the awful conditional claim that a chaste Desdemona was more precious than a world formed of topaz (142–5)—perhaps another form of his desire to think of her as perfect and unchanging, except that this image is the comparative part of an hyperbole. And then, as Emilia calls for help, Othello becomes silent (save for his single line of confession at 187), until, having cried out wordlessly, he reverts to the calm he showed in I.ii. (The two speeches at 199–202 and 209–16 are surprisingly low-toned and factual, with their reliance upon short, laconic main clauses—'I scarce did know you'; 'there lies your niece'; 'Cassio confessed it'; 'I saw it in his hand'; 'It was a handkerchief.')

His teasing of Gratiano is important. In one respect his ironic mock is like his behaviour towards Brabantio and his servants (I.ii.59–61, 81–5, 87–91), even to the detail of the sword not used, in each case. In another, it leads on in sustained irony to a recollection of what he has been, and a rejection of all the postures that he might now adopt:

> But, O vain boast!
> Who can control his fate? 'Tis not so now.
> . . . .
> Man but a rush against Othello's breast,
> And he retires. Where should Othello go?   (V.ii.262–3, 268–9)

The two actions which, without ironic mockery, he can now perform, he does: he tries to kill Iago, and he believes and begs pardon of Cassio. But, having done that, and having learned that his authority is taken off, he seems to realize that although he has been stripped of all that belonged to him in the course of the play, he can once more recognize himself. To discover the truth about Iago's lies is to regain his own identity: he is no longer the General, nor the husband of Desdemona, but he *is* once more Othello, who can refer again to himself in the first person ('I have done the state some service and they know't'). The opportunity has at last offered itself, to bring his past and his present together (though the combination is destructive), so that he can, and does, truly unite word and act: 'And smote him thus. In acting so, he achieves something like what he intended to achieve with the killing of Desdemona (sacrifice, not murder; justice, not revenge), and he contrives to sum up the pattern which, effectually, the play's language has enacted, by dying upon a chiasmus:

> I kissed thee ere I killed thee: no way but this,
> Killing myself, to die upon a kiss.

But Othello, despite the purely formal elaboration of his last words, builds the structure of them from the simple binary pattern which was formerly characteristic of him. Iago, by contrast, produces a form of words ('what you know, you know') which is at once a tautology and an unsolved problem (for who can know what is known, or is yet to be known?); so that to refuse to speak is indeed the only course left to him.

NOTES

[1] V.ii.280–1. These and all subsequent quotations from the play are taken from the New Cambridge edition of Norman Sanders (Cambridge, 1984), unless otherwise indicated.

[2] The enthymeme is, strictly, an argument of probabilities (an imperfect syllogism) and was so explained by Aristotle, who thought it the most persuasive form of argument; but the word came by misunderstanding to be applied to the abbreviated syllogism, in which one term (usually the conclusion) was omitted.

[3] Of the examples of *yet* as a conjunction, Iago speaks 21 and Othello 16; all the other speakers account for 13.

[4] Such 'eavesdropping' and spying are usually comic devices (cf. *Much Ado*, II.ii and III.i, though the narration in III.iii has an unhappy consequence). In *Troilus and Cressida*, V.ii, eavesdropping takes a far more complex form. But here, Othello briefly hears the attack on Cassio and is, unfortunately, spurred to action, although the overhearing was not apparently intentional (V.i.28–36).

[5] Consider, for example, Hamlet, from IV.vi to V.i., or Lear, from III.vi to IV.vi.

Michael E. Mooney

LOCATION AND IDIOM IN *OTHELLO*

"The special pathos of our urge to intervene"

Commenting on Othello's deathbed speech in 1927, T. S. Eliot suggested that the Moor was only "cheering himself up" and that his suicide was as full of "self-dramatization," self-deception, and self-idealization as his fictional life. Taking this hint, F. R. Leavis in 1937 anatomized the sentimentalist's Othello, claiming that the tears Othello sheds at the end are for "the spectacle of himself." Othello was a subject for debate until Dame Helen Gardner reestablished the noble Moor in our minds in 1955. She recognized that the Eliot-Leavis view deprived Othello of the opportunity to reinstate himself and that it raised the "whole question of how the characters in a poetic drama present themselves, of the self-consciousness of the tragic hero by which he creates himself in our imagination."[1] Gardner responded eloquently to the challenge, and there seemed, for a time, to be something like a consensus of opinion about Othello's vulnerable yet powerful faith in the nobility of human action.

By 1980, however, Othello was once again reeling. Stephen Greenblatt cast Othello as a "self-fashioner" whose "identity depends upon a constant performance . . . of his story"; the psychoanalytic studies that followed accounted for Othello's loss of faith in Desdemona by uncovering various flaws in his character.[2] And in a powerful reading Mark Rose expanded Greenblatt's attack on another front by exposing the frailty of Othello's "romanticizing imagination."[3] Greenblatt and Rose had, in effect, anatomized Othello's "bumbast circumstance / Horribly stuff'd with epithites of war," and their analyses proved, once again, that Othello had "non-suited" his "mediators" (1.1.13–16).

In these analyses Othello's belief in the absolutes of conduct, valor, and love becomes a dangerous form of romantic absolutism, and the "tension" between this "absolutism and the antithetical values of the marketplace," held in balance in earlier

From *Shakespeare's Dramatic Transactions* (Durham, NC: Duke University Press, 1990), pp. 104–28.

plays, turns into a "contradiction" used "to drive the tragedy." Othello becomes a public figure and a stranger "we apprehend at a certain distance"; he and Desdemona are full of "an exquisite and dangerous romantic beauty." Iago becomes a "high priest" who sacrifices the lovers with our consent, drawing "the audience into dynamic engagement with his purposes, mobilizing destructive emotions that we may not wish to acknowledge," and inviting us to "participate in the splitting apart of Othello's martial pastoral."[4]

There is little question that Shakespeare sets static, idealized, upstage "pictures" of the lovers against the machinations of a downstage Vice, or that he juxtaposes the lyrical blank verse related to these upstage locations with a coarse, animalistic, and mercantile idiom associated with the "place." Othello and Desdemona's *Figurenposition*, like that of their sonnet-lover predecessors, Romeo and Juliet, holds them within the play's illusion and makes them vulnerable to Iago's predations. Iago's *Figurenpositionen*, on the other hand, allow him to speak to the spectators. But let us note that his figural positions are linked not only to his representational "role" as Othello's "Ensign" but also to his nonrepresentational "parts" as the play's "Villaine" and presenter and that Iago's transactions with the spectators are, ultimately, typical of the Vice. Othello has been an easy prey, but the discovery of his weaknesses does not do justice to the play's effect on an audience that "feels the possibility of tears rising throughout an action" it yearns "in vain to interrupt."[5] Although there may appear to be valid reasons for thinking so, Othello is not to blame for what Iago does to him. The spectators provide a mediating presence here, and they must avoid falling into the trap Iago sets for them.

"I' th' alehouse"

Let us begin by distinguishing between the play's idioms and recalling the way Iago invites others to share his perspective. At the end of 2,1 Iago lets us know that he intends to put Michael Cassio "on the hip" to "Abuse him to the Moor in the rank garb" (305–306). By bringing Cassio down, Iago hopes to take Iago's place as lieutenant and to set into motion his revenge against Othello. But Cassio proves difficult to bring down. When he enters in 2,3, Iago finds Cassio ready to guard the citadel while Othello and Desdemona enjoy the "fruits" of their union. For his opening gambit Iago claims that Othello deliberately advanced the watch so he could spend more time making the night "wanton":

> IAGO: Our general cast us thus early for the love of his Desdemona; who let us not therefore blame. He hath not yet made wanton the night with her; and she is sport for Jove.
> CASSIO: She's a most exquisite lady.
> IAGO: And I'll warrant her, full of game.
> CASSIO: Indeed, she's a most fresh and delicate creature.
> IAGO: What an eye she has! Methinks it sounds a parley to provocation.
> CASSIO: An inviting eye; and yet methinks right modest.

IAGO: And when she speaks, is it not an alarum to love?
CASSIO: She is indeed perfection.
IAGO: Well—happiness to their sheets.   (14–29)

Iago's words invite Cassio to see Desdemona as "sport for Jove" and "full of game," her eye "a parley to provocation." But Cassio matches Iago's images with ones that identify her as "a most exquisite lady," "fresh and delicate," her eye "inviting" but "right modest." Indeed, Cassio so upholds Desdemona that Iago soon gives up trying to persuade Cassio to see things his way: "Well—happiness to their sheets."

Iago will not bring "happiness" to Othello and Desdemona's "sheets": he will transform those wedding "sheets" into winding ones, and Othello will "strangle" Desdemona in "her bed, even the bed she hath contaminated" (4.2.105; 4.1.207–208). As we will see, the love-in-death or *Liebestod* theme is as powerful in *Othello* as it is in *Romeo and Juliet*. For the moment, however, I would like to draw attention to the patterning of this exchange. Here, as in Desdemona's questions about being a "whore" in 4,2 (115ff.) and in her and Emilia's words about women who might commit adultery "for all the world" in 4,3 (61ff.), Shakespeare sets distinct idioms and opposed value systems at odds. As in act one, he dramatizes different ways of perceiving and defining value. Not believing in "virtue," Iago rationalizes love as "merely a lust of the blood and a permission of the will" (1.3.334–335). In Desdemona's declaration of love for Othello, on the other hand, love is a kind of religion. Defending her marriage after her own quietly powerful entry, she insists that her "heart's subdu'd / Even to the very quality of my lord" and explains that "I saw Othello's visage in his mind, / And to his honors and his valiant parts / Did I my soul and fortunes consecrate" (1.3.250–254). Readers and scholars have long recognized that *Othello* contains contrasting idioms, that of the "alehouse" and that of the sacramental world of love. As the exchange between Iago and Cassio makes clear, the perspectives are diametrically opposed. They provide the play with distinct linguistic "worlds."

The dramaturgical significance of this opposition has not been fully understood. In *Othello* one idiom infects the other, thematically *and* dramaturgically, and the coarse, animalistic, obscene, relativistic, and prosaic language of the "place" taints the lyrical, idealized, poetic, and spiritual values found in Othello's and Desdemona's *locus*-centered language. In *Othello,* as in *Romeo and Juliet,* Shakespeare sets mercantile value against the spiritual absolutes embodied by the lovers. Indeed, the relation between place and location, and the corresponding idioms associated with these figural positions, remind us of the opposition between downstage, prosaic language and bustling movement, and upstage lyricism and stillness in *Romeo and Juliet.* What most distinguishes *Othello* from *Romeo and Juliet* is of course the source of this downstage idiom, Shakespeare's finest Vice, Iago, who controls and envelops the action and whose sheer number of lines asserts his dominance. Indeed, when Iago's way of seeing and valuing comes to dominate Othello's, the results are tragic.

Iago's ability to turn "virtue into pitch" (2.3.360) is apparent from the start. As readers note,[6] Iago uses economic, light, diabolic, and animal images when he awakens Brabantio to warn him about the loss of his daughter, to "poison" his "delight," and to "Plague him with flies" (1.1.68, 71). "Awake! what ho, Brabantio! thieves, thieves!/Look to your house, your daughter, and your bags!" (79–80). " 'Zounds, sir, y'are robb'd" (86). Desdemona is itemized as an object to be stolen— and violated. "An old black ram/Is tupping your white ewe . . . your daughter . . . [is] cover'd with a Barbary horse," is "making the beast with two backs," is in the "gross clasps of a lascivious Moor" (88–89, 111–112, 116–117, 126). Indeed, Iago will again and again "begrime" Desdemona's "visage," as "fresh as Dian's," with "black" (3.3.386–387).

Iago "poisons" Roderigo's and Brabantio's minds just as he will try to poison Cassio's and will succeed in poisoning Othello's when he convinces the Moor that Desdemona is not "honest" (3.3.325–326). "Exchange me for a goat,/When I shall turn the business of my soul/To such exsufflicate and blown surmises," says Othello when Iago first leads him to question Desdemona (3.3.180–182). "If I do prove her haggard,/Though that her jesses were my dear heart-strings,/I'ld whistle her off, and let her down the wind/To prey at fortune" he continues later, "plagued" with thoughts that, like "flies," "quicken" "even with blowing" (3.3.260–263, 273, 276–277; 4.2.66–67). Recalled from his advice to Roderigo in 1,3, Iago's homily on his purse is part of the seduction. Setting the loss of "good name" and "reputation" against the "theft" of his purse, he introduces Othello to that monster, "jealousy." "It were not for your quiet or your good,/Nor for my manhood, honesty, and wisdom,/To let you know my thoughts," he tells Othello. " 'Zounds, what dost thou mean?" asks the Moor.

> Good name in man and woman, dear my lord,
> Is the immediate jewel of their souls.
> Who steals my purse steals trash; 'tis something, nothing;
> 'Twas mine, 'tis his, and has been slave to thousands;
> But he that filches from me my good name
> Robs me of that which not enriches him
> And makes me poor indeed.
> . . . O, beware, my lord, of jealousy!
> It is the green-ey'd monster which doth mock
> The meat it feeds on.   (3.3.152–161, 165–167)

Here an absolute ("Good name") undergoes a patently economic evaluation and is, despite being defined in contrast to such valuations, redefined and tainted. Iago's conflation of the "spiritual and the proprietary," of "the romantic and absolute with the commercial and contingent," will be common.[7] It is Iago, of course, who steals Othello's "soul" and separates him from his "chrysolitic" "jewel," Desdemona, and it is Iago who "robs" Othello and Desdemona of their "good name." Roderigo may bemoan the loss of his "jewels," which, he thinks, have been given to Desdemona (4.2.198); Brabantio may think Othello a "foul thief" who has "stol'n" his "jewel"

(1.2.61; 1.3.195). But it is Iago who robs these men, and Othello who most painfully feels the loss of "what is stol'n" (3.3.342).

Iago reveals to Othello "some monster in his thoughts / Too hideous to be shown" (3.3.107–108). He corrupts Othello's mind by perverting his imagination, acknowledging, even as he does so, the power by which "jealousy / Shapes faults that are not" (147–148). Desdemona *would* rather lose her valueless "purse" or her handkerchief than the love of her "noble Moor," so "true of mind" (3.4.25–27). When he redefines her, she will "understand a fury in [his] words / But not the words" themselves (4.2.32–33) or the "reasons" why his "clear spirit" is "puddled" (3.4.142). She knows that she never "gave" Othello "cause" to be jealous, but Emilia, a benign inhabitant of the "alehouse," knows that jealousy is "a monster." Desdemona may hope that "heaven keep the monster from Othello's mind!" (3.4.158ff.). But his words are indeed infected, his "tranquil mind," "content," and belief in the nobility of conduct and valor utterly "gone"—as his "Farewell" speech makes clear (3.3.345–357). Othello's "occupation" is gone, and with it his belief in a world defined by romantic absolutes; the values of the marketplace invade and destroy Othello's beliefs, and Iago exposes the vulnerability—and fragility—of a romanticizing imagination. Othello's ideals lose their meaning, become begrimed black as pitch. Instead of turning back thoughts of infidelity, he turns "Turk," becomes an infidel. "Love" becomes carnality, and faith is reduced to testimonial facts, "ocular proof," "causes," and "satisfying reasons."[8] Othello loses command of the imaginative shapes that define him, moving outside a relationship based on faith and reducing his love to the equivocal evidence of things seen. Iago's cruelest line is, predictably, his suggestion that Desdemona's "honor is an essence that's not seen" (4.1.16).

By the end of the third act Othello turns into the figure of darkness his nobility and language so belie in the opening scenes. His eloquent responses to Brabantio and to the Venetian senators thwart Iago's earlier attempt to make him into a "devilish" Moor. When Iago urges him to avoid Brabantio, Othello insists that he "must be found." "My parts, my title, and my perfect soul / Shall manifest me rightly" (1.2.30–32). His behavior gives the lie to Brabantio's accusations, and his powerful words, "Keep up your bright swords, for the dew will rust them" (59), disarm his enemies and assert his nobility. His self-command, poise, and presence, his control, make everyone in the theater "incline"(1.3.146) to him just as Desdemona did when he told his story. He *is* a magnificent, dominating figure we observe "at a distance, just as we might observe a public figure or a stranger." His actions and bearing fuse in his words, and the allure of exoticism draws us to this romantic figure with "poetry in his casual phrases,"[9] so much so that after listening to him, the Duke admits, "I think this tale would win my daughter too" (171). But when Iago burdens Othello with an "aspic's tongue," Othello turns into a figure of darkness, invoking "black vengeance from the hollow hell" (3.3.446, 450).[10] "In the due reverence of a sacred vow" he betroths himself to Iago, engages his "words" to him, promising himself "bloody thoughts." He now speaks in Iago's idiom. Once Othello's "fair warrior," Desdemona is now a "fair devil" and a damnable "lewd minx" (2.1.182; 3.3.479, 475).

"Goats and monkeys"

When Othello falls to Iago, he loses his bearing and the sense of value that sustain him. As one of the play's most influential commentators, Robert B. Heilman, puts it, "the breakdown of Othello from Act III on is a collapse of certain props of assurance—the assurance of being loved and the assurance of position—upon which his personality rests."[11] *Breakdown, collapse, props,* and *position* are crucial, for Othello loses the very *Figurenposition* and special relationship with the audience established in the opening scenes when he falls into incoherent babbling at Iago's feet in 4,1. Here is eloquence broken into shards:

> Lie with her? lie on her? we say lie on her, when they belie her. Lie with her! 'Zounds, that's fulsome! Handkerchief—confessions—handkerchief! To confess, and be hang'd for his labor—first to be hang'd, and then to confess. I tremble at it. Nature would not invest herself in such shadowing passion without some instruction. It is not words that shakes me thus. Pish! Noses, ears, and lips. Is't possible? Confess? Handkerchief? O devil!
> [*Falls in a trance.*]   (4.1.34–43)

Incoherent, yes, but psychologically precise. As Michael Goldman points out, "Othello is raving, and in his agitation pieces of the items Iago has planted in his brain whirl before him."[12] Later in 4,1 he will also fall in our minds when, assuming one of Iago's *Figurenpositionen* "outside" a scene, he eavesdrops on Cassio's conversation with Bianca and misperceives from his false "downstage" position; when, after plotting the double murder of Desdemona and Cassio, he welcomes Lodovico and slaps Desdemona in the play's most "intolerable spectacle"[13]; and when, in the course of formal, dignified conversation with Lodovico, he berates Desdemona, erupting with irrational harshness:

> Concerning this, sir—O well-painted passion!—
> I am commanded home.—Get you away;
> I'll send for you anon.—Sir, I obey the mandate,
> And will return to Venice.—Hence, avaunt!
> [*Exit Desdemona.*]
> Cassio shall have my place. And, sir, to-night
> I do entreat that we may sup together.
> You are welcome, sir, to Cyprus.—Goats and monkeys!   (257–263)

His reference to Cassio resonates. Othello's tortured and splintered mind cannot contain what is within, and he concludes with the words Iago used to picture Cassio and Desdemona "prime as goats, as hot as monkeys" (3.3.403; cf. 3.3180–182). Hardly the stuff of his address to the senators, his words indicate the loss of the *position* and stage presence he once so calmly and eloquently commanded.

Indeed, no matter where he "stands," literally or figuratively, Othello is trapped inside one of Iago's false illusions, and the alterations in his language and position are governed by the conventions associated with down- and upstage speech. These changes in Othello's *Figurenpositionen* are embedded in his speech and in the play's action. And yet, while Heilman's acute analysis of the relation between action and language hints at these changes in *Figurenpositionen* and begins to consider the "techniques of infiltration" by which Iago "flows" into the community of the play,[14] we have yet fully to understand the dramaturgical means by which this infiltration occurs or the relation it bears to the play's effect upon the spectators. In this sense it is important to remember that, when Iago invites a character to share his perspective, he often plays upon the very idea of "overhearing" so fundamental to the nature of dramatic performance, in which the spectators eavesdrop upon the action. In *Othello* the spectators witness an action in which scenes are often staged by Iago, scenes in which what they hear and see is at variance with what the characters appear to perceive and during which the spectators are helpless observers. Indeed, when Othello literally "sees" and "hears" from Iago's perspective, he substitutes the equivocal evidence of things seen for a belief in things unseen. The most familiar of these moments occurs in 4,1 when Othello overhears Iago and Cassio, apparently talking about Desdemona but actually about Bianca. When Othello "withdraws," Iago tells us what he intends to do:

> Now will I question Cassio of Bianca,
> A huswife that by selling her desires
> Buys herself bread and clothes. It is a creature
> That dotes on Cassio (as 'tis the strumpet's plague
> To beguile many and be beguil'd by one);
> He, when he hears of her, cannot restrain
> From the excess of laughter. Here he comes.
>   *Enter* Cassio.
> As he shall smile, Othello shall go mad;
> And his unbookish jealousy must conster
> Poor Cassio's smiles, gestures, and light behaviors
> Quite in the wrong. How do you now, lieutenant?   (93–103)

Set "outside" the illusionistic scene, Othello eavesdrops upon a scene of misunderstanding and misperception. Here Iago greets Cassio after he "reenters" the illusion, just as he appears to "step out" of it after Othello withdraws. He does not actually "move," but he has, as it were, stepped outside the illusion to address the audience. And because they have been privileged, the spectators know that Othello will misinterpret the following conversation: standing on the fringes of the scene, he will construe things clean from the meaning of the things themselves, and the spectators will not be able to help him.

In this "staged" scene Iago "blocks" the actors and is helped by a walk-on, Bianca. The scene is representative of the play's dramaturgy and use of fluid and undifferentiated settings. Throughout *Othello* Iago engages the audience and the characters in his soliloquies and private conversations. The spectators and the characters then "withdraw," so to speak, to witness a scene, and are addressed or reengaged in private conversation at its end. In a way typical of Shakespearean scenic construction, these conversations often begin in undifferentiated "places" that are localized only in the course of the scene. The first scene is exemplary, for during its course Iago moves from an undifferentiated place to a particularized location.[15] In 1,1 the spectators overhear Iago and Roderigo in conversation in a Venetian "place" that will be transformed into a location beneath Brabantio's "house," at one "window" of which the aroused Brabantio will respond to Iago's and Roderigo's taunts. At the opening of 1,2 Othello speaks privately with Iago before confronting Brabantio in another unlocatable "street," and at the end of 1,3, localized as a Venetian "council chamber" by use of a table and some lights, we again overhear Iago and Roderigo in conversation before Iago offers us his first soliloquy. In 2, 3, as we have seen, Iago and Cassio initially engage in private conversation. At the scene's end Iago and Cassio and then Iago and Roderigo speak alone before Iago addresses the audience in a closing soliloquy. This pattern of withdrawal and re-union is repeated in the temptation and fall scene, 3,3, in which, as in 4,1, Iago moves into and out of the illusion, alternately assuming his representational role and speaking to the spectators in his presented self. Indeed, this scene falls into two parts, with Iago's soliloquy (321–329) placed between Othello's temptation and fall. Dialogue, soliloquy, and dialogue map the dramaturgical contours of the scene, which concludes with Othello's outcry: "Damn her, lewd minx! O, damn her, damn her!" (476).

By 5,1 Othello has only to stand aside and listen in the dark to believe the "brave Iago, honest and just," has kept "his word" (31,27) by murdering Cassio. Iago has "taught" Othello, who steels himself for revenge:

> Minion, your dear lies dead,
> And your unblest fate hies. Strumpet, I come.
> Forth of my heart those charms, thine eyes, are blotted;
> Thy bed, lust-stained, shall with lust's blood be spotted.
> [*Exit Othello.*] (33–36)

Othello is cast into darkness, unable to see or to hear accurately, captured within an illusory and false "downstage" position. In his concluding couplet he gives his "worst of thoughts / The worst of words" (3.3.132–133).

"I kissed thee ere I kill'd thee"

These scenes seem "staged" because the spectators know Iago's true inten-tions. They are dramatically possible because Iago establishes his downstage *Fig-urenposition* early in the play. But there is another reason why his "practices" work so well. He is diabolically effective because his victims, like those of his villainous predecessor, Richard III, are "cast in darkness." Othello and Desdemona simply do not know what is going on. They are "ignorant as dirt" (5.2.164).

In this sense Othello and Desdemona, like Romeo and Juliet, are bound within the illusion, their language and manner of portrayal holding them within the play's pictorial frame. Indeed, in his portrayal of the lovers, Shakespeare draws upon a number of literary and iconographic traditions. There is little need to rehearse in detail the mythological and iconographic backgrounds Shakespeare drew upon to relate Othello and Desdemona to such mythological figures as Mars and Venus. They have been examined fully and well.[16] His borrowings from the sonnet tradition, however, have not received full credit. As we know, Romeo and Juliet first meet at Capulet's feast, where, after the servingmen's banter, the Capulets, Tybalt, the Nurse, and the guests enter, and the masked ball begins amid the whirling measures of masked dancers. Those fluid movements "stop" when Romeo asks the Servingman, "What lady's that which doth enrich the hand / Of yonder knight?" (1.5.41). And after Romeo's lyrical and rhapsodic description of Juliet's beauty (44–53), he approaches her. "The measure done," he has "watched her place of stand" (50) and advances to her. Here the lovers create an onstage, fixed picture that remains in our minds. Here, in an elegant verbal and visual duet, they "make blessed" their hands, and their kiss appropriately supplies their embedded sonnet (93–106) with its couplet. Juliet's "Saints do not move, though grant for prayers' sake" is embraced and held by Romeo's "Then move not while my prayer's effect I take" (105–106), with their accompanying kiss holding time in suspension. When Romeo and Juliet first intertwine their hands and lips, their interlocking words create a moment of suspended action and separate them from the surrounding movement. Juliet recalls Romeo's paradoxes when she finds out his name ("My only love sprung from my only hate!" [138]), and she supplies the play's dominant topos in saying that if Romeo "be married, / My grave is like to be my wedding bed" (134–135). This still point within a turning circle will be revisualized at the play's end, when Romeo and Juliet lie intertwined in deadly stasis upon the bedlike *locus* of the tomb while all the others hasten around in confusion.

These elements are recalled at those moments in *Othello* when movement is contrasted with stasis, energy with lyricism, and images of death with feelings of love. These contrasts are linked to the play's staging. Indeed, although the relation they bear to "sonnet figures" may be less noticeable, Othello's and Desdemona's characterization owes a great deal to sonnet narrative and to the *Liebestod*. Repeatedly, Juliet and Desdemona receive the idealizing praise common in the sonnets. Both pairs of lovers are "lifted" from literary love traditions and are created from the naturalization of poetic convention.[17]

Shakespeare establishes these iconographic and poetic contexts in 2,1, a carefully constructed scene that invites us to view the characters from a unique perspective. Cassio is the first of the Venetian force to land at Cyprus after the tempest that separates Othello's ships and destroys the Turkish fleet. His comments raise expectations about the arrival of the "divine Desdemona" (73), a transcendent maid who, like Juliet, Petrarch's Laura, and Dante's Beatrice, "paragons" poetic "description and wild fame" and "excels the quirks of blazoning pens" (61–63). When she appears, Cassio tells all the men of Cyprus to kneel:

> O, behold,
> The riches of the ship is come on shore!
> You men of Cyprus, let her have your knees.
> Hail to thee, lady! and the grace of heaven[.]
> Before, behind thee, and on every hand,
> Enwheel thee round!
>
> (82–87)

Here the men encircle her. The action "stops." Desdemona is set apart, held in everyone's eyes, frozen in our view much as Juliet is. And here Desdemona's mythological and religious iconography as Venus and the Virgin is established.[18] She silently stands at the still point of a turning circle of figures. The neo-Platonic, syncretic traditions Shakespeare draws upon to create this "chrysolitic" "jewel" crystallize in her dramatic entry.

All this lyricism is of course negatively defined when Desdemona asks Iago, "Come, how wouldst thou praise me?" His encomium comes in couplets that play with the very words and conventions Shakespeare so often mocks and upholds in the sonnets:

> IAGO: If she be fair and wise, fairness and wit,
> The one's for use, the other useth it.
> DES.: Well prais'd! How if she be black and witty?
> IAGO: If she be black, and thereto have a wit,
> She'll find a white that shall her blackness hit.
> DES.: Worse and worse.
> EMIL.: How if fair and foolish?
> IAGO: She never yet was foolish that was fair,
> For even her folly help'd her to an heir.   (129–137)

We hear echoes of Sonnet 127, of the tone of Sonnet 130. Later the alternation will be between "Lie" "with her," "on her" (4.1.33), recalling Sonnet 138's moral and sexual distinctions. "These are old fond paradoxes to make fools laugh i' th' ale-house." They are also menacing, as the reference to Iago's "invention" coming from his head like "birdlime does from frieze" (126) and the meaning "white" and "black" bear in the play remind us.

Iago is a poor versifier, as his frustrated sonnet proves (148–160), and he cannot praise a "deserving woman." His apparently playful view of women is actually cynical and sinister, and his folk wisdom and punning humor are laced with profanity. With Othello's arrival, however, poetry once again becomes musical. "Lo, where he comes," says Cassio (181). "O my fair warrior!" says Othello; "My dear Othello!," answers Desdemona. This is Mars greeting Venus, love and war commingled. The lovers' kiss joins them before our eyes:

> DES.:   The heavens forbid
> But that our loves and comforts should increase
> Even as our days do grow!
> OTH.: Amen to that, sweet powers!
> I cannot speak enough of this content,
> It stops me here; it is too much of joy.
> And this, and this, the greatest discords be
>   [*They kiss.*]
> That e'er our hearts shall make!   (193–199)

As we know, Othello will again kiss Desdemona before he murders her. And when he dies, his couplet draws from the *Liebestod* topos underlying the action: "I kissed thee ere I kill'd thee. No way but this, / Killing myself, to die upon a kiss" (5.2.358–359). Like Romeo and Juliet, the lovers reunite when they lie in stasis on the *locus* of their bridal-and-death bed. Othello's couplet returns him and Desdemona to the tradition from which they emerged. Although Othello's "spirit" has been expended in a "waste of shame," he is able, in his final action, to fall again into "Desdemona's arms" (2.1.80).

"I lack iniquity"

There is, of course, another dramaturgical force and another style at work throughout the play. Othello and Desdemona are set within the illusion. Iago is not. His voice and downstage *Figurenposition* provide a different perspective. When Cassio takes Desdemona by the hand in 2,1, Iago offers his own commentary:

> IAGO: [*Aside.*] He takes her by the palm; ay, well said, whisper. With as little a web as this will I ensnare as great a fly as Cassio. Ay, smile upon her, do; I will gyve thee in thine own courtship. You say true, 'tis so indeed. If such tricks as these strip you out of your lieutenantry, it had been better you had not kiss'd your fingers so oft, which now again you are most apt to play the sir in. Very good; well kiss'd! an excellent courtesy! 'Tis so indeed. Yet again, your fingers to your lips? Would they were clyster-pipes, for your sake!   (167–177)

Iago condemns Cassio's gentlemanly kissing of his hand by using his characteristic metaphors of hunting and trapping. Standing on the edge of the illusionistic scene, he alternates comments and nods to Cassio and Desdemona with glosses on their actions. And when Cassio kisses his fingers once more, Iago adds vulgarity to the description. He will similarly "set down the pegs that make this music" (260) when he sees Othello and Desdemona kiss, striking a discordant note that clashes with Othello's aria of love by commenting on an upstage action from his downstage place.

None of the characters "hears" Iago, of course. His comments are audible only to the spectators, with whom he has developed a privileged relationship. In this sense Iago recalls Richard III, that other figure of Iniquity who moralized "two meanings in one word." Like Richard III, Iago is an identifiable symbolic Vice who maintains a realistic facade. But with Iago, as with Richard III, critics seem torn between the poles of psychological analysis and theatrical convention—as the later editorial addition of *Ensign* to the *Villaine* of the Folio's *Dramatis Personae* suggests. Although there is little doubt that Iago is a type figure, it is also clear that Shakespeare conflates his persona as the Vice with his representational role. His motives for behaving as he does so multiply during the play that he seems, finally, to be a figure of "motiveless malignity"—a phrase that suggests his innate depravity. It seems to me, however, that discussion of Iago's psychology and motivations have obscured not only his theatrical lineage but also the nature of his transactions with the spectators. "Motive-hunting" flattens out the process by which the spectators are led to recognize Iago's lineage and to condemn him for what he is.[19]

In order to trace the process by which the spectators come to recognize Iago's lineage, we need to keep in mind that he possesses distinct psychological and theatrical personae and that each corresponds to a different *Figurenposition*. Indeed, the subtle shifts in his position relative to the illusion are not easily noted when we conflate the psychological and the emblematic. From his Vice-like perspective "near" the spectators, Iago encourages the audience to indulge in devilry; he invites the spectators to participate in the duping of Othello and his other victims. His psychological persona, on the other hand, distances him from the spectators and invites them to examine his motives. The degree of his association with and dissociation from the spectators and the illusion varies from moment to moment and from scene to scene, of course, and the way an actor decides to play the role will determine which persona is to dominate at any particular moment. Indeed, to play Iago well, one must blend devilry and depravity.

When we first see Iago, however, he is a "character" set in the world of the play, and his morality persona is not evident. In the opening dialogue he reveals himself only as a disgruntled, envious subordinate who dislikes the Moor because Othello passed him over by appointing Cassio as his lieutenant. " 'Tis the curse of service; / Preferment goes by letter and affection, / And not by old gradation, where each second / Stood heir to th' first" (1.1.35–38). His "reasons" for not loving the Moor are, apparently, justifiable: even though he had seniority, practical experience, and the support of "three great ones of the city" (8), Othello overlooked him in favor of an "arithmetician" and a Florentine outsider. His grievance seems legitimate enough, and certainly would have seemed so to those in the audience who, even today, appreciate his remarks and side with him, drawn into complicity with his prejudices and complaints. Not until he explains that he follows the Moor "to serve my turn upon him" do we realize his disappointment is laced with deep-seated hatred and a desire for revenge. But even now there is nothing to indicate he is a figure of Iniquity. His code of self-interest and his hypocrisy are deplorable, but the reasons he provides seem "satisfying" and seem to grow, naturally enough, from losing a position he thought should be his.

In the final line of his well-known speech to Roderigo, Iago may suggest another dimension:

> In following [Othello], I follow but myself;
> Heaven is my judge, not I for love and duty,
> But seeming so, for my particular end;
> For when my outward action doth demonstrate
> The native act and figure of my heart
> In complement extern, 'tis not long after
> But I will wear my heart upon my sleeve
> For daws to peck at: I am not what I am.   (58–65)

Although the last phrase, with its diabolical inversion of God's "I am that I am," hints at his underlying part (and may be delivered in precisely this way), it is better understood as confirming his hypocrisy rather than truly revealing "the native act and figure" of his "heart." It may be more effective and dramatically engaging, in fact, if, at the start of *Othello,* Iago possesses only the unattractive but identifiably human feelings of jealousy, envy, and hate. Indeed, by subordinating his morality to his realistic persona, Shakespeare invites us to consider his motivation. No wonder analysis of his character follows a psychological path. By providing us with "satisfying" reasons, Iago elicits psychological responses. Here is a character who does evil not for its own sake but because he believes he has been wronged. His egocentricity and hypocrisy contribute to his psychological makeup.

Unlike Richard III, that is, who admits that he is "determined to prove a villain" in his opening soliloquy, Iago does not immediately identify himself. Shakespeare may not have wanted Iago to reveal himself at the start because he wished to play upon an audience's response to the Moor's devilish blackness. He may also, I think, have wished to draw the spectators into complicity with Iago, the better to lead them to a revelation about Iago's underlying part and to suggest the dehumanization that occurs when a man steeps himself in sin. Like Richard III, Iago will be a presenter of, a participant in, and a commentator upon the action. But the order in which Iago introduces his personae is different from Richard's. Unlike Richard, Iago does not delineate these personae in a play-opening soliloquy, and he does not conclude scene one or two with asides, soliloquies, or scene-ending couplets.

When scene two begins, Iago is again a "character" in a play engaged in conversation with another character:

> IAGO: Though in the trade of war I have slain men,
> Yet do I hold it very stuff o' th' conscience
> To do no contriv'd murder. I lack iniquity
> Sometime to do me service. Nine or ten times
> I had thought t' have yerk'd him here under the ribs.
> OTH.: 'Tis better as it is.   (1–6)

His hypocrisy is obvious, and his speech may even contain a deeply embedded reference to the Vice, Iniquity. But there is no clear indication, here or in the final conversation with Roderigo in 1,3, that Iago will be more than a "naturalistic" character. Act one concludes as it began, with Iago duping Roderigo and articulating his code of self-interest. Not until the end of his soliloquy, after he gives another reason for hating the Moor ("it is thought abroad that 'twixt my sheets / H'as done my office" [387–388]) and after we hear him "thinking aloud," does Iago's natural complexion truly begin to emerge:

> Let me see now:
> To get [Cassio's] place and plume up my will
> In double knavery—How? how?—Let's see—
> After some time, to abuse Othello's ear

That [Cassio] is too familiar with his wife.
He hath a person and a smooth dispose
To be suspected—fram'd to make women false.
The Moor is of a free and open nature,
That thinks men honest that but seem to be so,
And will as tenderly be led by th' nose
As asses are.
I have't. It is engend'red. Hell and night
Must bring this monstrous birth to the world's light.   (1.3.392–404)

The soliloquy closes act one, asserts Iago's dominance, and establishes his unique relationship with the spectators. Iago muses in a psychologically realistic way, offers his plans to the spectators as a presenter might, and then, in his scene-ending couplet, hints at the presentational figure lurking beneath his representational role. As Iago shifts, that is, between his representational role and his presentational parts, he subtly alters his *Figurenpositionen* in relation to the illusion.[20]

Here Iago establishes a rapport with the spectators that, like Richard III's, provides them with privileged knowledge. At times it will be like the "rapport established by the comedian in the music-hall."[21] Full of "an unholy jocularity and a blasphemous wit,"[22] Iago will taunt and torture his victims with glee. "How do you now, lieutenant?" (4.1.103), he greets Cassio, never missing an opportunity. "I see this hath a little dash'd your spirits," he comments after reminding Othello that Desdemona deceived "her father, marrying you" (3.3.214, 206). "How is it, general? Have you not hurt your head?" he asks after the Moor *"Falls in a trance." "*Dost thou mock me?" answers Othello (4.1.43, 59–60). Iago is indeed a devilishly witty thrill seeker who skirts close to revealing himself.[23] He delights, most of all, in puncturing the hyperbolic praise heaped upon Desdemona, as his reply to Roderigo's claim, "she's full of most bless'd condition," makes clear: "Bless'd fig's end! The wine she drinks is made of grapes. If she had been bless'd, she would never have lov'd the Moor. Bless'd pudding!" (2.1.250–253). At times his stratagems are so successful that he cannot believe it. When Othello declares that his "occupation's gone," Iago questions, "Is't possible, my lord?"; this refrain is heard when Cassio laments the loss of his "good name" and "reputation" (2.3.287) and becomes part of Othello's incoherency in 4,1 (42–43). A savage comedian, Iago clearly enjoys telling Othello about Cassio's dream and about Desdemona's being "naked with her friend in bed / An hour, or more, not meaning any harm" (4.1.3–4). He equally delights in awakening people in the night. On each of these occasions Iago's sardonic humor depends upon the perspective he shares with the spectators, who simultaneously delight in and are repulsed by his fascinating devilry and whose own devilish pleasure comes from seeing how Iago's plans actually work.

Iago also provides a running commentary on the action in the manner of a chorus. From 1,3 to 5,1 he speaks at least one soliloquy or aside in the scenes in which he appears. All these strategically placed speeches make him the play's presenter, underscore his dominant role in the action, and ensure our dramatic engagement with him. At times they deepen his psychological makeup, since in them he often adds reasons for his actions and formulates his plans by "thinking aloud." They are psychological and expository. In one important soliloquy, however, Iago sheds his persona as a psychologically believable "character" to disclose his underlying theatrical lineage, and this soliloquy best reveals the relationship between him and the spectators.

"How am I then a villain"

At the end of 2,3 Iago convinces Cassio to enlist Desdemona's "help" to put him in his "place again" (319). After Cassio bids the "honest" Iago good night, Iago turns to the audience, assuming an undifferentiated position "downstage" and dissociating himself, momentarily, from the action. Iago mockingly questions the spectators.

> And what's he then that says I play the villain,
> When this advice is free I give, and honest,
> Probal to thinking, and indeed the course
> To win the Moor again? For 'tis most easy
> Th' inclining Desdemona to subdue
> In any honest suit; she's fram'd as fruitful
> As the free elements. And then for her
> To win the Moor, were't to renounce his baptism,
> All seals and symbols of redeemed sin,
> His soul is so enfetter'd to her love,
> That she may make, unmake, do what she list,
> Even as her appetite shall play the god
> With his weak function. How am I then a villain,
> To counsel Cassio to this parallel course,
> Directly to his good? Divinity of hell!
> When devils will the blackest sins put on,
> They do suggest at first with heavenly shows,
> As I do now; for whiles this honest fool
> Plies Desdemona to repair his fortune,
> And she for him pleads strongly to the Moor.
> I'll pour this pestilence into his ear—
> That she repeals him for her body's lust,
> And by how much she strives to do him good,
> She shall undo her credit with the Moor.
> So will I turn her virtue into pitch,
> And out of her own goodness make the net
> That shall enmesh them all.   (336–362)

Here Iago plays, ironically and self-consciously, with the adjective so often associated with him. His advice is "honest." And with "As I do now," Iago admits that he is like the devil, turning good into evil. The terrible pathos of acts three, four, and five is anticipated, and the utter helplessness of the audience is made plain. It might even be said that Iago teases and taunts the spectators, who are powerless to prevent what will occur. As records of performance indicate, spectators have often felt compelled to shout warnings to Othello and Desdemona, they have wept and "cried out," and they have observed the scenes, "not at all with that uneasy curiosity which changes moment by moment from fear to hope but with something of that inexpressible anguish that possesses us while, in a court of justice, we participate in the vain efforts of the unhappy ones dragged toward a fatal and indubitable condemnation."[24]

Here, at the threshold of the great temptation and fall scene, Iago not only tells the spectators what he intends to do but also reveals his kinship with other stage Vices. Appearing to deny it, he consciously acknowledges his histrionic part and toys with the audience's knowledge ("what's he then that says I play the villain"; "How am I then a villain"). This theatrically self-conscious soliloquy is revelatory, not of his character, but of his underlying "part." He *is* a "villain" who "puts on" the "blackest sins" with "heavenly shows." This "zestful malice" is spoken by a "lover of footlights," an actor the spectators "Curst for Acting an Ill part" so well.[25]

"Knavery's plain face" is seen at last (2.1.306). Although Iago has been self-seeking and Cassio's lieutenancy is in sight, he now intends to commit evil for its own sake and will use Desdemona's goodness to "make the net / That shall enmesh them all." A "diabolical personality" emerges "from the multiple folds of humane seeming,"[26] and his hypocritical "seeming" now becomes his "being." It is not a question of acknowledging, as in *Richard III,* that we have known what Iago truly is all along, but of discovering what he is. In this soliloquy Iago provokes the spectators and creates the "special pathos of our urge to intervene" in the action.[27] In the scenes that follow, our participation in Othello's dilemma will shift between what we know and what we see occurring and will depend upon our having, as Othello has, two images of Desdemona—his image and the truth.[28] And during all the painful scenes of her arraignment the pace never lets up, the events tumbling forward in "accelerating speed" toward the catastrophe.[29] All this contributes to the play's grip upon the emotions of the audience, a grip more relentless and sustained than in any other tragedy. And throughout it all our moral judgment is at war with our theatrical engagement. Shakespeare "plays" the dynamics of one against the other,[30] creating a tension between the perspective we continue to share and our sense of mock outrage. We have entered the action from Iago's perspective and have stood outside the illusionistic scene, eavesdropping, observing, and mediating in our minds: we now find ourselves part of a process over which we have little control. Iago's allure has been so powerful, our perspective so ensnared within his, that we have been caught. In keeping with his hypocritical ways, Iago has caught all the credulous. This tension explains why the slap Othello gives Desdemona is so "intolerable" and why the Willow Song is so poignant. It may also explain why Othello has always been so easy to blame for his downfall and why Desdemona has become too good to be true, her "innocence" so "uniquely annoying."[31]

After we discover that Iago is the Vice, however, his reasons for behaving as he does turn into rationalizations. As Iago adds more and more reasons to justify his hatred of Othello, he becomes less and less believable. As those reasons multiply, they strain our credulity and undercut their claim to truth. After this soliloquy, however, we understand why he is so motiveless. He no longer provides us with reasons, and he becomes more and more like a dehumanized Vice. Only his "credulous fools," Roderigo, Cassio, and Othello, continue to be caught. They still receive "satisfying reasons" (4.2.244–245; 5.1.9). Othello's "It is the cause" soliloquy, with its unclear referent, betrays his faulty reasoning. There have been no "causes," and Cassio's words to Othello, "I never gave you cause" (5.2.299), only remind us how superficial are all the reasons given in the play.

Iago never completely sheds his representational role, as his aside in 5,1 makes clear: "This is the night / That either makes me, or fordoes me quite" (128–129). And he reinforces the psychological sense of self-contempt by condemning Cassio as one who "hath a daily beauty in his life / That makes me ugly" (19–20). But that representational role is laminated upon a presentational part, with Iago's lineage as the Vice determining his stage movements and devilish machinations. We see flesh and blood figures, not abstractions, even in morality plays. From this soliloquy forward, however, Iago is as much the play's Vice as one of its representational characters, and he becomes increasingly viperous, more and more like a tempting, uncoiling, diabolical snake, whose

> Dangerous conceits are in their natures poisons,
> Which at the first are scarce found to distaste,
> But with a little act upon the blood
> Burn like the mines of sulphur.   (3.3.326–329)

When Othello reenters here, Iago greets his victim with relish: "Look where he comes!" (330).

Envenomed, Othello murders Desdemona in "the bed she hath contaminated." After he realizes what he has done, he knows that he will "roast ... in sulphur" and that when he and Desdemona meet "at compt," her look "will hurl" his "soul from heaven, / And fiends will snatch at it" (5.2.279, 273–275). But "heaven" will also requite Iago's actions "with the serpent's curse" (4.2.16). Emilia's words to Othello and her advice to Desdemona that some "eternal villain, / Some busy and insinuating rogue, / Some cogging, cozening, slave" has "devis'd this slander" (130–133) are insights, teasing revelations about Iago's true nature as one who "proves" himself a "villain" and whose "plots" and "inductions" set characters "in deadly hate the one against the other" (*Richard III* 1.1.30ff.). Emilia's words raise the hope that the characters will recognize Iago as the source of evil in time to save Desdemona and increase the pathos of our urge to intervene. Only at the end, however, is Iago's symbolic dimension apparent to all. "Where is that viper? Bring the villain forth," Lodovico orders (5.2.285). Othello will not believe what we know to be true. He looks "down towards" Iago's feet to see if they are cloven, and then wounds him, saying,

If that thou be'st a devil, I cannot kill thee.
> [*Wounds Iago.*]

LOD.: Wrench his sword from him.

IAGO: I bleed, sir, but not kill'd.   (287–288)

This "demi-devil" will not die, nor will he tell why he "ensnar'd" Othello: "Demand me nothing; what you know, you know:/From this time forth I never will speak word" (303–304). He will no longer provide "reasons" or "motives" or "causes," nor will his words infect. He no longer lacks "iniquity" to do him "service" (1.2.3). In drawing Othello into bestiality, Iago loses his humanity. He is correctly identified as a "demi-devil" and a "viper."[32]

Now recognized as a "hellish villain" (368) whose "words" have poisoned Othello, Iago will speak no more. Othello is again articulate. He will punish the "circumcised dog" *he* has become. And he will recover the calm, controlled, lyrical, and exotic musical purity of a voice that was so tainted. We hear Othello's renewed voice in the play's final moments:[33] "Soft you; a word or two before you go." When Emilia recognized the "villainy" of Othello's action, Othello fell *"on the bed,"* crying out as he did when he fell at Iago's feet in 4,1 (5.2.198). *"Rising"* again, he challenged Emilia, justifying his action: "O, she was foul!" (200). Now that he knows of Iago's villainy and understands the enormity of his action, he once again rises to full stature. In this private court scene, as in the formal scene in 1,3, he retells his story, aware of his loss of a "jewel" he threw away. He speaks as he did at the play's opening, knowing full well that the "services" he has "done the state" will not be sufficient to extenuate or "out-tongue" all "complaint" (1.1.18–19; 5.2.339). "No more of that," he says, manifesting himself rightly. He appeals for an objective assessment of a lifetime of heroism tainted by a moment of folly, and he splits himself, in his recounting of the Aleppo incident, into a servant of the state and an alien presence, concluding his tale with a "thus" that murders the Turk within himself. He may be only "cheering himself up," but it is more accurate to realize that Othello reasserts his nobility by passing judgment upon his crime.

The "rhetoric of his self-definition," tenuous though it may be, requires us to reawaken our faith.[34] As G. K. Hunter put it in 1967, in words that respond to later criticism, "Othello's black skin makes the coexistence of his vulnerable romanticism and epic grandeur with the bleak or even pathological realism of Iago a believable fact. . . . We admire him—I fear that one has to be trained as a literary critic to find him unadmirable—but we are aware of the difficulty of sustaining that vision of the golden world of poetry. . . . We are aware of the easy responses that Iago can command, not only of people on the stage but also in the audience. The perilous and temporary achievements of heroism are achieved most sharply in this play, because they have to be achieved in *our* minds, through *our* self-awareness."[35] The deep seated, "curiously compelling" "reasons" for Iago's appeal need to be recognized and denied in favor of Othello's tragic stature.[36] As his couplet makes so clear, Othello dies upholding the romantic and poetic absolutes of conduct "by which he creates himself in our imagination." Iago's valuations do not triumph. He will live on, only for a while, in tortured silence. A terrible and yet triumphant sense of pathos sweeps over the spectators when, dying with a kiss, Othello "falls" onto the bed that defines the lovers' dramaturgical and poetic *locus*.

NOTES

[1] T. S. Eliot, "Shakespeare and the Stoicism of Seneca," *Selected Essays, 1917–1932* (New York, 1932), p. 130. F. R. Leavis, "Diabolic Intellect and the Noble Hero," *Scrutiny* 6 (1937): 259–283; rpt. as "Diabolic Intellect and the Noble Hero: or The Sentimentalist's Othello" in *The Common Pursuit* (London, 1952). Helen Gardner, "The Noble Moor," *Proceedings of the British Academy* 41 (1955): 189–205; cf. Emrys Jones's comments in *Scenic Form in Shakespeare* (Oxford, 1971), p. 132: "Othello . . . acquires full reality only in the presence of a theatre audience." The Eliot-Leavis view is upheld by L. C. Knights in *An Approach to* Hamlet (London, 1960), pp. 15–20; it is challenged by John Holloway in *The Story of the Night* (London, 1961), pp. 55–56.

[2] Stephen Greenblatt, *Renaissance Self-Fashioning: From More to Shakespeare* (Chicago, 1980), pp. 222–257. Edward A. Snow, "Sexual Anxiety and the Male Order of Things in *Othello,*" *English Literary Renaissance* 10 (1980): 384–412; Stanley Cavell, *The Claim of Reason: Wittgenstein, Skepticism, Morality and Tragedy* (Oxford, 1979), pp. 485, 491; Carol Thomas Neeley, "Women and Men in *Othello,*" *The Woman's Part*, ed. C. R. S. Lenz, Gayle Greene, and Carol Thomas Neely (Urbana, Ill., 1980). Cf. A. P. Rossiter, *Angel with Horns and Other Shakespeare Lectures* (London, 1961), pp. 199–200.

[3] "Othello's Occupation: Shakespeare and the Romance of Chivalry," *English Literary Renaissance* 15 (1985): 293–311, esp. 298, 304. Also see Antoinette B. Dauber, "Allegory and Irony in *Othello,*" *Shakespeare Survey* 40 (1988): 123–133.

[4] Rose, pp. 302, 299, 311.

[5] Michael Goldman, *Acting and Action in Shakespearean Tragedy* (Princeton, 1985), p. 46.

[6] Robert B. Heilman, *Magic in the Web: Action and Language in* Othello (Lexington, Ky., 1956), pp. 45–98.

[7] Rose, p. 298.

[8] The most influential reading of the play in these terms is Winifred M. T. Nowottny's "Justice and Love in *Othello,*" *University of Toronto Quarterly* 21 (1951–1952): 330–344.

[9] A. C. Bradley, *Shakespearean Tragedy* (London, 1904), p. 188.

[10] S. L. Bethel, "Shakespeare's Imagery: The Diabolic Images in *Othello,*" *Shakespeare Survey* 5 (1952): 62–79, Heilman, pp. 64–68.

[11] Heilman, p. 139.

[12] Goldman, p. 53.

[13] Bradley, pp. 179, 205.

[14] Heilman, p. 45.

[15] Harley Granville-Barker, in *Prefaces to Shakespeare* (Princeton, 1946–1947), vol. 2, pp. 3–98 passim, notes how frequently the stage location is indefinite.

[16] In Rosalie Colie's *Shakespeare's Living Art* (Princeton, 1974), pp. 135–177. In her discussion of sonnet influence Colie cites Harry Levin's "Form and Formality in *Romeo and Juliet,*" *Shakespeare Quarterly* 11 (1961): 3–11.

[17] Colie, pp. 149ff.

[18] Colie, p. 150, identifies relevant iconographic sources.

[19] Bernard Spivack's *Shakespeare and the Allegory of Evil* (New York, 1958) examines the morality play background. Daniel Seltzer's "Elizabethan Acting in *Othello,*" *Shakespeare Quarterly* 10 (1959): 201–210, esp. 206–207, distinguishes between the detail and variety of Iago's "formal *persona*" and the "recognizable emblem" of his morality persona, as does Bethell in *Shakespeare and the Popular Dramatic Tradition* (Durham, N.C., 1944), pp. 87–89. In "Iago—Vice or Devil?" *Shakespeare Survey* 21 (1968): 53–64, Leah Scragg adds some interesting refinements to Spivack's view. Also see Bradley, pp. 209ff., and Granville-Barker, *Prefaces,* 2: 98–112.

[20] See Peter Holland's "Resources of Characterization in *Othello,*" *Shakespeare Survey* 41 (1989): 128–131, for further comment on these shifts; and Stanley Edgar Hyman, *Iago: Some Approaches to the Illusion of His Motivation* (New York, 1970), for the multiple possibilities inherent in the role.

[21] Arthur Sewell, *Character and Society in Shakespeare* (London, 1951), p. 81.

[22] Rossiter, *Angel with Horns*, p. 19.

[23] Heilman, pp. 79–80; cf. W. H. Auden, "The Joker in the Pack," in *The Dyer's Hand and Other Essays* (New York, 1962).

[24] Marvin Rosenberg, in *The Masks of Othello* (Berkeley, 1961), pp. 19, 216, 5, 34, recalls Samuel Pepys's anecdote and reminds us that the play has always been notable for its power to cause tears; also see Goldman, pp. 46–47. Nowottny, p. 178, comments that act four is "hardly to be borne" and cites the words (here translated) of De Broglie.

[25] Heilman, p. 48; Rosenberg, p. 15. Granville-Barker, p. 22, calls this soliloquy the "nodal point" in the drama.

[26] Heilman, p. 99.

[27] Goldman, p. 69.

[28] Nowottny, p. 340.

[29] Bradley, p. 177.

[30] Rose, p. 299.

[31] Robert Grudin, *Mighty Opposites: Shakespeare and Renaissance Contrariety* (Berkeley, 1979), pp. 130–131. Cited by Dauber, p. 125.

[32] See Heilman, pp. 95ff. In *Shakespearian Players and Performances* (Cambridge, 1953), pp. 124–131, Arthur Colby Sprague describes Edwin Booth's portrayal of Iago as a "snake-like" "demi-devil," particularly in the final act but also, in later years, in his earlier soliloquies. Rosenberg also offers valuable information on Macready's portrayal of Iago as "a revelation of subtle, poetic, vigorous, manly, many-sided deviltry" (p. 124).

[33] On the recovery of Othello's exotic and powerful "voice" see Maynard Mack's "The Jacobean Shakespeare" in *Stratford-upon-Avon Studies*, vol. 1 (London, 1960); and G. Wilson Knight's "The Othello Music," in *The Wheel of Fire* (London, 1930), pp. 97–119.

[34] Howard Felperin, *Shakespearean Representation: Mimesis and Modernity in Elizabethan Tragedy* (Princeton, 1977), p. 85.

[35] "Othello and Colour Prejudice," *Proceedings of the British Academy 53* (1967): 139–163, esp. 163.

[36] Rosenberg, p. 171.

CONTRIBUTORS

HAROLD BLOOM is Sterling Professor of the Humanities at Yale University and Henry W. and Albert A. Berg Professor of English at the New York University Graduate School. He is a 1985 MacArthur Foundation Award recipient, served as the Charles Eliot Norton Professor of Poetry at Harvard University (1987–88), and is the author of nineteen books, the most recent being *The Book of J* (1990). Currently he is editing the Chelsea House series Modern Critical Views and The Critical Cosmos, and other Chelsea House series in literary criticism.

A. C. BRADLEY held professorships of modern literature at the University of Liverpool, of English language and literature at the University of Glasgow, and of poetry at Oxford. *Shakespearean Tragedy* (1904) established him as the preeminent Shakespeare scholar of the early twentieth century and remains a classic of modern Shakespeare criticism. His *Oxford Lectures on Poetry* were published in 1909, and *A Miscellany* in 1929.

CARROLL CAMDEN is chairman of the Department of English at Rice University. He is the editor of *Literary Views: Critical and Historical Essays* (1964).

W. H. AUDEN (1907–1973) was one of the preeminent British poets and critics of our time. Among his many works are *The Age of Anxiety* (1947), *The Shield of Achilles* (1955), *Reflections on a Forest* (1957), and *Collected Shorter Poems 1927–1957* (1966). With Christopher Isherwood he wrote *The Dog beneath the Skin* (1935), *The Ascent of F6* (1936), and other works. Much of his critical writing is included in *The Dyer's Hand and Other Essays* (1962).

MADELEINE DORAN taught for many years at the University of Wisconsin, where she is now Professor Emeritus of English. She has written *The Text of* King Lear (1931), *Endeavors of Art: A Study of Form in Elizabethan Drama* (1954), *Shakespeare's Dramatic Language* (1976), and a book of poems, *Time's Foot* (1974).

JANE ADAMSON is Senior Lecturer in English at Australian National University (Canberra, Australia). She is the author of Othello *as Tragedy: Some Problems of Judgment and Feeling* (1980) and *Troilus and Cressida* (1987).

RANDOLPH SPLITTER is Instructor of English at De Anza College (Cupertino, CA). He is the author of *Proust's Recherche: A Psychoanalytic Interpretation* (1981) and has also written on James Joyce.

MICHAEL NEILL has edited *John Ford: Critical Re-visions* (1988) and coedited *The Selected Plays of John Marston* (1986; with MacDonald P. Jackson). He is Senior Lecturer in English at the University of Auckland in New Zealand.

GARRY GRAY is continuing his studies at Howard University (Washington, DC).

KENNETH PALMER is Senior Lecturer in English at University College, London. He is coauthor of *English Renaissance Literature* (1974; with Frank Kermode and Stephen Fender) and has edited Shakespeare's *Troilus and Cressida* (1982).

MICHAEL E. MOONEY is Professor of English and Director of the University Honors Program at the University of New Orleans. He has written *Shakespeare's Dramatic Transactions* (1990).

BIBLIOGRAPHY

Ardolino, Frank R. " 'In Saint *Iagoes* Parke': Iago as Catholic Machiavel in Dekker's *The Whore of Babylon.*" *Names* 30 (1982): 1–4.

Babcock, Weston. "Iago—An Extraordinary Honest Man." *Shakespeare Quarterly* 16 (1965): 297–301.

Battenhouse, Roy W. "Iago's Pelagianism." In *Shakespearean Tragedy: Its Art and Its Christian Premises.* Bloomington: Indiana University Press, 1969, pp. 380–84.

Bayley, John. "The Fragile Structure of *Othello.*" *Times Literary Supplement,* 20 June 1980, pp. 707–9.

———. "Love and Identity: *Othello.*" In *The Characters of Love.* New York: Basic Books, 1960, pp. 125–201.

Berry, Ralph. "Pattern in *Othello.*" In *Shakespearean Structures.* London: Macmillan, 1981, pp. 64–86.

Bethell, S. L. "Shakespeare's Imagery: The Diabolic Images in *Othello.*" *Shakespeare Survey* 5 (1952): 62–80.

Bloom, Harold, ed. *William Shakespeare's* Othello. New York: Chelsea House, 1987.

Bournan, Thomas D. "A Further Study in the Characterization and Motivation of Iago." *College English* 4 (1942–43): 460–69.

Brock, J. H. E. *Iago and Some Shakespearean Villains.* Cambridge: W. Heffer & Sons, 1937.

Brockbank, Philip. "The Theatre of *Othello.*" In *On Shakespeare.* Oxford: Basil Blackwell, 1989, pp. 198–219.

Brooke, Tucker. "The Romantic Iago." *Yale Review* 7 (1917–18): 349–59.

Buchman, Lorne M. "Orson Welles's *Othello:* A Study of Time in Shakespeare's Tragedy." *Shakespeare Survey* 39 (1987): 53–65.

Bulman, James C. "The Integrity of the Noble Moor." In *The Heroic Idiom of Shakespearean Tragedy.* Newark: University of Delaware Press, 1985, pp. 107–25.

Burke, Kenneth. *"Othello:* An Essay to Illustrate a Method." *Hudson Review* 4 (1951–52): 165–203.

Calderwood, James L. *The Properties of* Othello. Amherst: University of Massachusetts Press, 1989.

Champion, Larry S. "The Private Dimensions of Tragedy: *Julius Caesar, Hamlet, Othello.*" In *Shakespeare's Tragic Perspective.* Athens: University of Georgia Press, 1976, pp. 92–154.

Coe, Charles Norton. "Aaron and Iago." In *Demi-Devils: The Characters of Shakespeare's Villains.* New York: Bookman Associates, 1963, pp. 25–46.

Cohen, Derek. "Patriarchy and Jealousy in *Othello* and *The Winter's Tale.*" *Modern Language Quarterly* 48 (1987): 207–23.

Coursen, Herbert R., Jr. *"Othello."* In *Christian Ritual and the World of Shakespeare's Tragedies.* Lewisburg, PA: Bucknell University Press, 1976, pp. 168–236.

Darlington, W. A. "The Court Iago." In *Through the Fourth Wall.* London: Chapman & Hall, 1922, pp. 64–69.

Dauber, Antoinette B. "Allegory and Irony in *Othello.*" *Shakespeare Survey* 40 (1988): 123–33.

Doran, Madeleine. "Good Name in *Othello.*" *Studies in English Literature 1500–1900* 7 (1967): 195–217.

Draper, John W. "Ensign Iago." In *The* Othello *of Shakespeare's Audience.* Paris: Marcel Didier, 1952, pp. 136–65.

———. " 'Honest Iago.' " *PMLA* 46 (1931): 724–37.

———. "The Jealousy of Iago." *Neophilologus* 25 (1940): 50–60.

Elliott, G. R. *Flaming Minister: A Study of* Othello *as Tragedy of Love and Hate.* Durham, NC: Duke University Press, 1953.

Elliott, Martin. *Shakespeare's Invention of Othello: A Study in Early Modern English.* New York: St. Martin's Press, 1988.

Evans, Bertrand. "The Villain as Practiser: *Othello.*" In *Shakespeare's Tragic Practice.* Oxford: Clarendon Press, 1979, pp. 115–46.

Evans, K. W. "The Racial Factor in *Othello.*" *Shakespeare Studies* 5 (1969): 124–40.

Everett, Barbara. "Reflections on the Sentimentalist's *Othello.*" *Critical Quarterly* 3 (1961): 127–39.

Farnham, Willard. "Diabolic Grotesqueness: Thersites, Iago, and Caliban." In *The Shakespearean Grotesque: Its Genesis and Transformations.* Oxford: Clarendon Press, 1971, pp. 128–69.

Fineman, Joel. "The Sound of O in *Othello:* The Real of the Tragedy of Desire." In *The Subjectivity Effect in Western Literary Tradition: Essays toward the Release of Shakespeare's Will.* Cambridge, MA: MIT Press, 1991, pp. 143–64.

Flatter, Richard. *The Moor of Venice.* London: William Heinemann, 1950.

Foakes, R. A. "The Descent of Iago: Satire, Ben Jonson, and Shakespeare's *Othello.*" In *Shakespeare and His Contemporaries: Essays in Comparison,* edited by E. A. J. Honigmann. Manchester: Manchester University Press, 1986, pp. 16–30.

Fraser, John. "*Othello* and Honour." In *The Name of Action.* Cambridge: Cambridge University Press, 1984, pp. 59–70.

Gerard, Albert. "Alack, Poor Iago! Intellect and Action in *Othello.*" *Shakespeare Jahrbuch* 94 (1958): 218–33.

Girard, René. "Shall We Desire to Raze the Sanctuary? Desire and Death in *Othello* and Other Plays." In *A Theater of Envy: William Shakespeare.* New York: Oxford University Press, 1991, pp. 290–96.

Glaz, A. André. "Iago or Moral Sadism." *American Imago* 19 (1962): 323–48.

Goldman, Michael. "Othello's Cause." In *Acting and Action in Shakespearean Tragedy.* Princeton: Princeton University Press, 1985, pp. 46–70.

Green, André. "The Psycho-analyst and *Othello:* A Tragedy of Conversion." In *The Tragic Effect: The Oedipus Complex in Tragedy,* translated by Alan Sheridan. Cambridge: Cambridge University Press, 1979, pp. 88–136.

Hapgood, Robert. "The Role of Othello." In *Shakespeare the Theatre-Poet.* Oxford: Clarendon Press, 1988, pp. 183–202.

Hawkes, Terence. "Iago's Use of Reason." *Studies in Philology* 58 (1961): 160–69.

Hecht, Anthony. *"Othello."* In *Obbligati.* New York: Atheneum, 1986, pp. 51–84.

Heilman, Robert B. "Dr. Iago and His Potions." *Virginia Quarterly Review* 28 (1952): 568–84.

———. "More Fair Than Black: Light and Dark in *Othello."* *Essays in Criticism* 1 (1951): 315–35.

Homan, Sidney R. "Iago's Aesthetics: Othello and Shakespeare's Portrait of the Artist." *Shakespeare Studies* 5 (1969): 141–47.

Hyman, Stanley Edgar. *Iago: Some Approaches to the Illusion of His Motivation.* New York: Atheneum, 1970.

Jepsen, Laura. *Ethical Aspects of Tragedy.* Gainesville: University of Florida Press, 1953.

Josipovici, Gabriel. "Everything and Nothing." In *Writing and the Body*. Princeton: Princeton University Press, 1982, pp. 34–63.

Kaula, David. "Othello Possessed: Notes on Shakespeare's Use of Magic and Witchcraft." *Shakespeare Studies* 2 (1967): 112–32.

Kay, Carol McGinnis. "Othello's Need for Mirrors." *Shakespeare Quarterly* 34 (1983): 261–70.

Kirschbaum, Leo. "The Modern Othello." *ELH* 11 (1944): 283–96.

Lake, James H. "Othello and the Comforts of Love." *American Imago* 45 (1988): 327–35.

Lerner, Laurence. "The Machiavel and the Moor." *Essays in Criticism* 9 (1959): 339–60.

Levin, Harry. "*Othello* and the Motive-Hunters." *Centennial Review* 8 (1964): 1–16.

Levitsky, Ruth. "All-in-All Sufficiency in *Othello*." *Shakespeare Studies* 6 (1972): 209–21.

McAlindon, T. "*Othello, the Moor of Venice*." In *Shakespeare's Tragic Cosmos*. Cambridge: Cambridge University Press, 1991, pp. 126–57.

McCloskey, John C. "The Motivation of Iago." *College English* 3 (1941–42): 25–30.

McCullen, Joseph T., Jr. "Iago's Use of Proverbs for Persuasion." *Studies in English Literature 1500–1900* 6 (1964): 247–62.

McElroy, Bernard. "*Othello:* The Visage in His Mind." In *Shakespeare's Mature Tragedies*. Princeton: Princeton University Press, 1973, pp. 89–144.

McFarland, Thomas. "The Anxiety of Othello." In *Tragic Meanings in Shakespeare*. New York: Random House, 1966, pp. 60–91.

McPeek, James A. S. "The 'Arts Inhibited' and the Meaning of *Othello*." *Boston University Studies in English* 1 (1955): 129–47.

Manlove, Colin N. "*Othello, Antony and Cleopatra*." In *The Gap in Shakespeare: The Motif of Division from* Richard II *to* The Tempest. London: Vision Press, 1981, pp. 62–100.

Mason, H. A. "*Othello*." In *Shakespeare's Tragedies of Love*. New York: Barnes & Noble, 1970, pp. 57–161.

Mercer, Peter. "*Othello* and the Form of Heroic Tragedy." *Critical Quarterly* 11 (1969): 45–61.

Miller, Donald C. "Iago and the Problem of Time." *English Studies* 22 (1940): 97–115.

Moore, John Robert. "The Character of Iago." In *Studies in Honor of A. H. R. Fairchild*, edited by Charles T. Prouty. Columbia: University of Missouri, 1946, pp. 37–46.

Muir, Kenneth. "The Jealousy of Iago." *English Miscellany* 2 (1951): 65–83.

Murphy, G. N. "A Note on Iago's Name." In *Literature and Society*, edited by Bernice Slote. Lincoln: University of Nebraska Press, 1964, pp. 38–43.

Neely, Carol Thomas. "Women and Men in *Othello:* 'What Should Such a Fool/Do with So Good a Woman?'" *Shakespeare Studies* 10 (1977): 133–58.

Neill, Michael. "Unproper Beds: Race, Adultery, and the Hideous in *Othello*." *Shakespeare Quarterly* 40 (1989): 383–402.

Nevo, Ruth. "*Othello*." In *Tragic Form in Shakespeare*. Princeton: Princeton University Press, 1972, pp. 178–213.

Nowottny, Winifred M. T. "Justice and Love in *Othello*." *University of Toronto Quarterly* 21 (1951–52): 330–44.

Paris, Bernard J. "Iago's Motives: A Horneyan Analysis." *Revue Belge de Philologie et d'Histoire* 62 (1984): 504–20.

Porter, Joseph A. "Complement Extern: Iago's Speech Acts." In Othello: *New Perspectives*, edited by Virginia Mason Vaughan and Kent Cartwright. Rutherford, NJ: Fairleigh Dickinson University Press, 1991, pp. 74–88.

Rand, Frank Prentice. "The Over Garrulous Iago." *Shakespeare Quarterly* 1 (1950): 155–61.

Ribner, Irving. "The Pattern of Moral Choice: *Othello*." In *Patterns in Shakespearian Tragedy*. London: Methuen, 1960, pp. 91–115.

Rosenberg, Marvin. *The Masks of* Othello. Berkeley: University of California Press, 1961.

Rossiter, A. P. "*Othello*: A Moral Essay." In *Angel with Horns and Other Shakespeare Lectures*. Edited by Graham Storey. New York: Theatre Arts Books, 1961, pp. 189–208.

Rosslyn, Felicity. "Nature Erring from Itself: *Othello* Again." *Cambridge Quarterly* 18 (1989): 289–302.

Rozett, Martha Tuck. "*Othello, Otello,* and the Comic Tradition." *Bulletin of Research in the Humanities* 85 (1982): 386–411.

Ryding, Erik S. "Scanning This Thing Further: Iago's Ambiguous Advice." *Shakespeare Quarterly* 40 (1989): 195–96.

Schwartz, Elias. "Stylistic 'Impurity' and the Meaning of *Othello*." *Studies in English Literature 1500–1900* 10 (1970): 297–313.

Shaffer, Elinor S. "Iago's Malignity Motivated: Coleridge's Unpublished 'Opus Magnum.'" *Shakespeare Quarterly* 19 (1968): 195–203.

Shakespeare Survey 21 (1968). Special *Othello* issue.

Shaw, Catherine M. "'Dangerous Conceits Are in Their Natures Poisons': The Language of *Othello*." *University of Toronto Quarterly* 49 (1979–80): 304–19.

Siegel, Paul N. "*Othello*." In *Shakespearean Tragedy and the Elizabethan Compromise*. New York: New York University Press, 1957, pp. 119–41.

Smith, Gordon Ross. "Iago the Paranoiac." *American Imago* 16 (1959): 155–67.

Snow, Edward A. "Sexual Anxiety and the Male Order of Things in *Othello*." *English Literary Renaissance* 10 (1980): 384–412.

Snyder, Susan. "*Othello* and the Conventions of Romantic Comedy." *Renaissance Drama* 5 (1972): 123–41.

Spivack, Bernard. *Shakespeare and the Allegory of Evil: The History of a Metaphor in Relation to His Major Villains*. New York: Columbia University Press, 1958.

Stempel, Daniel. "The Silence of Iago." *PMLA* 84 (1969): 252–63.

Sterling, Brents. "'Reputation, Reputation, Reputation!'" In *Unity in Shakespearian Tragedy*. New York: Columbia University Press, 1956, pp. 111–38.

Stewart, William E. "Does Iago Die?—The Problem of His Motivation in the Light of Elias Canetti's Theory of Survival." *Deutsche Shakespeare-Gesellschaft West Jahrbuch*, 1985, pp. 78–93.

Stilling, Roger. "*Othello*." In *Love and Death in Renaissance Tragedy*. Baton Rouge: Louisiana State University Press, 1976, pp. 145–65.

Stoll, Elmer Edgar. "Iago." In *Shakespeare and Other Masters*. Cambridge, MA: Harvard University Press, 1940, pp. 230–80.

———. "Iago Not a Malcontent." *Journal of English and Germanic Philology* 51 (1952): 163–67.

———. Othello: *An Historical and Comparative Study*. (University of Minnesota Studies in Language and Literature, Number 2.) Minneapolis, 1915.

Suchet, David. "Iago in *Othello*." In *Players of Shakespeare 2*, edited by Russell Jackson and Robert Smallwood. Cambridge: Cambridge University Press, 1988, pp. 179–99.

Tannenbaum, Samuel A. "The Wronged Iago." *Shakespeare Association Bulletin* 12 (1937): 57–62.

Wall, John N. "Shakespeare's Aural Art: The Metaphor of the Ear in *Othello*." *Shakespeare Quarterly* 30 (1979): 358–66.

Wangh, Martin. "*Othello:* The Tragedy of Iago." *Psychoanalytic Quarterly* 19 (1950): 202–12.

Watermeier, Daniel J. "Edwin Booth's Iago." *Theatre History Studies* 6 (1986): 32–55.

Weisinger, Herbert. "Iago's Iago." *University of Kansas City Review* 20 (1953–54): 83–90.

Whitaker, Virgil K. "The Way to Dusty Death: *Othello* and *Macbeth*." In *The Mirror up to Nature: The Technique of Shakespeare's Tragedies*. San Marino, CA: Huntington Library, 1965, pp. 241–75.

White, Richard Grant. "On the Acting of Iago." *Atlantic Monthly* 48 (1881): 203–12.

Widdowson, H. G. "Othello in Person." In *Language and Literature: An Introductory Reader in Stylistics,* edited by Ronald Carter. London: George Allen & Unwin, 1982, pp. 41–53.

Young, David. "Storytelling and Complicity in *Othello*." In *The Action to the Word: Structure and Style in Shakespearean Tragedy*. New Haven: Yale University Press, 1990, pp. 45–76.

ACKNOWLEDGMENTS

"Images of the Devil, of the Hero, and of God" by Maud Bodkin from *Archetypal Patterns in Poetry: Psychological Studies of Imagination* by Maud Bodkin, © 1934 by Oxford University Press. Reprinted by permission of Oxford University Press.

"Diabolic Intellect and the Noble Hero: A Note on *Othello*" by F. R. Leavis from *Scrutiny* 6, No. 3 (December 1937), © 1937 by *Scrutiny*. Reprinted by permission of Cambridge University Press.

"Dramatic Illusion in *Othello*" by Hoover H. Jordan from *Shakespeare Quarterly* 1, No. 3 (July 1950), © 1950 by The Shakespeare Association of America, Inc. Reprinted by permission of *Shakespeare Quarterly*.

"*Othello*" by Harold C. Goddard from *The Meaning of Shakespeare* by Harold C. Goddard, © 1951 by The University of Chicago. Reprinted by permission of The University of Chicago Press.

"The Economics of Iago and Others" by Robert B. Heilman from *PMLA* 68, No. 2 (June 1953), © 1953 by The Modern Language Association of America. Reprinted by permission of The Modern Language Association of America.

"The Noble Moor" by Helen Gardner from *Proceedings of the British Academy* 41 (1955), © 1955 by The British Academy. Reprinted by permission of The British Academy.

"'Strength's Abundance': A View of *Othello*" by J. K. Walton from *Review of English Studies* 11, No. 1 (February 1960), © 1960 by Oxford University Press. Reprinted by permission of Oxford University Press.

"*Othello* and the Dignity of Man" by G. M. Matthews from *Shakespeare in a Changing World*, edited by Arnold Kettle, © 1964 by International Publishers, Inc. Reprinted by permission of International Publishers, Inc.

"*Othello, the Moor of Venice*" by T. McAlindon from *Shakespeare and Decorum* by T. McAlindon, © 1973 by T. McAlindon. Reprinted by permission of The Macmillan Press, Ltd.

"Plays within Plays: *Othello, King Lear, Antony and Cleopatra*" by Howard Felperin from *Shakespearean Representation: Mimesis and Modernity in Elizabethan Tragedy* by Howard Felperin, © 1977 by Princeton University Press. Reprinted by permission of Princeton University Press.

"Improvisation and Power" by Stephen J. Greenblatt from *Literature and Society: Selected Papers from the English Institute 1978*, edited by Edward W. Said, © 1980 by the English Institute. Reprinted by permission of The Johns Hopkins University Press.

"Othello's Orotund Occupation" by Tom McBride from *Texas Studies in Literature and Language* 30, No. 3 (Fall 1988), © 1988 by University of Texas Press. Reprinted by permission of University of Texas Press.

"Iago's Wound" by David Pollard from Othello: *New Perspectives*, edited by Virginia Mason Vaughan and Kent Cartwright, © 1991 by Associated University Presses, Inc. Reprinted by permission of Associated University Presses, Inc.

"In Defense of Iago" by Marvin Rosenberg from *Shakespeare Quarterly* 6, No. 2 (Spring 1955), © 1955 by The Shakespeare Association of America, Inc. Reprinted by permission of *Shakespeare Quarterly.*

"The Joker in the Pack" by W. H. Auden from *The Dyer's Hand and Other Essays* by W. H. Auden, © 1962 by W. H. Auden. Reprinted by permission of Random House, Inc. and Faber & Faber, Ltd.

"Iago's 'If' " (originally titled "Iago's 'If': An Essay on the Syntax of *Othello*") by Madeleine Doran from *The Drama of the Renaissance: Essays for Leicester Bradner,* edited by Elmer M. Blistein, © 1970 by Brown University. Reprinted by permission of University Press of New England.

" 'Pluming Up the Will': Iago's Place in the Play" by Jane Adamson from *Othello as Tragedy: Some Problems of Judgment and Feeling* by Jane Adamson, © 1980 by Cambridge University Press. Reprinted by permission of Cambridge University Press.

"Language, Sexual Conflict and 'Symbiosis Anxiety' in *Othello*" by Randolph Splitter from *Mosaic* 15, No. 3 (September 1982), © 1982 by *Mosaic*. Reprinted by permission of *Mosaic.*

"Changing Places in *Othello*" by Michael Neill from *Shakespeare Survey* 37 (1984), © 1984 by Cambridge University Press. Reprinted by permission of Cambridge University Press.

"Iago's Metamorphosis" by Garry Gray from *CLA Journal* 28, No. 4 (June 1985), © 1985 by the College Language Association. Reprinted by permission of *CLA Journal.*

"Iago's Questionable Shapes" by Kenneth Palmer from *"Fanned and Winnowed Opinions": Shakespearean Essays Presented to Harold Jenkins,* edited by John W. Mahon and Thomas A. Pendleton, © 1987 by Kenneth Palmer. Reprinted by permission of the author.

"Location and Idiom in *Othello*" by Michael E. Mooney from *Shakespeare's Dramatic Transactions* by Michael E. Mooney, © 1990 by Duke University Press. Reprinted by permission of Duke University Press.

INDEX